THE CIA AND THE
U.S. INTELLIGENCE SYSTEM

WESTVIEW LIBRARY OF FEDERAL DEPARTMENTS, AGENCIES, AND SYSTEMS

Ernest S. Griffith and Hugh L. Elsbree,
General Editors

†*The Library of Congress,* Second Edition, Charles A. Goodrum and Helen W. Dalrymple

†*The National Park Service,* William C. Everhart

The Forest Service, Second Edition, Michael Frome

The Smithsonian Institution, Second Edition, Paul H. Oehser; Louise Heskett, Research Associate

The Bureau of Indian Affairs, Theodore W. Taylor

The United States Fish and Wildlife Service, Nathaniel P. Reed and Dennis Drabelle

†*The CIA and the U.S. Intelligence System,* Scott D. Breckinridge

The Foreign Service of the United States: First Line of Defense, Andrew L. Steigman

†Available in hardcover and paperback.

ABOUT THE BOOK AND AUTHOR

Foreign policy—including economic policy and national security policy—and the appropriate planning, decisionmaking, and execution of that policy depend upon foreign intelligence, which must be collected on a global scale, checked, compared, sifted, analyzed, and coordinated. The collection, analysis, and delivery of this body of information requires a multilevel, multiagency governmental system.

Our understanding of the national intelligence system is often incomplete. This book by former CIA veteran Scott Breckinridge explains the complexities of the system, with a concentration on the National Security Council (the system's center) and the Central Intelligence Agency (its main coordinating instrument and also a principal collection arm). Mr. Breckinridge reviews the origin and development of modern intelligence systems with special emphasis on the U.S. establishment. He analyzes the main fields of intelligence and the characteristics of special intelligence sectors, the reasons for their existence, and their missions, targets, and problems. Particular attention is given to the vexing dilemma of overt versus covert activities, the sharp differentiation between the basic mission of intelligence collection and the CIA's additional, massive task of actively influencing conditions abroad. The author also deals with the dramatic changes in intelligence gathering and analysis that have resulted from the accelerating evolution of technical surveillance equipment. Finally, he discusses the status of intelligence under U.S. and international law and the principles and standards of conduct to be observed by those engaged in intelligence work.

Scott D. Breckinridge served with the CIA for more than twenty-six years, both overseas and in Washington. For three years, he was the agency's briefing officer for the White House staff. He represented the agency before the 1975–1976 congressional investigating committees. He also served as liaison officer with the intelligence organizations of an allied nation and coordinated assignments with other units or committees of the government's intelligence community. His last sixteen years were spent with the CIA's Inspector General's detachment, with six as the Deputy Inspector General. Mr. Breckinridge was twice awarded the CIA's Distinguished Intelligence Medal, the agency's highest award.

CIA headquarters building in Washington, D.C.

THE CIA AND THE U.S. INTELLIGENCE SYSTEM

Scott D. Breckinridge

Westview Press / Boulder and London

Westview Library of Federal Departments, Agencies, and Systems

Copyright © 1986 by Westview Press, Inc.

Published in 1986 in the United States of America by Westview Press, Inc.; Frederick A. Praeger, Publisher; 5500 Central Avenue, Boulder, Colorado 80301

Library of Congress Cataloging-in-Publication Data
Breckinridge, Scott D.
  The CIA and the U.S. intelligence system.
  (Westview library of federal departments, agencies,
and systems)
  Bibliography: p.
  Includes index.
  1. United States. Central Intelligence Agency.
2. Intelligence service—United States. I. Title.
II. Title: CIA and the United States intelligence
system. III. Series.
JK468.I6B74 1986   327.1'2'0973   85-20377
ISBN 0-8133-0282-X

Printed and bound in the United States of America

The paper used in this publication meets the minimum requirements of the American National Standard for Permanence of Paper for Printed Library Materials Z39.48-1984.

10   9   8   7   6   5   4   3   2   1

This book is dedicated to six unusual men—
former Inspectors General of the Central
Intelligence Agency—whose unpublicized
achievements should stand as a guiding beacon
for all public servants:

Lyman B. Kirkpatrick
John S. Earman
Gordon M. Stewart
William V. Broe
Donald F. Chamberlain
John H. Waller

Theirs was the mission to find the truth and
advance its cause. They did.

CONTENTS

FIGURES AND TABLES

PREFACE

The genesis of this book lies in a course on U.S. intelligence in support of national policy, which was taught by the author for the Department of Political Science at the University of Kentucky. No single book covered all the points and issues that seemed appropriate to that course, although authors with experience in the field had written valuable books on some aspects of intelligence. A number of people without direct experience or knowledge also had written on that subject, but much of this literature suffered from both limited experience and a negative bias that often distorted the facts and sometimes concealed the complexity of the issues.

The initial plan of this book was to provide a descriptive and explanatory review of the major intelligence activities of the government. That is an ambitious undertaking in itself, as the government's intelligence organizations are numerous and their interrelationships complex. Beyond that, many of the issues raised about intelligence in the mid-1970s remain alive and had to be addressed. Finally, it was important that the book be a single volume of manageable size, which demanded a difficult balance between detail and summary.

The author's background for undertaking such a book derives from over twenty-six years with CIA, both in Washington and overseas. The last sixteen years were spent in the Office of the Inspector General, and in the last six of those, the author served as Deputy Inspector General. The assignments provided a unique exposure to the range of activities in CIA, as well as recurring contact with other government agencies in the United States and abroad. The perspectives and insights gained from this experience were augmented by considerable involvement with the investigative groups of the mid-1970s. This experience, combined with the writing of others known to the author and details in reports of the investigating bodies,[1] has provided the basis for the present work.

There is considerable erroneous writing about intelligence, but one directly familiar with its actual nature can pick a way through most of the myths and legends that have been created and produce a reasonably reliable and authoritative manuscript. This cannot be done with total certainty, however, as some facts are beyond recapture, differing individual perceptions result in varying recollections and descriptions, and summaries sometimes omit details that people think important.

A comprehensive book such as this can be written from the vantage point of CIA because of its unique position in the government under its head, the Director of Central Intelligence (DCI). The DCI is, by statute and presidential directive, a strong centering influence for the government's planning and conduct of intelligence activities. The agency not only conducts programs assigned to it; it also provides staff support for the DCI in this role as a leader in the government's work in this field.

CIA is, in effect, the nucleus around which some twenty major intelligence organizations operate. Nevertheless, it spends only about 5 percent of government appropriations for intelligence. The Department of Defense, which includes several of the major intelligence organizations, accounts for some 90 percent of government expenditures in this field. It is useful to keep this generally unrecognized fact in mind for a balanced view of the U.S. intelligence community.

Some ten years have passed since the drama of the mid-1970s, when the intelligence agencies were under fire. The mark of that era is clear among university students, as it is among older citizens addressed by the author, many of whom shared the misunderstandings of the younger generation. Not only are the issues of the 1970s still with us, but impressions from that period complicate communications problems that normally would be expected in discussing any unfamiliar subject. As a result, the decision was made to address those matters in the book. If initially this decision was something of a distraction in terms of how the book was first envisioned, it served the purpose of broadening discussion and opening lines of thought to some of the more complex problems.

One factor eased organization of the subject matter. Each separate category of intelligence activity has the same basic characteristics, regardless of where or by whom it is carried out. Analysis is analysis. Espionage is just that. Counterintelligence and security operations are very much the same wherever they occur. As a result, broad description of an activity can be considered as generally applicable wherever it appears. This made it unnecessary to discuss separately every activity of each organization. Generic descriptions fit readily across the board.

Modern intelligence programs of the United States government are a product of the dangerous times in which we live. These programs will continue so long as international disorder continues. Many of the programs will be secret, with only occasional details of organization and activity appearing in media reports that usually will suffer from errors of omission and of unsupported assertion.

It now is possible to discuss earlier incidents more fully than at the time of their occurrence because of the release of certain previously classified information. Although some individuals may remain critical of specific intelligence activities, a fuller appreciation for the facts and the problems they present is possible. This opportunity to review the past and to compare earlier judgments with what now is known, should give rise to caution in rushing to judgment when breathless headlines make some new "revelation."

Criticism of errors in public affairs is an important feature of our society. However, false and ill-founded criticism makes more difficult the sober and responsible management of complex problems. Intelligence activities carried on in secrecy are difficult to follow publicly, but if they are to be effective they must remain secret. Even when superficial aspects of intelligence operations are publicized legitimately, some aspects of operations should never be divulged in order to protect those involved and the techniques they use. It must be kept in mind that intelligence activities are not unauthorized independent adventures but, rather, constitute part of a national policy decided at the highest levels of government. On occasion, problems may arise in which some operational detail of a larger program may turn out in ways not anticipated— functioning, as it does, in an unconventional environment—but the basic thought remains correct: that the main details of a program are approved however controversial they, or aspects of them, may become.

It is useful to remember that despite the charges and rhetoric of the 1970s, the basic organization and missions of the intelligence agencies were left essentially unchanged. Every president from Truman to Reagan has turned to the intelligence agencies for help in conducting foreign policy. Our presidents will continue to do so. That is not so much an abstract consideration as a reflection of the difficulties of the times in which we live. It behooves the public and their elected representatives to better understand the function of intelligence and to deal responsibly and realistically with the work of our intelligence agencies. It is hoped that this book will contribute to such an outcome.

Scott D. Breckinridge
Lexington, Kentucky

NOTE

1. Dramatic charges in the *New York Times* in December 1974 led to the appointment of a presidential commission to look into the charges against CIA,

followed by two congressional inquiries into the government's entire intelligence program. Each of these inquiries produced some controversy in itself, but two of them produced reports with considerable factual detail not readily available from other sources. One may have considerable reservation about some of the editorial treatment of the facts on some issues; nevertheless, the reports of the presidential commission and one of the congressional committees are cited throughout this book where relevant. They are described below, with a statement of how they are cited when used: (1) *Report to the President by the Commission on CIA Activities Within the United States.* June 1975. Government Printing Office, Stock Number 141-015-00074-8. The presidential commission was headed by Vice President Nelson A. Rockefeller, and will be cited hereafter as the *Rockefeller Commission Report.* (2) *Final Report of the Select Committee to Study Governmental Operations with Respect to Intelligence Activities.* United States Senate, 94th Congress, 2d Session, April 26, 1976. Report No. 94-755. The Senate Committee was chaired by Senator Frank Church, and will be cited hereafter as the *Church Committee Report.* (3) A House of Representatives Select Committee on Intelligence conducted an inquiry during the same period. It was the victim of erratic management, and members of the committee were unable to agree on presentation of issues as well as on major conclusions. When brought to the floor of the House, it was contested and rejected by the members. As a result there is no official report of that investigation. A copy of one of the various drafts of the report was leaked to a sympathetic left-wing publication in New York. The management of the inquiry was such as to place in doubt the validity of much of the leaked version, and thus it is not cited in this book.

ACKNOWLEDGMENTS

The author would be ungrateful if due recognition were not given those who made valuable contributions to this book. The book may not have been undertaken at all—much less completed—without the help of others.

It was Dr. Vincent Davis, director of the Patterson School of Diplomacy and International Commerce at the University of Kentucky, who first suggested the project upon hearing expressions of concern about the absence of a satisfactory textbook in this subject area. His encouragement and advice were a continuing spur afterward, right up to publication. Not just another academician speaking from general principle, he has been involved directly in national security affairs as a consultant with various government agencies in that field. In particular, as a consultant to the Director of Central Intelligence during the Carter administration, he saw the government's intelligence activities from the inside. Dr. John M. Rogers, of the University of Kentucky College of Law, made some pointed comments on an earlier shorter version of the chapter on the status of intelligence under international law. His remarks led to modified language, although he might not recognize the changes.

Former colleagues in the government—John F. Blake, Gordon M. Stewart, Ruth E. Gillard, and Robert O. Derrick—read some early trial drafts and made helpful suggestions that influenced later drafts. Lt. Col. Jack H. Taylor, a retired Air Force intelligence officer who followed his military career with ten years at CIA in various staff capacities, helped talk out a number of tangled issues, broadening the approaches that were taken and refining some of the presentation.

Bobbie Taulbee Smith, a former secretary in the Political Science Department at the University of Kentucky who had retired to raise a family, typed the manuscript. She had to deal with second-thought changes and displayed a rare talent for reading an unusual hand, crowded into tight places with confusing arrows and instructions. Her patience and good humor helped lessen the tedium of that part of the work. Col. John Frisbee, an editor with a magical pen, transformed turgid prose on difficult subject matter into a readable form, which must lighten the task of the readers.

An acknowledgment would be incomplete without an expression of gratitude for the patience of the author's wife, as her husband disappeared for long periods to hover over a typewriter in a room piled with books and papers that were not to be touched under any circumstances.

It must be emphasized that the mistakes—which a work such as this cannot avoid—are those of the author alone. The opinions, where expressed, are his, although he hopes others share them. Security approval of government authorities—a requirement of a work such as this—is just that and no more. It does not connote verification of facts or approval of opinion. Any errors that these authorities may have recognized are not their responsibility, and the errors go unchallenged if they do not raise issues of security.

For those who helped and encouraged, many thanks.

S.D.B.

Part One

BACKGROUND, HISTORY, AND ORGANIZATION

THE ROLE AND NATURE
OF INTELLIGENCE

> *Nam et ipsa scienta potentas.*
> *(Knowledge itself is power.)*
> —Francis Bacon

There is nothing novel in the relationship of governmental intelligence activities to international affairs. Throughout history national leaders have gathered information about other peoples and lands to guide their decisions. Without adequate information, they often have had to act on instinct and general familiarity with a situation, but when they had relevant facts, their judgment was more likely to be correct. Sometimes the best available knowledge can tell a leader only that there is no sure road to his or her objective, but the decisions made by this leader are at least informed, better balanced, and less subject to chance.

The history of mankind is filled with examples of both religious and secular leaders gathering information about a potential enemy and using it as best they could. A short trip through history helps illustrate the point.

The Book of Numbers in the Bible tells that Moses sent twelve men to explore Canaan and report back on the sort of land it was. He dispatched them into different parts of that land, instructing them:

> See what the land is like, and whether the people who live there are strong, few or many. See whether it is easy or difficult country in which to live, and whether the cities are weakly defended or well fortified; is the land fertile or barren, and does it grow trees or not.[1]

Most of Moses' spies felt that the land was too rich and its people too strong to be conquered by the Israelites. There was an inconclusive debate over evaluation of the information. A decision to attack Canaan was made only after Moses received guidance from on high. Those who counselled caution were punished by banishment and plague.

That ancient story contains most of the elements of strategic intelligence. The intelligence "requirements" included information on the economic qualities of the land, the vitality of its people, and their military strength as a basis for policy judgments. That this information produced disagreement emphasizes the historic uncertainties of major decisions.

Some 800–1,000 years after the conquest of Canaan by the Israelites, knowledge of the organization and fighting qualities of a foe made it possible for another greatly outnumbered army to win a historic victory. In 490 B.C. Athenians faced a Persian force that outnumbered them more than two to one. An Athenian general, Miltiades, who had served with the Persians, knew that they were lightly armored and relied on relatively undisciplined mass formations. He reasoned that if the Athenians did not fight immediately, the Persians would break out of the coastal plain on which they were gathered and overrun the area. He believed that the relatively heavily armored Athenians, with their long spears and disciplined formations, could defeat the Persians at that spot. Miltiades' views prevailed and the Battle of Marathon is remembered as one of the fateful engagements of history, allowing the culture of Greece to flower and to leave its mark on Western civilization.[2]

More than a thousand years after Marathon, the Prophet Mohammed fled from Mecca to Medina. In 624 authorities at Mecca gathered some 10,000 armed men to attack and destroy him. Mohammed had left behind in Mecca agents who reported these plans to him. He ordered defensive works to be built at Medina—a surprise to the army that marched against him. As the enemy camped outside the walls and debated their course of action, heavy rains so disrupted the camp that the army dwindled and finally departed without making an assault. But for Mohammed's intelligence about his enemies, and the lack of comparable intelligence on their part, Islam might not have survived to become a force in world affairs.[3]

Nearly a thousand years later, another historic event demonstrated the effect of intelligence on history. The rulers of the Ottoman Empire learned that there had been a major fire at the powder factories in Venice, with vast explosions that destroyed the Venetian fleet. A decision was made to move against Venice while it was weakened, and to deliver an ultimatum to the Venetians. In fact, although there had been a fire and explosions, only four galleys of the large Venetian fleet were lost.[4] On receiving the ultimatum the powerful Venetians enlisted support from other European powers. In 1571 a European naval force met the Ottoman fleet at Lepanto and defeated it decisively. The Ottoman Empire continued as a power for many years, but that event marked the end of its uninterrupted westward expansion.

The Turkish campaign originated with inaccurate information that could have been corrected with the communications of modern times. Lest one seek comfort in the thought that modern communications now afford a form of protection from major adverse developments, it is appropriate to consider the problem of timely warning today, given the fewer than thirty minutes between the launching of an ICBM and its arrival on target half a world away.

The French and Indian wars in North America provide another example of the effect of intelligence on the strategy and tactics of opposing sides. In 1759, the French commander in Canada, Montcalm, planned his defenses against the English along the line of Lake Champlain and Fort Niagara, the waterways of western New York having long served as avenues for military expeditions. Montcalm learned from an intercepted letter of the British commander, Wolfe, that the campaign against Quebec was to be by sea and the St. Lawrence River, instead of following the western route. With this warning the French were able to assemble their defensive forces at Quebec, which were then considered virtually impregnable. Wolfe, having lost the element of strategic surprise, resorted to tactical intelligence. In his army was a man who had been a prisoner of the French at Quebec, where he had learned of a steep trail up the high embankment from the river to the plain behind the fort. The French, considering the trail too steep and narrow for use by significant military forces, left it undefended. Wolfe moved his forces up the trail,[5] took the French by surprise, and won the battle that ensued on the level fields behind the fortified city.

There are more familiar instances of the role of intelligence in recent times. Most readers are aware of the lack of warning of the Japanese attack on Pearl Harbor in December 1941. Subsequent investigations disclosed that in the various military and civilian departments of our government there was information that, if brought together, analyzed, and reported promptly, should have provided warning adequate for essential defense measures. It was a failure of organization, not a lack of information, that allowed surprise. That tragic experience was an important factor behind the reorganization of the nation's intelligence structure under the National Security Act of 1947.[6]

Another event in this selective scan of history that provides additional insight into the use of intelligence is the Vietnamese communist Tet offensive in early 1968. A pending offensive by the communist forces had been reported. Accordingly, U.S. and South Vietnamese forces were redeployed in defensive positions. However, it was judged that a truly all-out offensive would result in such extensive losses to the communists—

6

who, it was felt, would realize this fact—that the likelihood of such an assault was discounted, although widespread lesser activities were expected. Many South Vietnamese troops were given leave for the religious observances of the Tet season, under a cease-fire declared by both sides. Despite the deployment of Saigon's reserve forces, there was a reduced level of readiness.

The communists launched a major offensive on the night of January 30–31. While this offensive met with dramatic initial successes, communist losses were some 32,000 in the first two weeks, with another 10,000–15,000 in the following two weeks. The offensive collapsed. The losses were so great that the communists required several months' reinforcement and regroupment to regain offensive capabilities in the South.[7]

The intelligence reporting on the impending offensive was correct, so far as it went. The military projection of the losses that the communists would incur also proved to be correct. What the U.S. estimators failed to appreciate were the ideological considerations that led the communists to undertake an offensive with such risks. The communists had convinced themselves that the South Vietnamese would welcome the invaders from the North, and that there would be a "general uprising" that would reduce the number of casualties and help gain major communist objectives. The general uprising failed to materialize. Since the Americans could not believe the communists would be so foolhardy, early communist successes appeared more dramatic than they actually were. Both sides would have handled the situation differently had they managed their intelligence more effectively. Neither side could have foreseen the political repercussions in the United States occasioned by media coverage that reported a great communist victory and heightened antiwar sentiment in this country.[8]

A final example of disastrous strategic hypotheses based on incomplete and mishandled information is the Argentine seizure of the Falkland/Malvinas Islands in 1982. The Argentine government obviously misjudged the strength and resolve of an England in decline as a major world power since the dissolution of its empire. It became dramatically clear that the government of Argentina, in occupying a territory that England considered its own, had reached erroneous conclusions. The humiliating defeat of the Argentine forces, leading two years later to the country's return to civil government, highlights the need for both knowledge and understanding in making major military decisions. Argentina's miscalculation is not unlike what must have been the Soviet view when the Kremlin launched the North Koreans against South Korea in 1950.

These examples of the uses of intelligence (and sometimes of its misuse) emphasize the role of intelligence as a tool of policy-making.

Among the problems in employing intelligence is the ever-present awareness that what is known may be flawed in important respects.

Today it is generally accepted that comprehensive, accurate information on the nations of the world is essential to the policymakers and military leaders of any major power, including the United States. Our information needs range from the numbers and capabilities of Soviet military forces through international political and economic matters, down to the internal stability of a small Central American country with which our nation has friendly relations. Given such broad interests, the requirement for the best knowledge possible is high. It is an unavoidable fact that a modern government must have a large, complex national intelligence structure. The future of our nation rests on sound political and economic policy and on strong defense, none of which can be shaped confidently without comprehensive and accurate knowledge of the world in which we live.

Since World War II the United States has developed complex machinery for managing national security policy and programs, and intelligence has been given a key place in that structure. A summary overview provides an introduction to the subject.

U.S. NATIONAL SECURITY STRUCTURE

The lessons of Pearl Harbor and World War II led to the conclusion that a formal structure for managing major national security affairs was needed. Pre–World War II arrangements were inadequate for guarding against a breach of the peace, and the various organizational arrangements during the war left much to be desired, although they demonstrated the usefulness of government-wide arrangements. While the war was under way, several studies of postwar organization for national security were conducted. Some of these studies are mentioned in the *Church Committee Report*.[9] Out of the process emerged the proposal that, with congressional review and action, became the National Security Act of 1947.[10]

Although the 1947 Act established a framework for policy-making and a new central mechanism for intelligence, some will recall that the most publicized feature at the time of its passage was "unification of the armed services." The U.S. Air Force was plucked from the rib cage of the Army—much as the scripture tells us Eve was created from Adam—and made into a third military service equal to the Army and Navy. The 1947 Act also created a National Military Establishment (redesignated the Department of Defense by a 1949 amendment to the Act), which was headed by a Secretary of Defense who held cabinet rank and presided over the three military services. This new overlord of the national military defense system was to coordinate military policy, and harness and direct the intense competition for roles, missions, and resources anticipated among the three services.

As substantial as these legislative innovations may have been, they were but part of a broader concept of providing for coordination of national security policy. Beyond military organization, the 1947 Act created a National Security Council (NSC) composed of senior government officials. The NSC was presided over by the President, with the Vice President, Secretary of State, and Secretary of Defense as permanent members.[11] It became customary for the Secretary of the Treasury and the Attorney General to attend NSC meetings, but the latter is no longer listed among those attending regularly. The Director of the Office of Management and Budget now attends.

In essence, the National Security Council is a special cabinet group, focusing on all facets of national security. It is more than a microcosm of what some refer to as "cabinet government," although it is limited to those departments having a special responsibility for or interest in foreign affairs, defense, and internal security. The role of the NSC, as stated in the 1947 Act, is

> to advise the President with respect to the integration of domestic, foreign and military policies relating to the national security so as to enable the military services and other departments and agencies of the Government to cooperate more effectively in matters involving the national security.[10]

Key to the function of those brought together in the Council is the word "advise." The basic authority of the President remains intact. Any attempt to replace presidential responsibility and decision by some sort of collegial organization, acting in consensus, would invade the President's constitutional prerogatives. In explaining this point, some have cited an anecdote concerning Abraham Lincoln's consideration of the Emancipation Proclamation with his seven-man cabinet. Opposition to the proposal was reported as initially unanimous, which Lincoln is supposed to have summarized in his quaint but pointed way: "The Nays seven. The Ayes one. The Ayes have it." In essence, the NSC provides the formal machinery by which the President can meet with his senior advisers on security matters, with the assurance that their advice is available should he wish it.

Among the non-members of the NSC who attend its meetings are the President's adviser on national security affairs (the exact title has varied over the years, but the job has remained essentially the same— adviser to the President and director of the NSC staff), the Chairman of the Joint Chiefs of Staff (a post formalized in a 1949 amendment to the National Security Act of 1947), and a new statutory position, the Director of Central Intelligence (DCI).[11]

DIRECTOR OF CENTRAL INTELLIGENCE AND CIA

The title of Director of Central Intelligence, as its phrasing suggests, was to have a central role in the activities of the government's intelligence organization. The Director was more than a disembodied head without organizational substance or support. He also was to direct a new organization named the Central Intelligence Agency. In the vernacular of government bureaucracy he was to wear two hats: one in his government-wide role as coordinator of intelligence activities and one as head of CIA. There have been a number of questions regarding the specific authorities for the intelligence programs of CIA. These questions will be treated more fully later, but a brief comment is appropriate here.

The fact that CIA has a legislative charter, provided in the 1947 Act, seems to have stimulated a special line of legalistic argument. The other intelligence organizations—at that time the three military services, for example, and later the Defense Intelligence Agency and the National Security Agency—were not creatures of the law but, instead, were created through departmental organization or by presidential directive. As a result, their organizational charters provided little statutory language on which lawyers could focus. Most of the technical legal contentions were directed at CIA and its programs.

If legislative charters are desirable—and the staff of the Church Committee thought so—there is no practical reason why such charters could not be provided. The follow-on U.S. Senate Select Committee on Intelligence agreed, up to the end of 1980. It seems, however, that those who pressed for such charters were excessive in their zeal and profuse in their drafting, and their proposals failed to win support. But with or without such magic as legislated charters may provide, the various intelligence organizations other than CIA seem for the most part to have functioned reasonably well over the years without them. They remain subordinate to the NSC structure, which in turn is subject to congressional oversight on intelligence matters as well as on foreign policy and military affairs.

The position of the NSC under the President, who is at the apex of foreign policy and military functions in the Executive Branch, is apparent. The relations of the Director of Central Intelligence and his agency (CIA) to the NSC, and to the other government organizations involved with intelligence, are stated in the 1947 Act as follows:

(d) For the purpose of coordinating the intelligence activities of the several government departments and agencies in the interest of national security, it shall be the duty of the [Central Intelligence] Agency, under the direction of the National Security Council—

(1) to advise the National Security Council in matters concerning such intelligence activities of the government departments and agencies as relate to the national security.

(2) to make recommendations to the National Security Council for the coordination of such intelligence activities of the departments and agencies of the government as relate to the national security.

. . . .

(4) to perform, for the benefit of the existing intelligence agencies, such additional services of common concern as the National Security Council determines can be more efficiently accomplished centrally.

(5) to perform such other functions and duties related to intelligence affecting the national security as the National Security Council may from time to time direct.[12]

Additional provisions authorized CIA to obtain the intelligence held by other departments or agencies, thus ensuring that vital information would not be withheld from others in the national security establishment. This was one of the reasons for which this machinery was created—a reason harking back to the Pearl Harbor experience. Some critics have alleged that there are no arrangements for dissemination of intelligence; not only does the law provide for it, but such arrangements do exist.

Although stated generally, the central role intended for the DCI and his agency in the intelligence activities and programs of the United States government under the NSC seems clear. Government being what it is, the broad legislative provisions needed to be translated into more specific arrangements. The first and second numbered paragraphs under item "d" in the 1947 Act resulted in a wide array of directives issued by the National Security Council on how the government's intelligence affairs would be managed. The fourth and fifth numbered paragraphs were the subject of more special directives. Known as National Security Council Intelligence Directives (NSCIDs), these instructions served for many years as the guidelines for the system that evolved, and under which the departments and agencies conducted their intelligence activities. The NSCIDs were modified as experience indicated by presidential Executive Order and other forms of NSC directives. But the stated central role of the DCI—coordination of intelligence activities—was not reduced. If anything, it has grown. This subject will be treated in greater depth in later sections of the book.

CIA, as distinguished from the DCI's community role, is an operating agency subject to additional specific legislative provisions. Section (d)

(3)—omitted from the sections cited earlier, in which the emphasis was on CIA's relations to the NSC and the Intelligence Community—described the following CIA functions:

> (3) to correlate and evaluate intelligence relating to the national security, and provide for the appropriate dissemination of such intelligence within the Government using where appropriate existing agencies and facilities.[13]

This mission of analysis and dissemination was not exclusive. The following language of the 1947 Act made it clear:

> *Provided further,* That the departments and other agencies of the Government shall continue to collect, evaluate, correlate, and disseminate departmental intelligence.

Some have seen this provision as a legislative mandate for duplication, but the concept is more sophisticated than that.

The original thought was that the departments would concentrate on their respective areas of competence and concern—for example, that the Army would address intelligence concerning Soviet Ground Forces, and so on. The phrase "departmental intelligence" is to be distinguished from the statutory reference to CIA's concern with "intelligence relating to national security," a phrase that eventually was shortened simply to "national intelligence." These concepts proved to be artificial in some respects, if applied literally and narrowly. Obviously, modern weapons systems and the global missions of the armed forces carry with them broad strategic considerations that unavoidably produce an overlap between departmental intelligence and national intelligence. The NSCID system undertook to delineate departmental responsibilities, as well as to provide for joint attention in the broader areas. Years of experience established working practices for dealing with these problems.

This portion of the 1947 Act dealing with distinctions between national and departmental intelligence has additional significance. Some congressional authorities seem to feel that intelligence organizations, other than CIA, lacked statutory charters of any sort[14]—hence their sense of a need for detailed proposals that, in lawyerly language, were intended to resolve all problems. Yet this provision of the Act clearly authorizes the intelligence organizations to continue doing the things that were already occupying them—and were known to the Congress— although they were not specified in the Act.

The important point here is that the National Security Act of 1947 established broad outlines for presidential organization of key elements of the Executive branch. The Act brought together those departments and agencies that make policies and the plans for carrying them out and, more specific to the purpose of this book, the elements of government that contribute to support of those functions—the intelligence organizations. It was within the NSC framework that the President was to organize, direct, and control this aspect of the government's function. There is sufficient leeway for modifying, from year to year and from national administration to administration, the ways in which the President's management of this function was to be handled, but it is clear that the national security apparatus is always under presidential control.

NOTES

1. *The New English Bible*, Oxford University Press and Cambridge University Press, 1970, pages 162–165.

2. *Decisive Battles of the World*, by E. S. Creasy, Harper & Brothers, New York, 1858, pages 21, 37.

3. *War of Wits*, by Ladislas Farago, Funk & Wagnall, New York, 1954, pages 9–10.

4. *A Military History of the Western World*, Volume I, by J.F.C. Fuller, Funk & Wagnall, New York, 1954, page 560.

5. *A Military History of the Western World*, Volume II, by J.F.C. Fuller, Funk & Wagnall, New York, 1955, pages 247–270.

6. *Donovan and the CIA*, by Thomas F. Troy, Center for the Study of Intelligence, Central Intelligence Agency, 1981, pages 211, 409. Subsequent analyses of the failure of intelligence in the Pearl Harbor attack have developed into further theses. See *Pearl Harbor: Warning and Decision*, by Roberta Wohlstetter, Stanford University Press, California, 1962. The original view that the failure was due to absence of satisfactorily institutionalized coordination and dissemination of intelligence remains valid. It certainly was the prevailing view at the time of enactment of the National Security Act of 1947, which created the current framework for centralized intelligence in the U.S. government.

7. *Report on the War in Vietnam* (as of June 1968), Government Printing Office, Washington, D.C., 1969, pages 157–162.

8. *The Big Story: How the American Press and Television Reported the Crisis of Tet 1968 in Washington and Vietnam*, by Peter Braestrup, Freedom House-Westwood Press, 1977. This remarkable two-volume study need not be read if one is uninterested in depth of detail. Braestrup gave his conclusions in articles in the *Washington Star*, Section E, 29 January 1978, and in the *Washington Post*, magazine section of the same date.

9. *Church Committee Report*, Book I, pages 20–22; Book IV, page 8. The most detailed and extensive review of the actions leading to organization of a postwar intelligence system, especially the creation of CIA, is in the authoritative book *Donovan and the CIA*, by Thomas F. Troy, issued first by the Central Intelligence Agency in 1981 and later in the same year by University Publications of America.

10. Title 50, U.S. Code, Section 402, et seq.

11. Two positions originally included as statutory members of the NSC were those of Director for Mutual Security and Chairman of the National Security Resources Board. Both positions have been abolished. Other posts were named subject to presidential appointment, two of which (Chairman of the Munitions Board and Chairman of the Research and Development Board) also have been abolished. See *Rockefeller Commission Report,* page 275.

12. Title 50, U.S. Code, Section 403 (d).

13. Ibid.

14. *Church Committee Report,* Book I, pages 426–427.

2

ORGANIZATION AND OPERATION OF THE NATIONAL SECURITY COUNCIL

There is established a council to be known as the National Security Council. . . . The President of the United States shall preside over the meetings of the Council. . . . The function of the Council shall be to advise the President with respect to the integration of domestic, foreign, and military policies relating to the national security. . . .

—National Security Act of 1947

The government's intelligence program is carried on as a subordinate function within the structure of the National Security Council (NSC) (see Figure 2.1). To understand the role of intelligence in support of national policy, it is necessary to understand the organization and operation of the NSC beyond the introductory summary in the preceding chapter.

The position of the President at the apex of the government's national security machinery has always been clear. He has constitutional authority for the conduct of foreign affairs, and is commander in chief of the armed forces. As international affairs grew increasingly complex, earlier methods for handling foreign policy and national security became increasingly inadequate. Military matters were mixed to an unprecedented degree with foreign policy, and the President's cabinet had difficulty in focusing on problems in which both were intertwined. The National Security Act of 1947 provided formal arrangements to assist the President in managing these intricate affairs. In many ways this organizational approach to broad governmental problems is unique.

As the main points of the 1947 Act are noted in Chapter 1, they will not be repeated here. Suffice it to say that the NSC does not compromise in any way the President's constitutional authority, but merely provides him with the mechanism for drawing together the many considerations involved in policy-making and planning. The President

14

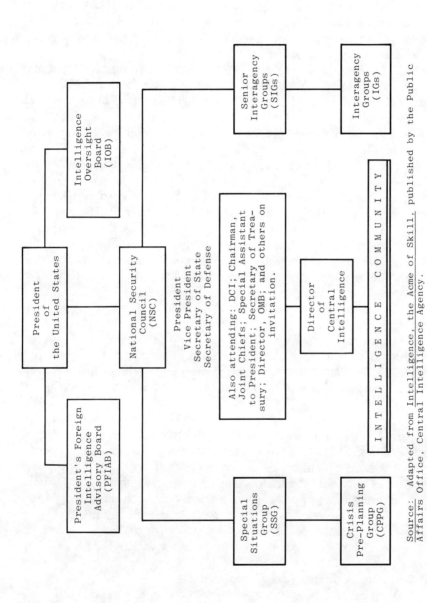

Source: Adapted from Intelligence, the Acme of Skill, published by the Public Affairs Office, Central Intelligence Agency.

FIGURE 2.1. The President's National Security Organization

is not bound by NSC recommendations, nor is he obliged to consult the Council. But regardless of whether a policy has been developed by the Council or by the President and his personal advisers, the NSC is responsible for its implementation. The Council looks to the intelligence agencies for support in its policy roles.

Prior to passage of the 1947 Act, President Truman directed the creation of a National Intelligence Authority and a Central Intelligence Group. The focus of his directive was on this one aspect of the national security problem. The concept was broadened in the 1947 Act inasmuch as the NSC had a wider role than the National Intelligence Authority, which was abolished. The Council is concerned not only with intelligence but also with broad policy matters affecting the entire range of national security—foreign policy, defense matters, international economic programs, and internal security. Under the 1947 Act, the Central Intelligence Group was replaced by the Central Intelligence Agency. The Agency's role in support of policy, and its intended central influence in what became known as the Intelligence Community, was clear from the language of the Act. As new intelligence organizations came into existence to meet the requirements of the post–World War II world, they have been brought into the system.

To be effective on a continuing basis, the NSC must function on more than an *ad hoc* basis. The NSC has a staff that serves as a secretariat for the Council and is headed by the Assistant to the President for National Security Affairs, who is known informally as the President's national security adviser. The nature of that position has depended very much on the personality of the individual holding it and the preferences of the President.

As with all human institutions, the NSC is subject to the play of the personalities and objectives of those involved. The Secretaries of State and Defense will have departmental interests that may diverge within the same overall policy. On occasion, their energies and purposes may lead to important differences. For instance, the Secretary of Defense may support military approaches to problems in which diplomacy seems to have limited potency, with the Secretary of State feeling that such an option is undesirable. This situation may lead to what is sometimes called the "Third Option," in which one of the intelligence agencies— most often the CIA—is directed to try to achieve by covert means objectives that otherwise seem unobtainable.

Cabinet officers have direct access to the President, and when more normal options are unpromising, the recommendations of a particular cabinet member may produce proposals that otherwise might not emerge from the NSC framework. Not to be overlooked in considering the influence of individuals is the President's national security adviser. Many of the papers dealing with a policy issue are blended into a policy position by his staff. If the occupant of the post is a person of strong views and personality, some important decisions may be shaped by him. The final decision is the President's, but the influence of this adviser can be critical in the decision-making process. This influence is believed to have been a very real factor during Henry Kissinger's tenure in the post, prior to his succeeding William Rogers as Secretary of State. Again, Zbigniew Brzezinski, President Carter's national security adviser, was perceived as more hawkish than Secretary of State Cyrus Vance. Vance resigned after the failed Iranian rescue mission of 1980. Criticism of previous strong national security advisers has been seen by some as the basis for the conservative instructions given Richard Allen, President Reagan's first national security adviser. Allen's conservative approach is believed by some to have been a factor in his replacement,[1] although his instructions seemed to have been to serve in a staff capacity rather than as a policy manager.

Others who were not statutory members of the NSC have had special influence on its deliberations. In an earlier time, Allen Dulles, as Director of Central Intelligence, had considerable personal access to President Eisenhower in addition to his influence in the NSC process. His influence doubtless was enhanced by his relationship with his brother, Secretary of State John Foster Dulles. Attorney General Robert Kennedy also had a unique influence on a number of decisions and programs during his participation in the NSC meetings, particularly in connection with clandestine operations against Cuba.

Director of Central Intelligence William Casey seems to have had considerable influence during President Reagan's first term. He was the first DCI to be given cabinet rank. Although this rank may reinforce Mr. Casey's status in the hierarchy, it could raise questions about the objectivity of his Agency. CIA was created as an impartial organization with an important role in carrying out policy, as distinct from initiating it. If major intelligence appraisals, known as National Intelligence Estimates, seemed to support a policy for which CIA was responsible, its conclusions would be subject to challenge on grounds of objectivity, regardless of its merits. Mr. Casey's cabinet status probably does not change his position in any material way, but in an age when perceptions often are as important as fact, cabinet status for the DCI must be considered a negative asset.

NSC STRUCTURE

In the Reagan administration the NSC staff is made up of people from various civilian agencies of the government, including the military, and of persons on leave from the academic profession or from private organizations specializing in certain aspects of national security policy. The staff is directed by the President's national security adviser and is organized along both geographical and functional lines, namely: West European Affairs, East European/Soviet Affairs, African Affairs, Latin American Affairs, Asian Affairs, Middle East Affairs, Defense Programs, Intelligence Programs, Global Issues, and International Economic Affairs.[2] This arrangement can be modified as deemed desirable.

The NSC staff members follow developments in their respective areas of responsibility, relying extensively on intelligence reports and analysis. They also initiate inter-agency studies that may lead to presidential security policy directives. This process begins with a proposal to the President for study of an important issue. If the President agrees, he will issue a National Security Study Directive (NSSD). The departments and agencies that have an interest in the particular issue, including members of the Intelligence Community, contribute to the work, which ultimately is submitted to the President. After he and his advisers, including the NSC, have arrived at a decision, a National Security Decision Directive (NSDD) is issued over the President's signature.[3] That becomes the basis for action by appropriate departments and agencies.

The NSC serves as the President's clearinghouse for many policy considerations, and its staff is his personal staff for national security matters. The President's national security adviser, as head of the NSC staff, stands between the executive departments and the President, although the prestige of the departmental secretaries ensures that their views are heard in NSC meetings. The mere description of this arrangement emphasizes the delicacy of these relationships. Eventual implementation of policy is the responsibility of one or more departments or agencies. Quite naturally, the organizations that will be responsible for carrying out a policy want to have a voice in its formulation.

Organization of the NSC to ensure involvement of the departments and agencies can be handled in a number of ways. President Reagan has elected to use a series of committees or groups. He directed creation of Senior Interagency Groups (SIGs) to support the NSC in its work, and Interagency Groups (IGs), composed of representatives of the SIG members, apparently to support the SIGs. In practice there is only one SIG, the membership of which remains constant, although there may be changes in procedure as the subject matter before it changes. The members are the Director of Central Intelligence, the Assistant to the President for National Security Affairs, the Deputy Secretary of State, the Deputy Secretary of Defense, the Chairman of the Joint Chiefs of Staff, the Deputy Attorney General, the Director of the Federal Bureau of Investigation, and the Director of the National Security Agency. When the group considers intelligence policy and activities on which it will advise the President, it becomes SIG (Intelligence) and its meetings are chaired by the DCI.[4]

A number of Interagency Groups (IGs) have been established to support SIG work. There is no fixed number, and their methods of operation can vary with the subject matter. A representative of the DCI chairs the meetings that deal with national foreign intelligence. A representative of the Director of the FBI presides when the subject is counterintelligence. The responsibility for terrorism is divided, with a State Department representative chairing meetings when the subject is terrorism abroad, and a representative of the Attorney General chairing when it involves terrorism in the United States.[5]

One arrangement, reserved for special problems, has to do with crisis situations. In early 1982 the President created a Special Situations Group (SSG), under the Vice President, for what is known in the government as "crisis management." Within the NSC staff, a working-level group headed by the deputy to the President's security adviser supports the SSG. It is named the Crisis Pre-Planning Group (CPPG).[6]

The Reagan Executive Order also specifies that there be NSC committees reporting to the President on "special activities" and "other sensitive intelligence operations,"[7] but later published material does not repeat those references. It is assumed that the Interagency Group concerned with intelligence matters considers such questions when they arise, sending them to the Senior Interagency Group for review and forwarding them to the President and the NSC.

The subject of Special Activities (covert action) received considerable attention in the Reagan Executive Order. Beyond provisions in that order for review and approval of Special Activities within the Executive branch, there remains, of course, a requirement of the Intelligence Oversight Act of 1980 that such activities be reported to the Congress (as will be discussed in more detail later on). Although Special Activities receive recurring attention in the Executive Order, sensitive intelligence operations (operations that may involve extra risk or political considerations and require individual review at senior policy levels) do not.

OTHER PRESIDENTIAL INTELLIGENCE REVIEW

In 1956, in response to a proposal by the Hoover Commission, President Eisenhower established a Board of Consultants on Foreign Intelligence Activities to conduct independent evaluations of the U.S. foreign intelligence program. The Board had a short period of inactivity after President Kennedy took office but was reactivated following the Bay of Pigs, when it was renamed the President's Foreign Intelligence

Advisory Board (PFIAB). The PFIAB has been credited by the Church Committee with significant contributions to the government's intelligence program, such as reorganization of Defense intelligence, revision of National Security Council Intelligence Directives (NSCIDs), development of the overhead reconnaissance program, and new technology for the National Security Agency.[8] One source cites 108 meetings of the PFIAB over the 18-year period from its creation through the Nixon Administration, with 200 recommendations to the President,[9] and a long list of subjects considered by the Board. Despite its achievements in strengthening the government's general intelligence program—or because of them—critics of intelligence activities subjected the Board to attack.[10]

The PFIAB was abolished by President Carter shortly after he took office, perhaps on the advice of his Vice President, who had been a member of the Church Committee. The rationale for eliminating this independent source of review and suggestion was never clear. President Reagan felt the need for additional advice and reestablished the PFIAB in 1982. Its members are prominent citizens from outside the government, serving at the pleasure of the President and without compensation. The PFIAB reviews all phases of intelligence activity and and advises the President of its findings and recommendations.[11]

In addition to the PFIAB there is an Intelligence Oversight Board (IOB), which was created in 1976 by President Ford following the charges about intelligence that had led to the investigations of 1975–1976. The IOB has three members from the private sector, appointed by the President. It functions in the role of independent watchdog within the Executive Branch, reporting to the President on questions of legality and propriety of intelligence community activities.[12] Senior officials in the intelligence community are responsible for ensuring that their employees cooperate with the IOB.[13]

There is probably no area of Executive Branch activity so comprehensively organized as the government's intelligence program. The provision for formulation of programs, their review in the approval process, and the monitoring and evaluation of achievement and failure, as well as the manner in which the programs are conducted, are unmatched. Reviews within the individual intelligence agencies, and in the Intelligence Community under the central coordination of the DCI, produce thoroughly considered proposals that move up in the NSC complex for further review. This process is separate from that of legislative oversight by the Congress, which will be discussed in a later chapter.

The President's Office of Management and Budget (OMB) also has an indirect role in intelligence. Although the DCI has the formal authority—and machinery—for developing the government's intelligence program and submitting it to the President, it still has to be fitted into the federal budget. The Director of OMB monitors the intelligence program and, on occasion, has made contributions, especially when the overall budget needed reduction. While his contributions are seldom substantive, the results often are, and they may require reassessment of priorities when the appropriations for intelligence are affected.

If uncertainty is the basic nature of intelligence activity—in fact, the reason for it—that uncertainty has been reduced to the extent that organization and review have been able to do so. There probably are no comparable procedures outside the national security field for comprehensive planning and eliminating unnecessary duplications. Whatever the complexity of these arrangements and procedures, they are designed to present the President with the best-considered programs possible.

NOTES

1. *National Journal*, 17 July 1982/No. 29, page 1244, article entitled "Clark Emerges as a Tough Manager," by Dick Kirschten.

2. Ibid., page 1245.

3. National Security Council unclassified statement of November 1982, given to the author on 22 December 1982 by the NSC Director of Public Affairs.

4. *Intelligence, The Acme of Skill*, Public Affairs Office, Central Intelligence Agency, Washington, D.C., 1982, pages 10–11. See *Church Committee Report*, Book I, pages 42–48, 427–431, on the NSC in 1976.

5. Ibid.

6. *National Journal*, supra, page 1245.

7. *Executive Order 12333*, section 1.2 (b).

8. *Church Committee Report*, Book I, pages 62–63.

9. *The President's Foreign Intelligence Advisory Board* (PFIAB), pamphlet issued by the Hale Foundation of Washington, D.C., 1981, pages 8–9.

10. *The President's Foreign Intelligence Advisory Board* (PFIAB), pages 10, 13.

11. *Intelligence, The Acme of Skill*, page 11.

12. *Church Committee Report*, Book I, pages 64–69. See also *Intelligence, Acme of Skill*, page 11.

13. *Executive Order 12333*, Section 1.7 (h).

3

THE DIRECTOR OF CENTRAL INTELLIGENCE AND THE CIA

The heavens themselves, the planets and this centre,
Observe degree, priority and place. . . .
        —*Troilus and Cressida* I.iii.85
        William Shakespeare

The National Security Act of 1947, with its new organization of the Defense area, as well as its creation of the National Security Council and the Central Intelligence Agency, was the end result of an extended process of study, review, debate, and legislative enactment.

Late in 1944, the State-War-Navy Coordinating Committee (SWNCC) was formed as the culmination of a series of arrangements to improve the way World War II was planned and fought.[1] The lessons from that war were convincing. First there had been the failure of peace-time intelligence organization prior to the attack on Pearl Harbor, emphasizing the desirability of better organization in that specialized field of national security. Then came the difficult task of developing national and allied strategy on a global basis, and of coordinating the resulting joint and combined operations. Today, some forty years later, the necessity of drawing together key national security organizations and activities in arrangements for coordinating policy and programs seems obvious. At the time, however, there were established organizations and programs responsible for various elements of security, each with vested interests. Without such existing entities there would have been reservations about how far to go organizationally, and how fast. With such organizations on the scene it was inevitable that countering questions would arise, some of which would assume the status of major issues. It is useful to review a few of these issues, as they contribute to an understanding of later developments.

Several studies of government organization were conducted during the war, although everyone agreed that any major changes should come after the war, when major innovation would not disrupt the war effort. One study, conducted in the summer of 1945 by Ferdinand Eberstadt, a New York banker who had served as head of the Army-Navy Munitions Board, seems to have made the most lasting impression. Some of its major unique suggestions survived the debates that followed. The intelligence section of that report was drafted by Rear Admiral Sidney Souers, a St. Louis businessman who had become Deputy Director of Naval Intelligence during the war.[2] Another study, also in 1945, was conducted by Robert Lovett, then Assistant Secretary of War for Air (there was no independent Air Force then; when it gained independence with the 1947 Act, the Secretary of War's title changed to Secretary of the Army). The Lovett study paralleled the Eberstadt report in important respects, particularly as it concerned the future Central Intelligence Agency.[3] The Joint Chiefs of Staff also made a study of the same general subject. In what proved to be a preliminary step, President Truman in 1946 directed establishment of a National Intelligence Authority (NIA) and a Central Intelligence Group (CIG). NIA was chaired by the Secretary of State, with the Secretaries of War and Navy as members, and with a personal representative of the President. NIA was to serve in a supervisory capacity for the CIG.[4]

Under the Truman directive, the CIG was to be responsible for coordinating the government's intelligence activities and for evaluating and disseminating intelligence.[5] Not without some back-and-forth, it was agreed that the CIG had the additional mission of overt collection of intelligence.[6] The CIG was limited in the extreme. Starting with some 165 employees, it had no budget of its own but, rather, looked to the services for both personnel and funds. The first man to hold the title of Director of Central Intelligence was Rear Admiral Souers, who had drafted the intelligence section of the Eberstadt report. For six months, before returning to private life, he presided over the task of organization, translating broad instructions into an administrative arrangement and initiating operation of the new organization and its machinery. He was succeeded by Air Force Lieutenant General Hoyt Vandenberg, who quickly sought amplification of the new organization's mission and capabilities. In June 1946 the NIA broadened the role of the CIG to include independent analysis, as distinguished from coordinating the work of others. This move seemed necessary to overcome a narrow interpretation placed on the Truman directive. Perhaps more significant, in terms of later issues, was the specific addition of the role of clandestine collection.[7]

In its brief life, from inception of the Truman directive at the end of January 1946 until passage of the National Security Act in September 1947, the CIG was the scene of interesting developments. The concept of its role, in conjunction with that of the NIA, grew into recognition of a need for a national policy group, as had been proposed by the Eberstadt study. These considerations combined to produce the National Security Council, reporting directly to the President. One part of the comprehensive approach to organizing national security was the concept of a Secretary of National Defense, who would preside over the military services.

The military services were concerned generally about being subordinate to a new czar, with a loss of cherished prerogatives. Moreover, they thought some of their important intelligence functions would be absorbed by the new central intelligence service that was being proposed. Although the CIG had not been regarded as posing a threat to the intelligence roles of the services because of military membership on the supervisory NIA, the proposed new intelligence service presented problems. The services' activities and maneuvers during this period have been detailed in the *Church Committee Report* and in Thomas F. Troy's *Donovan and the CIA*, and will not be dwelt on here. The services were not alone in their opposition. Some of the considerations presented during congressional hearings on the 1947 Act are of interest and will be noted below.

THE NAZI SYNDROME

Americans cherish so deeply their special institutions of freedom and personal liberties that their reactions, when threats to those liberties are perceived, border on paranoia. It is understandable that some would have reservations about creating an organization as unfamiliar as a secret intelligence agency, especially if it were portrayed as a possible danger to traditional rights.

Some asserted that the proposed organization was an incipient *Geheimes Staatspolizei*, or Gestapo—the brutal, oppressive secret police of Hitler's Nazi Germany. Having fought a great war to defeat the regime that the Gestapo had come to symbolize, it was not difficult to attract support for opposition to the creation of such an organization in the United States. Where the Gestapo comparison originated is not known for certain, but it is clear that the military services and the FBI were active in advancing their reservations before important members of the Congress and, in some instances, the press. Ironically, the alleged parallel was translated quickly into the public issue of a military dictatorship.

A few believed the proposed unification of the armed forces was a dangerous centralization of power. One senator declaimed that the bill would create "a vast military empire," with "untrammeled power over the entire social and economic structure of the Nation." He regarded the proposed CIA as "an invaluable asset to militarism."[8] One organization, calling itself the National Council for Prevention of War, saw it all as moving "in the direction of an imperialist military dictatorship."[9]

Questions about the intelligence portion of the legislative package settled on two main points. First, the three men to hold the post of Director of Central Intelligence during CIG's brief existence (Rear Admiral Roscoe Hillenkoetter succeeded Vandenberg) had been military men. This was seen as an ominous sign of things to come. Next, unless the proposed new organization was limited in its domestic activities, it was depicted as having the potential of a secret police. The question of limitations on CIA's functions inside the U.S. is a bit more complicated than that.

In 1944, when William Donovan, wartime head of the Office of Strategic Services, looked ahead to a postwar organization for intelligence, he drew up a proposal for a central intelligence service. Among the provisions he included was one stating that the new service would "have no police or law-enforcement functions either at home or abroad."[10] That or similar language appeared in nearly all subsequent studies. Rather than deriving from some philosophical considerations, Donovan's language seems to have been intended to exclude the FBI from the foreign intelligence field.[11] The Bureau had both intelligence and police functions, and the concept of separating the two would strengthen Donovan's objective.

While Robert Lovett was engaged in his study in 1945, he was approached by the FBI, which requested his support in protecting its primary jurisdiction within the United States for investigation of subversives and for "domestic intelligence." In a sense, the Bureau sought a formula not unlike Donovan's, but for the purpose of excluding independent operations by the new organization in the Bureau's established jurisdiction.

The FBI Director, J. Edgar Hoover, had long defended the Bureau's jurisdiction. He had complained about attempts of other agencies, as he saw it, to "literally chisel into this type of activity [domestic intelligence]," and stated that "we don't want to let it slip away from us."[12] He probably was referring to the Department of Treasury services, which at that time had intelligence functions: the Secret Service, the Customs Service, and the Division of Monetary Research.[13] The military services, which had a traditional interest in protecting their personnel and facilities, also had been given a role in this function of intelligence.[14]

Hoover doubtless wanted to avoid further erosion of his authority in an already crowded field.

The Lovett study included language similar to that in the earlier Donovan paper, denying the proposed new intelligence organization any police powers. Among the recorded considerations that may have influenced Lovett is his reported feeling that it was necessary to separate police and intelligence functions to avoid creating a Gestapo. If he actually did entertain such a thought, it may have been the first time the rationale was tied to this subject. He did not express a similar reservation toward the merging of the two functions in the FBI. However, it is clear that Lovett's discussion with the Bureau contributed to the way he viewed the government's overall organization in the field. The Bureau's influence, through the Department of Justice, was also reflected in the language of the President's 1946 directive creating the CIG:

> No police, law enforcement or internal security functions shall be exercised under the directive.
>
> Nothing herein shall be construed to authorize the making of investigations inside the continental limits of the United States and its possessions, except as provided by law and presidential directives.[15]

The most authoritative and detailed review of how the limitation on CIA domestic activities was developed, later to become part of the National Security Act of 1947, is found in Troy's book, *Donovan and the CIA*. The author states: "Undoubtedly these changes represented a Department of Justice contribution."[16] Lawrence Houston, the former General Counsel of both the CIG and the CIA is quoted as saying that the domestic limitation was added at the request of the FBI.[17]

The language limiting the domestic activities of the proposed central intelligence service originated in jurisdictional considerations that continued during the legislative process as a negotiable issue between governmental entities. The final language of the 1947 congressional act—"That the Agency shall have no police, subpena [sic], law-enforcement powers, or internal security functions"—will be considered in more detail later.

On the face of it, the prohibition of CIA police powers and internal security functions seemed a reasonable formula for avoiding jurisdictional problems in the future. As with the distinctions between departmental intelligence and national intelligence, the attempt to delineate between domestic security and foreign activity sometimes fell short of the test. For instance, if a CIA overseas employee or agent came to the United States representing a foreign government, how should he be handled?

He remained a foreign intelligence source, peculiarly within CIA's jurisdictional authorization. Yet he could present a security problem, especially if assigned to the diplomatic installation of an unfriendly nation. This is the sort of problem that should be amenable to reasonable arrangements between the FBI and CIA. But in the early days, as the problem seems not to have been anticipated, there were no established ground rules.

One incident highlights this point. In the early 1950s a CIA foreign agent came to the United States, just as postulated above. CIA kept its eye on the man to make sure he did not go astray, and he was contacted from time to time to keep the association alive and for intelligence purposes. He also came to the attention of the FBI, which first placed him under surveillance and then attempted to take him into custody. CIA personnel, also on the scene independently, came to the man's defense and an unseemly tussle occurred between FBI and CIA personnel at a major intersection in downtown Washington. The incident led to a more detailed set of ground rules. Such incidents have not recurred.

Beyond the question of the CIA agent who comes to the United States is the problem of foreign nationals who visit this country, to whom CIA has no access in their native lands. CIA's responsibility for foreign intelligence gives reason for approaching such individuals to gain their cooperation when they return home. Such cases, of course, may raise issues similar to those in which foreigners with established operational relationships visit the United States. Such cases led to further agreements between CIA and the FBI—agreements that represent realistic accommodations to unanticipated circumstances. The FBI's jurisdictional primacy in the United States is preserved, and CIA's effort to advance its assigned mission is reinforced. The arrangements are formalized in the Executive Orders of the presidents and reviewed and accepted by the Congress, as will be noted later.

At the time the 1947 Act was passed, a combination of provisions was viewed as laying to rest the perception of intelligence organizations as creating the basis for a military dictatorship. In the larger context— unification of the armed services—the provision of direct responsibility over the entire Defense system by the President as Commander in Chief satisfied those who saw danger there. The intelligence structure, too, was subordinated to the National Security Council, which was headed by the President, thereby ensuring responsible political control. The DCI, if a military man, was restricted by law in his relations with the military. Finally, the CIA was forbidden a police role in the United States. Echoes of the issues raised during the legislative process were heard from time to time over the ensuing years. But when the 1947 Act became law, it appeared to those involved that the intelligence organizations were controlled in their activities and that they would be responsive to direction under the system established by the legislation.

CIA: THE ORGANIZATION

The 1947 Act, which created CIA, left intact the functions of its predecessor, the CIG. New functions were added by the National Security Council in the early months of CIA's existence.

If the relationship of the Director of Central Intelligence to the CIG had been uncertain, as it was felt by some to be,[18] that uncertainty was resolved by the provisions of the 1947 Act. The DCI's role as coordinator of the government's intelligence activities was tied by the language of the 1947 Act to his agency. Further, direct subordination to the NSC and the President ensured that CIA would not be subjected to the supervisory control of the intelligence services as the CIG had been under the NIA arrangement. This was a major elevation of the DCI and his agency in the government's hierarchy; in addition, it provided the basis for a degree of future independence apparently not fully recognized by the other intelligence services at the time.[19] CIA was not only made an independent agency; it had clear statutory direction to coordinate the government's intelligence programs, to advise the NSC about the government's intelligence activities, and to make recommendations about them. It was to have access to the intelligence of the other agencies, as well as to conduct its own analysis (a function that had been contested) and see to its dissemination in the government. The Agency was to conduct services of common concern for other organizations in the government, at NSC direction, and it was to "perform such other functions and duties . . . as the National Security Council may . . . direct." These provisions are the specified responsibilities, the last of which is something of a catch-all provision to handle the unforeseen. Although not specified in the 1947 Act, the CIA was expected to continue to engage in overt and clandestine collection of intelligence, as the CIG had done; this subject will be treated in more detail later.

As had happened to the CIG, CIA's mission was augmented in its early days. In December 1947, at the first meeting of the NSC, CIA was directed to develop a program of covert operations to meet the emerging expansionist policy of the Soviet Union.[20] That activity, which became controversial, will be treated more extensively in later chapters, both in terms of what it involves and its legality.

Although the 1947 Act assigned CIA a number of missions and responsibilities, enabling legislation normally given an independent agency was not enacted at the time. Such legislation was discussed during the processing of the National Security Act of 1947, with the understanding that a legislative proposal would be introduced later.[21] Legislation was introduced early in 1948, but congressional scheduling problems and procedures delayed final passage for almost two years, after which it finally emerged as the Central Intelligence Agency Act of 1949.[22] The CIA was unique among the intelligence organizations in having its own legislative charter, combined in the provisions of the 1947 and 1949 Acts. During the interim, however, CIA found itself functioning very much as an organization created within the Executive branch, not entirely unlike CIG, which had to rely on the military services for funds and personnel. CIA did have its own personnel structure, and, although it did not yet have statutory financial authority, arrangements were made for it to conduct its affairs as if it did.

Initially, the DCI and his agency had three basic tasks to accomplish. First, they had to work with the new National Security Council to develop formal terms of reference for carrying out the broadly stated legislative mandate of both the CIA and the other intelligence organizations. Next, relationships had to be worked out with the other intelligence organizations, under the new legislative provisions, that would cope with the tendency of the services to cling to their established prerogatives. Finally, CIA had to develop its own organization under its new legislative charter. The new agency profited from the fact that the CIG had been built up from a very small group to a larger and more comprehensive organization, in anticipation of the missions that clearly would be included in the 1947 Act. General Vandenberg, as DCI, had gained clear authority for the CIG to engage in independent analysis of intelligence, and this authority was continued in the 1947 Act. Under Vandenberg the roles of both overt and clandestine collection had been established, and although the 1947 Act did not so specify, the Congress understood that those roles would be continued. After the 1947 Act was passed, the NSC added the new mission of covert operations mentioned above. The organizational forms established to carry out these functions are no longer relevant, but a brief description of them will help in understanding how the CIA evolved.

CIA ORGANIZATION FOR ANALYSIS

CIA inherited CIG's Office of Reports and Estimates (ORE), which consisted of personnel with varied areas of interest and expertise. Organized primarily on a geographic basis, ORE was conceived as the instrument for "producing objective estimates for the use of senior American policy makers." The military services had been inclined to keep their raw military data to themselves in order to preserve what they considered their "prerogatives in providing policy guidance to the

President, making CIG's primary mission an exercise in futility." To this end, military personnel assigned to CIG had not been authorized by their parent services to participate in "production of coordinated intelligence."[23] In 1946 CIG was authorized to conduct an independent analysis, in lieu of a coordinated procedure.[24] CIA inherited this function from CIG, along with the staff of ORE. With limited coordination by the military sources, ORE conducted its own analyses, which were often focused somewhat narrowly on the short term instead of taking the longer view that had been envisioned for the national intelligence estimate. The failure in 1950 to predict the Korean War more precisely led the new DCI, General Walter Bedell Smith, to establish a separate Office of National Estimates (ONE). This office was launched with a staff of some fifty professional analysts. Reviewing its work was a panel, the Board of National Estimates, composed of seven senior people from government and academia.[25]

Upon establishment of this separate estimative unit, ORE was reorganized into the Office of Research and Reports, with three components: Basic Intelligence Division, Map Division, and the Economic Research Area. In the following year a group that had been specifically formed to analyze communications intelligence (COMINT) on a compartmented basis was merged with personnel in ORE that focused on current intelligence reporting; the new group was titled the Office of Current Intelligence (OCI). The combination of normal intelligence with that available from COMINT provided the analysts with a broader data base, thus improving the quality of their work. COMINT was handled on a very restricted basis at the time, and its merger with less sensitive materials resulted in a highly classified system of reporting known as "all-source" intelligence. Analysts still produced material of lesser classification, without citing COMINT, but it was less valued because of its more limited data base. The establishment of OCI not only resulted in better-quality intelligence, but it also institutionalized the high level of responsiveness demanded of intelligence reporting by policy and planning levels.[26]

Earlier, in a separate area of analysis, the Office of Scientific Intelligence (OSI) had been created. After some difficult jurisdictional contests with the military, this office centered its attentions on basic sciences, scientific resources, and medicine. The military was given responsibility for studying weapons and weapons systems, along with related topics. The responsibilities of the OSI and the military obviously presented problems in the relation between new scientific developments and their military application.[27] As usually proved to be the case, tidy jurisdictional arrangements left gray areas to be worked out among those involved.

THE DCI AND THE CIA

In 1952 the various intelligence offices were consolidated in the Directorate of Intelligence under a Deputy Director for Intelligence, with ORR, OCI, OSI and ONE joined by the Office of Operations (OO), which handled the overt collection functions of interviewing American tourists and businessmen who traveled abroad.[28] Also assigned to the Office of Operations was the Foreign Broadcast Information Service (FBIS), which reported on open foreign broadcasts, and the Foreign Documents Division (FDD), which handled and translated foreign materials.[29] These organizations constituted the main elements of the Directorate of Intelligence for years afterwards. Under DCI Stansfield Turner, in the Carter administration, the Office of Current Intelligence was reduced to a staff that expedited current reporting by the substantive offices. Under DCI Casey, in the Reagan administration, the Intelligence Directorate was organized again along geographic lines, as in ORE years, with a small number of special functional offices.

CIA ORGANIZATION FOR CLANDESTINE OPERATIONS

When the CIG was assigned the responsibility for clandestine collection of intelligence, it was given two elements engaged in clandestine activity overseas. The first came into being when former OSS units, which came to be known as the Strategic Services Unit (SSU), were transferred from the Army in the spring of 1946. SSU had operational facilities in North Africa and the Middle East, with equipment, personnel, codes, and communications.[30] There were also elements in Berlin and Shanghai. In mid-1947 the FBI's Latin American mission was reassigned to the CIG, with some reservations on the part of the Bureau.[31] In fact, the transfer was phased over an extended period. To manage these functions, the CIG created an office named the Office of Special Operations (OSO). Inasmuch as the main Soviet threat was believed to be in the European area, efforts were made to develop a presence and capability there, as well as in the two areas in which existing resources had been given the agency.

It was something of a surprise when, at the very first meeting of the National Security Council, in December 1947, the new CIA was instructed to undertake covert psychological operations against Soviet programs. The consensus had been that the Department of State should be given this mission, but Secretary of State George Marshall had opposed it.[32] Earlier, the State-War-Navy Coordinating Committee (SWNCC) had become concerned with the aggressive policies of the Soviet Union and had proposed countering action. To meet this added responsibility, CIA created a new Special Procedures Group in its Office of Special Operations. Within six months it had a number of psychological operations functioning in Central and Eastern Europe. These actions involved propaganda in various forms, including radio broadcasting into Eastern Europe, balloons dropping propaganda materials to the East, and printed materials being distributed in the area. The Communist coup in Czechoslovakia in 1948 heightened the sense of crisis, and strongly pessimistic evaluations from General Lucius Clay, the U.S. commander in Europe, further intensified the sense of international danger.

In June 1948 CIA's instructions were broadened to include political warfare, economic warfare, and paramilitary activities.[33] As a result the Office of Policy Coordination (OPC) was created, replacing the Special Procedures Group. Although the organization was to be located in CIA, its head was designated by the Department of State. The instructions to OPC came from the Departments of State and Defense, which treated the office as an extension of the State Department and the military services. The DCI found himself with a new, active organization, but with very limited control over its growing program. Pressures within the government for increasing activities led to dramatic growth. In 1949 OPC had 302 employees, with a budget of $4,700,000; in three years the number of employees had risen to 2,812 (with an additional 3,142 contract people overseas) and the budget had increased to $82,000,000.[34]

Inevitable growing pains led to reorganization. General Smith, while DCI, sought improved guidance—and especially formal approval—for OPC programs. In 1951, a newly formed body, the Psychological Strategy Board, was given this task. However, there were anomalies in the role of OPC. The DCI still had no authority over its direction, although it was financed under the CIA budget. Further, competition overseas between OSO and OPC for staff personnel and operational resources led to a variety of working problems. In 1951 General Smith designated Allen Dulles as Deputy Director of Plans, a new position. Dulles worked with both organizations, but each retained its individual management. In August 1952 the Directorate of Plans was formally created, and the head of OPC, Frank Wisner, was named Deputy Director for Plans.[35] Although the basic organization of the directorate for clandestine and covert operations abroad was thus completed, evolutionary change and organizational consolidation within the basic structure became almost routine over the years to follow. It was later renamed the Directorate of Operations, but its basic mission was established.

The Directorate of Operations is organized into six geographic or area divisions, not unlike the geographic bureaus of the Department of State.[36] These are considered the operational divisions, each of which is subdivided into "country desks" that focus on activities in those countries where CIA has representation. Two additional operating di-

visions conduct foreign intelligence collection within the United States—
one overt and one clandestine.[37] In support of the operational divisions
are a number of specialized organizations, among them the Foreign
Intelligence Staff, Counterintelligence Staff, and Covert Action Staff,[38]
which conduct special studies pertaining to operations and provide
advice. On occasion, direct operational support may also be provided.

CIA ORGANIZATION FOR ADMINISTRATION, AND FOR SCIENCE AND TECHNOLOGY

General Smith also gathered the various administrative support
elements into a single organization named the Directorate of Administration, which included the offices one would expect: finance, personnel,
logistics, security, training, and medical services.[39] But this move was
not without some discussion. The clandestine operators wanted to retain
their individual support functions for reasons of operational security.

Until 1962 the three directorates—Intelligence, Plans, and Administration—constituted the basic organization of CIA. In 1962 DCI John
McCone gathered the various technical and scientific activities and
disciplines into one organization, thereby preparing the agency for a
more coherent approach to what was becoming a major aspect of modern
military defense and intelligence—advanced technology. The existing
directorates resisted the loss of operational resources that had been
important to their work. After a first try, which proved to be unsatisfactory,
McCone created the Directorate of Science and Technology in 1963.
The Office of Scientific Intelligence (OSI) was moved from the Directorate
of Intelligence. The Directorate of Plans had developed the U-2 overhead
reconnaissance program in a unit named the Development Projects
Division (DPD); this unit was also made a part of the new directorate,
as was the Technical Services Division (TSD), which had worked on
special support for clandestine operations. Signals Intelligence (SIGINT)
activities were shifted to the new Directorate, from the Directorates of
Plans and Administration. The Data Processing Staff was lodged there
for awhile, although it finally came to rest in the Directorate of Administration. Then a new unit, the Office of Research and Development,
was formed.[40]

LATER DEVELOPMENTS

Organizations change with requirements and with the perceptions
of new management. Tasks come and go, and for the most part are
handled within the basic organization. In transitory situations it was
the usual practice in CIA for special task forces to be formed for the

problem at hand and dissolved when the problem was concluded. The basic organization remained essentially as it was at the end of 1963, after the Directorate of Science and Technology was created (see Figure 3.1). New offices may be formed within the directorates as specialized problems present themselves on a permanent basis (e.g., the Offices of Strategic Research and Weapons Intelligence in the Intelligence Directorate).

Two major developments that affected staffing and organization should be noted to illustrate how novel requirements affect management. First, the U-2 program, under DPD in the Directorate of Plans, produced photography that previously had been unavailable. This photography necessitated the formation of a special unit in the Office of Research and Reports, in the Directorate of Intelligence, designed to process the material and evaluate it. CIA's involvement in overhead reconnaissance did not end with the downing of the U-2 flown over the Soviet Union in 1960 by Gary Francis Powers. As stated in the *Church Committee Report*:

> The Agency's technological capabilities have made a sustained contribution to policymaking. By providing the first effective means of verification, CIA's reconnaissance systems facilitated the United States' participation in arms control agreements with the Soviet Union, beginning with the 1972 Interim Agreement limiting strategic arms.[41]

The photography and other materials gathered by the overhead reconnaissance programs led to an entire new era of analysis, moving far beyond the techniques of World War II photographic interpretation. The small unit in ORR, that had handled analysis of materials from the U-2 flights expanded rapidly, and the National Photographic Interpretation Center (NPIC) became an important new processing and analytical unit in the government. Initially located in CIA's Directorate of Intelligence, it eventually became part of the Science and Technology Directorate, staffed by representatives from various organizations in the Intelligence Community in addition to those from CIA.

A second major development affecting both the Plans and Intelligence directorates was the war in Southeast Asia. At one time the Directorate of Plans had some 700 people working on Southeast Asia matters, 600 of them in Vietnam. The Intelligence Directorate gradually became engaged in increasingly detailed analysis, including military analysis, which is usually considered the jurisdictional domain of the armed services. Both OCI and ORR personnel worked on problems created by the war. In addition, a staff was created under a Special Assistant for Vietnam Affairs (SAVA), who reported to the Director.[42] In sum, the

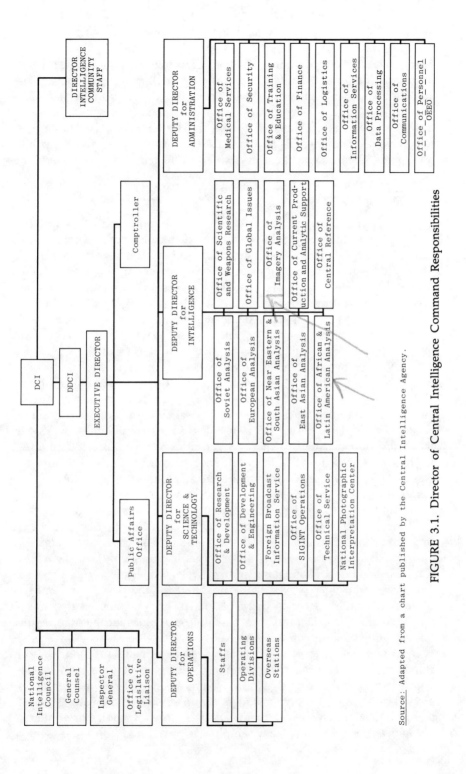

FIGURE 3.1. Director of Central Intelligence Command Responsibilities

Source: Adapted from a chart published by the Central Intelligence Agency.

agency was deeply committed both to carrying out policy in the field, in a paramilitary sense, and to conducting intelligence operations. The analytical elements inevitably were enmeshed in controversies that swirled around the uncertainties of the war and its progress. Some of the tasks given to CIA at that time—and the actions expected of it— may have seemed beyond the normal scope of its duties, yet it was but one of the government agencies similarly affected.

PERSONNEL

Intelligence organizations seek the cooperation of all types of individuals who may help achieve some difficult objective. Whatever the standards of those people—and they vary widely—the regular employees of the intelligence agencies must have a degree of stability and dependability materially above the standards set for agents. From the nation's earliest times this necessity has been recognized. As George Washington said early in the American Revolution, "I wish you to take every possible pains in your power by sending trusty persons . . . to obtain intelligence." And so it is with the employees of the CIA.

CIA's employment practices have passed through several stages with respect to administrative considerations. Following the creation of the CIA and its rapid growth during the early days of the Cold War, a number of different ways of hiring emerged. Former OSS and other military intelligence personnel were taken in, as were some FBI people when the Bureau's Latin American activities were transferred to CIA. Units transferred to CIA from other government organizations—the North African, Middle East, and Berlin and Shanghai activities of the Army, and FBIS—brought in personnel. Employees who knew individuals with appropriate talents recommended them; there was enough of this for some to refer to the informal practice as "the old boy net." The sense of international crisis stimulated some to seek government service, and the challenge of the new secret organization's unknown activities was an added attraction. Rapid growth resulted in the hiring of some employees who later proved to be unsuited for the work, from both a professional and a security point of view. This outcome created management problems later on, but overall the Agency profited from the high quality of the people it attracted.

With the passage of time, personnel recruitment, procedures, and standards have become more formal. The Office of Personnel in the Directorate of Administration now assigns personnel recruiting officers around the country to contact students at universities. Of greatest interest are individuals with special qualifications in foreign studies or academic disciplines; on occasion, new employees are hired for more senior positions because of experience and qualifications, but the majority enter at lower levels. But the suitability of individuals is not assessed on the basis of job qualifications alone; stability and security standards also form a part of the total evaluation of applicants. This issue will be considered in more detail when the general subject of security is examined.

COMMUNITY STAFF

This chapter has focused on the development of CIA to its present state. The organizational arrangements for carrying out assigned missions are not unusual, except in the case of tasks that are not common to other governmental organization. The DCI's coordination role in the Intelligence Community, now known as the Intelligence Community Staff, will now be discussed briefly (for further details, see in Chapter 5).

The National Security Act of 1947 specifies that many of the coordination functions are the duties of the Agency, as distinguished from their assignment expressly to the DCI—thus making clear that the DCI has a firm relationship with CIA. This relationship had not always been clear in the earlier NIA/CIG arrangement. It follows, of course, that the DCI, as head of the organization, exercises the powers of his Agency, whatever minor consideration this fact may present for those who pursue fine distinctions. The legal title of the officer heading CIA is "Director of Central Intelligence," not "Director of CIA," as it is referred to popularly in the media. The title thus refers to more than just the head of an organization; indeed, it is properly interpreted as reflecting the unique role intended for the DCI in reference to the Intelligence Community.

As the role of the DCI in actual coordination of the government's intelligence programs grew, there was an increasing need for greater staff support for that work. Previously the DCI had called on different elements of the Agency for support in the specialized committees of the National Foreign Intelligence Board (variously known over the years as the Intelligence Advisory Committee and the United States Intelligence Board). This board had limited authority, working by consensus, whereas the DI's role as coordinator—especially as it grew—was of a different quality.

In the drawing of those organizational charts, which consumes so much time and energy of administrators, there was a problem of how to show the DCI's special staff, as the DCI developed a separate mechanism for support in his Community role. Some DCIs have shown the IC Staff as a separate body attached to him but outside the normal organizational elements of the agency, and some have shown the staff alongside the other elements but set off by different colors to emphasize the different functions. DCI Turner used coloring to show the difference, whereas DCI Casey depicts the IC Staff as attached to him directly, outside the agency. This latter arrangement is revealed in Figure 3.1, and a more detailed discussion of the IC Staff is given in Chapter 5.

NOTES

1. *Church Committee Report*, Book IV, page 27.
2. *Church Committee Report*, Book IV, pages 6–9. For those interested in the blow-by-blow account of the studies and ensuing debates, see *Donovan and the CIA*, by Thomas F. Troy, Center for the Study of Intelligence, Central Intelligence Agency, 1981, pages 325–410.
3. Ibid.
4. *Church Committee Report*, Book IV, pages 8–9.
5. See President Truman's directive of 22 January 1946, recorded in full in *Donovan and the CIA* at page 464.
6. *Donovan and the CIA*, page 357. See also *Church Committee Report*, Book IV, page 12.
7. *Church Committee Report*, Book I, pages 101–102. With the clandestine mission came transfer from the War Department of the remnants of a former unit of the wartime Office of Strategic Services (OSS), which had seven field stations in North Africa and the Near East, as well as the necessary personnel, communications facilities, and equipment. See *Church Committee Report*, Book IV, page 14.
8. *Donovan and the CIA*, page 396.
9. *Donovan and the CIA*, page 385.
10. *Donovan and the CIA*, pages 445–446.
11. *Donovan and the CIA*, page 221.
12. *Church Committee Report*, Book II, pages 33–34. For a summary of the Bureau's position over the years, see *Church Committee Report*, Book VI, page 226.
13. *Church Committee Report*, Book VI, pages 226–227.
14. *Church Committee Report*, Book II, pages 24–27. A presidential order in 1939 directed that the FBI and Army and Navy intelligence coordinate their activities.
15. *Donovan and the CIA*, page 322.
16. *Donovan and the CIA*, page 347.
17. *Church Committee Report*, Book I, footnote on page 137. The second provision was omitted from the later legislative package because of an agreement between the FBI and CIG that the latter would engage in overt collection of intelligence from American businessmen.
18. *Donovan and the CIA*, pages 346–347, 402.
19. *Donovan and the CIA*, page 385.
20. *Church Committee Report*, Book I, pages 490–491. It is clear that assignment of a covert operations program was based on the NSC's understanding of the

legislative provision that CIA should "perform such other functions and duties
. . . as the National Security Council may from time to time direct."

21. *Donovan and the CIA*, pages 374, 380, 385.

22. *Church Committee Report*, Book VI, page 253.

23. *Church Committee Report*, Book IV, page 13.

24. *Church Committee Report*, Book I, page 102; Book IV, pages 13–14.

25. *Church Committee Report*, Book I, page 74; Book IV, pages 18–19. See also *Secrets, Spies and Scholars*, by Ray S. Cline, Acropolis, Washington, D.C., 1976, page 111, for a discussion of some of the thinking that went into the creation of the Office of National Estimates.

26. *Church Committee Report*, Book IV, page 22.

27. *Church Committee Report*, Book IV, pages 22–23.

28. *Church Committee Report*, Book IV, page 23.

29. *Church Committee Report*, Book I, pages 262–263; Book IV, pages 12–13; Book VI, pages 236–237.

30. *Church Committee Report*, Book I, page 102; Book IV, page 14.

31. *Church Committee Report*, Book IV, footnote on page 11; Book VI, page 284. See also *Donovan and the CIA*, page 547, footnote 51.

32. *Church Committee Report*, Book IV, page 28.

33. *Church Committee Report*, Book IV, pages 28–29.

34. *Church Committee Report*, Book IV, pages 30–31.

35. *Church Committee Report*, Book IV, pages 33–39.

36. *Church Committee Report*, Book VI, page 261.

37. *Church Committee Report*, Book I, page 438; Book VI, page 261.

38. *Church Committee Report*, Book VI, page 261; the Technical Services Division was transferred to the Directorate of Science and Technology.

39. *Church Committee Report*, Book I, page 108.

40. *Church Committee Report*, Book IV, pages 77–78.

41. *Church Committee Report*, Book I, page 124.

42. *Church Committee Report*, Book I, page 120.

4

THE DCI AND THE
INTELLIGENCE COMMUNITY

The whole is greater than the sum of its parts.
—Unattributed

The intelligence provisions of the 1947 Act mandate a special role for the DCI and his agency in central coordination of the government's intelligence work. Even with the full cooperation of all the intelligence organizations it would have been a formidable task to develop a coherent and balanced program out of the numerous independent activities already in being. A lack of enthusiasm on the part of the other organizations had been evident during the legislative process, and early achievement of a system of strong central influence would remain for the future.

The 1947 Act created a new legal framework for the government's intelligence activities, but attitudes and patterns of conduct had already been fixed in the period preceding it. The military intelligence organizations were accustomed to carrying on their independent analysis and reporting, and felt it their duty and prerogative to continue—even in light of the aforementioned distinctions between department and national intelligence and the specified broader duties of CIA. While the existing organizations were authorized to continue what they had been doing, their continuation was subject to the effect of having CIA and its functions superimposed on the old system.

The National Security Council undertook to establish jurisdictional boundaries, but in doing so it encountered the practical problem of complex subject matter. Extensive interrelationships of political, economic, and military affairs confounded tidy jurisdictional arrangements. After considerable debate among the agencies, the NSC issued National Security Council Intelligence Directives (NSCIDs) that spelled out ground rules. The Department of State, for instance, was responsible for economic analyses of the noncommunist world, and CIA was assigned coverage of the communist bloc. Logically, the military services were responsible for analysis on matters related to their special interests. CIA was given authority for clandestine operations abroad; other services wishing to engage in such activities were to coordinate with CIA. As noted earlier, CIA was also given the task of conducting covert actions abroad, although the initial directives preceded the NSCID series. The details are not important today, other than to note that problems were recognized and that an effort was made to handle them.

Despite the provisions of the law and the NSCIDs, a number of considerations that militated against complete success in tackling the problem of a strong central influence on the government's programs. In retrospect, it probably was inevitable that organizational progress would be evolutionary rather than precipitate. In any case, it is useful to review how arrangements for coordination developed and why these arrangements took the shape they finally did.

EARLY COORDINATION

When CIA was created, a forum on which the intelligence organizations could address their problems already existed. During the short life of CIG, a panel composed of the heads of the military and civilian agencies was established.[1] The function of this panel, named the Intelligence Advisory Board (IAB), was envisioned as advising the Director of Central Intelligence. The name of the body has changed over the years, as have its membership and scope of interest, but its basic approach—meetings among the different agencies to consider general problems—has continued. Upon passage of the 1947 Act, the IAB became the Intelligence Advisory Committee (IAC). Its membership consisted of the DCI as chairman and representatives from the Departments of State, Army, Navy, and Air Force, the Joint Chiefs of Staff, and the Atomic Energy Commission.[2] The IAC has been described as intended "to serve as a coordinating body in establishing intelligence requirements among the departments." However, not only the IAC, but the DCI as well, lacked the power to enforce decisions; the DCI

> was to "establish" priorities for intelligence collection and analysis. [He] did not have budgetary or administrative authority to control the departmental components. Moreover, no Department was willing to compromise what it perceived as its own intelligence needs to meet collective needs of policy makers as defined by the DCI.[3]

The absence of authority was clear. Whatever definition administrators and lawyers may have intended for the word *coordination*, it was a limited application. One dictionary offers the meaning of "harmonious adjustment of interaction,"[4] suggesting that easy consensus was the way things were to be handled. But easy consensus hardly fit the attitudes and circumstances of the time. In a real sense, progress on difficult jurisdictional issues depended in large part on the perceptions, preferences, and priorities of the DCI, as centralizing initiatives were not to be expected from the others. Whatever the defects of the committee arrangement, it did provide the means for facing problems and solving them, always with the knowledge that major unresolved issues could be taken to the National Security Council.

Rear Admiral Roscoe Hillenkoetter, who succeeded General Vandenberg as DCI prior to passage of the 1947 Act, was too junior an officer to meet the demands of rank-conscious Washington. He was unsuccessful in his efforts to advance the interests of the new agency in its central role. He, in turn, was succeeded in 1950 by General Walter Bedell Smith, who had been General Eisenhower's chief of staff in Europe. Smith was not only a senior and respected officer, well acquainted with Washington officialdom, but a forceful personality as well. Early in his tenure, the CIA General Counsel pointed out that the IAC had come to function as a supervisory body of the DCI and as an advisory body to the NSC—a reversal of the intended roles. In fact, just such an arrangement had been proposed at one point during the legislative processing of the 1947 Act.[5] General Smith advised the IAC that he expected it to serve him in an advisory capacity, and that he would report to the NSC in his capacity as DCI. At the same time, Smith sought the cooperation of the IAC members in producing a national intelligence estimate,[6] one of the purposes for which CIA was created. The military services had refused to cooperate in such work prior to passage of the 1947 Act, when CIG had been given the role of coordinator, which had not changed after passage of the 1947 Act.

The IAC was not the only intelligence advisory body to take form in the earlier days. A United States Communications Intelligence Board (USCIB) was also created to advise the Secretary of Defense on the important subject of Communications Intelligence (COMINT). COMINT involved the interception of foreign communications. The members of USCIB were the Secretary of Defense, the Secretary of State, the Director of the Federal Bureau of Investigation, and representatives of the organizations engaged in the operations—namely, the Army, Navy, and Air Force.[7] In 1957 the President's Board of Consultants on Foreign Intelligence Activities (PBCFIA)—which was later renamed the President's Foreign Intelligence Advisory Board (PFIAB)—recommended merger of the IAC and USCIB, which was achieved in 1958.[8] This step was opposed by the military services (i.e., the main collectors), which had a special interest in the intelligence derived from the activity. The military services feared that the merger would reduce their dominance in the work to that of an advisory role to the DCI.[9] The fact that this change did not find its way into an agreed NSC directive until 1960[10] reflects the care with which the various roles were defined. The combined board was named the United States Intelligence Board (USIB).

THE UNITED STATES INTELLIGENCE BOARD (USIB)

The USIB was not merely an administrative device for coordinating government intelligence programs, with the limitations that function already had experienced. It also served as a forum for the various members to advance their interests. Although the situation was not always one of perfect accord among the members, USIB served as a forum, to the satisfaction of most. Issues that could not be worked out by the members could be referred to the NSC if deemed sufficiently important.

The USIB, and the IAC before it, worked through committees made up of representatives from the USIB. Each committee was assigned specialized topics for consideration.[11] One source reports fifteen such committees; the Church Committee stated that the number was down to eleven at the time of its inquiry.[12] A list of some of the committee names may help convey something of the subject matter involved: the Security Committee, which deals with standards and practice; the Communications Intelligence (COMINT) Committee, which became the Signals Intelligence (SIGINT) Committee;[13] the Economic Intelligence Committee (EIC);[14] the Scientific Intelligence Committee (SIC);[15] the Guided Missile Intelligence Committee (GMIC), created by DCI Allen Dulles against Army, Navy, and Joint Staff opposition,[16] and later to become the Guided Missiles Astronautics Intelligence Committee (GMAIC);[17] the Joint Atomic Energy Intelligence Committee (JAEIC);[18] the Human Intelligence (HUMINT) Committee, formed with some reluctance on the part of the DCI, given the CIA's sensitivity over clandestine operations, and later to become the Human Resources Committee.[19]

THE COORDINATED ESTIMATE

The USIB approved and issued the National Intelligence Estimate (NIE), which had been such a source of early disagreement. In 1950, when DCI Smith took firm steps to develop coordinated national estimates, he formed an Office of National Estimates (ONE) under CIA's Deputy Director for Intelligence (DDI). ONE was designed to play a central role in producing the NIEs. Essentially, the ONE staff drew upon members of the Community, combining contributions into a draft paper, which in turn was reviewed by a panel of senior officers titled the Board of National Estimates (drawn from government and academic circles). The approved paper was then circulated to the USIB members for review. After that, meetings were scheduled so that representatives of the USIB members could engage in detailed review of the papers. The process was laborious—and sometimes filled with controversy—but meticulous attention was given to detail and conclusions. When consensus could not be reached, provision was made for a statement of dissenting views.[20] It was intended that sterile compromises popularly associated with committee drafting be avoided, in order that important issues be highlighted. Unresolved differences usually took the form of dissenting footnotes, which clearly stated the disagreements in question.

In the 1960s the Board of National Estimates was removed from the internal jurisdiction of CIA's Intelligence Directorate and began reporting directly to the DCI in his Community role. Then the Office of National Estimates itself was moved to join the Board,[21] thereby emphasizing the Community role in the estimating process. Although the NIE has traditionally been considered the DCI's paper (as well as that of the CIA), in fact it has been very much a Community product. Nevertheless, some have directed their criticism of the NIEs to the DCI and CIA, which surely bear a share of responsibility for such flaws as are perceived from time to time. Even so, the system for producing the NIE does not fit the narrow focus of that particular criticism.

The Office of National Estimates was replaced in 1973 with an arrangement of National Intelligence Officers (NIOs), each assigned a special area of substantive responsibility. Each NIO could draw on the various members of the Intelligence Community for support. Known collectively as the National Intelligence Council, the NIOs are assigned to the office of the DCI. The basic process for community coordination continued essentially along the same lines as those previously established.

ORGANIZATION OF THE NFIB IN
THE REAGAN ADMINISTRATION

In early 1978 the USIB was renamed the National Foreign Intelligence Board (NFIB) in President Carter's Executive Order 12036.[22] The NFIB's function is to advise the DCI on a range of intelligence problems. Its new name has been continued by the Reagan administration.[23] The Carter Executive Order was replaced in December 1981 by Executive Order 12333 in the Reagan administration.

In March 1981, prior to the eventual issuance of the Reagan executive order, DCI William Casey promulgated a directive outlining the responsibilities of the new NFIB as follows:[24]

a. Production, review and coordination of national foreign intelligence;
b. Interagency exchanges of foreign intelligence information;
c. Arrangements with foreign governments on intelligence matters;
d. Protection of intelligence sources and methods;
e. Activities of common concern;
f. Other matters referred to it by the DCI.

Preceding the Reagan Executive Order as it did, Casey's directive referred to the Carter order and, indeed, followed it closely in stating NFIB responsibilities. Although Reagan's Executive Order revoked the Carter order, the Casey directive continued in effect.

NFIB membership, with the DCI as chairman, is as follows: the Deputy Director of Central Intelligence (DDCI) as Vice Chairman and CIA representative; Director of the National Security Agency (DIRNSA); Director of the Defense Intelligence Agency; Director of Intelligence and Research, Department of State; Assistant Director of the Federal Bureau of Investigation; Principal Deputy Assistant Secretary for International Affairs, Department of Energy; Special Assistant to the Secretary of the Treasury (National Security); and appropriate representatives of offices for reconnaissance programs within the Department of Defense. Senior representatives of the military intelligence services attend as observers and may participate at the invitation of the DCI.

The Casey directive stated that the committees will continue to function, thus, in effect, continuing the NFIB committee structure that had existed over the years. Although the current titles and functions of those committees have not been published, it is assumed that they cover the same subject matter as that covered by the committees of the USIB and Carter NFIB.

Participants in the Intelligence Community have changed over the years. The Air Force and Joint Chiefs were added to the IAC with passage of the 1947 Act. The FBI and NSA were added with the merger of IAC and USCIB in 1958. It is interesting to note that the NSA was held in the position of technical adviser for many years, and the FBI restricted itself to matters directly related to its functions. When the DIA was created in 1961 by the Secretary of Defense, it became a member; at the same time, the Joint Chiefs ceased to attend. The Drug Enforcement Agency (DEA) was a member for several years, but during the Reagan administration it was absorbed by the Department of Justice and the FBI represented it.[25] The Marine Corps was given representation on the NFIB in recognition of its special global tactical missions. The Atomic Energy Commission ceased to be a member when it was absorbed into the Department of Energy, which now provides a member to the NFIB. The reconnaissance offices also participate when their problems are under consideration.

Through the first two decades of the post–World War II intelligence system of the U.S. government, the DCI lacked effective authority over a national intelligence budget. In fact, there was no identifiable national budget in this field, each organization having its own financial arrangement. The absence of such authority on the part of the DCI served for many years to prevent his exercising effectively the central function that had been implicit in the 1947 Act. The gradual growth of a role for the DCI in this area is a full and separate story that will be treated in the next chapter. The limitations under which the DCI labored in achieving his central role is well documented. His part in the National Intelligence Estimate had been the main exception to the problems he had experienced in establishing his central role in other areas.

The 1981 Casey directive had another basic provision that reflects the growing role of the DCI in the budget area. Provision was made for a National Foreign Intelligence Council (NFIC), which was to

> assist and advise the Director of Central Intelligence on matters concerning priorities for national foreign intelligence, the National Foreign Intelligence Program budget, and other matters as the Chairman may direct.[26]

The membership of the NFIC is essentially the same as that of the NFIB, with additional senior representatives from the Departments of Defense and Commerce, as well as from the office of the Attorney General and that of the Assistant to the President for National Security Affairs. Such confusion as may arise over the names of these two groups can best be kept clear if we emphasize the difference in their purpose: the National Foreign Intelligence *Board* (NFIB) is concerned with general intelligence problems, whereas the National Foreign Intelligence *Council* (NFIC) is concerned with the national intelligence program and budget.

Over the years, the Intelligence Community has come together as a working, coordinated entity. The jurisdictional rivalries have not disappeared, and not all issues have been easily resolved. But the structure for raising the issues came to function as the forum for orderly consideration of collective problems in lieu of petty contests between competing autonomous fiefdoms. The coordinating mechanism envisioned in the 1947 Act has evolved into a working system that provides a rational approach to numerous government programs, making them a unified whole.

It is not an exaggeration to state that the Intelligence Community has made great strides toward becoming a comprehensive, coherent system. The individual members carry out their separate missions, but they adjust their activities to fit the collective requirements of the government. Reflecting on the shaky beginning of the system, which began as a concept that flew in the face of existing practice and preference, one may find the fact of its eventual functioning an impressive achievement. This is not to say that differences will cease to exist or that the system will totally avoid intelligence failures in the uncertainties of our times, but merely to recognize that the complex system does work.

PRESENT INTELLIGENCE COMMUNITY MEMBERSHIP

Administrators tend to spend a good deal of time attempting to illustrate on charts how bureaucratic systems are arranged, as a way to show how organizations relate to one another in the line of command and where they stand in the overall system. Although such charts often omit material information, relating to particular special interests, they do serve a purpose. The circular chart in Figure 4.1 has been used by several DCIs to indicate the Community members and how they relate to the centralizing influence while retaining their separate relative autonomy.

The principal players in the Intelligence Community are the Departments of State and Defense and the Central Intelligence Agency. The first two are headed by senior cabinet secretaries, whose departments have the major share of national security policy and programs. Although the DCI has been given cabinet rank in the Reagan administration, the importance of his role lies in his position as a point of coordination for government intelligence matters. First assigned by statute, that role has evolved over the years. The responsibilities of the members are outlined here, based on a CIA summary:[28]

- *Director of Central Intelligence.* Primary intelligence adviser to the President and the National Security Council. Heads CIA and such staff elements as are required to discharge his responsibilities, develops the National Foreign Intelligence Program budget, and directs analytic and collection tasking of Intelligence Community elements.

- *Intelligence Community Staff.* Coordinates, for the DCI, the collection of all agencies and departmental elements to minimize duplication

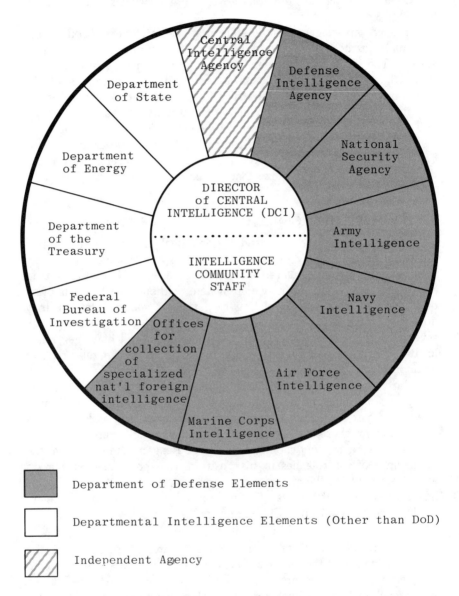

Department of Defense Elements

Departmental Intelligence Elements (Other than DoD)

Independent Agency

Source: Adapted from Fact Book, Public Affairs Office, Central Intelligence Agency, Washington, D.C., July 1982.

FIGURE 4.1. The Intelligence Community

and ensure coverage of major targets, under a program emphasizing topics of priority interest. Also advises on the National Foreign Intelligence Budget, develops its presentation to Congress, and monitors its implementation.

- *Central Intelligence Agency.* As distinct from the DCI in his community role, the CIA has primary responsibility for clandestine collection of foreign intelligence and for counterintelligence operations abroad. Also responsible for research and development of technical collection systems, and production of political, military, economic, biographic, geographic, sociological, and scientific and technical intelligence.

- *Defense Intelligence Agency.* Responsible for the foreign and counterintelligence requirements of the Secretary of Defense, Joint Chiefs of Staff, Unified and Specified Commands, and Defense Department components, and provides the military contribution for national intelligence. Also coordinates intelligence activities of the military services and manages the Defense Attaché System (see Figure 4.1).

- *National Security Agency.* Coordinates and directs the SIGINT programs of the government and performs highly specialized technical operations to protect U.S. communications.

- *Army Intelligence.* Responsible for the collection, production, and dissemination of military and military-related foreign intelligence, including the intentions and capabilities of possible enemies. Also reports on counterintelligence and develops and operates tactical intelligence systems and equipment.

- *Naval Intelligence.* Responsible for the intelligence, counterintelligence, investigative, and security requirements of the Department of the Navy, and conducts specialized collection and analysis related to the naval environment.

- *Air Force Intelligence.* Conducts collection, processing, and analysis to meet worldwide Air Force and national intelligence needs. Has the largest intelligence program among the services, and its Foreign Technology Division is a leading source of analysis of foreign aircraft and missiles.

- *Marine Corps Intelligence.* Provides intelligence support to Marine Corps tactical commanders, primarily for its amphibious warfare mission, on a worldwide contingency basis.

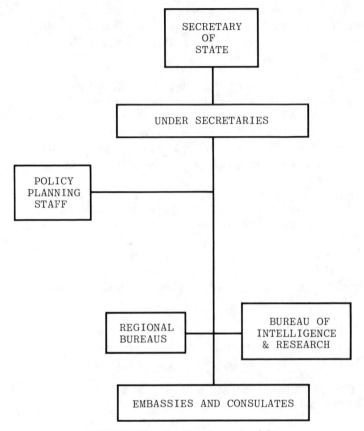

FIGURE 4.2. The Department of State

- *Department of State*. Disseminates reports from overseas posts and participates in preparation of National Intelligence Estimates (see Figure 4.2). The Bureau of Intelligence and Research produces political and economic intelligence for the State Department.

- *Department of Energy*. Openly collects political, economic, and technical energy information concerning foreign energy matters, and is primarily a consumer of intelligence.

- *Department of the Treasury*. Openly collects foreign financial and monetary information, and assists the State Department in collecting economic data.

- *Federal Bureau of Investigation*. Has primary responsibility for counterintelligence within the United States, including detection, penetration, prevention, and neutralization (by lawful means) of espionage, sabotage, and other clandestine intelligence activities directed against the United States by hostile intelligence services. The Drug Enforcement Agency (DEA) was merged into the FBI during the Reagan administration.

The organization charts of the Departments of State and Defense illustrate the overall administrative arrangements for intelligence in these departments. There are, of course, many informal channels of communication that do not appear on these charts. The Department of Defense is the most complex, given its many organizations, and its chart shows both command and intelligence entities (see Figure 4.3).

One Department of Defense organization, the Defense Mapping Service, has not been mentioned in the preceding discussion. Many of its functions are only marginally related to intelligence activities, whereas others are of vital importance.[28] The various maps it produces are of considerable usefulness to military commanders and in intelligence analysis. Because of this relationship the service is mentioned here, but it is not considered a major intelligence function.

The Department of State chart (Figure 4.2) shows only the Bureau of Intelligence and Research (INR) as actively and specifically engaged in intelligence, yet diplomatic missions abroad report events to the State Department, and its country desks and regional bureaus also review developments and form conclusions about the significance of events. The interchange between policy and intelligence is mutually stimulating. The State Department is considered the collector and producer of the largest quantity of political information.

The complex structure of the National Security Council for coordinating major policy and planning is impressive in itself. Its direction and control extends to the intelligence activities of the government as well. That system, with the subordinate machinery of the Intelligence Community as has been brought together in the National Foreign Intelligence Board and National Foreign Intelligence Council, adds to the entire coordination process. The DCI's arrangements for developing a comprehensive and coherent basis for the conduct of his central function in the Intelligence Community can only emphasize the extent to which the Executive branch has organized its work in the intelligence field. It is doubtful that any other government activity is so extensively and thoroughly coordinated and controlled.

NOTES

1. *Church Committee Report*, Book I, page 100.
2. *Church Committee Report*, Book I, page 71, footnote 4.

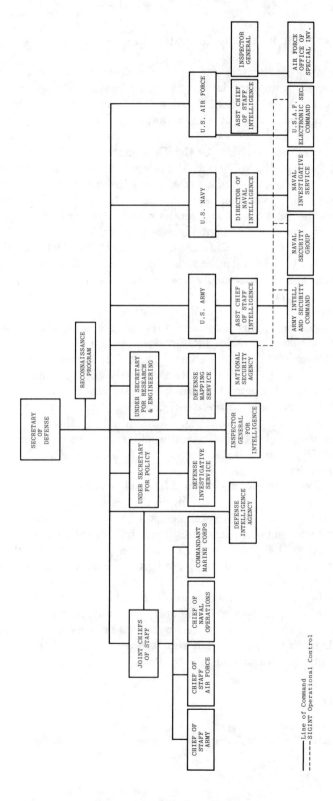

FIGURE 4.3. The Department of Defense (Intelligence Related Functions)

——— Line of Command
------- SIGINT Operational Control

3. *Church Committee Report*, Book IV, page 25.

4. *The American Heritage Dictionary of the English Language*, Houghton Mifflin/American Heritage, New York, 1969.

5. *Church Committee Report*, Book IV, page 25.

6. *Church Committee Report*, Book IV, page 18.

7. *Church Committee Report*, Book I, page 71, footnote 4; Book I, page 114, footnote; Book IV, page 62.

8. *Church Committee Report*, Book I, pages 114–115.

9. *Church Committee Report*, Book IV, pages 62–63. Disagreement over USCIB was not new. The establishment of USCIB occurred against the objections of the DCI. When the Secretary of Defense formed the National Security Agency in 1952, USCIB was reorganized with the DCI as chairman but in an advisory position relative to NSA and the Secretary of Defense. When USCIB was merged with IAC, thereby forming the new USIB, a COMINT Committee was created to deal with communications intelligence. In 1962 the COMINT Committee became the SIGINT Committee when ELINT (which is concerned with various electronic signals) was added to its responsibility. See *Church Committee Report*, Book I, page 85.

10. *Church Committee Report*, Book VI, page 311.

11. *Church Committee Report*, Book VI, page 63.

12. *Church Committee Report*, Book VI, page 260.

13. *Church Committee Report*, Book I, page 85.

14. *Church Committee Report*, Book IV, page 21.

15. *Church Committee Report*, Book IV, page 78.

16. *Church Committee Report*, Book IV, pages 60–61.

17. *Church Committee Report*, Book IV, page 78.

18. Ibid.

19. *Church Committee Report*, Book I, page 85, footnote 42, page 86.

20. *Church Committee Report*, Book IV, pages 18–20, 97.

21. *Church Committee Report*, Book IV, pages 100–101.

22. *Executive Order 12036*, Sections 1–4.

23. Letter of 6 January 1983 from the Public Affairs Office of CIA, with a 9 March 1981 statement by DCI William Casey establishing a "DCI Advisory Board and Council."

24. Ibid.

25. Although the DEA has a specialized focus on drug matters, it also provides the FBI with an overseas operational capability should the occasion for it arise. In such cases, related intelligence activities would presumably be subject to coordination with the CIA—an issue that could well become a future source of controversy.

26. Ibid. The National Foreign Intelligence Council (NFIC) is not to be confused with the National Intelligence Council, whose members are charged with writing National Intelligence Estimates.

27. *Intelligence, The Acme of Skill*, Public Affairs Office, Central Intelligence Agency, Washington, D.C., 1982, pages 12–13.

28. *Church Committee Report*, Book I, pages 329–330.

5

THE DCI AND MANAGEMENT OF INTELLIGENCE COLLECTION

Set thine house in order.
—Isaiah, xxxviii, I

Approximately three-quarters of the entire national intelligence budget is spent on the Intelligence Community's collection programs. An apparent imbalance between the cost of collection and other activities reflects two main considerations: the importance of acquiring information from around the world; and the high cost of modern technological systems for collection, which absorb some 90 percent of the collection budget.[1] With the increasing technical sophistication of these systems and the growing number of techniques being applied, this seeming imbalance may be increasing.

The United States must have detailed facts on a global basis in order to understand the forces at work on the international scene. This information is an essential ingredient in the judgments and decisions of those responsible for shaping policy and implementing it. Collection cannot be an aimless, unfocused activity, yet it must cover a seemingly infinite range of detailed subject matter. A sense of purpose and direction is necessary to shape and balance the overall program, which requires some central influence on planning and performance if the end product is to be both adequate and accurate. Throughout a good part of the post–World War II period central direction was limited. As discussed in the preceding chapter, considerable progress has been achieved in more recent years, although much remains to be done.

The design of a national program for collecting intelligence obviously must ensure that emphasis be placed on the most critically needed information. Accordingly, judgments must be made on the relative importance of the subjects and priorities for the amount of effort each is to receive. At the same time, of course, the lesser requirements must not be neglected. The task is to determine what subjects are to be included in the overall program, given the fact that financial constraints impose irrelevant imperatives on substantive judgments. Determining the highest priorities results in downgrading the importance of other requirements, with some emerging at such a low level that they may be neglected, if not entirely omitted from the operating plans.

We must keep in mind that every collection requirement reflects questions for which answers are not known. Decisions to deemphasize some questions in favor of others entail the risk that the nation's security may, in some unforeseen way, be affected adversely by lack of coverage. This is an unsettling consideration for those responsible for ensuring the highest quality of intelligence possible. Perhaps some consolation can be taken from one study, which found no evidence to indicate that any intelligence failure could be attributed to lack of operating requirements.[2] Failures usually result from gaps in knowledge—information sought and not obtained—or from misinterpretations of what is known.

In short, a knowledge of how the Intelligence Community has handled the problem of directing and managing intelligence collection over the years is necessary to understanding current collection activities.

THE EVOLUTION OF COLLECTION MANAGEMENT

Since the creation of the Intelligence Community following World War II, experience and administrative evolution have produced a combination of system, procedure, and practice that has acquired a character of its own. In the early days there was such a broad array of unknowns that almost any information was welcome. Initially the requirements were for information on relatively limited geographic areas, before the global character of the Cold War took form. In the four decades since World War II, general government policies and programs reflecting growing U.S. interests have been extended around the world. The scope of intelligence programs has expanded accordingly to support those activities.

The postwar years have witnessed a substantial accumulation of basic knowledge and background information on the world. This data base provides the basis for identifying gaps in knowledge. It now constitutes a solid point of departure for the annual planning cycle that takes place in the government's intelligence effort, during which a statement of current collection requirements and guidance is prepared.

The range of requirements does not diminish with the increased level of knowledge. The Intelligence Community must continue to monitor known situations to verify the continued validity of earlier appraisals if no significant change has occurred, as well as to keep abreast of normal change. This necessary precaution helps identify significant developments that may modify previous judgments and policies. The monitoring of known situations is relatively routine in most instances, but when the subject pertains to one of the more critical topics, such as Soviet military organization and activity, there is a greater sense of urgency. The general Soviet posture, with its swift-striking, long-range weapons systems, makes this emphasis a matter of basic importance to national security. The high priority accorded the USSR is reflected in the fact that it receives well over half the national intelligence collection budget.[3] Beyond that, the Department of Defense engages in additional collection activities that are not included in the national intelligence budget.[4]

The Intelligence Community has made a continuing effort to define and refine the statements of requirements for intelligence collection and the setting of collection priorities. General priorities were first stated in a National Security Council Intelligence Directive (NSCID) bearing the title of "Priority National Intelligence Objectives (PNIOs)." Initially a relatively simple statement, it expanded somewhat and for years was divided into three levels of importance, with Soviet military and foreign policy topics at the highest level. In the early 1960s a fourth level was added to the PNIO format. One result of this modification was a narrowing of the range of subject matter in the highest categories, thus further emphasizing their importance. The PNIO was a general directive from which broad guidance could be taken, but there was wide agreement that the document was an uncertain source of specific guidance.

Over the years the problems of collection guidance were the subject of a number of special studies. One by CIA's Inspector General in 1966 (known as the Cunningham Report) judged the PNIO to be a "lamentably defective document."[5] James Schlesinger, when he was with the Office of Management and Budget (he later was to serve both as Director of Central Intelligence and as Secretary of Defense), conducted a study in which he described the formal requirements as "aggregate wish lists" that could mean "all things to all people."[6] In the light of such criticism it should be no surprise that the imprecise guidance provided by the system left the collectors some leeway in translating priorities into collection programs. Studies conducted in 1970 (in the Department of Defense) and 1971 (the Schlesinger study) specifically concluded that it was the operators and program managers of the collection systems who determined the collection effort—to greater degree, that is, than did the priorities set by the intelligence consumers.[7] While there was, indeed, some latitude for independent initiative on the part of the collectors, the studies were somewhat overstated on this point.

To balance the critical views, the national Signals Intelligence (SIG-INT) collection programs (managed by the National Security Agency) did not formulate their own requirements.[8] Further, the overhead reconnaissance programs have from the earliest times been subject to a closely coordinated management arrangement—namely, a succession of Community committees that guided those collection programs throughout their history.[9] SIGINT and overhead reconnaissance are the two major programs in the technical collection area that account for nearly 90 percent of the national collection budget. It is correct to say that the program managers translate requirements into collection programs and capabilities, but that is not the same as formulating requirements or setting priorities.

Although those who designed the collection programs tried to reflect faithfully the broadly stated requirements and priorities, the ultimate consumers probably were not close enough to the actual collection work to be aware of this fact. As a result, there was some restiveness on their part, especially when the information they needed was not always forthcoming.

THE IMPACT OF TECHNOLOGICAL COLLECTION

A major increase in the information gathered by the technical collection systems created stronger pressure for more central management and control of the collection programs operated by the various intelligence organizations. Increased sophistication in SIGINT collection (especially on Soviet missiles) and the new materials available from overhead reconnaissance caused a precipitate rise in costs, at the same time producing such vast quantities of raw information that a new set of management problems appeared. The Schlesinger study of 1971 pointed out that technical collection programs were then producing a nearly unmanageable volume of material without an accompanying improvement in the ability to process and analyze it.[10]

There were some actions that management could take to bring the volume of this material under some control. Some programs were cut back or terminated. Redundant and purely confirmatory reporting from the field could be reduced, even though collection continued. Headquarters elements could be more selective in disseminating the materials received from the field. Processing capabilities at headquarters could be strengthened. In short, corrective action was taken in these areas.

Many of the problems resulting from the rising volume of reporting were brought within manageable limits, though not entirely eliminated. In 1976 the Church Committee stated that

The period of rapid growth in Intelligence costs that undoubtedly motivated much of the concern about overcollection has passed. Although the total of real spending has now returned to what it was during the late 1950s, the efficiency with which intelligence resources are being apportioned among the collection, processing, and production functions remains an issue.[11]

Thus although costs could be reduced and the volume of material brought within manageable limits, allocation of resources remained an issue, as did the establishment of requirements and priorities and control over the collection programs. These questions related to the functioning of the Intelligence Community, in which the role of the Director of Central Intelligence under the provisions of the National Security Act of 1947— or someone in a similar position—was a key to the problem. There had been earlier moves to enhance the central role of the DCI, but tangible progress had been limited.

CENTRAL DIRECTION OF COLLECTION

Prior to 1963 the Director of Central Intelligence had limited influence over the collection programs of the Intelligence Community members. Allen Dulles, who was DCI from 1953–1961, has been criticized for his "neglect of the community management or coordination aspect of his role as DCI."[12] Practically speaking, the DCI was limited in his power to control such activities (as has been noted earlier). Dulles probably appreciated this limitation more than those who criticized the absence of more tangible and forceful action on his part, in Community affairs. If his predilections might have led him in different directions, in 1960 he did in fact launch an investigation of NSA's practice in assigning collection tasks to the SIGINT collectors. The findings of that inquiry were too tenuous to justify major changes, although they did seem to support the belief that there was room for some modification in assignment practices. Committees of the IAC and USIB also considered such matters. There was, for instance, the PNIO system—whatever its degree of usefulness—but other matters consumed Dulles' main attention. Dulles was succeeded by John McCone who, in 1963, created an office of National Intelligence Programs Evaluation (NIPE) subordinate to him in his Community role, as distinguished from his position as head of CIA. That office was to deal with other intelligence organizations by reviewing and evaluating Intelligence Community programs as a whole, establishing an inventory of intelligence activities as a basis for judging cost effectiveness, and assessing actions by the United States Intelligence Board (USIB). Procedures were established for data gathering and evaluation. Work progressed to the point that the first consolidated national intelligence budget was produced in 1965. That, in turn, led to the creation in 1968 of a National Intelligence Resources Board (NIRB), which was designed to study resources for intelligence work.[13] The NIRB reflected the recognition that requirements must be accommodated to collection resources.

Although NIPE's work produced a comprehensive statement of the government's intelligence programs, authority for separate budgets remained with the various departments and agencies. NIPE did develop the data base for more ambitious work, if authority was provided, but for the time being its main contribution was that of an information resource.

In 1971 President Nixon directed then-DCI Richard Helms to review all intelligence activities in the government—including tactical intelligence programs of the military services, not usually considered part of the national intelligence budget—and the allocation of resources, for the purpose of rationalizing national intelligence priorities within budgetary restraints.[14] The need for this review was indubitably a result of the Schlesinger study the same year. Helms created the Intelligence Community Staff, and NIPE provided the cadre for its initial personnel. Helms used NIPE to prepare a consolidated budget for submission to the President. However, he was not given authority to press for adoption of a consolidated budget but, rather, continued in the more limited role of coordinator, seeking to influence by persuasion.

Although the DCI lacked authority in this field, he was able to exercise effective influence on occasion. An example of his influence occurred in 1971, when the Air Force reduced its missile test program. This development led to plans to deactivate the ships used to monitor test firings at Cape Canaveral. Helms was successful in keeping the ships in operational status to monitor Soviet missile tests and in sharing the costs involved with the Department of Defense.[15]

Quite clear is the practical problem confronting the DCI, who could not proceed very far without explicit presidential authority. The Department of Defense not only controls some 90 percent of the national intelligence budget, but it is also the government's primary consumer of intelligence information.[16] The DCI, with direct control over something less than 10 percent of the total budget resources,[17] would be hard-pressed to assert direction over the resources of a senior cabinet officer unless he had clear authority to do so. Furthermore, in those days, informational arrangements were such that IC Staff work was too far behind the Department of Defense budget cycle to have much influence over the DOD budget[18]. James Schlesinger, who became DCI in 1973, clearly came to the job with ideas developed during his term with the Office of Management and Budget. He was known to believe that a need existed for "a fundamental reform of the intelligence community's decision-making bodies and procedures."[19] Perhaps symbolic of his thinking was his emphasis of the status of the IC Staff, the location of which he advertised with signs erected along approaches to the CIA headquarters building in Langley, Virginia. Schlesinger left to become Secretary of Defense in July 1973. In that capacity he had an opportunity to cooperate with the new DCI, William Colby. The two men apparently reached close agreement on a number of issues during Schlesinger's brief stay at CIA.

REFINEMENT OF THE PROCESS

Although Colby's tenure as DCI was preoccupied with congressional inquiries, he still found time to address the problems of Community organization. The IC Staff received his support in developing its capabilities and extending its role under the Nixon directive. Colby sought to eliminate the defects of the PNIO's catchall format. He also developed a new formulation of key requirements for collection, and prepared to take the bull by the horns. He described his approach as follows:

> As a first step, I outlined what I thought were the important subjects that we should be working on; then I asked all the agency heads on the U.S. Intelligence Board to either accept or modify them. My object was to replace the enormous paper exercise called the "requirements" process—which pretended to tell the community precisely what it should be reporting on— with a simple set of general questions about the key problems we should concentrate on. A wag promptly labeled this the KIQs, or Key Intelligence Questions. . . . Once each KIQ was formulated, the various agencies discussed what each would do to answer the question. This then was to be followed by a statement of the resources that each agency would apply, so that an initial judgment could be made as to whether too many or too few were involved in the resolution of each KIQ.[20]

In 1975 there were sixty-nine separate KIQs, about one third of which were concerned with Soviet foreign policy and military technology. The others dealt with issues such as the negotiating positions of the Arabs and Israelis, terrorist threats, and so on. Colby envisioned a follow-up assessment of the performance of the various agencies. In his book he states his sense that things were moving in the right direction. It is clear that his initiative, despite the absence of clear authority, achieved material successes.

Shortly after Colby's replacement as DCI, President Ford, in early 1976, issued an Executive Order that provided for DCI authority over the national intelligence budget. Armed with this authority, the new DCI, George Bush (later to become Vice President), continued the direction commenced by Colby. In 1977 Bush was succeeded by Admiral Stansfield Turner under the Carter administration.

President Carter issued a new Executive Order in 1978, describing in some detail the organization of the National Security Council. The directive gave the DCI "full and exclusive authority for approval of the National Foreign Intelligence Program budget submitted to the President." In a fairly specific description of NSC organization, the DCI was given two staff groups to assist him in this Community role. One group came under the authority of a Deputy to the DCI for Collection Tasking, who had responsibility for assigning intelligence collection objectives and tasks within the Intelligence Community and for establishing priorities for those tasks. The other group, under a Deputy to the DCI for Resources Management, was to assist the DCI in formulating budget recommendations and overseeing implementation of the budget program. Each of these groups was staffed with personnel from both the various consumer organizations in the national security establishment and from intelligence organizations. Their staffing patterns, with established channels of communication, ensured familiarity with the programs. This organizational description made public certain details of planning that had not been publicized before. The functions—whatever the arrangements—were not unlike those of the IC Staff, which the new organization replaced.

DCI Turner also devised a system for stating priority intelligence questions, which constituted something of a lineal descendant of the earlier PNIO and KIQ approaches. Turner named his approach the National Intelligence Topics (NITs), which took the form of ninety-nine questions that were deemed to be the highest-priority intelligence subjects, broken down into current and long-range issues. These were to be reviewed periodically to ensure that changing events and perspectives were reflected in the collection guidance.[21]

An unclassified CIA study in 1980—perhaps the last such authoritative unclassified study that will be seen publicly for some time—concluded that there was a general feeling that the procedures for handling the NITs had tended to bureaucratize the approach, thus reducing its relevance with the passage of time.[22] An interesting feature of this study was the reappearance of the belief on the part of some policymakers that they had little effect on formulating the intelligence requirements that guided collectors. The requirements were seen as the independent product of the intelligence organizations. This view has a curious aspect, given the fact that the main consumers—State, Defense, Army, Navy, and Air Force—had representatives on the committees preparing the requirements, as well as in the organizational machinery under the DCI, where the more detailed management actions were taken.

The reservations found at policy levels can be attributed, at least in part, to preoccupation with other matters. The 1980 study found that policymakers generally were unfamiliar with Intelligence Community resources,[23] thus suggesting that although the policymakers' organizations were represented in the intelligence process, they had not personally become consciously involved in influencing it.

The 1980 study also found that gaps in personal knowledge about the intelligence organizations had produced a lack of confidence on the part of policymakers. As a result, their own staffs were called upon to rework the intelligence reports and analyses received by them. That negative attitude was found to be strongest among those whose communications with the intelligence components were the least developed, and nonexistent among those who dealt regularly with the intelligence organizations.[24] The study concluded that there was need for stronger working relationships between policy levels and supporting intelligence organizations. Such strengthened relationships are sought by intelligence organizations, but actual achievement of them depends on recognition of the value of such arrangements by those at policy levels.

In December 1981, President Reagan issued Executive Order 12333, which replaced the Carter directive for the Intelligence Community and its work. The DCI's authority in budget matters has continued, but the structure for the NSC to address various policy and operational issues was not spelled out in the detail provided by the Carter directive. The new executive order provides only that "the NSC shall establish such committees as may be necessary to carry out its functions" and that the DCI "shall establish such boards, councils and groups as required."

New managers usually rearrange their organizations to suit their perceptions and taste, and DCI Casey was no exception. An organization chart published by CIA in July 1982 showed the reappearance of a single Intelligence Community Staff (IC Staff), which meant the elimination of both the Deputy to the DCI for Collection Tasking and the Deputy for Resources Management. Although the arrangement of the IC Staff was subject to change in any case, it is interesting to note the titles of the new "offices" in the Staff, as they reveal something of the early feeling under DCI Casey as to what was important in his Community management function. These are the offices of Assessment and Evaluation; Community Coordination; HUMINT Collection; Imagery Collection and Exploitation; SIGINT Collection; Planning; and Program and Budget Coordination. Apparently DCI Casey then discovered that the various committees of the NFIB were confronted with the same problems that faced the IC Staff. At some point during the period 1983–1984, he drew a number of the NFIB committees into the IC Staff, as shown in Figure 5.1. It would appear that not all the NFIB committees were involved in this move, as some of long standing do not appear among those moved to the IC Staff. As the functions of those committees continue to be significant, it is assumed that they continue to exist within the NFIB structure.

In addition to the committees appearing in Figure 5.1, provision was also made for staffs among the various elements of the new organization. Particularly significant are the Program and Budget Staff, and the Planning and Policy Staff, both of which pertain to the DCI's continuing budget authority. Two of the committees also seem to relate to the functions of these two staffs: the Foreign Intelligence Priorities Committee and the Critical Intelligence Problems Committee, which apparently develop positions on major problems that will affect where and how substantial parts of the budget are to be spent. Among the various subordinate units is a Secretariat Staff, which provides house-keeping services for various committees and boards. Those groups listed on the chart as being served by the Secretariat Staff are the President's Foreign Intelligence Advisory Board (PFIAB), the National Foreign Intelligence Board (NFIB), the National Foreign Intelligence Council (NFIC), the NSC's Senior Interagency Group on Intelligence (SIG-I), the Intelligence Research and Development Committee (IR&DC), and the Scientific and Technology Advisory Panel (STAP).[25]

The current arrangements have clearly been designed to fit present perceptions and working relationships without significantly modifying the DCI's central role or overall authorities.

This review of the Intelligence Community's system for directing collection, which grew with the DCI's authority over the budget, suggests that from the earliest times there was both a basic and a long-range need for strong overall or quasi-executive direction of the government's collection activities. In retrospect, such a systematized approach would not have been practical at the beginning. Earlier arrangements probably served the needs at the time, in terms of available resources. However true that may have been, the need for increasing central direction and control has become an obvious requirement.

The thought that the unstructured approach of earlier times met the needs of the moment may not seem entirely credible in an age of systems-oriented management. Yet the course that was followed was the product of then-perceived needs. The more comprehensive, and at the same time more sharply focused, procedures that have developed since then were needed to cope with the high-cost, high-volume technical collection systems.

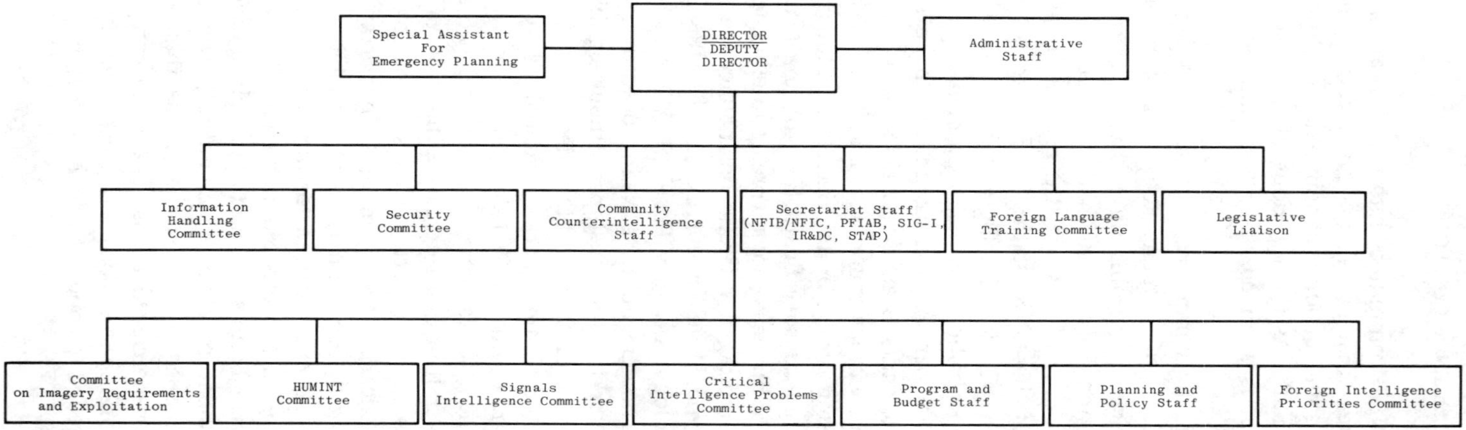

Source: Courtesy of the Public Affairs Office, Central Intelligence Agency.

FIGURE 5.1. Intelligence Community Staff

The data base has grown considerably over the years, and the availability of automatic data processing equipment facilitates its use. Now that the organization and evaluation of collection activities is centralized and planning for the future is structured on a comprehensive basis, many of the perceived problems of the past should be reasonably well in hand. The future concern will be to avoid the tendency of structured bureaucracies toward rigidity and inflexibility, and the need to retain the essential qualities of resiliency that were a positive feature of less formal times.

The 1980 study recorded a considerable working-level exchange among the various organizations in the government. The study praised the effectiveness of these informal channels of exchange, referring to them as "ad hoc networks."[26] There is considerable working-level exchange on a continuing basis, with a tendency toward intensification in special situations. Although the informal, working-level exchanges may not show up in broad or high-level studies—not to mention organizational charts—it is a real and continuing feature of the Intelligence Community, both within the internal operation of the separate agencies, as well as among the agencies themselves.

Keeping the annual statement of intelligence priorities (PNIO, KIQs, NITs) current can be handled in many ways. New statements of requirements are given to the collectors. Less formal guidance also has a place in the system. For years an administrative unit of CIA coordinated a statement of immediate interests known as the Current Intelligence Requirements List (CIRL), which served as a general presentation of the consumer's current special information interests. The CIRL was something of a supplement to more formalized statements of requirements, giving guidance rather than binding directives. It was taken over from CIA by one of the subcommittees of the Intelligence Community's central body[27]—namely, first by the USIB and then by the NFIB.

Basic problems will continue to present themselves as the members of the Intelligence Community continue to carry out their assigned collection responsibilities. It is realistic, however, to anticipate differences among the various consumers as they press for coverage of the subject matter of primary importance to them. The central system will be the forum—and the target—of such controversies as arise.

NOTES

1. *Church Committee Report*, Book I, page 344. Although the source for this figure is dated, it probably holds true given the nature of things. Technological collection has probably increased, but it has also been reported that CIA has

received additional funding under the Reagan administration. Exact figures are not critical to a general sense of the balance of the program.

2. *Church Committee Report*, Book I, page 347.

3. *Church Committee Report*, Book I, page 348.

4. *Church Committee Report*, Book I, pages 329, 336.

5. *Church Committee Report*, Book I, pages 343 (footnote), 347.

6. *Church Committee Report*, Book I, page 347.

7. *Church Committee Report*, Book I, page 346.

8. *Church Committee Report*, Book I, page 355.

9. *Church Committee Report*, Book IV, page 75. See also Book I, page 84. For years NSA employed a Consolidated Cryptologic Program, in which members of the Community participated, as the basic device for planning. See *Church Committee Report*, Book I, page 334. In 1975 USIB approved a National SIGINT Requirements System, which handled Community review and approval of all SIGINT requirements. See *Church Committee Report*, Book I, page 85.

10. *Church Committee Report*, Book I, page 343.

11. *Church Committee Report*, Book I, page 344.

12. *Church Committee Report*, Book IV, pages 60–61.

13. *Church Committee Report*, Book IV, page 76.

14. *Church Committee Report*, Book I, page 87.

15. *Church Committee Report*, Book I, page 88.

16. *Church Committee Report*, Book I, pages 319, 344. Although the Department of Defense's share of the total national intelligence budget may seem high, it constitutes less than 5 percent of the Defense budget. See *Annual Report to the Congress*, by Caspar W. Weinberger, Secretary of Defense, Fiscal Year 1983, 8 February 1982, Government Printing Office, Washington D.C.

17. *Church Committee Report*, Book I, page 333.

18. *Church Committee Report*, Book I, page 333.

19. *Church Committee Report*, Book I, page 341.

20. *Honorable Men: My Life in the CIA*, by William E. Colby, Simon & Schuster, New York, 1978, page 361. See also *Church Committee Report*, Book I, pages 84, 90–92, and Book IV, page 87.

21. *The Impact of Intelligence on the Policy Review and Decision Process: Findings*, by Arthur S. Hulnick and Deborah Brammer, Center for Study of Intelligence, Central Intelligence Agency, Washington, D.C., January 1980, page 14.

22. Ibid.

23. Ibid., page 13.

24. Ibid., pages 13–14.

25. Letter from the CIA Public Affairs Officer, 29 November 1984, amplified in a conversation on 4 December 1984.

26. *The Impact of Intelligence on the Policy Review and Decision Process*, pages 13–14.

27. *Church Committee Report*, Book I, page 86.

6

THE CONGRESS
AND INTELLIGENCE

Vox Populi

The arrangements within the Executive branch of government for direction and control of intelligence activities are about as complete as reasonably can be designed. But overview of the activities does not stop there. The Congress created both the National Security Council, with its authority over intelligence, and the Central Intelligence Agency, with its role in coordinating the government's intelligence programs. As a result of this legislation, the Congress became responsible for exercising its oversight of the new activities. The CIA has always been sensitive to congressional interest and responsive to its wishes. As former DCI William Colby stated on several occasions, the Agency was always prepared to deal with the Congress in the manner that Congress preferred. Despite Colby's statements, it was he who closed the door on an investigative committee when it flagrantly abused agreements about protecting intelligence sources and methods, deliberately leaking highly classified materials to the press.

The need for congressional oversight should be matched by responsible conduct on the part of the members of Congress in handling sensitive materials. As the Congress is a political body, some of its members are tempted to act dramatically on occasion, thus inevitably creating some tension in its relationship with Executive departments. Whatever the issues that may occur from time to time in this respect, the oversight role of the Congress is important.

Under the Constitution, the President traditionally has had primary authority and responsibility in the field of national security. His preeminence in the conduct of foreign relations and his role as Commander in Chief of the armed forces make clear his status in these matters. Under our system of checks and balances, however, the Congress shares responsibility and authority in important ways. The "advice and consent" of the Senate is needed for treaties. If implementing a treaty requires expenditures or positive legislation, both houses take the necessary action. Under the Constitution it is the Congress that "provides for the common Defense." It "raises" the army, "provides" the navy, and pays them both. It is the Congress that declares war, and it has additional authority, extended in the early 1970s, to limit what the President can do in an emergency, prior to consideration and action by the Congress.[1]

Whatever the source of proposals for new governmental programs, if they are to become public law it is the Congress that enacts enabling legislation and raises the funds for them. Toward these ends, the Congress must inform itself on existing problems and past performance as a basis for making judgments on future plans, all the while ensuring that current programs are performing as intended and taking appropriate remedial action if they are not. Arrangements between the Legislative and Executive branches usually provide for such oversight. The system permits constructive cooperation between the Legislative and Executive branches, but more often than circumstances justify, cooperation deteriorates into an adversarial relationship.

Under our system, Congressional oversight of Executive activities differs in material respects from that of a parliamentary system. In the latter system, cabinet ministers are members of the legislature, and they participate in the legislative process. It is more difficult for members of parliament who hold cabinet portfolios to dissociate themselves from past government policy and practice about which they were aware and perhaps at least partly responsible. Although a member of parliament may recant on past policy, he or she is less likely to attack the departments and agencies for actions carried out under what is tantamount to parliamentary direction.

It may be interesting in this connection to recall an incident that occurred in Great Britain in 1982. Labor party members were quick to challenge the government over its security procedures when Soviet penetration of a sensitive intelligence organization was revealed, and even quicker in dropping the challenge when it became apparent that most of the damage had been done when Labor was in power. Indeed, continuity of responsibility has a tempering effect on certain types of partisan excesses.

An example of the ability to avoid responsibility in our system is Democratic opposition to Nixon's conduct of the war in Southeast Asia. Full involvement had occurred under Democratic administrations, with congressional support. Nixon declared the intent to disengage and continued to fight the war while seeking a way to extricate U.S. forces. Democrats, who had supported the original commitment, attacked the incumbent administration for being involved at all. Doubtless this complicated the search for a way to withdraw while heartening the communists in stands they felt safe in taking during the negotiations.

A by-product of this period was the War Powers Resolution of 1973, which limits presidential power in reacting to international crises on the rationale that involvement in Vietnam had been the result of uncontrolled presidential excesses. The Congress tried to put the blame on the presidency while avoiding responsibility for its own role. President Nixon's unpopularity, compounded by his involvement in the Watergate affair, reinforced the congressional move. There is little question that the virulent tone observed during congressional investigations of intelligence was due, in part, to the larger contest over Executive and Legislative roles.

CONGRESSIONAL OVERSIGHT OF INTELLIGENCE

The National Security Act of 1947 was considered to be primarily defense legislation. The subject of unification of the armed forces had been the major issue at the time of its passage. In spite of the broader implications of policy formulation at the NSC level, the House and Senate Armed Services Committees were assigned authority for overseeing the new Central Intelligence Agency, which was to support the NSC. Those committees already had oversight responsibility for the military services, which included their intelligence activities. It is safe to say that, because of the other major issues involving military preparedness, the service intelligence activities received relatively limited attention. Intelligence information coming from the services was followed more closely than were the details of how it was collected.

The Foreign Relations Committee of the Senate and the Foreign Affairs Committee of the House (since renamed the International Relations Committee) had oversight responsibility for the Department of State's intelligence function. The Judiciary Committees of the two houses conducted oversight of the Department of Justice, where the Federal Bureau of Investigation was located. The Atomic Energy Commission and the Treasury Department were subject to oversight by different committees. The committees could have requested appearance before them of representatives from organizations assigned for oversight to other committees, although this was not the regular practice. CIA did appear before the committees concerned with foreign affairs. The Agency considered the Armed Services and Appropriations Committees of the two houses to have an oversight function. Although the Armed Services Committees were felt to have the primary substantive role, the Appropriations Committees conducted detailed review of programs and budget.

Given such arrangements, it is clear that there was considerable fragmentation in congressional oversight of intelligence matters. The Armed Services Committees did, however, have oversight of the larger part of the government's programs in the military services and CIA.

As noted in Chapter 17, it was the practice for many issues before some of the congressional committees to be handled by their powerful chairpersons. One result of this practice was that the details of numerous intelligence activities were held to a relatively small number of committee members.[2] In addition, there was some sense among the members that national security activities, and apparently intelligence in particular, involved matters of such sensitivity as to inhibit them in raising questions of detail.[3] The majority generally accepted the role correctly understood to have been assigned to the intelligence organizations. In fact, as admitted in the *Church Committee Report*, "there were occasions when the principal role of the Congress was to call for more intelligence activity, including activity which infringed the rights of citizens."[4] Whatever the majority view, some held reservations about it.

Following publicity concerning CIA's involvement in ousting Guatemala's Arbenz regime during 1953, and in the overthrow of Mossadeq in Iran the following year, Senator Mike Mansfield introduced a proposal to establish a Joint Congressional Committee on Central Intelligence as a permanent oversight committee to replace the jurisdiction over CIA of the Armed Services Committees. This 1959 proposal was defeated in the Senate. Debate on the proposal reported the detailed responses by CIA to questions put to it by members of the oversight committees (Armed Services and Appropriations) to demonstrate the satisfactory relationships between Congress and CIA. The original Mansfield proposal was renewed a number of times over the years, by Mansfield himself as well as by others.[5] The Congress rejected such proposals until the mid-1970s, although the proposal for a joint committee of the two houses gained some support within the Intelligence Community during the investigations. As intelligence officials tend to be sensitive to the propensity of some members of Congress to engage in willful disclosure of secrets, they prefer arrangements that reduce the number of members and staff employees who would have access to sensitive information.

The organization of the Congress began to undergo significant changes that would have a lasting effect on the way it does business. Between 1960 and 1983 the staff employed by the Congress increased from some 7,000 employees to about 19,000.[6] The Congress had not been given sufficient staff support to conduct much independent research, thus making it dependent on the Executive for much of the detailed factual material pertinent to its oversight. The expansion made it possible to conduct considerable independent research on behalf of its members.

The quality of the resulting staff support and the control exercised by members over their employees—and vice versa—have been debated, but there is little doubt about both the concurrent increase in the assertiveness of the Congress and its members in relations with the Executive branch, and the increased disagreement over the facts.

The generally supportive attitude of the Congress toward the Cold War policies of the United States—and, for that matter, toward intelligence as well—continued well into the Southeast Asia war. This congressional attitude began to change in the mid-1960s. Moreover, something of an insurrection within the Congress in the early 1970s, against its long-standing seniority systems, affected the more settled patterns for doing business.

Perhaps the first major innovation in the nature of congressional oversight of intelligence came at the initiative of the Executive branch in 1973. William Colby—then Executive Director of CIA and DCI-designate—volunteered to the armed services oversight committees the results of a survey completed within CIA, that covered past instances of questionable activities involving the Agency. The survey, begun during James Schlesinger's brief tenure as DCI, was to identify all activities in which CIA had been involved that raised questions of legality or propriety. The CIA Inspector General gathered materials from throughout the Agency, including a number of items from the files of his own office. These were assembled into a set of files, which were divided into activities involving the separate directorates, including a section for specially sensitive material. CIA's Director of Security forwarded records held in his office, referring to them jocularly as the "Family Jewels." Although the final package bore a more formal title, that name caught on and came to be applied familiarly to the entire collection. Later, when the files were reviewed by the Department of Justice to determine if there were prosecutable offenses, each piece of paper was numbered in sequence. Including routing slips, blank pages, and dividers between sections, the total came to slightly more than 690. The media, upon learning of that number, reported some 690 instances of wrong-doing. As it happened, no prosecutions resulted from these cases. In fact, as Colby later commented in his book, *Honorable Men*, most of the reported incidents were found to be proper and legal, and most of those judged otherwise already had been identified over the years and either terminated or corrected.

Colby, in discussions with Schlesinger, decided that the collection of papers should be reported to the oversight committees. He briefed Senator John Stennis, chairman of the Senate Armed Services Committee (then hospitalized with gunshot wounds suffered in a street assault), and followed that with a more detailed briefing of Senator Stuart

Symington, acting as chairman in the absence of Stennis. Colby also reported to Representative Edward Hebert, Chairman of the House Armed Services Committee, who referred him to Representative Lucien Nedzi, Chairman of the Intelligence Subcommittee. Nedzi required a series of followup reports on the matter, although without public fanfare. At the end of August, Colby issued a series of instructions within CIA on how such problems would be handled if they arose in the future, proscribing some activities and requiring various procedures for how decisions would be made on others.[7] There is little question that a number of the ideas produced by the Church Committee for future regulation of clandestine operations had their origin in the Colby instructions, although they were rephrased in a restrictive way that contributed to their rejection by the Congress several years later in 1980. There were low-key statements of reservations on the part of White House personnel about Colby's reporting of the matter to the oversight committees prior to clearance with the White House.

In 1974, as a direct result of allegations by Representative Michael Harrington about CIA's role in Chile, the Hughes-Ryan Amendment to the Foreign Assistance Act of that year was passed. As discussed in Chapter 17, passage of this act required CIA to report specifically to the Congress on Covert Action programs, thus adding the Senate Foreign Relations Committee and the House Foreign Affairs Committee to the Armed Services and Appropriations Committee of both houses, to which the Agency already reported. This increase in the number of committees also increased the number of members of Congress and their staff employees who would have access to information regarding some of the most sensitive operational programs. Accordingly, questions of security were raised, in addition to the administrative burden involved in the repeated reporting on the subject of security to a succession of committees.

After a number of investigations in the period 1975-1976—by presidential commission and the two houses of Congress—the Senate formed a permanent Senate Select Committee on Intelligence (SSCI) in May of 1976. The House of Representatives, in some disarray after the debacle of its investigating committee,[8] did not establish its permanent oversight committee until July of the following year. As a result, the prospect of a joint committee of the two houses—which had, indeed, been considered—fell by the way. Formation of this new set of oversight committees did not initially divest the other committees of their roles. Accordingly, CIA became responsible for reporting to two more committees, totaling eight in all, but not including such special occasions as those requiring it to appear before other committees.

The existence of permanent oversight committees offered the advantage—from the point of view of the Intelligence Community—of bringing together all the government's substantive intelligence programs before one committee in each house, thus providing a comprehensive view of the total effort while broadening the understanding of the members. Also ensured was a degree of substantive continuity that would contribute to a growing comprehension of the problems at hand—a comprehension that had not always been a distinguishing characteristic of special investigating committees. As actual knowledge and understanding replaces uninformed perceptions, a less aggressively critical attitude usually emerges. Critics describe this attitude as "co-option" of members of Congress and attribute it to clever intelligence operatives. How offensive such an assumption was to the members themselves, whose intelligence and integrity were thus questioned, is not clear. But the point, as noted, does help convey some of the attitudes encountered on the Hill.

In 1978 the Foreign Intelligence Surveillance Act was passed, thereby establishing procedures for approval of electronic surveillance in intelligence work in the United States. The Act also required annual reports to the Congress of warrants issued by court order; in those instances in which the Attorney General authorized such an operation, a report of the incident was required at the time. The working assumption was that the requirement to obtain warrants and to report on them would inhibit those responsible for counterintelligence. However, as noted in Chapter 13, the Act did not reduce the number of such operations (as had been publicly stated).

In 1980, after the opponents of intelligence failed to gain approval for wide-ranging legislation restricting intelligence activities, the Intelligence Oversight Act of that year was passed, reducing the number of committees to which certain reports should be made. The permanent select committees of the two houses (SSCI and House Permanent Select Committee on Intelligence, or HPSCI) now have what amounts to primary Congressional oversight of the government's intelligence programs. Membership of the committees reportedly includes representatives from the committees dealing with appropriations, the armed forces, and foreign affairs, thus ensuring that those former oversight committees remain substantively aware of issues that may possibly concern them. The role of the Congress is recognized formally in the Reagan Administration's Executive Order 12333 of 1981 on the National Intelligence effort, which provides in Section 3 that departments and agencies cooperate "with the Congress in the conduct of its responsibilities for oversight of intelligence activities."

The arrangements for oversight have matured. Machinery for orderly and responsible oversight is in place. The problem confronting the committees is that of monitoring performance, determining what is needed, and, where necessary, providing the resources to support adequate intelligence capabilities.[9] How these committees will function in the hurly-burly that sometimes characterizes the Congress is for the future to reveal.

FINANCIAL OVERSIGHT

The exclusive authority of Congress to levy taxes and allocate funds to proposed programs ensures that its role in oversight of Executive activities will be honored. In recent years Congress has sought to extend its authority through judicial enforcement of expenditures for programs enacted by the Congress, on those occasions when the Executive felt it desirable to spend less than had been appropriated.

Congressional oversight committees have been involved with the programs and budgets of the intelligence agencies on a regular basis over the years. The Armed Services and Appropriations Committees had the major function in this respect, by virtue of their oversight responsibility for the Defense intelligence budget and that of CIA. At the time of the Church Committee inquiry, the Department of Defense managed its various intelligence budgets by combining them in a Consolidated Defense Intelligence Budget (CDIB), which ensured that its parts would not be lost in larger Defense programs.[10] CIA and the other departments and agencies with intelligence activities had a somewhat simpler task and, in this respect, presented the oversight committees with less complex problems.

The manner in which the the Intelligence Community, under the Director of Central Intelligence, now coordinates the National Foreign Intelligence Program and its budget was discussed in Chapter 4. The machinery of the Intelligence Community and the National Security Council for developing intelligence programs was covered in Chapters 2 and 4. The program produced by this process must be accommodated in the overall Executive budget, which is done in cooperation with the President's Office of Management and Budget (OMB). If the oversight committees had no knowledge of the national intelligence program until after it had been produced—with all the backing and filling that is involved—they would be at a considerable disadvantage in judging the final product. Under those circumstances, they could, at best, try to reconcile separate budget items with overall explanations of the program. Accordingly, there are continuing exchanges between Intelligence Community personnel and the staff of the oversight committees, thus ensuring that in areas of agreement, the uncontested items can be approved without delay. Where there are disagreements, the issues often can be worked out.

In a world of unexpected contingencies, new developments may produce new requirements that demand "reprogramming" of funds— that is, the transfer of money from established programs to deal with an unforeseen situation. Such deviations from major budget provisions must be approved by the oversight committees. This reprogramming of funds is the subject of Section 1.5(o) of Executive Order 12333, which provides that the DCI shall review all requests for reprogramming in accordance with OMB procedures, prior to reporting to the Congress. Of course, the Congress must approve supplemental appropriations when they are required. The Department of Defense and CIA are allowed to have unexpended funds held by the Treasury for possible future contingencies. Such deviations from major budget provisions must be reported to the oversight committees.

These practices, reinforced by the improved arrangements for oversight of intelligence, put Congress in a better position to work with budgetary problems than in the past. Prior to 1974 the Congress was generally limited in its arrangements for handling the Executive budget proposals, with controls uncertain at best. In 1974, passage of the Congressional Budget and Impoundment Act resulted in formation of a Committee on the Budget in each house, and a Congressional Budget Office (CBO) was created to provide staff expertise to the committees.[11] Even when CBO personnel are not cleared for intelligence matters, they are in a position to provide technical assistance in budget matters.

For current monitoring of financial details, the oversight committees must rely on continuing exchanges with Intelligence Community representatives. The Congress does not have the same auditing function for some intelligence activities that it has, through its General Accounting Office (GAO), for the rest of the government.[12]

The question of public disclosure of classified intelligence budgets remains unresolved. That issue arises out of a sense of need in the Intelligence Community to protect certain types of information, regardless of a constitutional provision stating, in part, that "a regular Statement and Account of the Receipts and Expenditures of all public Money shall be published from time to time."[13] Although the Church Committee felt that some form of publication was both desirable and required, no steps to that end have been taken. The Executive branch believed that intelligence receipts and expenditures were included in the overall reports, and that confidentiality was necessary. A single judicial opinion has treated the question and upheld the position of the Executive branch. It found that the phrase "from time to time" was added in the last

week of the Constitutional Convention, on the initiative of James
Madison, to provide confidential funds for the President's use in military
and foreign matters.[14] In the absence of a ruling by the Supreme Court
overturning the decision, it is unlikely that the Executive branch will
agree to publication of this information in the foreseeable future.

THE RESPONSIBILITY OF OVERSIGHT

In the light of tensions inherent in our system of checks and balances,
it behooves Congress and the Executive branch to devise ways of
ensuring general agreement on the conduct of the government's intelligence programs. If an atmosphere of responsibility and trust is well
established, *bona fide* disagreements can be faced on their own merits
rather than developing into a general attack on the entire system, as
happened during the congressional investigations of the 1975–1976
period.

If the Congress expects responsibility from the Executive branch,
its members must themselves display a reasonable degree of responsibility.
Although I have had the privilege of dealing with a number of responsible
individuals among the Church Committee members and investigators,
I am also aware of examples of uncertain standards on the part of some
members and their staff employees. The experiences cited here are
selected from these less reassuring incidents to point up the problem
of irresponsibility.

The present author met with the senior staff employees of one of
the investigating committees to discuss how the final report would be
reviewed for security purposes, under an agreement between the President
and the committee chairman. This agreement had been made following
DCI Colby's reaction to inappropriate security practices by the committee
and its staff. The committee's senior representative explained at some
length why agreement should not be honored. As the meeting came to
a close, the man declared that it was his ambition to be able to say,
when the investigation was completed, that he had conducted "a tough,
adversary investigation." He resented the response that it was his
responsibility to conduct a fair and objective investigation, and that to
the extent he did not do so the public would have been done a disservice.
The measure of his achievement was rebellion in the committee and
rejection of the report by the House of Representatives—an unheard
of development.

On one occasion, I met with a senator about a portion of a report
produced by his staff at his initiative. Source material was cited to
demonstrate flaws in certain contentions advanced in the draft we were
discussing. When he eventually came to understand the point, though

not without tedious repetition (and finally through confirmation by his staff assistants), he dismissed the source as "lies" and proceeded with his highly suspect conclusions.

There is clearly room for serious consideration of the opinions of public servants involved, in good conscience, with complex problems not always clear to those who visit the subject matter only briefly. It is not enough to commend "the capacity and dedication of the men and women serving in our intelligence services"[15] and then proceed as though those qualities were lacking, as some did. Not all agreed with such negative approaches or attitudes, as demonstrated by the House of Representatives' rejection of the irresponsible offerings of its investigative committee. Some members of the Church Committee refused to sign its report because of what they considered to be its excesses.

Security is critical to successful intelligence activities. Those who must live with the problems on a continuing basis develop a deep appreciation for the intricate ties between information and its sources and an awareness of how indiscriminate disclosure of one can compromise the other. Disclosure of activities can also have disastrous effects on those foreign citizens who cooperate with U.S. representatives in programs directed from the highest levels of the United States Government. There is something very wrong in attacking a government organization that has carried out an approved government policy as though the policy did not have that approval. Yet there are those whose understanding of these difficult situations is reflected in their announced belief in the salutary effect of "disclosure."[16] Such notions may be understandable in the context of the fox-and-hounds spirit of an investigation, but it must be restrained in the environment of more permanent oversight situations, where problem solving should be the focus.

A line must be drawn between disclosures for the sake of exposure and those that serve a real public purpose. During the Church Committee inquiry it was agreed that the identities of agents should be protected, and the committee accepted this limitation on its access to files and records. It was also agreed, in principle, that "the details of sensitive methods used" would not be revealed,[17] but that "the details of illegal acts should be disclosed."[18] In the latter instance it was understood that disclosure could identify those involved, unless it would jeopardize their personal safety.

Although specific details were not given in all of the reports, in many cases they were provided. The nature of the disclosures frequently revealed enough information that knowledgeable foreign counterintelligence officers were able to analyze the intelligence methods used and identify those involved. Even when the activities in question were clearly not illegal, some operations were fully described in the report. Despite the agreements, there was extensive publication of intelligence methods. The intelligence agencies found themselves faced with pressure to agree to publication of the reports under implicit threat of greater disclosure. The *Church Committee Report* occasionally attributes the reluctance of personnel to reveal certain specific details to embarrassment. That opinion has limited stature in fact, but it does serve as a reflection of attitudes prevalent among some of the investigators. More details were published than required to achieve the proper purposes of the Committee, owing to the propensity among some members and staff employees to engage in full disclosure, regardless of the sensitivity of the information.

It should be apparent that investigators venturing into a complex, unfamiliar field will likely experience communications problems. The tendency to revert to irrelevant but comfortable approaches from other disciplines—as some investigators with legal training were wont to do—carries with it the hazard of basic error. The need to learn a great deal in a relatively short time, and to master the nuances in a politically charged atmosphere, is difficult enough in itself. To burden that task with the extra baggage of political bias and negative preconceptions is to compound problems. Hence the investigations sometimes seemed out of control.

In the case of the intelligence investigations, the follow-on step was formation of permanent oversight committees. The employment of investigators from the special investigation committees is understandable. These investigators had at least been introduced to the subject matter, however far they still had to go to fully understanding it. Staffing must start somewhere, and if there is responsible management of the new staff, hiring can reasonably proceed from among the investigators. The SSCI was able to exactly that with a fair degree of success. One of the management tasks, then, was to curtail the crusading tone of some investigators in favor of sober professionalism—not an easy task, but one worth noting.

There is little doubt that those attracted to congressional staffs are in large part motivated by the appeal of public issues. The heady atmosphere of the Congress adds to that appeal, even among those with relatively mundane tasks (as there always is the chance that one may land a more dramatic assignment). Congressional staffs generally include a number of people with radical convictions, some of whom joined as younger workers during the 1960s and 1970s when the staffs were expanding. A few others, disaffected with U.S. society, may have special causes to advance. In some work such tendencies might not matter much, but in those committees concerned with national security they can matter a great deal.

A recent incident points up the problem. In October 1982 the House Permanent Select Committee on Intelligence (HPSCI) issued a study entitled *U.S. Intelligence Performance on Central America*. This study, which leaked to the *Washington Post* before being officially issued, criticized CIA's reporting on communist influences in Central American dissident movements. If such reporting had been in error, it would have been proper for the staff to challenge it. However, to toss the issue into the public domain for its impact on public opinion concerning the issues in Central America, and to risk the exposure of intelligence sources and methods, is to commit an act of a very different and dubious nature. The report in question led to the resignation of Admiral Bobby Inman as consultant to HPSCI, with his flat statement that the assertions in the staff's study were "false." He declared that the release of the study had been decided on partisan political lines, with the Democrats voting for release and the Republicans opposing it.[19] One media source subsequently asserted that one of the apparent authors of the study had been a contact of "an agent of influence on behalf of the K.G.B. for the Cuban intelligence service."[20] The issue became that of Democratic sponsorship for a radical attack on Republican policy in Central America. The study by the committee's staff was refuted in detail in Congress by Representative C. W. Young.[21]

Obviously, if intelligence is used by members of Congress—with distorted accuracy—as an instrument of partisan politics, and if Congress employs staff members with a radical orientation, such action is likely to give rise to grave questions about the credibility of the oversight function. Such matters cannot be dismissed easily as a mere reflection of the erratic conduct of affairs that sometimes is attributed to House tradition.

Not only is the Executive branch being monitored to measure the quality of its performance, but the responsibility and integrity of the Congress is also on trial. Individual members can engage in eccentric partisanship, being accountable only to their constituents (who may never learn about it). However, if the machinery of the Congress is abused—as appears to have occurred in the case just mentioned— serious questions must be raised about the delicate balance between Legislative and Executive relations. If cooperation is to be constructive and of a high quality, both branches must enforce a high standard of professionalism in their respective operations. If the Congress is quick to criticize perceived error in the Executive branch, it must practice the standards it advocates for others or be viewed with less than total respect and trust.

Whatever the differences, when the Congress is in a crusading mood, with the intelligence people becoming increasingly defensive, there is room for even greater confusion than usually exists. Even when working relations are positive, a problem may exist with the best of intentions on both sides. Those working in intelligence—as with other walks of life—develop a vocabulary of their own. Even normal words come to have connotations not immediately clear to those not directly involved. Nuances obvious to intelligence people are sometimes lost on their listeners. And occasionally congressional investigators approach a subject with preconceived notions, which are based, perhaps, on allegations unknown to those being questioned. They may not even be talking about the same thing, as has been known to happen. Each side, then, is likely to end up frustrated with and irritated by the other, the purpose of neither being served.

One recent example of a breakdown in communications involved the mining operations of Nicaraguan ports in early 1984. The Congress was aware of a program to interdict the movement of arms from the Sandinista government in Nicaragua to the insurgents in El Salvador. The general U.S. program of opposing the communist campaign had been made controversial by those opposing the Salvadoran regime. The role given to CIA—to support the anti-Sandinista group (the "Contras")—was judged by some to be a form of illegal intervention, whereas those approving of the concept considered it to be support for the non-Marxist forces as well as a chance to strengthen democratic forms in the area. Early in 1984 CIA was to brief the oversight committees in both houses on the entire program. The House committee was briefed in detail. Delays and postponements of the Senate briefing held up that presentation to the end of the first quarter of the year. From one point of view it was, from all reports, a typical detailed review of what was happening, where and when and how. After the mining became controversial some senators disclaimed any knowledge of it; what developed, in fact, was that it had been reported.[22] Then followed complaints that the mining aspect of the briefing was but a small part of an indigestible whole. Perhaps the same could have been said about each segment of the briefing, but the real problem is that this particular part flared into an issue.

In retrospect, there is an explanation of why the senators felt they had not been told. First, they knew of the general program to interdict the movement of war materials from Nicaragua to the insurgents in El Salvador. It is likely that when they were told of the mining of the harbors from which arms were shipped to the insurgents in El Salvador, the mining seemed a logical part of what had been approved. Only one senator reacted to the point and requested additional briefing. Others, when approached by the media with the challenging question about violation of international law—an arguable point, in any event—were startled and claimed that they knew about nothing that would violate international law.

The way in which committee hearings are often conducted further explains the confusion. Those who have appeared before committees have observed the occasional preoccupation of committee members with such matters as draft legislation, correspondence to constituents, and discussions with their staff assistants who come to consult with them. A fragmented attention span can produce blank spaces in the consciousness of the committee members. The fact is that the members *were* told, and only one of them seems to have reacted to the point. Members of Congress are not known for acknowledging error; the initial reactions to the news of the mining were never corrected.

As such problems will not simply go away, the Congress must realize that a great care should be made to understand what it is told; intelligence people, for their part, must speak as clearly as possible to those who are unlikely to understand some nuances. The fact remains that congressional oversight is essential to effective operation of our governmental system. It is a responsibility of both Executive and Legislative branches to make it work as well as possible, especially in relation to intelligence.

NOTES

1. For a general discussion of this aspect of the balance between Legislative and Executive functions, see *Foreign Policy and Congress*, edited by Thomas M. Franck and Edward Weisband, Oxford University Press, New York, London, and Toronto, 1979, pages 61–82, 210–211. See also "Congress Versus the President: The Formulation and Implementation of American Foreign Policy," by John G. Tower, in *Foreign Affairs*, Winter 1981–1982, pages 229–246. Senator Tower has observed that "over 150 separate prohibitions and restrictions were enacted [in the 1970s] on Executive Branch authority to formulate and implement foreign policy." In his view, "not only was much of this legislation ill conceived, if not actually unconstitutional, it has served in a number of instances to be detrimental to the national security and foreign policy interests of the United States."

2. *Church Committee Report*, Book I, page 11.

3. Ibid., page 149.

4. Ibid., page 11.

5. *Central Intelligence and National Security*, by Harry Howe Ransom, Harvard University Press, Cambridge, Mass., 1958, page 146. A fairly full discussion of the issues that existed at that time appears on pages 146–158.

6. James Reston, in the *New York Times*, 18 December 1982.

7. *Honorable Men: My Life in the CIA*, by William Colby, Simon & Schuster, New York, 1978, pages 340–349.

8. See Note 1 in the Preface of this book.

9. Admiral Bobby Inman, a recognized authority on intelligence who spent years in naval intelligence and served in the posts of Director of the National Security Agency and Deputy Director of Central Intelligence, has declared that the nation's intelligence capabilities have experienced "a 40 percent drawdown." See *Washington Inquirer*, 8 October 1982.

10. *Church Committee Report*, Book I, pages 328–330. It should be in this connection that the Defense intelligence budget is projected at less than 5 percent of the entire Defense budget for FY 1983, and is projected to average at some 4 percent for the FY period 1983–1987. Given the requested total of $258 billion for FY 1983, this brings the Defense intelligence budget to some $10 billion. See *Report of Secretary Caspar W. Weinberger to the Congress on the FY-1983 Budget, FY 1984 Authorization Request and FY 1983–1987 Defense Program*, of 8 February 1982, Table IA.1 and Chart III.J.4.

11. For a fairly simple and up-to-date summary of the budgetary process of the Congress, see "Congress and Budget-Making," by Robert W. Harman, in *Political Science Quarterly*, Vol. 97, No. 3, Fall 1982, pages 381–402.

12. See the testimony of Comptroller General Elmer Staats before the House of Representatives special investigating committee, in which he described the termination of the GAO audit of CIA and the restrictions operating in the audit of FBI funds. The National Security Act of 1947 specified that "the sums payable to the [CIA] shall be expended without regard to the provisions of law and regulations relating to the expenditure of Government funds." In practice, this meant that clandestine expenditures were not to be audited by personnel other than those subject to CIA security disciplines. Further, the annual appropriations for the Department of Justice provide that certain FBI funds are to be accounted for on certification of the Attorney General. See *Hearings Before the Select Committee on Intelligence*, U.S. House of Representatives, Ninety-Fourth Congress, First Session, Part I, July 31, August 1, 4, 5, 6, 7, and 8, 1975, pages 4–11, 519–527. See also *Rockefeller Commission Report*, pages 77–78.

13. See *U.S. Constitution*, Article I, Section 9, and *Church Committee Report*, Book I, pages 367–384. At page 369, the *Church Committee Report* contended that the "constitutional provision was intended to insure that Congress would control the governmental purse and that the public would be informed of how Congress and the Executive spend public funds." Through its oversight arrangements the Congress does have access to this information, but it is correct to state that the public is not similarly informed. Testimony of DCI Colby is cited, as are a number of historical statements of the intent of the provision, over which there was disagreement. Intelligence officials argued for security, as well as for the need not to expose for hostile study information about the size and nature of our intelligence effort—information the United States spends considerable time trying to figure out about the other side. The Executive branch cited as precedents the confidential funds from the earliest times, as proof that the founding fathers had understood this to be appropriate under the Constitution. See the *Church Committee Report*, Book I, at pages 469–471, and page 500, footnote 105. See also the testimony of Comptroller Elmer Staats, *Hearings Before the (House) Select Committee on Intelligence*, pages 12–13.

14. *Halpprin v. Central Intelligence Agency*, 629 F. 2d 144 (DC Cir. 1980).

15. *Church Committee Report*, Book I, page 15.

16. Ibid., page 567.

17. Ibid., page 14.

18. Ibid.

19. *Periscope*, Vol. 7, No. 4, Fall 1982, publication of the Association of Former Intelligence Officers, McLean, Virginia. See also *Washington Inquirer*, Vol. 2, No. 41, 8 October 1982.

20. *Review of the News*, 27 October 1982, article entitled "The Choice Is Intelligence or Propaganda," by Julia Ferguson.

21. *Congressional Record* of 1 October 1982, E 4631/2.

22. *New York Times* column, by William Safire, 28 May 1984.

Part Two

SECRECY, ACTIVITIES, AND TECHNIQUES

7

SECURITY

The necessity of procuring good Intelligence is apparent & need not be further urged—All that Remains for me to add is, that you keep the whole matter as secret as possible. For upon Secrecy, Success depends in Most Enterprizes of the kind, and for want of it, they are generally defeated, however well planned & promising a favourable issue.

—General George Washington, 1777[1]

Beyond the questions of policy, politics, and bureaucratic organization, secrecy is a basic factor that has an important influence on the conduct of intelligence activities. The need for secrecy is obvious to those familiar with what happens when its requirements are violated—people's lives are endangered, sources of information dry up, operations fail. Secrecy accounts for much of the working environment for the activities that will be covered in this section.

Security—secrecy in many forms—permeates the world of intelligence. It affects the way in which those engaged in intelligence work must handle their papers, discuss subject matter, carry out programs, and even how they treat the results. The indirect approaches that security considerations impose on some operations, and the additional administrative procedures required in many usual daily activities, add to the time and cost of the work. That not only is unavoidable; it is necessary.

Security procedures protect vital collection activities, both human and technological. They also safeguard what is collected; to reveal it may disclose the window through which it was acquired, helping the other side locate the window and close it. Not only the intelligence process, but also the factual basis for decisions in policy and planning circles must be protected. To the extent that the opposition does not know the information on which policy is made, it must have less confidence in its appraisal of our most likely courses of action, and will find it more difficult to design its own policies.

Recognition of these considerations led to the provision in the National Security Act of 1947 placing upon the DCI the charge that he "shall be responsible for protecting intelligence sources and methods."

The nation's secrets—*the public's secrets*, to state the thought in its paradoxical essence—are many and varied. Some secrets in themselves may not seem important or sensitive, but when viewed in conjunction with other information they may have great significance. The varying levels of sensitivity—relating to both source and importance—and the interrelationships among the different subject matters, complicate the administration of sensitive materials. Application of the principle known as the need-to-know control adds to the difficulties of managing internal controls. Even in "classified" or protected areas, in which individuals are cleared for all levels of general security information, some individuals may not be given access to certain types of reporting. Then there is the question of responding to pressures from both within and outside the government to release material to the public.

When controversy flares up on some issue involving national security in either military or diplomatic areas, those debating the issue need better information than may be publicly available. Reasonable persons can disagree on issues, but when they share the same knowledge—and thus have some share in the responsibility—the chance of reducing the disagreement, or resolving it, is improved. To this end, arrangements have been made between the Executive and Legislative branches of government to ensure detailed reporting to the Congress. In a constitutional republic such as ours, that is the way to handle it.

In a major debate, both sides of an argument may occasionally wish to reveal classified information that they believe may reinforce their views. Sometimes the revelations seem more dramatic than relevant, having almost the character of an act of reckless defiance. There is no completely satisfactory formula for handling such a problem. Legal prescriptions will not fit all situations. Circumstances and judgment in a given instance, which, one would hope, have been influenced by a sound sense of responsibility, will provide the basis for decisions on what secrets—and how much of them—can and must be made public.

Beyond the question of what information must be made public in contested issues, there are those who hold that any secrecy in government is incompatible with the essential principles of our open society. Although this attitude is not a prevalent one, it does often color and influence discussion of proper arrangements for publication of secret information. There was an undercurrent of such thinking in the Church Committee, although in general the committee's report accepted the principle of security and observed it in much of its work.

PRECEDENTS IN HISTORY FOR SECURITY

In the *Church Committee Report*, a philosophical and historical essay on secrecy in the United States declared that there were no directives regarding protection of information, or for guarding against foreign military intelligence, until the Civil War.[2] This statement may reflect a belief among the members of the committee that the founding fathers had some compunctions on this score. To the contrary, the leaders of the American fight for independence were sensitive to the practical considerations of security. George Washington's instructions, quoted at the head of this chapter, are but one example of such sensitivity.

In 1775, when the Continental Congress began to meet regularly following the skirmishes at Lexington and Concord, the members imposed a resolution of strict secrecy on themselves:

> RESOLVED, That every member of this Congress considers himself under the ties of virtue, honour and love of his country, not to divulge, directly or indirectly, any matter or thing agitated or debated in Congress, before the same shall have been determined, without the leave of Congress: nor any matter or thing determined in Congress which a majority of Congress shall order to be kept secret. And that if any member shall violate this agreement, he shall be expelled this Congress, and deemed an enemy of the liberties of America, and liable to be treated as such. . . .[3]

The Continental Congress took its security seriously. One of the committees it formed was the Committee of Secret Correspondence, designed to communicate with sympathizers in England, Ireland, and elsewhere. It also had an intelligence function—namely, to conduct secret missions in Europe and the United States. When the man it had employed as its secretary divulged information from the committee's files, he was dismissed from his post. He was none other than the gifted pamphleteer of the Revolution, Tom Paine, who had written *Common Sense*, and coined the stirring phrase, "These are the times that try men's souls."[4]

When it was discovered that a prominent American figure was a British agent, he could not be tried as there was no espionage law. To remedy this situation, the Congress appointed a Committee on Spies, which revised the Articles of War to make treason punishable by death. The Congress approved the committee's resolution (believed to have been drafted by Thomas Jefferson), which stated:

> RESOLVED, That all persons not members of, nor owing allegiance to, any of the United States of America . . . who shall be found lurking as spies in or about the fortifications or encampments of the armies of the United

States, or any of them, shall suffer death, according to the law and usage
of nations, by sentence of court martial, or such punishment as such court
may direct.[5]

Not only did the Congress take steps to establish laws for punishing
espionage, it further tightened the authority that it had for observing
secrecy. In the Articles of Confederation—our first national constitution—
the following provision appeared:

The Congress of the United States . . . shall publish the journal of their
proceedings monthly, except such parts thereof, relating to treaties, alliances
or military operations, as in their judgment, require secrecy.[6]

Those who might discount the significance of these actions as
reflecting wartime pressures should consider the circumstances surrounding the writing of the present Constitution. When the delegates
gathered in Philadelphia, the war had been over for several years and
the task was that of creating a viable society. They voted secrecy for
their proceedings, as follows:

That no copy be taken of any entry on the journal during the sitting of
the House without leave of the House. That members only be permitted
to inspect the journal. That nothing spoken in the House be printed, or
otherwise published, or communicated without leave.[7]

It is not hyperbole to suggest that our present system of government—
our open society—was created under the protective cloak of secrecy.
The new Constitution produced in Philadelphia repeated the practice
of the Continental Congress, giving the United States Congress authority
to observe secrecy, but it broadened the language that had applied to
just three categories of subject matter into a provision that included
any subject matter judged to merit such protection. The provision read
as follows: "Article I. Section 5. Each House shall keep a Journal of its
Proceedings, and from time to time publish the same, excepting such
Parts as may in their Judgment require Secrecy."
The men who put those words into practice, through resolutions
during the Revolution and afterward, were students of government.
Liberty, to them, was more than an abstract notion. They knew the
problem of achieving practical balance in government, as opposed to
choosing one doctrinaire extreme or another. Over the years since those
days, secrecy has been practiced in many areas of national interest by
a succession of presidents and congresses. Whatever the contentions to
the contrary, most citizens recognize and accept the need for secrecy

in some matters. The continuing task is to establish and maintain a proper balance between secrecy and openness in our system of government.

CONSIDERATIONS AFFECTING SECURITY

The protection of secret, or classified, information is subject to occasional exception for public purposes, but its control within the government is managed under a complex system of security. A provocative little book by William J. Barnds, consisting of a series of essays debating the issue of secrecy in government, discusses the way in which the government manages its secrets as well as some of the thinking that influences the way it is done. Noting that "the Congress has at various times passed over 170 statutes *requiring* secrecy" (original emphasis), Barnds indicates in the following summary that:

> within the government there has developed a bewildering variety of security classifications that far outstrip the once simple breakdown of confidential, secret and top secret. Many of these new and esoteric classifications grew up because of the vast expansion of scientific and technical information and the strong determination to protect such information. Moreover, having a secret or even top secret clearance by no means allows a person to have access to all of the information so classified, for some of this information is available only to those people judged to have the need to know it in line with their official responsibilities. This is done because of the conviction, which is probably correct, that the fewer people that know about a piece of information the more likely the security will be maintained.[8]

The author goes on to outline the problem of balancing policies of strict application of the need-to-know principle with the more liberal preferences of our society.

The security system is administered by people, a fact that may point up one of the underlying reservations of those opposing it. This system surely appears to be subject to variations in interpretation from time to time, as perceptions of requirements shift. But circumstances usually account for such changes. Crisis situations may cause some deviation from usual practice. There may be pressures to open classified information to more people than is usually felt necessary. On the contrary, access rules may be tightened during a crisis if information is judged to require additional protection. New intelligence sources usually are held closely, although over ensuing years access may be broadened. Such was the case with communications intelligence, which for many years was restricted in its distribution to a limited number of people and organizations.

Information handled on a sensitive basis at the time of collection eventually loses its original sensitivity. An example is the once-guarded secrets of World War II intelligence coups such as Ultra—secrets that were publicized extensively in recent years. Although enforcement of the rules at any given time may be quite specific, security practices are not unchanging. Rather they exhibit realistic adjustments to changing times and requirements, thus reflecting a flexibility that is subject to human judgment.

While the emphasis of this summary has been on security in intelligence, security is not peculiar to that field; indeed, it is a general government practice in matters of defense and national policy. The purpose of this book is not to dwell on the legal issues of security, but some comment is appropriate.

The many laws requiring secrecy cover a wide range of subject matter, not all of which lies within the area of national security. The spectrum of subjects ranges from agricultural statistics to communications intelligence. Laws on the subject are complex, and those interested in more detail may refer to other works on the subject.[9]

The Constitution recognizes treason as a crime, defining it as "levying War [against the United States] or in adhering to their Enemies, giving them Aid and Comfort." Successful prosecution for treason requires either two witnesses to the same overt act or confession in court. As treason is seldom overt, in the usual sense of the word, prosecution is seldom undertaken for constitutionally defined crimes. The main operative law at present is the 1917 Espionage Act. These two key excerpts describe forbidden acts:

- Gathering or delivering defense information to aid foreign governments.
- . . . whoever, with intent or reason to believe that [defense information] is to be used to the injury of the United States or to the advantage of a foreign nation, communicates, delivers or transmits [it]. . . .[10]

It seems to be agreed generally that specific intent must be proved, and that it cannot be assumed from the act in question. As stated in one congressional study of the security of Communications Intelligence, "unauthorized revelation of information of this kind can be penalized only if it can be proved that the person making the revelation did so with the intent to injure the United States."[11] Amendments to existing laws to cover other categories of national security information and to eliminate the requirement for proof of specific intent have been attempted, but with limited success.[12]

In our society, unauthorized release of classified information frequently leads to its publication in the media. That involvement of the press raises the question of freedom of the press, a consideration that has inhibited stricter provisions to punish those who release classified information without the authority to do so. It is not enough to say that publication will surely bring the information in question to the attention of hostile powers, and that this fact is understood by even the most naive offender. Under present law, there simply is no doctrine of constructive intent applicable to such an unauthorized release. This somewhat anomalous status of the law probably influenced former DCI William Colby to propose legislation intended to impose criminal sanctions on CIA employees who violate the trust extended to them, and accepted by them, when they "leak" or publish classified information. Mr. Colby's proposal would have raised no legal obstacles to publication of the material by the media once it came into their possession. His formula, limited to intelligence matters, would provide for prosecution of the employee but—to meet the predictable defense that the secret did not deserve protection in the first place—also would require proof that the revelation "truly did expose a legitimate intelligence source or technique."[13] Press reports in early 1985 indicate that CIA briefly considered proposing similar legislation.

A more narrowly focused bit of legislation was passed in 1982— the Intelligence Identities Protection Act.[14] This act mandates criminal sanctions for unauthorized disclosure of information that identifies U.S. intelligence personnel and agents. There was no question about that portion of the law making it a crime for past or present employees of intelligence agencies to disclose such information, but some challenged a provision that would also punish those without access to classified information who engaged in such activity.[15] That contention was based on the proposition that this provision would violate constitutional rights established by the First Amendment of the Constitution. This view springs from an unqualified interpretation of the First Amendment, a position not supported by the courts or the Congress.[16] The underlying rationale for this legislation is that the publication of identities would threaten not only sensitive operations in which those individuals may be involved but their personal safety as well. Of course, unimpeded programs to publicize the identities of operational personnel can have no real purpose but to expose them to such risks, having what some prefer to call a "chilling effect" on the work. The present author interviewed one officer who returned from overseas and resigned when his name appeared in the media in connection with an intelligence matter with which he had only a peripheral connection.

Whatever the status of the law and the uncertainties of applying it to various acts believed to be in violation of clear security requirements, in the final analysis the heads of the government agencies must rely on their own security organizations and administrative procedures for maintaining their own security. In this context, the prohibition against domestic security functions on the part of CIA was not intended to apply to management of its own security. Every government agency has that function and can call on the FBI or other police as necessary.

No central administrative authority exists in the Intelligence Community to handle the day-to-day practice of official security in the separate agencies. While the DCI has the general legislated responsibility to protect intelligence sources from unauthorized disclosure, that responsibility is not accompanied by any specific authority outside his own agency, although the provision clearly was directed to his larger role in the Intelligence Community. The DCI can request other members of the Intelligence Community to take appropriate measures, and for the most part this procedure has not posed a problem. But beyond that, the prohibitions on police powers and internal security functions are an inhibiting consideration that places much action beyond the limits of CIA. On occasion, CIA has arranged with the FBI to handle some problems, but the procedure is not automatic and sometimes causes controversy because of the legislative prohibitions affecting internal security functions.

Under the 1947 act, the Director of Central Intelligence does have authority to dismiss CIA employees "whenever he shall deem such termination necessary or advisable in the interests of the United States." In practice this simply means that the cause for dismissal need not be stated for the record, nor does the DCI have to defend his action in the courts on general grounds. In courts martial, the military services can prosecute violations of security provisions by uniformed personnel, but civil service employees may present technical difficulties in dismissal because of procedures protecting them from arbitrary action. The government is limited in enforcing security, but there are instances in which it has been able to take action. In one instance it succeeded in removing the profit motive for violation of security procedures by appropriating in court action the author's income from a book written without submitting it for security review.[17]

As troublesome as the aforementioned problems might be, the truly serious one is the employee who has been subverted by a foreign intelligence operative and continues to work at his or her desk while passing secrets to the foreign power. The first practical difficulty is identifying such a case when it occurs. For security officials the case may initially involve only an unverified suspicion. Investigation may prove the suspicion unfounded, but even when it bears out, verification, much less success in catching the suspect in the act, is very difficult to achieve. The Fourth Amendment prohibits unreasonable search and seizure, and the Foreign Intelligence Surveillance Act of 1978 delineates what can and cannot be done by means of electronic surveillance techniques (see Chapter 13).

The crime of treason and espionage is more difficult to detect and prove than the more familiar crimes against persons and property. In the opinion of some, current law imposes unrealistically restrictive procedural requirements in limiting counterintelligence operations, in which time is often of the essence. In addition to the protections afforded personal privacy, even in the case of the common criminal, there seems to be something of a subliminal rationale that accords treason the same extra considerations extended to those who are engaged in legitimate political protest. The line between untrammeled personal right and the rightful interest of a government in treasonous acts by its citizens is not always easy to draw. The differentiation usually depends on the facts, which cannot be ascertained without some surveillance. The issue will remain alive while an acceptable standard is sought. Each new national administration in recent years has revised its regulations on how to proceed in such cases, and not without controversy.

ADMINISTRATION OF SECURITY

Traditionally, the Executive branch of the government has categorized the levels of sensitivity of materials to be protected as official secrets. To have access to such materials, one must be "cleared" on the basis of assigned responsibilities—the need-to-know principle. Current practice is to use the formal designations of Confidential, Secret, and Top Secret to indicate the primary levels of sensitivity. This classification of levels of security importance has made the phrase *classified information* one that is known generally. In the world of diplomacy, the level of classification usually relates to the importance of the subject matter, as it impacts on national interests. Similarly, in military matters, the importance of the subject matter determines the level of classification, with additional handling requirements if extra sensitivity is deemed to require special protection. In the Intelligence Community, these factors also affect classifications, with operational uniqueness and related risks of exposure being additional factors. This extra sensitivity is usually reflected in the use of "code words," which are added to the usual formal classifications.

The code words are essentially indicative of additional handling restrictions on access to the subject matter in question.

In the continuing contest between government protection of official secrets and those favoring the open-book school, semantics in legislation and regulatory language have provided some interesting controversy. For instance, the term *national security*, in itself, has presented a problem despite the term's formal status at least since the National Security Act of 1947, which provided for "the integration of domestic, foreign and military policies relating to the national security." Most observers can assign a generally acceptable meaning to that, but the Watergate episode brought the term into some disrepute, when it was used incorrectly—and unsuccessfully—to block an investigation into the Watergate break-in. That development seems to have provided a new basis in the continuing campaign to restrict the scope of the term *national security*.

On 8 March 1972, President Nixon issued Executive Order 11652 to refine procedures and practice in classification of national security information, and to administer compliance with the Freedom of Information Act (FOIA) of 1967.[18] EO 11652 set new standards for assigning classifications and materially reduced the number of persons with authority to classify documents.

The FOIA specified several areas of information that would be exempt from its operation. The most important exception, in the context of the present discussion, affected information "specifically required by Executive Order to be kept secret in the interests of national defense and foreign policy." EO 11652, in undertaking to clarify this position, first used the phrases *national defense* and *foreign relations*, and then combined them into the familiar phrase *national security*. While the term may not seem exceptionable to many, it came under attack as an attempt to broaden the exemptions under FOIA. The term *national defense*, itself, seems to cover a wide field, and it overlaps extensively with *foreign policy*. Yet, to some observers the phrase *national security* was new and raised an important additional category.[19]

CIA has had a continuing problem in handling the Freedom of Information requests that have been put to it. These requests have incurred unusually high administrative costs as files have had to be searched, with the frequent result that release is denied due to the nature of the information. The Congress enacted a bill in October 1984 that exempted "operational files"—those involving intelligence sources and methods—from FOIA requests. This action is expected to reduce CIA's backlog of requests.[20]

Basic classification of a particular subject is not difficult. Sources are assigned certain sensitivities, and material emanating from them can be marked accordingly. But from that can arise all manner of derivative classifications. For instance, papers that relate to a classified subject but may not themselves contain sensitive information necessarily acquire the same classification as the basic subject. Furthermore, in analysis work, one piece of information may not be very meaningful in itself, but when studied in conjunction with other materials it can assume increased significance. Accordingly, different reports with different classifications are often joined to provide a composite picture of a situation. Yet this procedure may mix materials of differing levels of sensitivity that lose their sensitivity at different rates. Thus, while substantive relevance is the controlling consideration in that marriage of information into one document, future handling is complicated by it. The highest classification can be assigned a paper when it is prepared, with separate items that are part of the document also showing their separate classifications.

When the question of declassifying "all-source intelligence" arises, especially when different sections bear the different classifications, the declassified paper may become pretty badly cut up. Some portions may retain their sensitivity, while others can be declassified. It should be apparent that it is easier to assign an overall classification to a paper than it is to either reduce its classification—"downgrade" it, in the vernacular—or totally declassify it. The bureaucratic burden is substantial. To ease this burden, automatic declassification after specified periods of time has been proposed. Unfortunately for those who propose arbitrary formulas, different types of intelligence lose their sensitivity at different rates. Classification review, and the resulting downgrading or declassification, will always seem slow, regardless of the thousands of people assigned to the task and the millions of dollars budgeted for it. Some members of the media are among those favoring automatic declassification procedures, and occasionally one will see humorous articles based on the chopped-up paper released for public consumption.

A sense of special mission shared by many members of the press, reinforced by a concept of the public's right-to-know, has expressed itself in an aggressive search for national secrets and "inside" stories. The pressure to publish or perish is one of the forces at work in journalism, as it is in academia. It has resulted in some serious breaches of security. The following examples illustrate the problem.

In early 1971 a prominent columnist learned of a sensitive source that had revealed numerous exchanges between key personalities in the Kremlin. Since the columnist knew of these exchanges, he presumably assumed this source to be no longer a secret, and it was discussed in one of his columns. It must be presumed that the source thereupon was lost and is unlikely to be replaced. The columnist's informant was not discovered.

Another interesting case was the CIA attempt in 1975 to recover a Soviet submarine that had sunk in the Pacific. Parts of the story became known, but journalists were persuaded at first to not write about it. The first phase of the operation ended with the recovery of a portion of the submarine, but then the recovery vessel itself had to return to port so that some of its equipment could be serviced. Members of the media, fearing that one of their colleagues might scoop the other, rushed to print. Ensuing developments in the recovery area made it unwise for the follow-up recovery attempt to be made. Former DCI Colby's account of his attempt to dissuade members of the media from publication makes interesting reading.[21] This exercise of freedom of the press was not exactly free. It cost the taxpayer full return on an investment of more than a quarter of a billion dollars spent on the project.

Personnel security, as pointed out earlier, is vital to intelligence work. Efforts are made to hire people who are stable, normal, dependable, and loyal, and who have the requisite professional skills. The employment process requires a "background investigation" by security investigators to ascertain the personal traits and character of the applicant. Are drugs or alcohol a problem? Does an applicant exhibit social conduct that suggests aberrant attitudes? Is there evidence of radical political tendencies that could influence the employee to disregard security rules? Prospective CIA employees must undergo both psychological evaluation and polygraph examinations.[22] New employees are instructed in security procedures and standards, and regular administrative measures are used to maintain their attention to this aspect of the work.

Physical security is a large part of the intelligence environment. It includes walls and fences, guards, safes and vaults, special alarms, separated areas, and control of papers and documents. "Compartmentation"—the segregated handling and storage of especially sensitive materials—is an established administrative security measure.

Secure communications,[23] care in disseminating materials, careful maintenance of records, and monitoring of the system's functioning are all parts of security. In clandestine work, operational tradecraft is largely a matter of caution and security. Meetings, communications between agent and case officer, attention to detail in conduct of the work—all pertain to the protection of operations from exposure (or "compromise," as it is known in the Intelligence Community).

Finally, beyond these obvious measures to strengthen security is the operational aspect mentioned before—counterintelligence. The objective of counterintelligence is to identify attempts to subvert Americans and to prevent penetration of secure areas in which classified material is stored. Counterintelligence will be treated in depth in Chapter 13.

All in all, security—the protection of national secrets—is a critical aspect of intelligence work. Although it requires an administrative structure and a set of procedural practices that add to the normal bureaucracy of large organizations, those who are engaged in intelligence work come to accept security as second nature and make it a part of their daily lives. Security, in its various forms, is challenged by some, but it is supported by the Congress, which itself practices secrecy. With rare exceptions, congressional respect for security is reflected in all its oversight work on matters of national security, including intelligence. Security will continue to be a central feature in these matters.

NOTES

1. *Intelligence in the War of Independence,* A Bicentennial Publication of the Central Intelligence Agency, Washington, D.C., 1976, page 5.

2. *Church Committee Report,* Book VI, pages 313ff. See also Note 22 in Chapter 4, supra.

3. Quoted in *Secrecy and Foreign Policy,* edited by Thomas M. Franck and Edward Weisband, Oxford University Press, New York, London, and Toronto, 1974, page 412.

4. *Intelligence in the War of Independence,* page 9.

5. Ibid., page 11.

6. *The Articles of Confederation,* by Merrill Jensen, University of Wisconsin Press, Madison, 1963, page 269.

7. *The Great Rehearsal,* by Carl Van Doren, Viking Press, New York, 1948, page 28. See also *Miracle at Philadelphia,* by Catherine Drinker Bowen, Atlantic Little, Brown, Boston, 1966, pages 4, 22–23.

8. *The Right to Know, to Withhold and to Lie,* by William J. Barnds, Council on Religion and International Affairs, New York, 1969, page 14.

9. See *Secrecy and Foreign Policy,* which deals primarily with foreign policy secrets but unavoidably also involves itself in discussion of defense information. Presumably the views of its various authors would extend to intelligence, but that special subordinate aspect of national security is not treated otherwise. The chapter entitled "The American Espionage Statutes and Publication of Defense Information," by Benno C. Schmidt, gives a valuable analysis of the current status of law on these subjects. Beyond this, Schmidt's views on what the law ought to be happen not to be the law. Pages 183–201 are detailed and illuminating. The chapter entitled "The Ellsberg Case: Citizen Disclosure," by Leonard B. Boudin, is also quite interesting. The Ellsberg case involved a government suit to prevent publication of what came to be known as the "Pentagon Papers," a collection of documents from the military sector of the government on the Vietnam War. Pages 296–303 further consider the espionage laws and provide useful reading.

10. Title 18, U.S. Code, Sections 793 and 794.

11. *Cryptographic Systems and Communications Intelligence Activities—Disclosure of Information*, U.S. Code Congressional Service, 1950, page 2298. See also Title 18, U.S. Code, Sections 798 and 952, on Communications Intelligence.

12. *Secrecy and Foreign Policy*, page 298.

13. *Honorable Men: My Life in the CIA*, by William Colby, Simon & Schuster, New York, 1978, pages 466–467.

14. Public Law 97-200.

15. "Secrecy, Foreign Intelligence, and Civil Liberties: Has the Pendulum Swung Too Far?" by Duncan L. Clarke and Edward L. Neveleff, *Political Science Quarterly*, Vol. 99, No. 3, Fall 1984, pages 499–503.

16. *National Security and the First Amendment*, by John S. Warner, Association of Former Intelligence Officers, 6723 Whittier Avenue, McLean, Virginia, 1984, pages 18–19. This pamphlet is the most complete treatment of the titled subject and is worth reviewing in its entirety.

17. *Snepp v. United States*, 444 U.S. 507 (1980). As a CIA employee, Snepp had signed a secrecy agreement. After resigning from the Agency, he published a book based on his work with CIA, but without submitting it for security review. The government did not contend that Snepp's book included classified information but based its case on the legal issues alone. Snepp lost the case, and the proceeds from the book were impressed with a constructive trust. See *National Security and the First Amendment*, op. cit., pages 23–24.

18. Title 50 U.S. Code, Section 552.

19. *Church Committee Report*, Book VI, pages 345–348; *Secrecy and Foreign Policy*, pages 102–108.

20. *Washington Post National Weekly Edition*, 15 October 1984, page 15.

21. *Honorable Men*, pages 413–418. See also *Los Angeles Times*, 7 February 1975, and *New York Times*, 19, 20, and 21 March 1975 at pages 15, and 27 March 1975 at page 18.

22. The whole business of clearing persons for employment in sensitive work is complex and detailed, with a history of statutory and regulatory provisions that have shifted with the sentiments of the times. For a full discussion of this history and related problems, see *The Federal Loyalty-Security Program: The Need for Reform*, by Guenter Lewy, American Enterprise Institute Studies in Political and Social Processes, Washington, D.C., and London, 1983.

23. Communications security (COMSEC) is essential today, even more so than in the past. Secure codes and coding machines and protection of electronic equipment employed in modern communications, are basic to protection of national secrets. The National Security Agency (NSA), which will be discussed in later chapters in relation to its intelligence role, is likewise responsible for the security of the government's communications. This function is important enough that the NSA letterhead includes the title of Central Security Service. Some sense of the NSA's work can be found in *The Puzzle Palace*, by James Bamford, Houghton Mifflin, Boston, 1982.

8

THE COLLECTORS AND
OVERT COLLECTION

Ask, and it shall be given you; seek, and ye shall find; knock, and it shall be opened unto you.

—Matthew 7:7

Chapter 5 outlined the high points in the development of the government's efforts initially to influence and guide, and eventually to control and direct centrally, the collection programs of the intelligence agencies. That chapter explained how and why the government's machinery for guiding intelligence collection took the shape it did, given the central role of the DCI. The system did not develop without some problems and recurring reservations have been voiced, up to and including the present, as to whether the consumers at policy levels have as much influence as they would like on what the collectors do. However, there is some doubt as to the validity of consumer reservations, for reasons that will be noted.

Once the machinery in Washington has produced its annual statement of collection requirements and priorities, it is up to the collectors to translate requirements into systems and programs, and then to implement them. They have help from the central machinery (under the DCI), which evaluates which system and methods did well and which did not, those that were marginal and should be strengthened, and those that seem unpromising and should be abandoned. But in the final analysis, it is the collectors who must run the programs. Sometimes the results will be incredibly successful, and sometimes disappointingly not so. Both the annual requirements statement and the system shaped to serve those needs are flexible and dynamic.

Although the collection organization and its resources are characterized by considerable stability simply because certain types of basic coverage continue from year to year, there is also a pattern of continuing

101

change. New developments on the international scene are the most obvious cause of such change, usually calling for additional detail on a situation previously covered in less depth. Information obtained by a collector may give policy levels a greater appreciation for what is known—or not known. Such developments produce new statements of requirements.

Sometimes new collection techniques will have a far-reaching effect on organization. Note, for instance, the dramatic impact of overhead reconnaissance systems on the entire intelligence organization as these systems came into operation. Budgets grew rapidly and raw reporting was produced in quantities that exceeded the abilities of the processing and analytical elements of the government (as noted in Chapter 5).

An example of increased demands coinciding with new techniques occurred during the 1960s and 1970s, when the expanded reporting requirements of the war in Southeast Asia had to be handled at the same time that new technological systems for covering the USSR were being added to the equation. But such major changes are not the rule. Change is usually incremental, consisting of day-to-day adjustments that occurr as developments indicate a need for them. That continuing process is an accepted part of the relationship between consumers in Washington and collectors in the field.

Some excess capability must be built into the collection systems to provide the ability to respond to change. Although some programs have experienced difficulty in recent years as a result of budget constraints, the response in the field to Washington requests has remained high. It is useful to review briefly some of the types of problems faced by collection managers.

SIGINT collectors have an extensive worldwide system for intercepting signals and communications (see Chapter 10). They have a number of fixed intercept sites, with basically stable collection assignments, and they exhibit some ability to shift coverage within a general geographic area. In this connection, so-called search operations are assigned to detect new targets for coverage. Among these basic facilities there is enough capability to allow for unplanned assignments.

The overhead reconnaissance programs monitor known Soviet weapons systems and activities while also keeping a watch for previously unidentified activities and facilities. These programs also have the ability to provide considerable geographic coverage (as further discussed in Chapter 10).

The collectors of political and economic intelligence have an established pattern for gathering information, both overt and clandestine. Normal work may produce significant new information, which often requires a special focusing of effort. Since manpower is limited, more routine work may be dropped for a time in order to concentrate on an issue judged to be more critical at the moment. Additional people may be assigned temporarily to help cope with an immediate problem. Sometimes a collector may happen on information that is not part of a collection requirement but meets interests in Washington. Such "targets of opportunity" reinforce reporting from the field.

The managers of the technological systems appear to have adequate flexibility in their programs. The same is not as true of collection from human sources (HUMINT) gathered by Foreign Service Officers, Defense Attachés, and CIA clandestine collectors, to name the major collectors in this category.

The Foreign Service has been caught between a continuing effort to lower the U.S. profile abroad by reducing overseas personnel and an increased congressionally imposed work load in consular responsibilities.[1] The Defense Attachés had a fairly viable pattern of staffing posts abroad, but that system, too, was cut back. CIA's clandestine service was reduced significantly as part of an overall CIA reduction of some 20 percent in the five years preceding the arrival of DCI Schlesinger. Schlesinger ordered further reductions in 1973. CIA felt there was room for still more reductions following termination of the war in Southeast Asia and planned for further personnel cuts to be executed over a period of years. When DCI Turner arrived with the Carter administration, he carried out that reduction on a shortened time schedule. Concentration on what was considered the classic clandestine target, Soviet Bloc activities, had been envisioned earlier. It soon developed that the Carter administration expected coverage of Third World matters as well (see Chapter 9). CIA found itself understaffed to meet this broadened requirement satisfactorily. The Reagan administration reportedly has increased the CIA clandestine staff to cope with this work load.

Whatever the problems in ensuring adequate resources, it should be clear that the various collection systems and programs must be designed to meet established needs, including some cushion of flexibility with which to meet unexpected but recurring contingencies.

The collection organizations are staffed with trained intelligence personnel who are familiar with the substantive issues on which they work. They are also sensitive to changes in existing situations and aware of the significance of new information they obtain. They have the latitude in which to exercise independent initiative on the scene but are expected to respond to formal requirements from headquarters as well. And so they do. Individual failures do occur from time to time, resulting from human frailties, but the basic system is designed to reduce the chance of error.

OVERT COLLECTION

The gathering of openly available information is the least difficult and least costly method of intelligence collection, yet it requires organization and effort. In 1949, Sherman Kent, in *Strategic Intelligence*, summarized overt collection as follows:

> By "overt" I mean the technique of finding things out by open and above-board methods such as are used in all kinds of scientific, commercial, and journalistic pursuits. I mean the kind of technique you might employ if you wanted to make biscuits for the first time or ascertain the market price of a railroad stock. In some kinds of intelligence work, especially positive foreign intelligence, you can learn a great deal by these overt methods. You study the current published technical literature, or you read the foreign press, or you listen to the official broadcasts of foreign radio stations, or you walk down the streets of a foreign city (with no attempt to conceal your identity) and observe what is going on. Some intelligence devotees have said that you can find out by overt means some 90 or more per cent of what you must know. The remaining percentage constitutes the very thing that the other countries regard as secrets of state, and these cannot be had without recourse to clandestine operations.[2]

In the time since publication of Kent's book, the advent of intercontinental missiles carrying nuclear warheads has affected his generalization about the proportion of critical information that can be obtained overtly. Technological means of collection have proliferated to cover such intelligence targets and the costs have multiplied, but Kent's basic description of the information that can be gathered overtly remains basically correct. Some sense of the nature of this activity can be found in a survey by Lyman Kirkpatrick, who described the process as it existed in Europe in 1975:

> Throughout Europe, the U.S. embassies also serve as a major source of information through liaison with host governments; by the ambassador or Foreign Service personnel; by military attachés; by CIA personnel; by legal attachés (FBI personnel assigned overseas for liaison on investigative and security matters); by Treasury Department representatives on economic intelligence and other matters; and by many others, depending on the size of the embassy.[3]

Formally accredited representatives routinely deal with the various departments of host governments on diplomatic and commercial matters. Accordingly, they are placed in contact with a broad range of knowledge about the nations in which they serve. In the military field, extensive exchange among allied nations, as in NATO, is typical.

Aside from the information afforded by normal official exchanges and liaison relationships, an individual placed "on the scene" is in a position to observe things in a way not possible from afar. Kent described the observer who, while walking down the street, absorbs a feel for the land in which he or she lives during the assignment. In addition, insights can be gleaned from associations in the diplomatic community, given the opportunity for informal exchanges of views and information with the representatives of other nations. It is popular to treat the so-called diplomatic cocktail circuit humorously, but informal and personal contacts always constitute productive additional sources of information as well as leads for further inquiry.

In his book, Kent included references to the usefulness of published technical literature and of the foreign press in general. The Department of State had managed the procurement of foreign documents prior to 1954, at which time it passed that responsibility to CIA.[4] Much of this procurement was handled as any library would handle it—that is, through commercial organizations that stock foreign publications from around the world, including books, professional journals, periodicals, and special publications. Representatives abroad follow the local press and provide special materials such as photography, maps, and biographical material on public figures.

Kent also noted the usefulness of listening "to the official broadcasts of foreign radio stations," much as one might listen to news broadcasts at home. In foreign lands, especially where radio and television are state controlled, the recording of such broadcasts provides exact statements of what public figures are saying on subjects of interest. In 1940 the Federal Communications Commission created the Foreign Broadcast Information Division to take on this task. Shortly after U.S. entry into World War II, this function was transferred to the U.S. Army, where it remained until it was transferred to the Central Intelligence Group in 1946. It was made a part of CIA on its creation, where it remains as the Foreign Broadcast Information Service (FBIS), maintaining for the government a worldwide system for monitoring foreign broadcasts.[5]

In addition to the procedures involved in acquiring overtly available information is a program designed to take advantage of the knowledge of private U.S. citizens who, while traveling abroad, provide unique information on the basis of their business interests or simple observations as tourists. This program was started during World War II by OSS and was described by Ray S. Cline as

an innovation in intelligence gathering that was to have a long history—
overt collection of useful data about foreign areas voluntarily provided by
U.S. citizens and foreigners. The information was given on the understanding
that their furnishing it was kept confidential. With Europe closed off during
the war, these sources proved valuable for analytical writing and planning
for both clandestine and military operations. They also provided leads to
many individuals who volunteered for secret work with OSS in regions
with which they were familiar. Basically, however, the function was simply
overt information collection, a task central to any national intelligence group.
It was preferable to collect needed data in this manner rather than risk
agent lives in searching for the same information abroad. This function was
preserved in the work of "domestic contacts" units that through the years
served CIA by collecting overt information from U.S. businessmen, scientists,
and travelers who wanted to help their government without it being known
that they had passed along data procured in the normal conduct of their
business or travels abroad.[6]

Under the principle of protecting intelligence sources and methods,
the identities of sources and often many of the details they report are
kept strictly within the Intelligence Community. Enforcement branches
of the government are not on the dissemination lists for some of this
private and commercial reporting; should it come to their attention,
they understand that it is not to be used in enforcement actions.

As collection by private citizens is not conducted by trained intelligence personnel working against fairly well-focused requirements,
recurring reservations have been voiced with respect to the quality of
the information gathered. In 1973 steps were taken to bring the activity
under strengthened direction, by transferring responsibility for the activity
from the overt side of CIA to management by the clandestine side,
where collection controls had been developed to a high degree.[7] The
work has continued, there, although it remains an overt function.

As one reflects on the global scope of the programs for overt
collection, what becomes apparent is the extensive range of materials
this makes available for current use and future reference in the Intelligence
Community and among policymakers and planners.

NOTES

1. *Church Committee Report*, Book I, page 316.
2. *Strategic Intelligence*, by Sherman Kent, Princeton University Press,
Princeton, N.J., 1949, page 214. Kent's book is one of the mere handful of works
on the subject of intelligence that can be considered classics. Although portions
are dated and some terminology has since been changed, it remains a clear
statement of the problems faced by national intelligence.

3. *The U.S. Intelligence Community*, by Lyman B. Kirkpatrick, Hill & Wang, New York, 1975, page 124.
4. *Church Committee Report*, Book I, page 263.
5. *Church Committee Report*, Book I, pages 262–263; Book VI, pages 236–237.
6. *Secrets, Spies and Scholars*, by Ray S. Cline, Acropolis Books, Washington, D.C., 1976, page 63.
7. *Church Committee Report*, Book I, page 262.

9

CLANDESTINE COLLECTION

> . . . the United States cannot forego clandestine human collection and classic
> espionage and expect to maintain the same quality of intelligence on matters
> of the highest importance to our national security.
> —*Church Committee Report, 1976*[1]

Not all human intelligence (HUMINT) comes from overt contacts and
activity. An important part of HUMINT is a product of secret—that is,
clandestine—intelligence collection. Secret intelligence operations have
received considerable attention over the years, not without controversy;
in popular treatment, their melodramatic aspects are generally emphasized
over the mundane. Often ignored in the resulting mystique attached to
these activities is the fact that many of the techniques employed are
present in more familiar lines of work.

The activities of law enforcement officers at both the local and
federal levels, or private detectives, or attorneys preparing a case for
trial, or investigative journalists, or even manufacturers attempting to
learn the secrets of competitors—all entail activities that are used in
clandestine operations. They differ primarily in subject matter, environment, and importance. Doubtless the sense of intrigue often associated
with international affairs has given secret intelligence activities an added
aura of mystery, which contributes to the romantic quality seen by
some. To others it is suspect. Yet, as reflected in the finding of the U.S.
Senate's investigating body cited at the head of this chapter, clandestine
collection of intelligence is an essential ingredient in the functioning of
our national intelligence system.

However much information is collected by overt and technological
means, critical gaps in the knowledge of other governments' actual
intentions and plans will remain. A great deal can be learned about
the general makeup of a foreign land—its population, its governmental
structure, the organization and functions of its society, its economy, its

transportation, and its communications. Reliable details can be gathered on national leadership, the preferences of the individuals who constitute it, and the impact they are likely to have on policy. Considerable information can be assembled on military organization and capabilities; one might refer, for instance, to such authoritative private publications such as the International Institute for Strategic Studies' annual publications, *Strategic Survey* and the *Military Balance*, which contain extensive information about military forces around the world, especially those of the great powers.

A nation's general policy and the resources on which it is based may be known, but it does not follow that specific plans will thus be revealed. In the absence of actual knowledge, or of a fairly sound basis for judgment, there is considerable room for error in judging another country. If U.S. policies and plans are to be focused properly for timely and relevant response, hard—that is, reliable—intelligence is required about decisions made by the leaders of the nations of prime interest. Yet this, of course, is the very knowledge that is most closely protected by governments. The *Church Committee Report*, continuing the comments at the head of this chapter, stated the issue as follows: "Agent intelligence can help provide valuable insight concerning the motivations for activities or policies of potential adversaries as well as their future intentions." But even in the absence of precise details on imminent major moves, there are times when enough can be learned to provide a basis for informed deductions with a high degree of reliability.

U.S. ORGANIZATION FOR CLANDESTINE COLLECTION

While CIA was predominant in U.S. foreign clandestine operations (espionage, counterintelligence, and covert action—now known as Special Activities), it never held an exclusive charter in any of these areas until the Reagan Executive Order in 1981 gave it general responsibility for Special Activities. The discussion that follows will touch on the clandestine activities of various organizations, but the emphasis will be on CIA operations. It will be evident that some of the activities of clandestine collectors, security investigators, and such are, in fact, overt.

Initial uncertainties among the organizations of the U.S. Intelligence Community about their clandestine missions under the National Security Act of 1947 continued until the mid-1950s, as described by the Church Committee:

> The most persistent and troublesome operational problem in intelligence community coordination involved the Army's espionage activities, particularly in Western Europe. The Army, Air Force, and to a lesser extent, the

Navy, had continued their independent clandestine collection operations after the war. Among the services, the Army had been the most active in the field and grossly outnumbered the CIA in manpower. The services' justification for their operations had been that during wartime they would need clandestine collection support. That capability required long-term development. Service activities, in particular the Army's, resulted in excessive duplication of the CIA effort and, frequently, competition for the same agents. . . .

In 1958 . . . an arrangement [was worked out] with the services, which attempted to rationalize clandestine collection activities. A National Security Council Intelligence Directive assigned CIA the primary responsibility for clandestine activities abroad. An accompanying directive gave the DCI's designated field representative a modified veto over the services' field activities, by requiring that disagreements be referred to Washington for arbitration by the DCI and the Secretary of Defense. Although issuing these directives theoretically provided the DCI with authority over espionage activities, in practice the directives only created a means for adjudicating disputes. Military commanders continued to rely on service intelligence personnel to satisfy their intelligence requirements.[2]

The central role of CIA in coordinating, if not controlling, clandestine activities abroad thus was based for years on the provisions of a National Security Council Intelligence Directive (NSCID No. 5);[3] subsequently, they were based on a succession of presidential directives commencing with that of President Ford in 1976, followed by that of President Carter in 1978, and finally that of President Reagan (Executive Order 12333) in late 1981, which remains in effect at this writing.[4] The FBI, similarly, was given the central coordinating role for secret operations within the United States. The military services—particularly the Air Force—reduced the size of their overseas clandestine effort over the years, but they continue to maintain an independent operating capability abroad.

DEFENSE AND MILITARY ORGANIZATION

Clandestine operations usually involve much the same organizational machinery, whether the operations be foreign intelligence collection, counterintelligence, or covert action. The various organizations involved directly, as well as peripherally, will be considered briefly here. As the Department of Defense has the largest overall intelligence program, its organizations will be described first.

The Department of Defense has four major intelligence organizations, which are engaged in varying degrees of clandestine activity abroad—namely, the Defense Intelligence Agency (DIA) and the three military services. DIA is organized into directorates. One of these, the Directorate of Attachés, is responsible for managing the Defense Attaché System (DAS). Basically, the DAS was formed through the convergence of the service attachés, who formerly had represented their respective services in embassies abroad. The Church Committee perceived unresolved problems between DIA and the three military intelligence services,[5] which continued to assign intelligence personnel abroad. The difficulties these unresolved problems may have caused were not reduced by the fact that DIA had no independent source for military personnel but, instead, relied upon the services for uniformed personnel detailed to it.[6] Of DIA's estimated 9,000 employees at the time of the Church Committee inquiry, more than half were professional personnel, of whom more than half in turn were civilians.[7]

The Defense Attaché System works with the DIA Directorate of Collection Management, which coordinates the requests of the military services for information. Traditionally, attachés assigned to allied countries conduct official liaison with the military services of those countries. They also maintain formal relations with the services of less friendly nations when stationed there; in addition, they may conduct limited independent collection activities in those countries. The Church Committee was concerned that protocol obligations of the military attachés interfered with their intelligence responsibilities. In any event, the Defense Attaché System has tended to minimize its involvement in direct clandestine activities, although those activities have not been eliminated entirely. The investigative services—the U.S. Army Intelligence and Security Command (INSCOM), the Naval Investigative Service (NIS), and the Air Force Office of Special Investigations (AFOSI)—also have operational capabilities overseas that are relied upon in some instances. These services will be discussed in Chapter 13.

Although the Church Committee did not devote much space in its report to the three military organizations, they do occupy an important place among the government's clandestine activities. These service organizations (as is the case with DIA) have no legislative charters, although they have existed in various forms for many years. They conduct independent collection activities, focusing primarily on subject matter relevant to their respective department's special interests; and they assemble the information, evaluate it, identify gaps to be filled, and issue collection requirements to other members of the Intelligence Community.

Army and Air Force intelligence organizations are headed by Assistant Chiefs of Staff for Intelligence (ACS/I); that of the Navy is headed by the Director of Naval Intelligence (DNI). Their established stature in the governmental hierarchy, despite the fact that their departments have been subordinated to the Department of Defense, has ensured them a place on the NFIB, which is the Intelligence Community group concerned with policies and programs.

The two organizations with basic jurisdictional authority over clandestine activities are the FBI (within the United States) and CIA, with which foreign clandestine operations must be coordinated.

FEDERAL BUREAU OF INVESTIGATION (FBI)

The FBI, which is subordinate to the Department of Justice, was designed initially as a law enforcement agency. The early public drama of its work came during Prohibition days. In addition to law enforcement, the Bureau was responsible for investigating subversive activities, a responsibility that expanded under the policies of President Roosevelt in World War II (as discussed in Chapter 3). The activities and responsibilities that developed during the war under presidential authority continued after cessation of hostilities.[8] These included centralization of authority over domestic intelligence, a role defended by the FBI's director, J. Edgar Hoover, and supported in various presidential directives (i.e., both in NSCIDs and the later Executive Orders of Presidents Ford, Carter, and Reagan).

As with some of CIA's functions, the FBI did not have explicit legislative authority for its intelligence operations,[9] although the Congress was quite familiar with the activities supporting this work on the part of the Bureau over the years. The absence of a legislative charter spared the FBI the imaginative legal arguments that CIA's charter seems to have attracted. However, to the extent that specific legislation is needed as a basis for authority, there is relevant federal legislation. The Internal Security Act of 1950, passed over President Truman's veto, contained two main sections: the Subversive Activities Control Act, which required registration of communist "front" groups and of communists; and the Emergency Detention Act, which, in emergencies, provided for internment of persons who might engage in espionage and sabotage. In 1954 the Congress also enacted a Communist Control Act, which was based on findings that the Communist party in the United States operated "under Soviet Union control" with the objective of installing a "Soviet style dictatorship." In essence, the Act denied the Communist party some of the legal protections that are usual in the United States.[10] All three of these acts envisioned FBI involvement in enforcement tasks arising under the laws and presupposed some intelligence activity in identifying the groups and individuals affected.

At the operational level within the United States, the FBI relies primarily on officers known as Special Agents, who number about 8,500 and are assigned to some sixty field offices in the United States and

Puerto Rico. The Bureau also maintains liaison officers with the title of Legal Attaché, who are assigned to embassies in some nineteen nations to conduct liaison with allied security services.[22]

The operations of the FBI are directed and coordinated by headquarters divisions, which usually report to Assistant Directors. The Domestic Intelligence Division and the Internal Security Division (these titles sometimes vary) are concerned primarily with intelligence and counterintelligence problems. There had been some feeling at one time that the FBI had neglected its counterintelligence function, but this was thought to be less true by the middle 1970s,[12] especially after FBI responsibilities were clarified in later presidential directives.

With only a few Legal Attachés abroad, the Bureau looks to CIA for reporting on foreign sources, which comprise either Americans in contact with radical or subversive groups abroad or undesirable foreigners seeking entry into the United States. A former FBI officer responsible for liaison with the CIA gave the Church Committee this description of one aspect of the working relationship between the FBI and CIA:

> CIA had penetrations abroad in radical, revolutionary organizations and the individual was coming here to attend a conference, a meeting, and would be associating with leading dissidents, and the question came up, can he be of any use to us, can we have access to him during this period.
>
> In most instances, because he was here for a relatively short period, we would levy the requirement or the request upon the CIA to find out what was taking place at the meetings to get his assessment of the individuals that he was meeting, and any other general intelligence that he could collect from his associations with the people who were of interest to us.[13]

The author of this section of the *Church Committee Report* offered the opinion that such a response by CIA to a Bureau request was engaging in "internal security functions" of the sort proscribed by the 1947 Act. This view by the Committee's report was advanced in spite of the arrangements between the FBI and CIA for a realistic way of handling the matter while protecting the FBI's jurisdictional authority. The author's literal-minded criticism failed to attract support, either from the Congress in subsequent legislation or from the succession of presidents who, since then, have provided for just such relationships in their Executive Orders. Those Executive Orders were cleared with the appropriate congressional committees, thus suggesting that if formal legislative clarification were to occur at some future time, it would parallel the provisions of the Executive Orders.

The FBI's dual role as both a law-enforcement agency and an intelligence organization has caused occasional confusion over the two missions. The distinction between secret counterintelligence operations and aggressive investigation in the law-enforcement mode has not always been clear.[14] On the other hand, the Bureau has occasionally been reluctant to investigate security "leaks" of government secrets to the press, given Director Hoover's belief that such investigation was a waste of manpower.[15] At one time, the Bureau had a statistical reporting procedure that measured effectiveness of investigations in terms of resulting prosecutions, which are not usually considered a primary goal of intelligence activities. CIA, given the DCI's statutory responsibility for protecting intelligence sources and methods, found this unsettling and on occasion conducted a few investigations of leaks, albeit with FBI coordination. These investigations led to criticism of CIA for violating its legislative charter. The problem was resolved by the presidential Executive Orders of 1976, 1978 and 1981.

At present, the FBI remains the central authority on the conduct of intelligence activities within the United States. The military services and CIA must coordinate with the Bureau on domestic operations.

CENTRAL INTELLIGENCE AGENCY (CIA)

The 1947 Act was passed with the understanding that CIA would conduct clandestine intelligence collection, although this function was not specified at the time because of reservations about disclosing such a mission in a public document. The reader may recall that CIA's organization was outlined in Chapters 3 and 4 of this book, with some discussion of how its Directorate of Operations—known as the "Clandestine Service"[16]—is organized into geographical operating divisions and supporting staffs. Not all of the operating divisions are intended to engage in overseas activities; indeed, two of them focus on foreign intelligence matters inside the United States. One of these, the Domestic Contacts Division, performs overt collection from U.S. travelers (as mentioned in Chapter 8). The other is involved in contacts with foreign visitors in the United States, as distinguished from security functions relative to these visitors. The current strength of the Directorate of Operations is classified. Although accurate figures are not available publicly, educated guesses provide a general sense of the size of the effort.[17] The chain of command in the directorate descends from the Deputy Director through the division chiefs, to the overseas Chiefs of Station. In some countries there may be subordinate installations, known as bases, headed by Chiefs of Bases.[18]

Although overseas installations may engage in clandestine operations, some may be involved entirely in liaison activities dealing with local intelligence and security organizations of the host government, where such relationships are established. Liaison was especially valuable in the early postwar days, when CIA's program was new, and it has continued to contribute significantly to U.S. intelligence. Our allies conduct intelligence programs of their own, and exchange with them is extensive.[19] Operations are not conducted against allied host governments,[20] but some operations may be directed against Soviet Bloc targets within an allied nation, with agreement and sometimes discreet support from the services of the host country. "Joint" operations are not at all unusual in the relations with some allied nations. Agents from a third country may travel to the country in which a station is located, to meet with a case officer from that station, and a case officer may visit a third country to meet an agent from yet another country who is there for the meeting. The possible variations are numerous, indeed.

CIA also has an Office of Security, located in its Directorate of Administration, that occasionally exercises an operational function much like that of the military investigative services. At times, the office's work involves counterintelligence aspects of security cases, thus bringing it into coordination with both the Directorate of Operations and the FBI.

DEVELOPMENT OF U.S. CLANDESTINE COLLECTION

Clandestine collection is responsive to collection guidance as are other collection activities of the Intelligence Community, but guidance and reporting have not always been handled on an orderly basis. In part this resulted from the procedures that developed in the early post–World War II period and partly as a result of the difficulty of the work itself. Some of the criticisms heard today date back to those earlier times.

The United States entered the postwar period with some capability for clandestine collection. The military services had an operational capability,[21] although it had been designed for wartime work against the Axis powers. A new and very different target began to emerge—the Soviet Union and the satellites it was acquiring in East Europe. The FBI was the central authority for operations with the United States,[22] but it also had foreign operations of a limited nature. The new CIA inherited resources that had been given to its predecessor organization, the Central Intelligence Group (CIG), following its formation in 1946. CIG had been provided seven stations in North Africa and the Middle East (stations that had been established by OSS during the war)[23] and the FBI's activities in Latin America had been transferred to CIA as well.[24] Thus, although CIA started with some capabilities, they proved to be limited for the task at hand.

The high state of flux in the post–World War II period presented unique intelligence problems for those assigned to report on events. So much was not known, both initially and as a result of the rapid changes occurring at the time, that almost any information could be useful. Hence considerable random reporting was a characteristic of that early period.

Europe had suffered extensive damage and dislocation during the war. The former Axis powers had fallen, and the emerging successor governments presented unique problems in themselves. The reestablishment of viable and stable governments and societies was uncertain.

The fate that befell the nations in Eastern Europe is a familiar story. Not so well known is the Soviet challenge in Western Europe, where an intensive campaign was mounted to exploit postwar instabilities in order to install pro-Soviet governments. The Soviet program was met by an array of U.S. programs, of which the Marshall Plan and the NATO alliance are the best known. Major efforts were made to shore up West Europe while it reestablished its own societies.

The considerable concern over the internal stability of a number of those countries led to intelligence operations designed to learn about internal political developments, especially those involving related Soviet subversive activities. Both the U.S. military intelligence organizations and CIA were involved. CIA was also thrust into a range of programs intended to counter Soviet activities. These took the form of support for organizations opposing the numerous communist front groups, highly organized and heavily financed, that were advancing Soviet objectives in the area. This situation put CIA personnel in touch with a broad range of social strata in Western Europe, thereby producing valuable contacts with access to a great variety of knowledge about events of the moment.

Intelligence personnel of the various U.S. government organizations worked out of official installations, moving in official circles where important contacts were to be established. Often CIA and the military reported on subjects traditionally considered the jurisdiction of the State Department. Some duplication, as well as uncertainty, occurred as a result. As it established itself, CIA was expanding and covering considerable territory.

CIA's initially limited capabilities rapidly gathered substance and momentum—a fact worthy of special note given that viable clandestine resources usually require long-range development. That was one of the rationales given by the Army for continuing its clandestine activities after World War II.

The postwar environment was made to order for the new U.S. clandestine service. Many Europeans were grateful for the United States' role in the defeat of Germany, and many supported its leadership in opposition to the Soviet threat. U.S. economic strength, readily visible to the prostrate European societies, served as an additional attraction during the postwar years. Refugees from Eastern Europe and the USSR also found a place in CIA for their special knowledge. Suffice it to say that the relatively inexperienced CIA operatives were able to establish relationships with a number of high-quality individuals who continued to play an important role in the clandestine activities in Europe and elsewhere over the years to come.

As Western Europe recovered and stabilized, and as the Soviet threat receded in the face of NATO, early postwar requirements for detailed coverage of the "internal target" in those countries declined, as did the requirements for the large programs to counter Soviet covert action in the area. Soviet initiatives, which shifted to what came to be known as the Third World, sought to exploit the disruptions accompanying the independence of former colonial lands. U.S. policy concerns turned to those areas as official diplomatic relations were established with the newly independent nations. Economic aid programs sought to play the role there that they had played in Western Europe. Given the uncertainties of the transition period, and Soviet interests, the reporting on the "internal target" in those countries became a requirement for both overt and clandestine collectors. This called for establishing contacts with new sources who had access to information. Not only were these people contacted in their homeland, but many such relationships were developed in locales away from Third World areas. Western Europe, something of a crossroad for world travelers, was the scene for this activity.

In the Third World, after some years of obvious turmoil, the internal situations in some of the new nations stabilized to a degree and the requirements for clandestine collection were reduced. As CIA operators could pay less attention to the internal target in these areas, duplication between State Department reporting and that of CIA declined.[25]

CIA's emphasis shifted from the Third World internal targets to so-called "denied area" subject matter.[26] Usually this term referred to Communist-controlled nations, although it can apply to certain unfriendly noncommunist countries as well. It had long been CIA doctrine to consider its primary intelligence target to be the Soviet Union and the satellite nations, to the extent that they provided a window to the USSR. The ability to emphasize the Soviet target often was preempted by other national policy priorities. During the Carter administration, as events such as the fall of the Shah of Iran—with its unsettling effects on Middle East policy—and growing troubles in Central America captured attention, the Assistant to the President for National Security Affairs pressed for increased coverage of the Third World internal target. This action posed substantial problems for management, considering the recent reductions in CIA manpower. Given the long-term problems of developing clandestine agents, who usually are directed at specific targets, it is difficult to turn such activities on and off; sometimes they cannot be redirected at all. A shift in collection priorities often requires considerable time, even when it is feasible. Considerations such as this have led CIA to accept requirements for clandestine collection only if they cannot be filled by other means.[27]

Many clandestine operations are tailor-made for a specific task, thus complicating the difficulties of redirection. Any additions to an agent's work-load may materially impair his or her performance on established targets without ensuring success on the new one. Further, security risks may be incurred when an agent's assignment is changed. A precipitate change in the agent's pattern of activity may attract attention and jeopardize the operation. Flexibility and responsiveness exist in the system, but the use of it occasionally occurs at the cost of other reporting, and with increased risk to the agents.

When existing operational arrangements cannot be redirected, new ones must be developed, thus raising the question of manpower and budgetary constraints. The Reagan administration reportedly has recognized the management problem of providing personnel for the sort of coverage required by policymakers, and it seems recently to have been rebuilding some of CIA's operating capabilities and manpower.

CONTROL OF CLANDESTINE REPORTING

The end purpose of clandestine operations continues to be reporting from the field on significant subject matter. The quality of reporting has persisted as a continuing subject of attention. Uncertainties inherent in clandestine intelligence, if not managed closely, can produce undesired results.

Operators are required to ensure the reliability of their agents by verifying that the agents actually have access to the targets on which they file reports. Assessment of the information they submit can be accomplished in a number of ways. An agent's reporting can be compared with existing knowledge and with other reporting on the same subject to develop a sense of its reliability. Over a period of time the accumulated reporting by an agent provides a record for measuring the quality of his or her work. This track record speaks volumes. The case officer's familiarity with the agent is an additional element in this evaluation. Given the uncertainties of reliability and loyalties, use of the polygraph provides some verification of the agent's motivation and sincerity.

It is customary to assign grade and letter evaluations to individual reports before they go to the consumers. This grading, based on knowledge of the sources, conveys some sense of their value. Occasionally information that cannot be assessed in terms of its reliability will be reported because it is important if true; in this case, it will be accompanied by a caveat as to its unverified reliability. Such reporting serves to alert consumers to a possible significant development for which verified reporting is not yet available.

As substantive reporting progressed over the years, it was felt that the graded assessments on disseminated reports left something to be desired in the overall improvement of reporting. By the late 1960s, CIA's Clandestine Service developed a process for grading performance within the reporting system. These separate grades would be used for internal administrative control and were not passed on to consumers. Individual reports disseminated to the Intelligence Community continued to carry the familiar gradings and comments. Internally, a fine report might be assigned a Roman numeral X, and a normal report a V. Over a period of time sources could be measured by a numerical average, with the case officers and field installations also being graded in comparison with others. This procedure stimulated heightened discrimination in the field with respect to what was forwarded to headquarters, with a decline in marginal and peripheral reporting. It also provided a basis for evaluating existing programs and the performance of officers, and for planning future activities.

Foreign Intelligence (FI) is not the only reporting done by the field stations. FI reporting, also termed Positive Intelligence (PI) to distinguish it from operational reporting, is disseminated to consumers. Operational Intelligence reporting (Ops Intell) is for internal operational management only. It addresses the details of activity and environment in areas in which clandestine operations are being conducted. Careful attention is given to the comings and goings of case officers and their agents, and to operational contacts in the field. This information is recorded in the field in considerable detail and is reviewed carefully to ensure that sound procedure is being observed and, to the extent possible, to detect unexpected risks. For instance, encounters of agents with certain persons may show, from records at headquarters, that the contacts involve hostile or suspect individuals (an issue that will be discussed further in Chapter 13). Sometimes operational reporting may suggest to officials in Washington certain courses of action that may broaden and improve procedures. Ops Intell reporting is treated as highly sensitive, giving, as it does, so much detail about operational activity.

TRADECRAFT

Once the several intelligence organizations have been created, their missions refined by experience, and administrative arrangements established for carrying out assigned tasks, the work of clandestine intelligence collection is passed down to operators in the field. Their techniques, personal style, and flair and their use of the organizational apparatus combine into what is referred to loosely as "tradecraft." The term is usually applied to those engaged in clandestine activity, and has the connotation of professional mastery of this special form of endeavor.

Although tradecraft usually refers to personal use of clandestine techniques in operational activity, it includes a varying mix of elements, depending on the specific mission at hand, the environment in which it is handled, and the available resources. It ranges from surveillance of others (sometimes with assistance) through the arrangement and conduct of clandestine meetings and the intricacies of clandestine communications, to the identification of potential agents and their development for eventual recruitment.

The activities vary with the task at hand and the resources that may be required to handle it. Operations officers pride themselves on their mastery and use of techniques and, despite the word *trade*, consider their work to have significant qualities of professionalism. Supervisory measurement of their performance judges not only the results but the professional quality of their tradecraft as well. Although clandestine operations often involve an element of daring, given the uncertainty and personal risk entailed, they are conducted with marked conservatism. Tradecraft provides the basic ingredient for continued success and operational security.

COVER

Clandestine collection of foreign intelligence requires that the operator, often referred to as case officer, is not known publicly for what he or she is. Operators must be able to move normally through the environment in which they work. The *Rockefeller Commission Report* effectively summarized this issue as follows:

> Many CIA activities—like those of every foreign intelligence service—are clandestine in nature. Involved CIA personnel cannot travel, live or perform their duties openly as CIA employees. Even in countries where the CIA works closely with cooperative foreign intelligence services, Agency personnel are often required by their hosts to conceal their CIA status.

Accordingly, virtually all CIA personnel serving abroad and many of the Agency's professional personnel in the United States assume a "cover." Their employment with CIA is disguised and, to persons other than their families and co-workers, they are held out as employees of another government agency or of a commercial enterprise.

Cover arrangements frequently have substantial domestic aspects. These include the participation of other United States government agencies, business firms, and private citizens and creation and management of a variety of domestic commercial entities. Most CIA employees in need of cover are assigned "official cover" with another component of the federal government pursuant to formal agreements between the CIA and the "covering" departments or agencies. Where official cover is unavailable or otherwise inappropriate, CIA officers or contract employees are assigned "nonofficial" cover, which usually consists of an ostensible position with CIA-created and controlled business entities known as "proprietary companies" or "devised facilities." On occasion, nonofficial cover is provided for a CIA officer by a bona fide privately owned American business firm.[28]

The considerations applying to CIA employees abroad, especially those engaged in clandestine operations, apply similarly to the collectors and operators belonging to military intelligence organizations. Military operatives can and do use nonofficial cover arrangements, although not usually with the complex of special arrangements described in the *Rockefeller Report*. It should be apparent that the need for nonofficial cover is not as great with military intelligence personnel as it sometimes is with CIA.

Clearly, clandestine operators cannot engage in their missions abroad if the purpose of their work is known, or if their identities are suspect. They must have some plausible cover that avoids special attention. Because of the publicity CIA has received, this principle applies to its administrative and clerical personnel abroad, as well as to those officers involved only in the relatively prosaic chores of liaison with allied services.

In friendly areas, the lightest cover often is acceptable for liaison officers. An individual assigned such work is officially accredited to the host nation, is known to many within the intelligence community there, and works with them much as other personnel in the official U.S. installation deal with people in the various ministries of the host government. Although the work is relatively overt, many of those assigned to liaison duties may belong to the Clandestine Service and remain subject to later assignment to operational tasks. For them, some continuity of sound cover is required. Their cover will be more complete, being known as "deep" cover, in contrast to the "light" cover of less sensitive personnel.

In practice, the very fact of cover presents some problems for clandestine operators. If integrated into the personnel system of another government organization, they may be expected to perform some work for it. These "cover duties" intrude on the time otherwise available for basic activities and tend to stretch the work day. Official protocol chores may become a part of the assignment, further trespassing on the time available. As mentioned earlier, the Church Committee expressed concern over the effect of protocol duties on Defense Attachés. Yet "living one's cover" is an important part of the work.

Official cover carries with it the inconvenience of having to work out of an official installation, where hostile counterintelligence officers are better able to identify a possible operator and establish surveillance of him or her. This situation complicates the mobility of the person under official cover, requiring extra activity to ensure that there is no surveillance before engaging in the more sensitive work, or eluding it if it is present.

Those serving under nonofficial cover are free from the burdens of official cover, often doing only enough work at their ostensible vocation to be convincing to the casual observer. That applies primarily to the person in a devised or proprietary facility, as mentioned in the *Rockefeller Report*. In a bona fide commercial organization, intelligence personnel must also perform normal duties within that company to avoid attracting attention. The advantages of mobility that may attach to the person under nonofficial cover are offset, at least in part, by problems of communication. The person "outside"—that is, not working in an official installation—has the same responsibility to report on a timely basis as does the person "inside." Sometimes this situation presents problems, one of which is the time consumed during observation of security procedures. Emergency contact can be established and occasionally special communications can be arranged, but the basic problem remains.

Clandestine intelligence operations are somewhat labor-intensive, involving detailed one-on-one meetings between agent and case officer. The problems of operational security and communications add to this labor-intensive situation, in which cover is but one aspect of the problem. Living one's cover is a built-in feature of the clandestine operator's tradecraft. To the experienced officer it becomes an accepted, though onerous, part of the work.

THE AGENT

The central and essential element of clandestine intelligence activity is the agent. The agent, usually a foreign citizen, is someone who accepts a clandestine mission from an American representative. An American who is not a regular employee of the government may serve as an agent, going abroad for that purpose or cooperating in a foreign country where he or she already resides, although the latter arrangement is far less frequent. The unique nature of the relationship between agent and case officer will be discussed in Chapter 16.

Working-level operators in the FBI are called "Special Agents" and their operational contacts are referred to as "informants," although some of the latter may have more positive functions as agents similar to those of CIA. The familiar title of Special Agent seems to have led much of the media to refer to CIA staff employees as "agents." CIA normally reserves that title for cooperating individuals not employed in a staff capacity by the Agency.

Agents are selected on the basis of their access to classified information of a foreign government that is of interest to the United States. Identification of a potential agent and assessment of his or her access to desired information and qualities of stability and reliability constitute the first step. Unstable individuals with access to such information cannot be used in a clandestine relationship; contact may be maintained, but the individual will be held at arms length. Once a person is determined to be a desirable candidate, a process of "development" begins, leading, if all goes well, to a proposal of clandestine relationship. This process is followed closely at headquarters, which makes the final decision on whether or not to proceed to recruitment. Once agreement is reached, indoctrination or even training will follow, if circumstances permit. An experienced, mature individual may require less training than would a person of untested quality.

Not all agents are primary sources of intelligence as such. Agents may develop to the point that their associations with others who have access to desired information become of primary importance. The agents' contacts may be so valuable that the emphasis turns to information they can collect from their contacts. One agent may then become the central figure in a "net," serving as "principal agent." However, such an arrangement presents problems in measuring access and suitability of the principal agent's contacts and in ensuring reliable reporting. Usually these matters can be worked out, but a difficulty may arise when the principal agent stands between the case officer and the members of his or her net. One important requirement of this arrangement is to protect against fabricated reports, which are handled through record-keeping; another is to provide for occasional direct contacts with the members of the net. Despite these problems, the arrangement has the benefit of reinforcing the quality of security. There are few contacts among members of the net and a given case officer since the principal agent serves as a "cut-out" between them. It also reduces the U.S. operative's work, freeing him for additional tasks.

Not all agents are sources of information. In larger cities, in which a number of operational targets may be present, a field station may develop a substantial operational support capability, consisting of local people who agree to carry out rather routine support assignments. They may simply collect mail at post office boxes or other locations, or they may conduct neighborhood inquiries to locate individuals. They are sometimes trained and formed into surveillance teams for special situations. They may also serve as "safehouse keepers," living in an apartment or house used for secret meetings. Safehouses, in turn, may serve as "observation posts" or "listening posts" in which photographic or electronic surveillance is maintained on targets of interest. Occasionally, an agent may have important connections over whom he or she is willing to exercise influence along lines favorable to U.S. policy—hence the term *agent of influence.*

TECHNOLOGIES EMPLOYED IN CLANDESTINE OPERATIONS

Brief mention should be made of the technology used in supporting clandestine operations. Soviet operations against U.S. personnel, such as the installation of an electronic device in the Great Seal of the United States in the ambassador's office in Moscow, or that in the heel of the shoe belonging to an American official (a shoe later sent out for repairs) are well known. U.S. intelligence organizations may use similar technology.

The Church Committee discussed a number of technologies that can be used for clandestine collection from individuals.[29] Although that discussion was in the context of intrusion on civil liberties in the United States, those technologies are applicable to foreign intelligence operations as well. They are generally known, in any case, and thus require only brief mention here. The activities listed in the *Church Committee Report* are as follows:

1. Breaking and entering offices and homes (known as "surreptitious entry," involving "picks and locks").
2. Opening letters in the postal system (known as "flaps and seals").
3. Bugging or use of hidden microphones (known as "audio operations"), the placement of which may involve surreptitious entry. Either a battery-powered device that transmits to a nearby listening post or a microphone connected to a recording device may be used in this connection.
4. Wiretapping telephone communications.

   5. Intercepting telephone communications without connecting to the
      telephone or wire.
   6. Intercepting facsimile or printer communications.

Some of these techniques may be used in the field, or may even be
operated jointly with a host security service. In both such cases, CIA
often provides the equipment and funds the operation, sometimes
including personnel, while the local officials provide authorization,
security, and additional personnel.

Beyond these means of collecting information clandestinely, operatives may rely on technical processes of communications for passing
information, including special codes or secret writing. The so-called
micro-dot—a process whereby a message is reduced to the size of a
typed punctuation mark and affixed to a letter—has been reported
publicly.

Clandestine collection is, in actuality, far more complex in its
intricacies and variations than the techniques discussed here. It often
provides valuable information that is not available from other sources.
Although it occasionally fails, overall it offers the best chance of filling
gaps in information obtained from all other sources. It is a function
that will be continued for so long as the Cold War and its central causes
exist.

NOTES

1. *Church Committee Report*, Book I, page 437.
2. *Church Committee Report*, Book IV, page 61.
3. *Church Committee Report*, Book I, page 310; Book II, page 98.
4. *Executive Order 11905* of 18 February 1976; *Executive Order 12036* of 24
January 1978; and *Executive Order 12333* of 4 December 1981.
5. *Church Committee Report*, Book I, page 325.
6. Ibid., pages 349–354.
7. Ibid., page 352; Book VI, page 290.
8. *Church Committee Report*, Book II, pages 33–34, 38, 41.
9. Ibid., page 41.
10. Ibid.
11. *Church Committee Report*, Book VI, pages 284–285.
12. *Church Committee Report*, Book I, pages 170–171.
13. *Church Committee Report*, Book III, pages 519–520. This portion of the
Church Committee Report offers yet another imaginative assertion about restrictions
on CIA authority against engagement in internal activities in the United States.
Some have contended that foreign intelligence collected by CIA should not be
passed to domestic law enforcement agencies. The *Rockefeller Commission Report*
felt it necessary to comment on this situation, stating that the Commission

"does not construe the proviso to prohibit the CIA from evaluating and disseminating foreign intelligence which may be relevant and useful to law enforcement. Such a function is simply an exercise of the Agency's statutory responsibility 'to correlate and evaluate intelligence relating to the national security'" (p. 62). Nor did the Commission feel the CIA was "barred from passing domestic information to interested agencies, including law enforcement agencies, where the information was incidentally acquired in the course of authorized intelligence activities." The Reagan Administration, in *Executive Order 12333*, Section 2.6, defined the relationships between the intelligence agencies and law enforcement authorities, the language of the directive having been cleared with the congressional oversight committees.

14. *Church Committee Report*, Book III, page 63.

15. *Rockefeller Commission Report*, page 56.

16. *Church Committee Report*, Book I, page 111; Book IV, pages 45, 66–67.

17. One source quoted by the *Church Committee Report* (Book VI, page 261), citing *CIA and the Cult of Intelligence*, by Victor Marchetti and John D. Marks, Alfred A. Knopf, 1974, gave a round figure of 6,000 staff members—about two-thirds of whom were described as professional employees, 45 percent of the total being overseas. Although the date of publication of that figure was 1974, the basis for it probably preceded the Schlesinger reductions in 1973. The *Church Committee Report* (Book I, page 437) stated that the size of the Clandestine Service had been reduced significantly over the decade prior to its inquiries in 1975–1976. Subsequently, DCI Turner, in the Carter administration, carried out a much-publicized further reduction. If the total dropped 5,000—near the 4,000 mark—there seems to have been a recent reversal of the trend, given that the press reported significant increases under DCI Casey. Although there is no published information available to the present author, one can speculate that over 5,000 employees are now working in the Directorate of Operations. The numbers are unimportant but a general summary provides a sense of the order of magnitude of staff strengths in the Clandestine Service.

18. *Church Committee Report*, Book VI, page 261.

19. *Church Committee Report*, Book IV, page 49.

20. *The U.S. Intelligence Community*, by Lyman B. Kirkpatrick, Hill & Wang, New York, 1975, page 124.

21. See Note 2, supra.

22. See Note 8, supra.

23. *Church Committee Report*, Book IV, page 14.

24. *Church Committee Report*, Book VI, page 284.

25. *Church Committee Report*, Book I, page 437.

26. Ibid.

27. Ibid., page 436.

28. *Rockefeller Commission Report*, page 215. See also *Church Committee Report*, Book I, page 252.

29. *Church Committee Report*, Book IV, pages 109–114.

10

TECHNICAL COLLECTION

Each Party shall use national technical means of verification at its disposal.
—Article XV, SALT II Agreement

In a technological era, it is to be expected that technology will be used to learn as much as possible about an adversary. Both the Soviet Union and the United States have important programs in this area. The existence of such technology has made it possible to develop formulas for some arms agreements, since intelligence systems permit verification of compliance with some agreements. Unfortunately, the present technology of these systems puts limitations on what can be verified, but much of the progress in arms control has been possible because of these intelligence systems.

The U.S.-Soviet agreements in the Strategic Arms Limitation Talks (SALT) of 1972 and 1979 achieved an historic first. Two major powers openly accepted certain forms of technical intelligence collection by one another, agreeing that there would be no obstruction by either side of the other's monitoring activities. It was this ability—to verify compliance with the agreements—that made the agreements possible. Those engaged in intelligence activity often have asserted that they help preserve the peace; moreover, the two major powers seem to have endorsed that view by providing for the critical role of intelligence in verifying compliance with the agreements.

Secretary of State Cyrus Vance, in his analysis of the SALT II Agreement in a pamphlet issued by the Department of State,[1] specified that the term *national technical means of verification* included "a broad range of systems for collecting intelligence [such as] photo-reconnaissance satellites, the ships and aircraft which are used to monitor Soviet missile sites, and ground stations such as the large U.S. radar at Shemya Island in Alaska." He also stated that "the deliberate denial of telemetric information by any means, such as encryption, is prohibited." The

127

reference to encryption has to do with the encoding of telemetry signals from missiles to ground stations, thereby concealing the data on test flights.

Future Soviet attitudes on the verification methods of SALT II cannot be predicted, but for the present this agreement represents a step forward in the ability of the two powers to agree on tangible steps that help ensure compliance with arms control accords. The complex technical systems serve very well in verifying compliance with agreements to limit the major strategic military systems. Yet, however remarkable as these systems may be, their capabilities are limited in important ways. The SALT II formulas reflect this fact. For instance, the formula of limitations regarding "launchers" and the number of warheads they are to bear are not readily transferable to all weapons systems. The term *launchers* is included in the agreement to refer to the submarines, aircraft, and ICBM launch sites that can be observed and counted (as will be noted below). This formula does not include all missiles—"delivery systems" to some commentators—simply because there is no sure way of observing them all from overhead, if some are stored in reserve. The same consideration applies to reserve warheads. The emphasis on "launchers" recognizes the fact that reserve warheads can be verified, whereas other elements of the systems are subject to greater uncertainty.

If realistic new arms control formulas are to be developed, a great deal depends on the ingenuity of the negotiators. Reductions in the numbers of deployed major strategic and theater nuclear systems can be verified by means of overhead reconnaissance, but general agreements on the total number of deployed and reserve delivery systems would prove difficult without dependable systems for verification. The progress that has been made encourages hope for more progress still, but caution must remain an essential balance to optimism.

The SALT Agreements appear to be something of a departure from the unequivocal rejection by the Soviet Union in 1955 of the Eisenhower "open skies" proposal, although agreement on aircraft overflight cannot be expected. Moreover, it is unlikely that the USSR would accept unrestricted on-site inspection, which seems the one sure way of having credible verification of compliance on broader arms control arrangements. The USSR's position concerning on-site inspection was first demonstrated in connection with the so-called Baruch Plan, which proposed international control of nuclear weapons. The UN General Assembly endorsed a modified version of the Baruch Plan in 1948, which included on-site inspection by international teams but failed to gain Soviet acceptance. The Soviet negotiators would not consider on-site inspection when this issue was raised in the course of the SALT negotiations. The massive logistical effort involved in creating an effective inspection system would be considered by the Soviet leadership to be an intrusion into their closed society, and therefore unacceptable. For the present, reliance must be placed on the technical collection systems of the parties to SALT II. The fact that the verification systems cannot cover all aspects of armaments must be kept in mind, as they impose limits on the matters that can be agreed upon—simply because compliance with some forms of arms limitations and reductions cannot be verified.

The technical means mentioned in the SALT II Agreement refer to the long-standing Signals Intelligence (SIGINT) programs as well as the more recent overhead reconnaissance activities, which owe their origins to the relatively new need to know as much as possible about Soviet missile developments. As noted earlier, these technological collection programs account for some 90 percent of the national intelligence collection budget. Traditional SIGINT activities have been expanded to supplement other programs targeted against the Soviet missile force. The following sections will focus on these two important types of collection activity.

SIGINT COLLECTION

SIGINT activities of the U.S. government consist of a number of different technologies. The oldest of these, Communications Intelligence (COMINT), involves intercepting and, where necessary, decoding the communications of other nations. As the eavesdropping aspect of this procedure offended the sensibilities of Secretary of State Henry L. Stimson in 1929, he was prompted to terminate the department's support for the work. The U.S. Army and Navy, viewing the requirements of national security differently, continued to intercept foreign radio communications and thereby produced intelligence from them.[2]

SIGINT also encompasses Electronics Intelligence (ELINT), once referred to as Electronics Intercept at a time when some questioned whether its technical contributions really constituted "intelligence." ELINT consists of technical and intelligence information derived from the interception of electromagnetic radiations emitted by radars and other special communications equipment. These electronic signals are studied to determine the equipment's unique characteristics. An outgrowth of this activity was the sophisticated study of missile telemetry, known as Telemetry Intelligence (TELINT),[3] provided for in the SALT II Agreement.

Secretary Vance's explanation of SALT II referred to the radar facilities at Shemya Island in Alaska, where reentry of Soviet test-missile firings is monitored. Such activities gave rise to the term RADINT, for Radar Intelligence. Mentioned here—not because it is SIGINT (it is not), but because of the electronic technology involved—is infrared photography[4], which will be discussed later in the context of overhead reconnaissance.

The U.S. government's SIGINT program is managed by the National Security Agency (NSA). Unlike CIA, which has a legislative charter, NSA was created in October 1952 by presidential directive. It replaced the short-lived Armed Forces Security Agency, which had only limited powers over the government's SIGINT activities. NSA, which reports directly to the Secretary of Defense, was given operational control over the military cryptologic agencies: the Army Security Agency (ASA), which subsequently was merged with other organizations into the Army Intelligence and Security Command (INSCOM); the Naval Security Group (NSG); and the Air Force Electronic Security Command (for many years known as the Air Force Security Service).[5] These three organizations, subordinate to their respective departments, are responsive to NSA operational direction. Estimates of the personnel engaged in the national SIGINT program range between 70,000 and 120,000;[6] a more accurate estimate would probably fall about halfway between these extremes.

NSA responds to both national and tactical requirements, political as well as military, but its major and primary collection effort is directed to military targets.[7] The scope of coverage by NSA and the three military cryptologic agencies requires that personnel be stationed around the world,[8] including an impressive net of facilities abroad. According to the *Church Committee Report* of 1976, the U.S. SIGINT program was then the largest and most expensive single program in the national intelligence budget.[9] The rapid growth of the overhead reconnaissance program, with its highly sophisticated technology and equipment, may have modified the balance somewhat.

One writer close to the SALT II process described the intelligence programs of which SALT II verification was a part. His description was general, but it included a specific reference to the SIGINT facilities that had been located in northern Iran prior to the fall of the Shah:

> The Iran stations were part of a varied and far-reaching network of American facilities that kept track of Soviet military activity, including missile tests. These facilities include airplanes, satellites, ships and ground stations outfitted with an array of equipment for taking photographs, detecting launches by infrared sensors, intercepting radio messages and tracking missiles and their warheads by radar. Many of the functions are overlapping. Redundancy is a deliberately designed and highly prized feature of the system.[10]

The Eurasian landmass occupied by the Soviet Union and its empire extends from 10° east longitude at the western limit of East Germany, through 170° east longitude at the end of the Chukotsk Peninsula across the Bering Strait from Alaska. The size of the collection task in this vast area is enormous. Numerous collection activities around the periphery of the Soviet Bloc are required. The reported loss of the valuable sites in Iran conveys something of the nature of the intelligence effort. The press has reported collection efforts in Turkey, where U.S. forces had at one time been ousted owing to a congressional initiative in relation to Cyprus. Unconfirmed press reports have stated that an arrangement exists with China for operation of a similar collection site in western China. Such widely separated activities suggests something of the scope and variety of the effort involved.

Europe has been considered an area of strategic priority among U.S. interests, both military and cultural. The largest military confrontation exists there, given the NATO forces aligned to oppose any armed aggression from the Warsaw Pact forces in East Europe. Probably the greatest concentration of U.S. SIGINT collection facilities is in the NATO area, where both the United States and its NATO allies conduct independent SIGINT programs, with arrangements for exchange of the "take" among them. SIGINT collection serves the essentially defensive purposes of NATO strategy and tactics, but it also exhibits a potential for offensive use in the event of war.

Permanent installations have been established along the length of the East European borders. As a rule, their locations are determined by terrain and radio reception conditions, although sometimes by the location of communications and other collection targets in East Europe. SIGINT facilities engage in electronic "listening" for all manner of signals emanating from the other side of the East European borders.

Soviet and other Warsaw Pact ground forces in East Europe can rely on ground lines (normal telephone systems) when not on maneuvers. But wireless communications systems must be kept active, and when the troops take to the field for seasonal exercises, or to move their location, they invariably use radio communications. During routine practice and "command post exercises," SIGINT collection on the ground forces is most active. Maneuvers are followed closely to verify continuation of known procedures and to identify new ones, as well as to learn what communications may reveal about organization. Exercises are monitored closely to ensure that they do not a cloak a real offensive. Air-to-air and air-to-ground radio communications also form a part of normal air force operations in peace or in war. Electronic observation of Warsaw Pact flight activity makes it possible to determine aircraft basing, movement, levels of flight experience and training, numbers, and organization.

As Warsaw Pact forces are relatively near and mobile, continuing watch is maintained by the United States for any indication of change in deployment and readiness. "Indications" and "warning" intelligence is crucial to Western readiness to meet possible military initiatives from the East. Against such an eventuality a list has been prepared of steps to be expected in the event the Pact began preparations for hostilities, and a watch is kept of developments in those areas. The U.S. European Command (EUCOM) has a "watch list" of some 500 discrete indicators (more than 700, counting subsets), and daily reports are assembled for review.[11] SIGINT is one of the more important sources of information to be included in these lists of possible preparations for war.

Similarly, there are collection programs targeted on the Soviet Navy, which has become a "blue water navy" in the past two decades in contrast to its traditional role as something of a coastal defense force.[12] Soviet ships can be observed visually when they exit the Black Sea, the Mediterranean, and the Baltic. This susceptibility to visual observation probably was a probable factor in the Soviet decision to base a considerable portion of its fleet, especially its submarines, along the Kola Peninsula on the White and Barents seas, which are quite inhospitable in winter. Other Soviet naval bases exist in East Asia, both in northern USSR and in Vietnam. The new global role of the Soviet navy makes it a more difficult SIGINT target than it was when it had a more limited mission. Although SIGINT facilities in the European and Mediterranean areas provide considerable coverage in those regions, other arrangements have had to be made for surveillance of Soviet naval forces in the South Atlantic, the Indian Ocean, and the Pacific.

The majority of the Soviet SIGINT targets are at fixed sites, although a number of the radar facilities have some mobility. Of special continuing interest are the large fixed-site facilities that would have to be dealt with in the event of retaliation against Soviet aggression in Europe. For example, the capabilities of the Soviet Bloc air defense system would have to be determined in order to design tactics to penetrate it.

SIGINT collection sites along the borders between West and East Europe can identify different types of Soviet radars—general search and aircraft-acquisition radars, anti-aircraft artillery radars, surface-to-air missile radars, tracking radars, interceptor radars for aircraft, and so on. To identify and locate these radars is not enough. It is necessary also to know how they function in operational situations. This information is acquired in part through so-called ferret flights, in which specially equipped aircraft fly along the borders of the East European line of demarcation. These aircraft will be picked up by Soviet Bloc radars and tracked, accompanied by routine precautionary measures in the Warsaw Pact air defense system. Bloc interceptor aircraft are often scrambled to move along with the ferret flights. Anti-aircraft systems will activate their equipment against the possibility that the ferret flights might turn to penetrate the East European airspace. Western SIGINT collection facilities, as well as the electronic equipment on the ferret aircraft, monitor these reactions as defensive responsibility is moved from sector to sector in the Warsaw Pact air defense system. These defensive responses usually provide subject matter for COMINT and ELINT collection. It also reveals a good deal about the organization, functioning, and capabilities of Pact air defenses, and contributes to the design of tactics and strategy for penetrating the system if that should become necessary. The Soviet Bloc is quite aware of what is happening, but it usually feels obliged to react in order to ensure that the ferret flights are not about to turn east over Warsaw Pact airspace.

Ferret flights along the demarcation line in Europe are in friendly airspace, often with accompanying fighter protection. They have proven to be basically safe patrol missions. But the same has not always been true of similar flights that approach Soviet or other communist coastal areas over international waters. These latter flights occasionally have been attacked and U.S. patrol aircraft downed. Such incidents occurred in 1955, 1956, 1958, and 1960[13] during the Eisenhower administration, and in 1969 during the Nixon administration.[14] Analysis of those incidents has indicated that the aircraft had invariably flown over international waters. Communist motives have not always been clear, although there doubtless is some irritation about the obvious purpose of the ferret flights.

In addition to the aircraft usually employed in ferret activity, the U.S. Air Force operates a special high-performance aircraft—the SR-71—capable of speed in excess of MACH-3 at very high altitudes. Originally designed as the follow-on to the U-2 aircraft, the SR-71 has been used on a limited basis owing, at least in part, to the performance of reconnaissance satellites. The SR-71 can perform SIGINT along with its other missions. Unmanned drone aircraft equipped with sensors have been flown into areas in which a hostile reaction is expected.[15] The Church Committee, concerned with the risks of overflight activity, both to human life and the possibility of escalating reactions if an aircraft is shot down, recommended that unmanned drones be used where possible in place of manned ferret flights.[16] Although surveillance satellites have eliminated much of this element of risk, manned flights may sometimes be necessary.

Ferret flights are supplemented by naval equipment. Secretary Vance has mentioned the use of ships to monitor Soviet missile tests. The role of DCI Helms in their use of these ships for this work was also mentioned in Chapter 5. There are other naval vessels equipped for more general SIGINT work. Naval communications ships designed for SIGINT missions execute more normal collection tasks, although their work is not always without risk. The USS Pueblo, engaged in a general SIGINT mission off North Korea in 1968, was attacked on the high seas and seized by North Korea. [17] The USS Liberty, conducting SIGINT operations in the eastern Mediterranean during the so-called Six Day War in June 1967, was attacked repeatedly by Israeli naval vessels and aircraft.[18]

Other forms of SIGINT collection were discussed by the Church Committee in the context of electronic techniques. Although these discussions concerned domestic activity in particular, the techniques obviously have application for foreign collection activities as well. Mentioned in the Church Committee summary were intercept of voice communications from microwave relay systems, intercept of non-voice communications from microwave relay links, and intercept of both voice and nonvoice communications from satellites.[19]

Not all SIGINT operations involve the intercept of signals on the air. One dramatic incident that received some publicity is known as the Berlin Tunnel Operation. In the mid-1950s a tunnel was dug from an empty building on the west side of the Berlin Wall to underground communications cables on the east side. CIA communications specialists installed banks of recorders tapped in to East German and Soviet communications cables in the tunnel.[20] The operation ended in a scramble in mid-1956 when Soviet authorities stumbled on it.

This general discussion should provide some sense of the scope and nature of both usual and unusual SIGINT collection. Although much of the activity is *pro forma* in nature, special opportunities may result in unique operations. Given the variety of modern technology, SIGINT has found a place in the overhead reconnaissance program as well.

RECONNAISSANCE

Analysts responsible for judging Soviet military capabilities and intentions—and in the late 1950s this came to include military missiles—labored under an inadequate supply of hard facts. Those who had served in World War II and remembered the value of aerial photography made it a natural subject for consideration as a possible means of collecting critical intelligence. The basic and twofold need was a vehicle that could fly over the USSR at an altitude beyond the reach of Soviet anti-aircraft weapons and interceptor aircraft, and that could carry special sensors and cameras capable of high-fidelity photography.

In 1953 CIA began to develop the new cameras, with optical equipment and film of unprecedented high standards. In 1954 work was begun on the air vehicle that was to carry the photographic equipment as well as other sensors. Known as the U-2, it first flew in 1955, conducting weather flights for the National Aeronautics and Space Administration (NASA), which had not been apprised of the plane's intelligence function. The first flights over the Soviet Union occurred in 1956 and continued until Gary Francis Powers' U-2 was downed by a missile in 1960.[21] President Eisenhower gave the following evaluation of the program:

> During the four years of its operations, the U-2 program produced intelligence of critical importance to the United States. Perhaps as important as the positive information—what the Soviets *did* have—was the negative information it produced—what the Soviets *did not* have. Intelligence gained from this source provided proof that the horrors of the alleged "bomber gap" and the later "missile gap" were nothing more than imaginative creations of irresponsibility. U-2 information deprived Khrushchev of the most powerful weapon of the Communist conspiracy—international blackmail (original emphasis).[22]

The "bomber gap" and the "missile gap" referred to by Eisenhower had stemmed from U.S. Air Force speculation in the absence of hard information.

It is a venerable and understandable tendency of some military officials, in measuring the strength of a potential enemy, to emphasize the worst-case scenario in a range of possibilities. A historical example familiar to modern observers is General McClellan's delay of operations of the Army of the Potomac during the Civil War because he had estimated Confederate forces to be twice their actual strength.[23] In the same vein, the missile gap referred to by Eisenhower was a contention by some military and civilian officials that the United States had fallen behind the USSR in missile armaments. Taken up by the media, the missile gap became an issue in the Kennedy-Nixon election contest of 1960, although the so-called missile gap was a subject of significant reservation within the Intelligence Community. Eisenhower's bitter characterization reflects something of his feeling as to how the issue should have been treated publicly if at all—especially as the U-2 had made it clear, by 1960, that the missile gap had not existed. The missile gap issue presents the question of indiscipline, which has plagued some government agencies, and of the distorting influence that selective leaking of intelligence to the media can have on public affairs. More basically, it has highlighted the need for hard facts to support responsible analysis.

When the U-2 program began, the CIA recognized that the aircraft would become technologically obsolescent in a few years. A program was launched to provide a follow-on capability to take over when the U-2 could no longer fly safely over the USSR. As it so happened, the loss of the U-2 in 1960 preceded the availability of the new systems, although they did become operational subsequently. These systems consisted of the prototype of the aircraft now known as the SR-71 and, more important, the satellite reconnaissance program. The latter became operational in 1961.[24]

It was clear that the overhead reconnaissance program would become a major feature of intelligence collection against Soviet intelligence targets. Its management and control would entail a considerable administrative establishment. CIA, which was centrally involved in early overhead reconnaissance developments, opted not to take on full management of the program, given the increased staff that would require. It made this decision in spite of the bureaucratic muscle that program management might have provided in the Intelligence Community for maneuvering purposes. Management was transferred to the Air Force, which wanted it badly. The Air Force had already lost control of the space program to NASA, and its manned bomber force had yielded primacy as a strategic weapon to the ICBM. Nevertheless, CIA did retain a major role in the design and development of space collection systems.

In 1961 central control for overhead reconnaissance was established in a small office composed of CIA, Air Force, and Navy personnel, who reported to the Secretary of Defense. Budget appropriations were arranged through the Air Force, which was to provide the booster missiles, bases, and recovery capabilities for the reconnaissance systems. CIA would continue to be responsible for research and development, contracting, and security. Collection requirements would be met through the United States Intelligence Board (USIB), which was chaired by the DCI.[25]

As the new systems developed, it became apparent that further arrangements were desirable. In 1969 the President, the DCI, and the Secretary of Defense agreed that CIA and the Secretary of Defense would have decisionmaking authority over the national reconnaissance program. An Executive Committee (EXCOM) of three was formed, with membership made up of the DCI, an Assistant Secretary of Defense, and the President's Scientific Adviser. EXCOM reported to the Secretary of Defense, and the DCI had the right to appeal to the President in the event of disagreement with the Secretary's decisions. The DCI, as head of the Intelligence Community, was to establish collection requirements in consultation with USIB.[26] This arrangement would involve at least two USIB committees: the Committee on Imagery Requirements Exploitation (COMIREX) and the SIGINT Committee.[27] CIA also established a National Photographic Interpretation Center (NPIC), staffed by personnel from members of the Intelligence Community for the purpose of processing and analyzing the materials collected by the program.[28]

The reconnaissance program has continued to operate under the basic arrangements summarized above. Some of the aspects of this program do not lend themselves to summary, and some remain highly classified, but quite a bit of literature has been published on the subject. As already noted, Secretary of State Vance sketched a broad outline of the technologies involved.

There are two general types of satellites associated with these technologies (see Figure 10.1). One type is placed in near-polar elliptical orbit above the earth. The earlier satellites had a perigee (the lowest point of the orbit) of about 100 miles above the earth. Some 90 minutes were required to complete an orbit. The earth rotates beneath the satellite so that over a period of time most of the earth's surface passes under the orbit path of the satellite. In earlier days a satellite's time in orbit was about seven weeks,[29] a period that has been extended significantly. These satellites offer high-resolution photography on targets of special interest.

The other type is the geosynchronous satellite, which, in essence, is "parked" some 22,000 miles out in a near-equatorial station, remaining in a relatively fixed position over a designated spot on the earth's surface, although there is a pattern of movement to help maintain its position.[30] The geosynchronous satellite can remain in place for prolonged periods. It is not unique to intelligence reconnaissance. The principle of geosynchronous positioning is used in international communications satellites, which are placed in space to relay normal communications.

Both types of satellites have features in common and must be equipped to carry out a variety of tasks. They cannot be allowed to tumble in space, but must provide stable platforms so that the sensitive equipment they carry can be pointed at the targets selected for them. This objective requires certain maneuvering capabilities, both to stabilize the satellites at a given attitude and to aim them at the designated targets. The satellites must also have a power source. Most people are familiar with the solar cells projecting from the vehicles sent on scientific exploration into outer space. In addition, there has been public comment regarding the use of nuclear power sources by the Soviets, usually in connection with the danger of radio-active damage that occurs when a satellite falls. Equipment in the satellites must be responsive to commands from earth, activation and deactivation of equipment, recording and transmission of information, and ejection of film packages for recovery. They must possess some redundancy in their systems so that if one part fails, operation can be continued through activation of fall-back systems. Photography satellites carry the high-quality optical equipment that is a lineal descendant of earlier breakthroughs in the U-2 program. For SIGINT missions, these satellites have the appropriate electronic equipment and antennae.

138

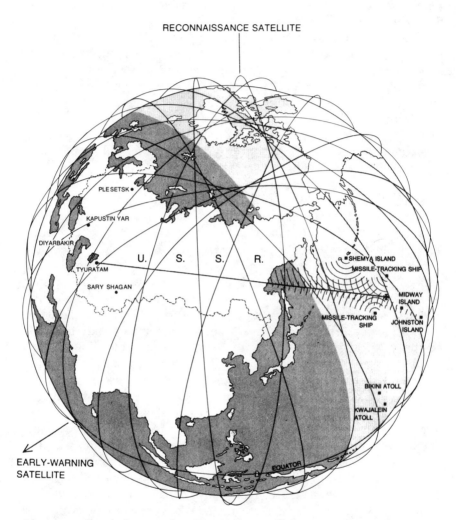

RECONNAISSANCE SATELLITE

PLESETSK

KAPUSTIN YAR

DIYARBAKIR

U. S. S. R.

TYURATAM

SARY SHAGAN

SHEMYA ISLAND

MISSILE-TRACKING SHIP

MIDWAY ISLAND

MISSILE-TRACKING SHIP

JOHNSTON ISLAND

BIKINI ATOLL

KWAJALEIN ATOLL

EQUATOR

EARLY-WARNING SATELLITE

Source: Arms Control: Readings from Scientific American, with introductions by Herbert York.   San Francisco, Calif.: W. H. Freeman Company, 1973, p. 234. Published with permission.

FIGURE 10.1. Reconnaissance and Surveillance Satellite Systems

An appreciation of the complexity of the camera systems can be gained from one source that described two photographic systems used in earlier nonmilitary programs. The techniques used by these systems are applicable to intelligence reconnaissance equipment. One of these camera systems was used to survey landing sites on the moon. A schematic diagram of the system shows lenses, a strip-film feed system that moves the film behind the lens, through a processor, dryer, and video system that transmits the picture back to earth, and then on to storage in the overall system. The other system, designed by General Electric for NASA's earth resources survey program, featured a series of multispectral cameras, with separate film capsules for ejection and recovery. Some of the reconnaissance film packages, after being ejected from the satellite, dropped toward earth by parachute, to be recovered by special aircraft.[31] Media reports indicate that satellite photography is of such high resolution that individuals and even manhole covers in the streets are clearly visible to the cameras.

Those who have seen color photographs of the rings of Saturn and of other heavenly bodies that have been transmitted from outer space can sense the sophistication of the technology available for reporting images not recoverable on film. Weather photographs that appear on television involve techniques similar to those first used in scouting for likely landing spots on the moon.

Although television transmissions serve a variety of purposes in general reconnaissance, such as identifying new targets or providing early warning of possible missile attack, they are not entirely able to meet certain objectives. A television image can be sharpened by addition of lines on the image tube, but in instances of special interest the clearer definition and additional detail available from film is preferable. Satellites with a lower perigee, which thus brings them closer to the target, serve this purpose.[32]

Not all overhead reconnaissance imagery is achieved by daylight photography. Both cloud cover and darkness serve to obscure critical targets at times. Infrared photography capable of reasonably high-quality imagery under adverse conditions fills this gap.[33] Infrared equipment can be installed in both orbiting and synchronous satellites, for purposes either of general reconnaissance or of early warning of missile attack.

Reconnaissance satellites can provide coverage of all communist countries. When satellites carry infrared sensors that are sensitive to heat, they can detect missile firings, thus providing the early warning capability mentioned above.[34] An interesting incident illustrates the sensitivity and reliability of the warning systems. On September 22, 1979, a U.S. nuclear-test-detection satellite recorded a single atmospheric explosion over a remote ocean area off South Africa. There was some question as to whether it was a nuclear explosion, but radioactive fall-out over New Zealand two months later led most to believe that it was.[35]

The source relied on for much of the foregoing review stated the general role of reconnaissance satellites as follows:

> By photographing missiles test sites [reconnaissance satellites] help to identify new missile systems, to detect changes in operational procedure that may suggest a change in hardware and to monitor testing programs. They can watch industrial facilities, including shipyards for the construction of sub-marines and plants for the assembly of missiles. Intermittent information on critical aspects of transportation networks can be obtained. The progress of construction of missile silos, ABM radars or ABM launcher sites can be monitored. Wide-area surveys can be made to determine if any activity is underway that violates the [SALT] agreements.[36]

There must be arrangements for communications systems to report intelligence to policy and command levels if significant developments are to be recognized on a timely basis. In an age when intercontinental weapons can strike halfway around the world in minutes, special attention must be given to rapid communications. Specifically, Executive Order 12333, Section 1.5 (i), requires that the DCI "establish uniform criteria for the determination of relative priorities for the transmission of critical national foreign intelligence, and advise the Secretary of Defense concerning the communications requirements of the Intelligence Community for the transmission of such intelligence." The Joint Chiefs of Staff maintain a World-Wide Military Command and Control System (WWMCCS), with special communications arrangements for strategic commanders and for "time-sensitive operations." In addition to the early-warning satellite information provided for in this system, a complex array of special land-based military radar systems across the Northern Hemisphere relies on the Department of Defense communications system for its reporting.[37] Although these detection systems are not intelligence in the usual sense, they do provide crucial information to responsible authorities in the event of attack, complemented by critical intelligence from other sources, including early warning satellites.

THE ROLE OF INTELLIGENCE IN VERIFICATION

The Intelligence Community has developed an excellent capability for detecting violation of agreements pertaining to strategic weapons—Intercontinental Ballistic Missiles (ICBMs), Submarine-Launched Ballistic Missiles (SLBMs), aircraft-delivered weapons, and Anti-Ballistic Missile

(ABM) developments. Reports of detected noncompliance are made, and from that point on the issue becomes a matter for political levels to handle.

The SALT Agreements provide for a Standing Consultative Commission (SCC) composed of Soviet and U.S. representatives, who handle issues of noncompliance. Neither side fully trusts the other, but this arrangement provides the forum for exchanges on such matters when they arise. The SCC has served its purpose well, but questions have recently been raised about it. At least as early as the spring of 1983 there were reports of an interagency committee advising the President that the USSR was developing more new ICBMs than allowed under the agreement, new ABM developments barred by the agreement, underground tests exceeding limits on the size of nuclear devices set in treaties, almost total encryption of missile telemetry, test attacks on U.S. intelligence satellites, and concealment of missile activities.[38] Restiveness on the part of the Congress resulted in a report from the President with considerable additional detail.[39] Oddly enough, given the political potential of those reports, neither major party made an issue of it during the 1984 presidential campaign. The issue seems to remain at dead center, whatever the ultimate answer may be.

OTHER SURVEILLANCE

In addition to SIGINT and overhead reconnaissance are certain other forms of strategic surveillance. The Navy has an obvious responsibility for knowing the location of USSR naval units, a more difficult task now than in the past, when the Soviet Navy's role was primarily one of coastal defense. The Navy's long-range shore-based patrol planes have an important ocean surveillance role, which could become a vital part of the antisubmarine (ASW) program in time of war.[40] Not as dramatic as the SIGINT and overhead reconnaissance programs, these planes nevertheless are an important part of the government's overall program.

The technical systems of collection are able to provide extensive information on critical subject matter. Comprehensive coverage of the Soviet Union's vast military machine is the most important function of modern intelligence, as reflected in the emphasis on military subject matter in the National Foreign Intelligence Program and budget. It will continue to be a major function so long as the present international situation exists.

NOTES

1. SALT II Agreement, Vienna, June 18, 1979 (U.S. Department of State, Bureau of Public Affairs, Selected Document No. 12B), pages 43–45.

2. For a more detailed summary of this activity, see Chapter 16 of the present volume.

3. *Church Committee Report*, Book I, page 354.

4. See *Arms Control: Readings from Scientific American*, with introductions by Herbert York, W. H. Freeman Company, San Francisco, 1973, Ch. 24. See also "Reconnaissance and Arms Control," by Ted Greenwood, pages 223–234, including a discussion of the role of infrared photography on page 225 and unclassified photographs on pages 229–231.

5. *Church Committee Report*, Book I, pages 325–326. A letter of 27 January 1983 from the Director of Counterintelligence, Office of the U.S. Army Assistant Chief of Staff for Intelligence, states that the Army Security Agency (ASA) was merged with the U.S. Army Intelligence Agency (USAINTA) and other units in 1977 to form the U.S. Army Intelligence and Security Command (INSCOM). A letter from the CIA Public Affairs Officer, dated 29 November 1984, stated that AFSS changed its name to Air Force Electronic Security Command in August 1979.

6. *Church Committee Report*, Book VI, page 268. See also *The Puzzle Palace*, by James Bamford, Houghton Mifflin, Boston, 1982, which estimates the number at 95,000 (at page 78).

7. *Church Committee Report*, Book I, page 354.

8. Ibid., pages 325–327, 353–355. The number of intercept stations has been reported publicly to be over 4,100. See *New York Times News Service*, 2 September 1983.

9. *Church Committee Report*, Book I, page 334.

10. *Endgame*, by Strobe Talbott, Harper & Row, New York, 1979, page 252.

11. *American and Soviet Military Trends*, by John M. Collins, Center for Strategic and International Studies, Georgetown University, Washington, D.C., 1978, page 343.

12. *Soviet Military Power*, with an introduction by Secretary of Defense Caspar W. Weinberger, U.S. Department of Defense, Government Printing Office, Washington, D.C., 1981, page 39.

13. *Waging Peace*, by Dwight D. Eisenhower, Doubleday, New York, 1965, page 568 ff. See also *The Puzzle Palace*, which lists attacks on U.S. aircraft in 1950, 1951, 1953, 1955 and 1958 at pages 137–138, and in 1959 at page 184.

14. *The Memoirs of Richard Nixon*, Grosset & Dunlop, New York, 1978, pages 382–383.

15. *Church Committee Report*, Book I, page 336.

16. Ibid., pages 364–365.

17. *Church Committee Report*, Book I, page 365; *The Vantage Point*, by Lyndon B. Johnson, Holt, Rinehart & Winston, New York, 1971, page 533.

18. *The Vantage Point*, pages 300–301.

19. *Church Committee Report*, Book IV, pages 112–114.

20. *Secrets, Spies and Scholars*, by Ray S. Cline, Acropolis Books, Washington, D.C., 1976, pages 161–162.

21. Ibid., pages 156–157; *Waging Peace*, pages 483, 544–545, 558.

22. *Waging Peace*, page 547. See also *Church Committee Report*, Book IV, page 59.

23. *Abraham Lincoln*, vol. 3, by Carl Sandburg, Scribners, New York, 1949; *The War Years, I*, pages 319, 491.

24. *Secrets, Spies and Scholars*, page 157.

25. *Church Committee Report*, Book IV, page 74. Not everyone in CIA agreed to this transfer of operational control. See footnote 8 on page 74. See also *Church Committee Report*, Book VI, page 271, on the machinery under Air Force aegis to handle this—namely, the National Reconnaissance Office.

26. Ibid., page 75.

27. *Church Committee Report*, Book I, page 84.

28. Ibid., page 263.

29. *Arms Control*, page 234.

30. See Note 28, supra.

31. *Arms Control*, pages 225, 228. See also *Cold Dawn*, by John Newhouse, Holt, Rinehart & Winston, New York, 1973, pages 14–15.

32. *Arms Control*, page 227.

33. An example of the technology in this area can be found in an unclassified infra-red photograph of an airfield in Texas at night time, displaying significant detail. The assumption is that technology has advanced since then. See *Arms Control*, pages 227–229.

34. Ibid., page 234. For a general review of the many applications to which satellites can be put, see *National Geographic Magazine*, Vol. 164, No. 3, September 1983, pages 280–335.

35. *Strategic Weapons: An Introduction*, by Norman Polmar, National Strategy Information Center, Crane, Russak & Co., New York, 1982, page 74.

36. *Arms Control*, page 225.

37. *American and Soviet Military Trends*, by John M. Collins, Center for Strategic and International Studies, Georgetown University, Washington, D.C., 1978, pages 25, 130–135.

38. "Soviets Have Violated Arms Treaties, Panel Says," by Hedrick Smith, *New York Times News Service*, 21 April 1983.

39. *Soviet Violation of Arms Control Agreements*, by Senator McClure, Congressional Record, Vol. 130, No. 8, Wednesday, 1 February 1984. An indication of the types of questions that can arise over technical collection, and the uncertainties of it, can be found in *Reader's Digest*, October 1985, pages 142–147, in an article entitled "U.S. Eyes over Russia: How much Can We See?" by Ralph Kinney Bennett.

40. *Church Committee Report*, Book I, page 330.

ANALYSIS OF INTELLIGENCE

The more extensive a man's knowledge of what has been done, the greater will be his power of knowing what to do.

—Benjamin Disraeli

Out of collected intelligence comes knowledge that has to be studied, if useful wisdom is to emerge. Between knowledge and decision—if the first is to influence the second—there must be a correlation and evaluation of what is known, and a judgment as to its significance.

The National Security Act of 1947 provides that the intelligence organizations of the government correlate and evaluate intelligence—a provision that is accepted as the legislative charter for intelligence analysis. Had the Congress omitted mention of this integral function of intelligence, this function would have been assigned by executive direction, as it had been prior to 1947.

Gathering and understanding information about other nations is the central purpose of National Intelligence. The available information must be assembled, sifted, weighed, and appraised as a basis for judgments about the present state of affairs and about what the future may hold. Knowledge of the past and present provides a sense of the continuing course of events; therefore, intelligence analysts are expected not only to identify key aspects of a current situation, but also to point to the future significance of what is known.

In attempting projections into the future, it is essential—when the facts are not complete—that the analyst keep in mind the limits of reliable prediction, delineating for the reader the distinctions between hypothesis and what is known. This point is critical if the highest professional standards are to be applied to intelligence work. It is in this context, where projections of opinion go beyond known facts, that the most controversy is generated in the analytical process.

No one challenges the need for balanced and responsible analysis, but there is no full agreement as to what this involves or how to achieve it. Some contend that "theoretical constructs"—that is, hypotheses—should be given full play in developing extrapolations of known facts,[1] with the understanding that important unknowns will often emerge. But this approach too frequently involves advocacy, which can hold many dangers for consistently reliable analysis. The more conservative approach is to control imagination when key facts are not known, thus limiting the liberties to be taken with what is known. The conservative approach attempts to consider the most likely directions of developments but, in doing so, presents them as possibilities rather than as firm probabilities. A disadvantage of the conservative approach, if carried to the extreme, is that it may suppress the insights of trained professionals. Balance between the two approaches is achieved through review procedures in the analytical process, testing and challenging the selection of facts and the conclusions, and confrontation among contesting views when they exist.

Even when analytical organizations are well staffed, equipped, and administered and are doing their work professionally, producing the best intelligence possible, they cannot be certain that the soundness of their work and its presentation will be well received by those for whom it is intended. The consumers of intelligence at policy and planning levels often are subject to a variety of political considerations and to fixed notions of their own that may inject some bias into their reactions.[2] Not only may they misread what they are told, but on occasion they may evince a strong preference for conclusions different from those given them.[3] Despite these considerations, analysts must try to provide the best summary of available knowledge, with the most objective appraisal possible. When opposing views arise, the differences among them must be made clear to policy levels to ensure their fullest understanding. This measure, not incidentally, guards both the quality and integrity of the analytical process.

The considerations affecting analysis that are noted in these introductory comments will appear from time to time in the discussion that follows in this and the next chapter.

SUBSTANTIVE SCOPE OF ANALYSIS

The breadth of knowledge that a great power must have to make policy and plan its implementation sometimes seems endless. The United States deals with problems in every corner of the world, ranging from sharply focused issues concerning single nations through regional questions to the activities of major international powers and organizations. Were it not for the unresolved issues of the Cold War, which currently exists at a reduced level of intensity, the requirements for such broad coverage could be reduced materially.

The experience of World War II demonstrated how much was not known about parts of the world where U.S. forces were involved. The gaps in which knowledge and familiarity would have facilitated decisions had to be filled through ingenuity and improvisation. Sometimes error was the product of ignorance.

In the early postwar days following creation of the new national intelligence structure, the members of the U.S. Intelligence Community undertook to assemble and organize an encyclopedic collection of information. Topics were assigned to the members of the Community, and a unit was formed in CIA to coordinate production of a compendium of "factual intelligence . . . of a fundamental and more or less permanent nature on all foreign countries."[4] Known as the National Intelligence Survey (NIS) program, it was to be a detailed, organized source on all the major nations of the world.

The objective of the NIS program was to organize basic intelligence of a "more or less permanent nature" with supporting files, for eventual incorporation into a printed reference work. The written materials on a major nation such as the USSR may have required a number of volumes, while those on a smaller nation may have called for only a single thin volume. In practice, the printed product has proved of limited use to those regularly assigned the analytical responsibility for a given nation or subject. Their expertise and regular working files usually provided all that was needed. Periodic review of the NIS materials ensured that the files were up-to-date, and also helped in the training of new personnel. But these measures alone hardly justified the NIS program. Scheduled maintenance of the program had a lower priority than other programs competing for budget support and was discontinued in 1974.[5] The publications (with security classifications) still exist as a resource "of a more or less permanent nature," subject to revision if required.

The NIS program did help develop an organized sense of the categories of information needed for national planning and policymaking. The exact form of the program is not available, but some authors have summarized typical lists of information similar to the NIS format, thereby giving an indication of the range and depth of subjects covered.[6] The following compilation of topics reflects the scope of the original undertaking as well as the continuing overall responsibilities of analysis work.

1. *Government.* Governmental system and structure of the country under consideration. Political arrangements and key personalities.

2. *General Background.* Summary of history. Social structure and special cultural characteristics. Religion(s). Language/dialects. Demography.
3. *Geography.* Cartographic information. Topographical, geological, hydrographic data. Climate.
4. *Economy.* Monetary, banking and financial system. Agriculture, mining, industry, services, trade. GNP. Role of government in economy and private sector. Allocation of resources.
5. *Communications.* Mail, civil telephone and telegraph systems. Radio and television systems. Newspapers. Publishers.
6. *Transportation.* Highway system (quality of roads, bridges, secondary and lesser roads). Motor transport. Rail system and capabilities. Civil air service and fields. Water ways (coastal and inland). Shipping. Ports.
7. *Science and Technology.* Organization and status of science and technology (private and government). Engineering, medicine, health. Education in science and technology. Research programs. Use of science and technology in military programs.
8. *Military.* Organization of national military system and forces. Subordination in the government. Numbers and equipment of separate services. Level of readiness and doctrine.
9. *Intelligence.* Subordination; organization and programs of intelligence and security organizations of the government.

Whether intended for the NIS program or for other reference purposes, the accumulation of printed materials and intelligence on foreign lands and its organization into libraries, files, and computer storage facilities present a major task. The variety of qualified personnel needed to use this material knowledgeably is equally extensive. All of this is basic to the organization of analysis activities.

A listing of subject matter categories does not, in itself, point up the various types of analysis that must be performed within the Intelligence Community. The concepts and practices of some general types of analysis are outlined in this chapter.

The final product of the intelligence system, intended for the upper reaches of government, is known as "finished intelligence."[7] This designation distinguishes the data in question from the "raw" information gathered by collectors, and from the interim forms that information takes as it progresses through the various steps of processing and review in the Intelligence Community. Finished intelligence is usually preceded by a number of analytical functions at different levels in the government. Specific details and interim conclusions may not appear in a final report, but they affect its form. A continuing thread runs from the collector in the field to the final product.

FIRST LINE ANALYSIS—THE FIELD

Collectors must be familiar with the subject matter in order to know what information is wanted, whether the information they collect meets a known requirement, and therefore whether or not it is to be reported at all. For instance, it may not be appropriate to report information from a clandestine source if it already is known. Similarly, if technical equipment monitors signals from known Soviet radar sites, the fact that the equipment is still in place and operating may be noted, but unless the information has some unique new quality it may not merit continual reporting. The reader may recall that the steps taken to reduce the flood of redundant reporting from the field were discussed in Chapter 5; judgments by the collector are part of that process, requiring intellectual discrimination not always credited to the collectors. This process is clearly a form of analysis in itself.

The screening out of redundant reporting is a negative aspect of the collector's evaluative function. If new and significant information is acquired, the collector has a positive contribution to make. The latter case involves, first, an evaluation of what has been collected, then the preparation of this information for transmission to headquarters with appropriate comments to ensure that any unique insights from the special vantage point of the collector are available for reviews at headquarters.

The decision to submit a report also requires a judgment as to its urgency. Should the report be submitted through normal official mail or the diplomatic pouch, as is customary for a great deal of nonpriority material? Or should it be reported by cable, and if so, what handling precedence should be given it? These decisions are based on substantive evaluation made on the scene, in the light both of events of the moment and of broader considerations.

Reporting by cable is not limited to headquarters. A variety of other consumers must also be considered. For instance, in HUMINT collection, significant reports will be given "lateral dissemination" to other field installations, usually embassies, with the understanding that official evaluation from Washington may follow. This procedure ensures timely awareness of new developments in addition to procedural requirements for review and evaluation at headquarters, in the broader context usually thought to be available there. Major military commands, such as CIN-CEUR and CINCPAC and the regional SIGINT processing centers, also have informational requirements that might include them among addressees in the field.[8] These lateral disseminations, before they are circulated with formal headquarters evaluation, may stimulate further analytical judgments and action from recipients in the field. This procedure does not conform precisely to the rigid confines of the bureaucratic organizational charts popularly associated with how governments prefer to function.

The treatment of reports from the field varies. A HUMINT report may not be given further dissemination in Washington, either because it does not add measurably to what already is known or because it is not considered reliable. Questionable reporting may, however, be circulated with a caveat if it serves as an alert to a possibly significant development. On the other hand, a report that is accepted in the form in which it was received from the field—which is usually the case— may be disseminated with or without additional comments by headquarters.

Technical reporting presents many of the same questions as those posed by HUMINT, although the processes differ given that the materials usually vary in form. SIGINT collectors receive all manner of electronic signals and communications, as discussed in Chapter 10. For instance, a new radar installation may appear or a change in the level of communications activity may occur, thus suggesting some possible new development. The collectors in the field are expected to make preliminary judgments and to report immediately to higher echelons for further analysis. An unencrypted communication—a plain language transmission—can present the same substantive questions as those faced in HUMINT collection, so far as judgments of significance are concerned. A single report may have great significance, requiring the most urgent attention at higher levels of the government. There are special communications procedures and facilities for such critical reporting.

The analytical function in the field is an integral part of the total process, not to be overlooked in preoccupation with analytical activities in Washington. If field analysis is often narrower in focus because of more limited local perspectives, it nevertheless is a first, and often lasting, contribution to later, broader reviews of a problem.

INTERIM AND SPECIAL ANALYSIS

Analytical functions in the field are invariably followed by reviews in Washington, where reporting is considered in the larger context available from reports produced by all sources. Additional reviews are conducted on technical data by special processing centers, the results of which become a part of the total data base used in producing reports for policy levels. Some of the major analytical contributions are made in these special processing centers. The technical form of the material with which they deal must be translated into meaningful forms that otherwise might not be apparent.

The SIGINT collectors—for the most part the military's so-called cryptologic agencies (the Army Intelligence and Security Command, Naval Security Group, Air Force Electronic Security Command)—report to their parent organizations, to the National Security Agency, and to the regional processing centers. Special situations may involve direct reporting to other elements of the Intelligence Community, but generally it is those four organizations that receive SIGINT reporting and review and process it for direct use and further dissemination.

Collection by the three military cryptologic agencies is conducted under the operational direction of NSA. Although much of what they collect serves the purpose of National Intelligence, their primary analytical focus is on the needs of their own services. Their work fits within the general description given NSA's work, which is "directed to foreign intelligence, obtained from foreign electrical communications and also from other foreign signals such as radars. Signals are interpreted by many techniques and procedures, sorted and analyzed . . . then reported to various agencies of the government."[9]

An intercept site in Europe may detect a signal indicating either a new communications or radar facility, or transmissions by previously unidentified equipment. The significance of that information may not be apparent at the site, but in combination with similar information from other sites it could assume material significance. The analytical process might result, for instance, in a reevaluation of Warsaw Pact/ Soviet air defense capabilities, thus leading to major revision of the Radar Order of Battle.[10] That knowledge could affect established operational planning. Analysis of Communications Intelligence (COMINT) may also contribute to revision of the Radar Order of Battle. Radio communications among radar sites, air defense centers, interceptor aircraft, and ground-to-air missile sites permit "traffic analysis" to chart relationships in the larger air defense system.

Analyses of SIGINT material may not reach policy levels in their original form. Such analyses serve primarily the requirements of the military services in the process of assessing what their own capabilities and plans must be. Yet impressive as these studies might be, they are not universally considered to be "finished intelligence" (although at one point the Church Committee seemed to refer to them as such).[11] The information in these studies will appear in summaries included in the eventual finished intelligence that is prepared for policy levels. That is not to denigrate the importance of the work, which is great, but to distinguish among the various types of study and analysis that are not intended directly for policy-level attention.

In addition to these long-standing technological means of collection and analysis are the procedures involved in overhead reconnaissance systems. Photography must be recovered and delivered to special centers for development—a process that sometimes involves complex retrieval and transportation methods. Moreover, electronic images involving special ground sites are received for study. There is much less field analysis in this functional area than in the other major technical collection systems.

The work of the National Photographic Interpretation Center (NPIC) in CIA might be equated with the analysis provided by the three military cryptologic services and NSA. NPIC is organized under CIA as an integrated Community operation, staffed with personnel from the military services and CIA, and with smaller scale participation by other government agencies.[12] Much of the photographic and imagery analysis serves the Departmental Intelligence interests of the services, but the results are also the basis for major measurements of Soviet military strengths—a prime objective of National Intelligence, especially as it bears on the missile issue. The overhead reconnaissance program provides considerable detail on the number and deployment of Soviet military forces, which can be combined with intelligence available from other sources to provide a remarkably comprehensive picture of overall Soviet military capabilities. Some of this work can be done in NPIC, and some is done in the other analytical facilities of the military services and CIA.

In addition to the broad sweep of knowledge available from these types of technical collection, the armed services need information such as that provided through samples of Soviet weaponry—carbines, side arms, armor, cannon, automotive equipment for logistical support and personnel transport, and aircraft, to name a few. Warsaw Pact capabilities can be measured with more confidence and our own tactics can be better focused when we know the quality of Soviet-made equipment.

The Soviet Union became a major international arms trafficker in the Third World, beginning with large arms sales to Egypt during the late 1950s, when Egyptian-Soviet relations were better than they became later. Since then the USSR has provided arms to a number of other countries. When Soviet arms are used in combat, as in Indochina and the Middle East, the Intelligence Community can make use of the opportunity to acquire samples for analysis. The range of samples for technical study may be broadened by clandestine means.

The Army's Edgewood Arsenal served in the past as a test center for foreign equipment, as has the Air Force Technical Intelligence Center (AFTIC) at Wright-Patterson Air Force Base. The Navy's Material and Sea Systems commands can provide qualified personnel to study foreign naval equipment if it is acquired. Detailed knowledge of Soviet equipment is not complete, but most important gaps can be filled with considerable success.

Still other areas of interim analysis are worthy of mention. One, usually associated with "finished intelligence," is the analysis of Soviet industry. Formerly a main area of concentration in CIA's economic analyses, such analysis was phased down gradually as the emphasis on a broader approach increased. Overhead reconnaissance has reduced the need for information on some industrial complexes, but that need still continues for certain industries as a basis for judging production outputs. Even economic studies have some of the characteristics of interim analysis, when the large economic reports are used as a basis for general conclusions in reports to policy levels. CIA also has an office concerned with scientific analysis that sometimes turns out finished intelligence but more often produces studies that are cited in the finished product.

Analytical work at every level and in all functional areas is directed at providing the best possible intelligence for decisionmakers. The unchanging objective is comprehensive, balanced, and responsible statements of what is known—statements that constitute essential elements within the final finished intelligence that ultimately serves as a basis for national policy.

NOTES

1. *Intelligence Requirements for the 1980's: Analysis and Estimates*, edited by Roy Godson, Consortium for the Study of Intelligence, Washington, D.C., 1980, page 2.

2. *Perception and Misperception in International Politics*, by Robert Jervis, Princeton University Press, Princeton, N.J., 1976. This intriguing book considers the forces that shape the decisions of policymakers. The entire book is worth reading by those faced with the problem of gaining policy-level attention for analytical judgments. The first chapter (pages 13–31) lays out the problem in general. The last chapter (pages 409–424), entitled "Minimizing Misperception," considers a number of factors relevant to the problem of analysis and the presentation of intelligence, although it is not the subject of the treatment.

3. "Ethics and Intelligence," by E. Drexel Godfrey, *Foreign Affairs*, April 1978, page 633.

4. *Church Committee Report*, Book I, page 260.

5. Ibid.

6. *Strategic Intelligence*, by Sherman Kent, Princeton University Press, Princeton, N.J., 1949, pages 12–13; *War of Wits*, by Ladislas Farago, Funk & Wagnalls, New York, 1954, pages 11–12.

7. *Church Committee Report*, Book I, pages 257–259.

8. *The Puzzle Palace*, by James Bamford, Houghton Mifflin, Boston, 1982, page 166.

9. *Church Committee Report*, Book I, page 327. See also *Church Committee Report*, Book VI, page 268, in which the NSA analytical function was described as follows: "interprets, traffic-analyzes, and crypt-analyzes the messages of all other nations."

10. The term *Order of Battle* had its origin in descriptions of military forces, organization, manpower, and equipment. The term, through evolution, came to be applied broadly to a wide variety of organizational descriptions. For instance, when all information on Soviet air defense radars is assembled, showing different equipment, their purpose, and command subordination, a comprehensive picture of air defense organization and capabilities emerges.

11. *Church Committee Report*, Book I, page 321.

12. Ibid., pages 263–264; Book IV, page 59.

FINISHED INTELLIGENCE

This is an unquestioned fact—that human beings do not have a foreknowledge of future human choices. In this field, therefore, we cannot make infallible predictions; we can only hazard guesses. This human inability to forecast what courses of action are going to be chosen by human beings makes it impossible for human minds to foresee the future course of human affairs on the basis of our knowledge of past human history.

Where prediction is impossible, guess work may be valuable so far as it goes—on condition, of course, that we recognize its limits.

—Arnold Toynbee[1]

Following initial and interim processing and specialized analysis of collected information, the resulting materials move to the final levels of analysis. There they are joined with the broad range of other information available. It is at this stage that the separate bits of reporting are fitted into a more comprehensive picture, the final product to be known as finished intelligence.

The policymakers and planners do not, themselves, have the time to sift through the mass of material that must be reviewed and digested. In fact, when they do their own analysis they risk reacting in inappropriate ways to a single bit of information that is out of context. The finished product of the analytical organization puts the information in context, points out its significance, and projects those judgments into the future.[2] It is the evaluation of current situations, and what they mean for the future, that moves the analytical effort into the realm of uncertainty.

When Dr. Toynbee formulated the dictum quoted at the head of this chapter, he did not have in mind the analysis of foreign intelligence. However, his broadly stated principle constitutes a basic truth that is applicable to the process. It is such an evident consideration that one would automatically think it a part of the attitude of those who use the finished product. Unfortunately, the reverse often seems to be the case.[3] Both the critics and supporters of intelligence frequently measure the results by unrealistic standards of perfection.

The remarkable achievements of intelligence over the years seem to have whetted the appetites and heightened the expectations of those who use the product, untempered by the failures that sometimes occur. Penetrating insights concerning still-developing situations are expected, and they have often been produced. Prescient forecasts are demanded, and they too sometimes have been possible. But frequently the sort of information necessary for definitive statements is not at hand. Not only are precise current insights sometimes difficult to achieve, but the Toynbee principle comes very much into play when it is a vision of the future that is wanted.

A demand for more accurate and complete knowledge, and the best and most balanced evaluation of it, is understandable. That is the ultimate purpose of intelligence. But perfection cannot be guaranteed, nor should it be expected. The certainty with which current developments can be evaluated varies with available facts. Projections into the future are even more difficult. Contributing to the confusion in the minds of some as to what reasonably can be expected is the fact that different topical areas are subject to different levels of certainty.

Analysts can speak with considerable detail and confidence on the composition and general capabilities of the Soviet armed forces. How those forces would be used in war can be described with considerable confidence. This confidence raise the expectations of consumers, but there is considerably less certainty as to when and where those forces may be used. General Soviet policy and posture can be described, but it is very difficult, in the absence of precise reporting on plans in the Kremlin, to forecast reliably the direction and the form of future Soviet moves. The uncertainties of intentions, as contrasted to capabilities, are so well recognized that special warning procedures have been provided to give as early an alert as possible when major new developments seem to be taking shape. (This matter will be discussed later in this chapter.)

A recent example of an unknown variable, relating to the predictability of events, was highlighted by the death of Soviet leader Leonid Brezhnev in 1982. Although the government intelligence organizations had considerable biographical information on key personalities, and on Brezhnev's most likely successor, they had only limited knowledge about the personal preferences of the new leadership and about the relationships among individuals holding key positions in the Soviet hierarchy. It was impossible to meet the requests of some prominent U.S. political officials for precise statements of what the changes in Moscow portended. As a result, one member of the U.S. Senate Select Committee on Intelligence received some publicity by proposing creation of a new Institute for Soviet Studies, to improve our knowledge of the inner workings of the USSR. Although such an organization could be useful, one doubts that it would improve analysis on a subject such as this. There would be no better information to work with. The senator surely would not relish being held to the same standard of analytical exactitude in evaluations he might make on the courses of action of U.S. politicians, about whom more is known (indeed, he might even know some of them personally).

The responsible analyst can produce the best conclusions professionally possible, given the facts available, and put them forward as the best understanding of the moment. He or she is also inclined toward candor in pointing out the unknowns and uncertainties. This candor may have an unsettling effect on some consumers, as seemed to be the case with the senator mentioned above.

Policy-level consumers have the right to demand the best intelligence possible. But if they do not understand the limits of the intelligence process and press for more than is known, their impact on the intelligence process can be negative. Intelligence analysts are conscious of the need to be responsive to higher levels. They try to give the breadth of coverage that seems appropriate to issues of the moment, including considerations that transcend current interests. When policy levels want the discussion narrowed, to reduce the complexity of the subject on which decisions are to be made, the analyst is faced with problems of adequacy and balance. And when policy levels expect conclusions that confirm decisions already made, that expectation can affect not only the quality of the process but its integrity as well. A result of too much responsiveness along these lines may be a subtle distortion that can lull or mislead the policy-level consumer in unintended ways.

Pressures generated on the analytical process from within the machinery of government are not the only factors that may have an adverse effect on analysis. Individual analysts are subject to normal human frailties. Some bring to their work personal attitudes that must be recognized and controlled. Some may be deluded as to their own intellectual prowess. There is always the hazard of carrying hypotheses too far beyond the facts. Or an analyst may seek to simplify complex matters to reach a conclusion that is firmer than the evidence warrants, perhaps to meet some inner personal need for certainty.

Given these considerations it is apparent that the administrative arrangements for achieving consistently high levels of performance in analytical work are important. Some provision must be made for reinforcing the positive aspects of the process while controlling the negative influences. The key to meeting this requirement lies in organization and management.

PRINCIPLES OF ORGANIZATION

The administrative organization for Departmental Intelligence and for National Intelligence presents many of the same problems. There are different problems as well. For instance, the military intelligence agencies must first meet the responsibilities of their respective departments, determining and measuring the military potential of unfriendly powers. These responsibilities are inextricably mixed with departmental interests, thus leading leading some to charge the military intelligence agencies with excessive parochialism. Yet, if we consider the matter in its full significance, we find an important rationale behind the shaping of military intelligence judgments to support their departments' plans and budgetary requests.

The military must plan and prepare for defense of the United States against possible aggression. This solemn mission demands a clear-headed judgment of the military capabilities of the most likely foe. That is the basis for planning. Unfortunately one will always find gaps in what is known about a potential enemy. Although long-range objectives of the other nation can often be discerned, specific actions cannot be foretold with much confidence. Modern systems of collection make it possible to observe changes in the structure and capabilities of another nation as they occur, but how large the program is intended to be or how long it will take to complete it seldom is known. When such changes begin, as they did in the Soviet Union in the period 1962–1964, when the USSR commenced its major military buildup, what lay ahead could not be foretold with much certainty. It could be observed as it developed, but the ability to predict with confidence was limited. That situation generated one of the more interesting periods of controversy within the U.S. Intelligence Community.

The conservatism of the military intelligence agencies, in seeking to ensure that our preparedness was adequate for the future, was offset by the conservatism of CIA in its reluctance to go very far beyond the known facts. The military did not dare to underestimate Soviet strengths, and CIA felt obliged to stand close to what the facts told its analysts.

These considerations must be kept in mind when considering the debates carried on within the Intelligence Community. The bias—if that word is read narrowly—is very real, deriving from important positions that demand respect. The missile controversy of the early 1960s presented the issue with unusual drama, but, in lesser ways, the conflicting positions are unavoidably present in many of the questions that analysts face.

The Department of State, which is responsible for advancing official policy abroad, may tend to see events as justifying earlier decisions or reflecting progress in achieving policy goals. By the same token, if CIA analysts were to become involved in the Covert Action programs of the operational side of the Agency, their involvement and resulting commitment might warp their objectivity. However, it is not desirable to keep the analysts screened off entirely from what is happening, for ignorance may produce erroneous conclusions. One example of such exclusion of professional analytical judgment from operational planning is the Bay of Pigs operation. The planners in that instance did not request an intelligence evaluation on the possibility of a popular uprising by the Cuban people in response to an invasion, but acted on their own judgment that an uprising had a good chance of occurring. At that very time an officer from the analytical side of CIA, assigned to brief the White House staff regularly but unaware of the pending Bay of Pigs landing, was advising that there was no organized opposition to Castro and no likelihood of a popular movement against him.

Protecting a high level of intellectual integrity in the analytical process must be a continuing concern; at the same time, analysts must be kept in touch with the real world. This is a consideration in the thinking of most senior officers, but not one that has received much formal attention in literature on the subject.

Sherman Kent has written most directly on the question of objectivity, or intellectual integrity, in the analytical process in his work entitled *Strategic Intelligence.*[4] Following publication of his book in 1949, he was called to Washington, where his influence was felt for nearly three decades. His approach was one both of principle and of practical application. He described the problem as follows:

> Now an intelligence staff which must strive for reasoned and impartial analysis, if it is to strive for anything, has its own difficulties with view, position, slant, and line. After all, it is made up of men whose patterns of thought are likely to color their hypotheses and whose colored hypotheses are likely to make one conclusion more attractive than the evidence warrants.[5]

Realizing that the analyst would be expected to produce more wisdom than available facts would usually support, Kent emphasized the ideal qualities of those involved in the work. He spoke of analysts making projections on the basis of what is actually known—that is, extending known facts into a reasonable evaluation of the future, an evaluation he called "speculative knowledge":

> Speculative knowledge is not common and it is not to be had for the gathering. It is the rarest ingredient in the output of intelligence and is produced only by the most competent students this country possesses. It requires of its producers that they be masters of the subject matter, *impartial*

in the presence of new evidence, ingenious in the development of research techniques, *sharp in the analysis of their own predilections or prejudices,* and skillful in the presentation of their conclusions. It requires of its procedures the best professional training, *the highest intellectual integrity,* and a very large amount of worldly wisdom[6] (Emphasis added.)

The qualities he described are intangible in many respects—hence the difficulty experienced in attempts to codify them. Yet these qualities are the central standards sought for every line of professional endeavor.

Sometimes aspects of other lines of work are compared with intelligence analysis, by way of trying to explain the latter. Journalism, which involves gathering information, sorting it, and making some coherent presentation based on an understanding of the situation, has been cited for its parallels. But a headline and a story often seem to be the driving force. More recently, the proclivities of some reporters to editorialize tend further to compromise professional standards. The legal profession also requires intellectual talents similar to those called for in intelligence analysis, but the institutionalized partisanship of our system of adversary justice does not always contribute to the objective pursuit of truth. If any walk of life offers parallel requirements for high professional performance and intellectual objectivity it is the academic world. Some attribute this fact to the removal of academic world from everyday reality. Traditionally, academia aims at unbiased research, although in modern times—in its attempt to be relevant—even such research, on occasion, becomes an instrument of ideological purpose.

The requirement for high professional performance and objectivity is greater for the intelligence analyst than for most social scientists. An academician who writes a book is frequently an advocate of some thesis, whereas the intelligence analyst is responsible for making judgments about the real world, in which his or her judgments will be evaluated accordingly. Achieving the appropriate standard and maintaining it is a continuing problem.

In addition to summarizing the ideal qualities to be looked for in an analyst, Kent described the environment that should exist in an analytical organization:

[A]n intelligence organization is a strange and wonderful collection of devoted specialists molded into a vigorous producing unit.

In a sense, intelligence organizations must be not a little like a large university faculty. They must have the people to whom research and rigorous thought are the breath of life, and they must accordingly have tolerance for the queer bird and the eccentric with a unique talent. They must guarantee a sort of academic freedom of inquiry and must fight off those who derogate such freedom by pointing to its occasional crackpot finding. They must build around a deference to the enormous difficulties which the search for truth often involves.[7]

Kent went on to say that beyond the resemblance to a university faculty there must be provision for a quicker pace and some orderly arrangements, which he likened to the metropolitan newspaper and business organization.

Moving from the analysts and the atmosphere in which they should function, Kent spoke of the managers of analysts, observing that

[t]o carry out this job the substantive managers must be exceptional indeed. For they must combine a high degree of professional ability with a high degree of practical sophistication and managerial talent. They must have professional standing in order to command the respect of a professional staff. That they have this respect and the good will which usually goes with it is of utmost importance. They will have great difficulty in obtaining either respect or good will without themselves possessing a reputation and a proven ability in an apposite field of systematic study. This experience in turn will favor their performance in another and almost equally important way: it will permit them a personal insight into the capabilities of the staff and a foreglimpse of the time necessary for the completion of a given project.

. . . What I am describing is not what every professional gets with his graduate training; in fact he is likely not to acquire it anywhere. Generally he has to be born with it. . . .

There can be no question of the importance of competent professional specialists and of this managerial control staff.[8]

Kent also advocated an organizational arrangement to reinforce the objectivity of analysts. Since the time of his writing, in the late 1940s, there has been recurring criticism of parochial bias in Departmental Intelligence, in support of positions of the department to which an intelligence agency is subordinate. For example, one author has alleged that U.S. Air Force intelligence on Soviet missile capabilities was distorted for the purpose of supporting "the role of the Air Force's missilemen."[9] This contention can be argued, as indeed it has been, but the assertion is an example of a perception. Aspects of the missile issue will be considered later in this chapter.

Kent, writing well before the controversy over the missile issues, reasoned that organizational subordination of analytical intelligence to policymakers and operators risked the objectivity of the analytical product. He cited author-journalist Walter Lippmann to the effect that "the only institutional safeguard [for impartial and objective analysis] is to separate as absolutely as it is possible to do so the staff which executes from the staff which investigates." He then offered the following organizational principle:

> The only way out of the dilemma seems to me to lie in the very compromise that is usually attempted: guarantee intelligence its administrative and substantive integrity by keeping it separate from its consumers; keep trying every known device to make the users familiar with the producers' organization, and the producers with the users' organization.[10]

In fact, the Intelligence Community is organized in both these ways. The military services have their controlled organizations, and CIA has an analytical organization separate not only from its own operational group but from the other departments as well. These arrangements protect the legitimate institutional right of the separate departments and agencies to develop their own position, from their own vantage point of legislated responsibility, based on the analysis of their own staff. And it provides for the *relatively* detached view of CIA, wherein the analytical organization is not expected to report the facts and conclusions differently than analysis judges them. Needless to say, these different approaches lead to disagreements, which can be expected to sharpen the focus of policy-level consumers. The Church Committee favored these expressions of difference, believing that where they occurred, they should be preserved in the final product instead of being diluted in the compromise language of consensus.[11] In fact, procedures for producing "community" papers provide for recording such differences.

One former senior CIA officer, who served with the analytic side of that Agency, wrote an article in *Foreign Affairs* describing how the CIA attempted to function:

> That element of the CIA whose job it is "to tell the truth," as opposed to collecting the truth overseas, is the overt Intelligence Directorate. It would appear at first glance to have the easier job. But this is not necessarily so. For one thing, truth is rarely simple fact; it is almost always a combination of fact and judgment and as such almost always subject to second guessing. The intelligence analyst has no monopoly on wisdom and prescience, but he does have one advantage. He is not subject to policy considerations of the operating departments, such as State and Defense. He is, in this respect, free to call the shots as he sees them, whether or not they substantiate or confirm some fundamental premise of U.S. policy. Ignoring the policy assumptions of the Administration in a search for the most defensible judgment can be an unhappy affair, as those analysts who toiled through the Vietnam years can testify. While support from Agency superiors for the views of the analysts was strong during the Johnson and Nixon

Administrations, the analytic product—that is, the truth as the analyst saw it—was not always palatable to higher consumers. The "truth" more often than not implicitly cast doubt on the outcome of the U.S. efforts in Indochina. Reaction to such judgments at White House and National Security Council levels was at worst unfriendly, and at best indifferent.[12]

This quotation may overstate the quality of CIA analysis during the period in question, but one can compare that analysis it favorably with some analysis emanating from other governmental organizations. The important point to be noted concerns the relative freedom of professional CIA analysts to follow the facts to their logical conclusion. They are not guaranteed that their conclusions will always be the best, or even correct, but that they will be relatively free from the warp of higher command decisions, and thereby free of the suspicion of institutional bias. They need only be reviewed on their merits.

Whatever the preferred approach to organization of analysis in theory, the different departments and agencies have obligations that affect their choices. Whatever the organizational forms they adopt, from beginning to end the main problem confronting them is the difficulty of the substantive problems they must solve. As each organization cannot give the same level of attention to all subject matter, responsibilities for analysis have been divided among them. Since there are some duplications of responsibilities and interest, no effort has been made to eliminate all overlapping assignments.

ASSIGNMENT OF RESPONSIBILITIES

With the development of what became known as the Intelligence Community, which came into being under the National Security Council following the National Security Act of 1947, there was a need to reduce excessive duplication in the government's intelligence agencies. Making room for the new Central Intelligence Agency presented some bureaucratic problems in itself. The existing intelligence organizations did not welcome a new member, feeling that they were well able themselves to take care of the government's intelligence problems. One example of the questions that arose concerned clandestine collection, which was handled by a mix of accommodation and evolution (as noted in Chapter 9).

The 1947 Act provided only very general terms of reference for analysis. CIA was instructed specifically to engage in analysis that related to national security—National Intelligence. The other agencies were to continue what they had been doing, including analysis, which was deemed by the 1947 Act to be Departmental Intelligence. Quite a bit was left for experience to clarify.

It was clear that the military services were to work on their traditional subject matter—analysis of the military organizations of the world—with primary emphasis on the Soviet Bloc armed forces. They had not wanted CIA added to the picture in the first place,[13] and CIA was excluded from analyzing military subjects in the early days.[14] How it could accept this restriction and still meet its mission of working on matters relating to national security remained for the future to determine. One of CIA's first major analytical efforts was made in the economic field. It was agreed that the Department of State would handle analysis on economic matters not involving the communist world, which would be reserved for CIA.[15] These arrangements were formalized by National Security Council directives.

The initial arrangements were reasonably effective. The military services were skilled in traditional military intelligence, but it was not clear as to how CIA's role would develop under its legislated responsibility for matters relating to national security. It became popular to refer to the arrangement as the military agencies "doing" Order of Battle while CIA "followed" Order of Battle; that is, CIA used the product of the military agencies' analysis and description of foreign military forces. The division of economic analysis between the Department of State and CIA was also a reasonable one, and it continued unchanged for nearly two decades.

Although the initial arrangements were satisfactory, they were also subject to change. Some of the developments will be reviewed below.

DEFENSE ANALYSIS

As noted in Chapter 5, the intelligence effort of the Department of Defense is by far the largest in the U.S. government, a fact that has resulted from the complex international relationships in which U.S. foreign policy is inextricably associated with U.S. strength. Military resources are an integral part of that strength. U.S. tactical and strategic military capabilities depend on knowledge about and appreciation for the capabilities and policies of the Soviet Union.

At the time of the 1947 Act there were three main military intelligence agencies: the Army and Air Force under Assistant Chiefs of Staff for Intelligence, and the Navy under a Director for Naval Intelligence. The Defense Intelligence Agency was not created until 1961, some fourteen years later. The military agencies follow developments in other nations of the world, with a primary focus on the Soviet Bloc armed forces. The following discussion will emphasize that aspect of their work. CIA will be treated not separately but in terms of its involvement in military issues, thus revealing a good deal about its function.

Military analysis involves the assembling of all available information and data on the Soviet services. Manpower is counted, organization is determined, and units are identified and located. Weapons systems and equipment, logistical organization, tactical and strategic doctrine, levels of readiness, and overall capabilities are studied. All of these factors constitute the traditional Departmental Intelligence mentioned in the 1947 Act. This knowledge is essential to measuring Soviet strengths as a basis for U.S. military planning. The success of the work has been impressive in terms of the detail and comprehensive coverage provided. The results have become known generally, partly owing to disclosures to the Congress in hearings before Armed Services and Appropriations committees. The information has been published by a number of authoritative sources.[16]

Given the global mission of the U.S. military services, which has derived from the geographic span of the Soviet Union, and its growing policy of projecting Soviet influence and power beyond its immediate borders, it follows that the range of the U.S. services' interest extends into the area of National Intelligence. The scope of military responsibilities has expanded, as has the task of intelligence analysis. The mobility of modern forces and the technology of advanced weapons systems have raised the level of urgency of what previously was a relatively mundane job of counting guns, tanks, ships, aircraft, and personnel.

Information gathered by modern systems for collecting intelligence provides a reliable basis for measuring potentially hostile forces and for planning the future shape of our own forces as a counter to the threat posed by unfriendly nations. Analysis generally discloses gradual or incremental change in overall strengths. It is important to detect such changes when they begin, for the development and deployment of new weapons systems involves long lead times. The recently publicized massive Soviet arms buildup started in the 1962–1964 period and has continued unabated to the present. In the Intelligence Community there was no argument over whether such a development was taking place. The controversy was over how far it would go, and how long it would last.

The composition and posture of armed forces is relatively static in the absence of major armed conflict. Collection and analysis are thus facilitated with respect to peacetime planning, but in times of armed conflict, operating conditions change. Programmed collection and analysis, which in peacetime may have taken on a stable character, are altered by war. Tactical contact of armed forces in the field calls for a different form of collection. Military forces move about and suffer combat attrition, so identification, location, and evaluation of units become less certain. Although headquarters elements will continue to watch developments, the more current and up-to-date information is in the hands of the combat commands. The ensuing discussion will address examples of these different analysis problems.

NAVY

During the Soviet buildup of the past twenty years, intelligence analysts have witnessed the gradual change of the Soviet Navy from an essentially coastal defense force into an ocean-going "blue water" navy. It is now designed to extend Soviet power to areas distant from the USSR. Although U.S. surface naval forces still generally appear to be stronger than the Soviet fleet, their former overwhelming dominance has been reduced materially and their freedom of movement has been challenged. One feature in the growth of the Soviet fleet has been the development of some seventy Soviet submarines with the capability of launching antiship missiles.[17] This development requires not only new U.S. defensive tactics but also "killer submarines" with the capability of seeking out and destroying enemy submarines. The ramifications of such a development are many, and detailed knowledge is the basic requirement for any planning in this connection.

The Office of Naval Intelligence is organized to provide both operational activity and analysis, with units for Intelligence Evaluation, and for Policy and Estimates. Another unit deals with Soviet Doctrine, Plans, and Strategy. Analysis of ship construction, observed from overhead reconnaissance, is an important aspect of the work. Another unit is concerned with plotting the location of all known Soviet shipping and naval vessels. In time of war, the "Plot" would provide the basis either for immediate action against surface vessels or for intensified search in areas where craft are believed to be.

As the U.S. Navy's mission includes the launching of strategic missiles from submarines in wartime, a new ingredient to the intelligence support is required.

AIR FORCE

The U.S. Air Force, the newest separate arm of the services, has tended to emphasize strong staff structures, which include recognition of the role of intelligence in providing the factual basis for long-range planning as well as in addressing current problems. The emphasis on strong staffs doubtless had its roots first in the pre–World War II struggle for a clear definition of the role for air power and then in the Air Force's quest for status as an independent military service. This emphasis has produced an aggressive approach to problems—an approach that is strongly supported by well trained staffs and operates with a sense of mission based on doctrinal concepts.

Air Force intelligence has the obvious task of locating and evaluating tactical and strategic Soviet air units. Knowledge of the capabilities of aircraft, operational doctrine, and tactical deployment is critical for planning.

For nearly two decades after World War II, the U.S. Strategic Air Command (SAC) fleet of long-range bombers was our main deterrent force. Plans for its possible use involved target selection programs and tactics for penetrating Soviet air defenses, thus placing a special intelligence task on SAC in cooperation with the Air Force Assistant Chief of Staff for Intelligence. The Air Force is also responsible for the land-based ICBM force, which is assigned to SAC. This responsibility involves careful attention to Soviet capabilities against our strategic forces, as well as to Soviet vulnerabilities. Over the years the Air Force concentrated on the strategic issues of long-range aircraft and intercontinental missiles. There have been some sharp differences over estimates of future Soviet missile strengths, particularly between the Air Force and CIA. These can be noted in summary fashion. President Eisenhower's comments, quoted in Chapter 10, point up the "bomber gap" (early to mid-1950s) and the first "missile gap" (late 1950s to early 1960s). The Church Committee summarized the first of these as arising out of service rivalries over financial resources, as a result of budget cuts following the Korean War. The Air Force made high estimates of the Soviet long-range bomber force and sought an increased share in the budget because of it. The Army and Navy questioned the Air Force, but CIA's entry into the question was a new development. The Church Committee's summary concluded as follows:

> In the midst of this controversy [CIA] . . . produced its estimates of Soviet bomber production. [These] assessments were more moderate than those of the Air Force. [The CIA] analysts argued that because of production difficulties, the U.S.S.R. could not operate as large a long-range bomber force as the Air Force was predicting. [This] marked the beginning of [CIA's] gradual ascendancy over the military in strategic analysis.[18]

In fact, CIA's analysis was not confined to studying Soviet production facilities; it involved additional intelligence and analytical techniques that supported the conclusions of the Army and Navy. CIA's conclusions were borne out later by overhead reconnaissance, as stated by President Eisenhower in his earlier comment.

Again in the late 1950s—culminating with the Kennedy-Nixon presidential contest of 1960—the Air Force concluded that a Soviet

Year	CIA Estimate of Projected Soviet ICBM Buildup	Actual Number of Soviet ICBMs at Time of Estimate
1966	800 ICBMs	About 250 ICBMs
1967	1,000 ICBMs	About 420 ICBMs
1968	1,200 ICBMs	About 700 ICBMs
1969	1,200 ICBMs	About 950 ICBMs

TABLE 12.1 National Intelligence Estimates

missile force was being developed to conduct a "first strike" against the United States. Senator Stuart Symington contended that the USSR was producing a missile force greater than that of the United States. CIA had a more conservative view, later borne out by the evidence. Intelligence collected by CIA agents and U-2 reconnaissance aircraft did not support the Air Force's contentions, which were discounted.[19]

Whereas CIA had been able to support its conclusions in the earlier disagreements, by means of intelligence collection and special analysis, it was not so successful in the second half of the 1960s on the question of missile production. This issue arose with the Air Force favoring the higher numbers and CIA taking a more conservative position. One critic of CIA described the situation as follows:

> While the Soviets were beginning the biggest military buildup in history the NIEs [National Intelligence Estimates] judged that they would not try to build as many missiles as we had. When the Soviets approached our number the NIEs said they were unlikely to exceed it substantially. When they exceeded it substantially the NIEs said they would not try for decisive superiority—the capability to fight and win a nuclear war. Only very recently [in 1978] have the NIEs admitted the possibility as an "elusive question." Now the NIEs say the Soviets may be trying for such a capability.[20]

One published chart records the NIEs from 1966 to 1969.[21] Exact numbers are difficult to extract, but they can be approximated. The estimates of ultimate Soviet ICBM deployments rose annually, always ahead of actual deployment until the end but below the eventual Soviet deployment. The U.S. Air Force estimates were materially higher than the CIA projections and much closer to the eventual figures. The estimates show a range of projected deployment, with high and low figures; the high numbers are listed in Table 12.1. The Soviet total actually rose to something over 1,500 at one point, and it leveled off at about 1,400 in 1970 when some older models were eliminated.

In the light of what happened next, one might wonder if anyone at policy levels was paying attention. The number of Soviet ICBMs was increasing without apparent slackening. Even though CIA's projections were incorrect, actual deployment was known as it progressed. What was lost was an advance appreciation for the eventual magnitude of the Soviet buildup. Yet, despite knowledge of levels eventually attained by the Soviets in 1970, no action was taken to increase the number of U.S. ICBMs to offset growing Soviet power. Instead, U.S. representatives completed negotiations on SALT I in 1972, fixing the maximum number of U.S. ICBMs at 1,054 and of Soviet ICBMs at 1,607.

The following summary throws some light on the other developments under way at the time:

In the winter of 1967 and 1968, Washington learned from intelligence reports that the Soviet Union was nearing parity with the United States in land-based ICBM's, and was believed to be deploying its first solid-fueled missiles. McNamara [then Secretary of Defense], in his January, 1968, posture statement told Congress that the Russians had more than doubled their ICBM force—from 340 to 720—in the space of a year. On December 13 [it was] announced that the United States had a weapon to counter the Soviet ICBM buildup. The weapon was MIRV, which . . . could send multiple, separately targetted warheads against the enemy.[22]

In other words, a single ICBM could launch several warheads at one time, thus obviating the need for additional numbers of missiles.

There is no question that CIA's projections of the Soviet ICBM buildup were too conservative. Although the estimates of numbers increased and then stayed ahead of actual deployment of new missiles by the USSR through 1969, the error was substantial. The 1966 estimate of the goal of 800 Soviet ICBMs was about half the actual number eventually reached in 1970. New weapons technology reduced such negative effects as the error might have had. Had it not been for the new technology, some compensating buildup presumably would have been undertaken, although with some time lag.

CIA analysts have been criticized for not reacting more strongly to the trend line of Soviet missile growth and not reexamining basic premises and approaches. Some critics believe that there was too great a tendency to accept Soviet protestations of moderation during détente, thus allowing the Soviets to obscure the less moderate statements also emanating from Soviet leaders.

In retrospect it appears that CIA analysts were influenced, at least in part, by estimates of the expenditures by the Soviet Union on its arms program. It was believed prior to the mid-1970s that the Soviet defense budget received some 8–10 percent of the USSR's gross national product (GNP). It was not until new evidence was received in the mid-1970s that the rate of investment by the USSR in defense was discovered to be closer to 13–14 percent of GNP.[23] What effect this might have had on CIA judgments in the second half of the 1960s is speculative.

The three cases summarized above—the "bomber gap" in the early 1950s, the "missile gap" of the late 1950s and early 1960s, and the underestimate of Soviet ICBMs in the second half of the 1960s—call to mind an observation made in the *Church Committee Report*, to the effect that "while analysts may be able to furnish fairly complete and reliable reporting on tangible factors such as numbers and make-up of Soviet strategic missile forces, they are not as good at asserting such intangibles as why the Soviets are building such a force."[24]

SIOP

In the age of strategic missiles, there arose a need to coordinate plans for the possible employment in wartime of the Air Force's inter-continental missiles (ICBMs) and the Navy's submarine-launched ballistic missiles (SLBMs) in order to eliminate unnecessary duplication in targeting and to allocate target assignments.[25] Initially, SAC had been the main strategic targeting agency, but with the deployment of SLBMs, that function had to be shared with the Navy. The Single Integrated Operations Plan (SIOP) serves that purpose, and a joint organization was formed to handle strategic targeting. Intelligence support is required for target identification, priorities, and assignment between the two services.

ARMY

In the absence of major conflict, the U.S. Army intelligence services have the least difficult task in measuring and evaluating Soviet ground forces. Knowledge of those forces is impressively detailed.[26] However, in time of war the task becomes severely complicated given the need for detailed, current knowledge.

In wartime, armed units move about and may be difficult to identify in combat. Communications may be less certain, and the fluidity of some situations will make it extremely difficult for current reporting to meet the usual interests of command echelons. Field commanders generally have enough on-the-scene information to direct tactics and develop new strategy, but the overall picture will often be blurred.

War in Europe would involve at least formal military forces, but a war similar to the recent conflict in Southeast Asia can be more complicated because of its political aspects and the mix of formal military forces and indigenous irregulars. This very question became an issue in the Intelligence Community during the Vietnam War, and has since attracted some attention in regard to questions about official strength figures raised by a CIA analyst, Samuel Adams, and others.

It should be noted, by way of background, that the U.S. Army's analysis of Order of Battle on Vietcong and North Vietnamese Army (VC/NVA) organization and strengths was handled in Vietnam by some 200 to 300 uniformed analysts assigned to the U.S. Military Advisory Command, Vietnam (MACV). The Department of the Army's charter for military analysis, under NSC directive, was, in effect, delegated to the field command with responsibility for conducting military operations.

CIA, under the existing assignment of responsibilities by National Security Council directives, seldom engaged in basic Order of Battle analysis. It used the results of Army analysis in most cases, especially in Vietnam. CIA analysts were of the general view that the reported official strengths of communist forces were lower than actual operating strengths. However, numbers were not believed to be a matter of central significance to the outcome of the war. There were sufficient communist forces to keep the war going, and progress depended on the morale and determination of the communists. The evaluation of communist resources and determination was reflected in *The Will to Persist*, a fortnightly CIA publication on the status of the war prepared for a select number of senior officials in Washington. This publication reviewed developments and reported VC/NVA casualties, desertions, and level of activity in an attempt to measure where things stood. Numbers were discussed, but the publication also sought qualitative measurements.

Adams was assigned to analyze communist military strengths. He is correct in saying that at one point he was the only full-time military analyst in CIA involved in that work, but he was not the only CIA officer with responsibilities for the subject. He soon reached the conclusion that the communists were suffering so many casualties and losing so many personnel through defection that their ability to continue must have been seriously impaired. His views led to special work, including travel to Vietnam with a team of psychologists to measure communist morale. In the course of his work, Adams found that other CIA personnel were not at all sanguine in their reactions to his thesis. He began to have second thoughts. In reading captured documents, in which communists from district and province levels reported to higher echelons on their progress in organizing their regions and on their military strength, he discovered that these documents reported greater strengths than those credited to the communists by MACV's official Order of Battle figures. Adams found that other captured documents gave the same picture for other areas. He concluded that VC/NVA strengths were about 600,000 instead of the 270,000 figure then in use. His account of this process and his attempt to win acceptance for his conclusions appeared in an article in *Harper's* magazine of May 1975, reproduced in full in a report of hearings before a committee of the House of Representatives.[27]

Adams presented his case before a number of forums within CIA and at conferences in Washington, Honolulu, and Saigon. But it was not accepted as presented. His case was considered flawed because of his acceptance at face value of all of the information he had gleaned from captured documents, which were believed to have an element of inflation in claims made to higher echelons. One analyst cited an area in which reported communist strengths exceeded the number of persons available for recruitment by both sides. Further, there was considerable variation in the level of success experienced by the communists in different areas of South Vietnam, thus subjecting straight arithmetical extrapolation to substantial distortion, when applied across the board. In addition, current VC/NVA casualties and defections affected the reliability of dated reports. Had Adams not tried to produce the absolute answer—as the military had done—but instead had showed existing flaws and sought an increase in personnel to work on the problem, he might have been more successful. The problem was obscured by the form of his criticisms. Even had he approached the issue with a broader understanding of the problem, CIA might not have taken on the task of producing more accurate strength figures, given the jurisdictional inhibitions against intruding into the Army's assigned role.

Adams pressed a campaign to gain support for his position, initially alleging false reporting on the part of CIA. In his own later testimony before the House of Representatives committee inquiring into the matter, he stated that he had never read the CIA regulations.[28] He probably was unaware of the NSC directives, mentioned earlier, that delineated jurisdiction for military analysis. Nor was he adequately trained in the sort of statistical work appropriate for the approach he had taken in processing the raw data he had found. Experienced as he was in a previous assignment involving fairly rudimentary military subject matter, he proved to be less than fully prepared for this larger task. That is not to detract from his instincts, which seem sound, but to suggest what went wrong when he tried to document his case.

In September 1967, at a conference on Order of Battle held in Saigon, the MACV Chief of Estimates presented what came to be known as the "cross-over" theory. In essence, a graph line that showed rising VC/NVA losses crossed a declining line showing replacements, and led to the conclusion that we were winning through attrition.[29] This theory was very similar to the earlier theory developed by Adams and then abandoned by him. CIA did not accept the cross-over theory. The new ingredient, however, was that MACV's theory gave the numbers strategic significance, attempting as they did to predict the outcome of the war. CIA then felt it necessary to increase its analysis of the subject.[30] The result was the eventual raising of official figures for communist Order of Battle. The final number was well above the former official MACV figure and not far from Adams' overall figure, although supported by more sophisticated analytical methodology.

As has not been the case with disagreements over bombers and missiles, there is no reliable subsequent intelligence to provide a guide for determining what VC/NVA strengths actually were. The authorities in North Vietnam probably knew the numbers they sent South, and probably had some idea of casualties and missing men. But VC strengths were something else. There was the problem of what to count, in determining how many irregular troops there were. For instance, irregular forces in provinces remote from the main action had limited relevance to the areas of main engagement. Political cadres, with their organizational infrastructure, were seldom counted among the effective military forces, but when military operations went into one of the relatively inactive areas these cadres could cause casualties. No one really knew then, and it is safe to say that no one really knows now, what the effective strength of the VC/NVA was at any given time.

The differences that can arise—and that actually arose over estimates of bomber, missile, and Vietnamese communist strengths—are in part a result of the difficulties of developing accurate and timely information on an important subject. The differences in these three cases help illustrate certain aspects of the task that confronts intelligence analysts.

DIMENSIONS IN TIME

Requirements of policy-level consumers vary with the subject matter, and with issues of the moment. The information they need takes on a sense of time, thus raising questions about past, present, and future. Intelligence organizations manage themselves so as to produce relevant finished intelligence for such purposes.

Chapter 11 noted the process involved in assembling and presenting a broad array of basic data about the nations of the world. This is general, rather than sharply focused, information. As inclusive as that data may be, however, specific issues do increase the range of detail needed to understand them. Different types of problems pose different analytical requirements.

DEEP RESEARCH

Personnel specializing in foreign subject matter should develop a broad range of familiarity with their assigned responsibilities. Such personnel must therefore have extensive factual knowledge and an understanding of the forces at work in a given nation or field of activity.

Closed societies such as the Soviet Union or the People's Republic of China present the most difficult analytical problems. A long time has passed since private Americans have been able to reside in those countries as they can in other lands; hence such countries are more difficult to learn about. Official contacts and careful study of all printed materials emanating from those countries provide some knowledge, and are studied in more careful detail than is necessary for more open societies. The result is fairly reliable information on the general structure of the economy and the system of government, including, in particular, the way the ruling hierarchy functions. Thus, when an event such as the death of Brezhnev occurs, knowledge of the workings of Soviet political forms, the broad nature of the careers of possible successors, and the problems to be faced within the system provide the basis for judgments as to what is most likely to occur next. In the case of Brezhnev's successor, the two most likely candidates were named (and both have risen to the top since then) with some cautious discussion of the tasks facing the new leader. But analysis could not, and did not pretend to, speak definitively on the subject. In the absence of specific information, that was the best to be expected. The analysts could convey the atmosphere in which developments would occur, but they could not predict with certainty precisely everything that would happen.

The Intelligence Community has extensive biographic data on a large number of foreign officials, with special attention directed to the major communist nations. Long range economic studies, inquiries into the social structures of the less advanced nations, and the military analysis reviewed earlier are parts of the regular process of research that contributes to the background for interpreting current developments and envisioning the future.

CURRENT INTELLIGENCE

The Church Committee was concerned with the effect on general intelligence analysis of what it called the Current Events Syndrome. General agreement was reached with respect to the need for more effort on "increasingly important long-term (and interdisciplinary) problems [such] as world food balances, raw material supplies, population pressures and pollution of the environment." CIA's analytical area was reported to be turning more attention to this work.[31] The committee recognized, however, that emphasis on current reporting was in response to "the growing demands for information of current concern . . . [and] for more coverage of more topics."

In today's dynamic world, change must be monitored closely. When change is gradual, current reporting keeps policy levels aware of the normal flow of events (in addition to contributing to the education of those at policy levels who come and go from private life, as they tend to do in the U.S. government). As policy-level support staffs grow, they require a broad feel for current developments pertinent to much of the day-to-day fine-tuning of policy so essential to the effective conduct of foreign affairs. These staffs cannot lose sight of events in one area while more critical events elsewhere occupy their attention. Current intelligence reporting keeps policy levels aware of changing conditions.

The authors of the *Church Committee Report* felt that pursuit of current intelligence obscured the broader vision of analysts. A more prevalent criticism of current intelligence personnel had been directed at their readiness to look beyond the event of the moment to its significance, an area that the estimators felt to be their special preserve. The problem was solved in CIA during the Carter administration through a reduction of the current intelligence office; but this action raised complaints—at least from certain levels in the NSC Staff—about the fact that the NSC then had to start doing its own current analysis because CIA's current reporting had fallen behind in quality and timeliness.

The CIA organizational chart drawn up at the time of this writing shows an Office of Current Production and Analytic Support, designed to focus especially on this type of reporting and thus coordinating among the various analytical elements. The reported reorganization under DCI Casey of CIA's Directorate of Intelligence along geographic lines seems to have caused some temporary dislocation, but recent press reports indicate that additional personnel are believed to have restored earlier reporting capabilities.

WARNING/INDICATIONS INTELLIGENCE

Warning of hostile actions against U.S. or allied forces and territory is a critical and continuing aspect of intelligence responsibility, underscored by the Pearl Harbor experience. In the context of discussing the military role, the Church Committee described the basic mission as follows: "U.S. technical collection systems are able to alert leaders to an imminent attack by detecting movement or changes in the status of the Soviet Union's strategic forces. . . . This so-called strategic warning may be essential to the survival of some components of the U.S. retaliatory force."[32]

Once known as "Indications Intelligence"—involving the detection of indications of preparation for hostilities—a National Indications Center (NIC) was formed in the Pentagon, headed by a senior CIA officer. Included was the so-called Watch Committee, headed by the Deputy Director for Central Intelligence, which regularly reviewed recent developments for possible indications of hostilities. The machinery for this committee has evolved over the years; most recently, the DCI had a National Intelligence Officer (NIO) for Warning, who serves as a special centralized reference point for the work.

The technical collection systems discussed in Chapter 10 are designed to provide timely comprehensive reporting of major indications that point to hostile preparations. A list of such developments would be considered by some to be a check-off list for a countdown of such preparations. As noted in Chapter 10, the U.S. military in Europe has some 700 "indicators" on its lists. If the Soviet Union were preparing for war, one would expect to see preparations checked off on the list of indicators, although one must keep in mind that deception is a part of starting war and that a single event of special importance may convey the same message as a full list of indicators.

ESTIMATES

The National Intelligence Estimate (NIE) can be considered the culmination of the intelligence process. Its purpose is to provide a synthesis of the Intelligence Community's knowledge and wisdom, telling policy levels what is known and what it means. Sherman Kent described his understanding of the Estimate in the one section in his book, under the section headed "Probable Courses of Action: Estimates."[33] Obviously, if reliable predictions can be made about what another nation will do, they are invaluable to those responsible for the conduct of national foreign policy.

Given the uncertainties of intelligence, one can entertain some reservation about Kent's description of the estimative product pointing out "probable courses of action." One would prefer a description of the conclusions as "most likely courses of action." Such a description has something to do with the state of mind in which estimators approach the analytical task, and with what policy-level consumers may feel entitled to expect in the reports they receive.

The hazards of estimating future events have been stressed in the preceding pages. Even if there is a report of a foreign leader's declared intention to do a certain thing, problems encountered in implementing the action may modify what actually is done, not to mention the influence that colleagues may have on that judgment. Moreover, an opponent's foreign policy may change in reaction to the United States' own response to some initiative or act of preparation.

The American word *estimate* has acquired the connotation of prediction, and some of those engaged in the work have come to believe that prediction is what they unerringly can do. The temptation to speak out clearly and to avoid "weasel words" sometimes causes one to make categorical statements. When this tendency replaces the careful distinctions of precise writing, it can prove embarrassing. The British, who tend to be more conservative and precise in their use of the English language, use the word *appreciation* to describe their review and appraisal of a situation, and what it may mean for the future.

Sherman Kent was called to Washington to put his principles into practice, and for about a quarter of a century presided over the center of the Intelligence Community's estimative function, giving it form, life, and purpose. His CIA Office of National Estimates (ONE) was unique, with a senior Board of National Estimates composed of officers from private life and other government agencies, supported by a staff of experts who labored with the substantive problems. In 1973 the Office of National Estimates was disbanded in favor of a new approach to the work.

The strength of the ONE arrangement was, initially, its function as a central mechanism for producing national estimates. Specialists on the office's staff worked on their areas of special interest. The board members, responsible for bringing to bear senior experience and knowledge of attitudes and developments outside the relatively cloistered life of ONE, had a direct influence on research. In addition, members of the board usually chaired meetings within the Intelligence Community on the various NIEs being processed. The ONE system provided direct and substantive support, centrally, with access to the agencies in the Intelligence Community. Among the perceived problems of the office was the tendency for personnel to stay on instead of rotating to other assignments after a period, as had originally been the practice. This tendency was seen as developing an in-grown quality that placed staff members at ONE increasingly out of touch with the activities and interests of others in the Intelligence Community. A system of rotational assignments might have prevented this problem. Some critics felt that members of the staff also developed attitudinal biases on certain issues in which objectivity was essential.[34]

Dissolving the Office of National Estimates seemed a drastic way of handling the perceived problems, especially as the new arrangement experienced some basic problems in the beginning. In place of a formally organized office, the new approach consisted of a group of senior officers attached to the Office of the Director of Central Intelligence. They were titled National Intelligence Officers (NIOs)[35] and were known collectively as the National Intelligence Council.[36] Each NIO was assigned an area in which he or she had special expertise. Six NIOs were responsible for specific geographic areas: Africa, China–East Asia, Latin America, Near East and South Asia, USSR–Eastern Europe, and Western Europe. Four NIOs had general assignments (not described in a chart published in late 1980), and three had special responsibilities: Strategic Programs, General Purpose Forces, and Warning. Presumably the categories of responsibility were subject to some variation to meet changing requirements.

In the earlier days of the system, its weaknesses were felt to be a result of both the loss of direct control over staff-level support on substantive matters and the reduction of institutional access to community resources (which, in turn, resulted from the loss of formal organization behind the NIO). As the NIOs came from different agencies, they were able to solve the problems incurred by loss of familiarity with the Intelligence Community, which were thought to have become a collective weakness of ONE. ONE had gathered a staff of superior writers over the years, and when the office was dissolved that reservoir of talent was lost. As a result, some of the papers produced by the new system were criticized as being too ponderous (however well documented they might have been as research papers) for busy policy-level consumers to read and digest. It was felt that the personal access the NIOs had to members of the Intelligence Community counterbalanced this problem as the new system developed.

With the passage of time, in the way of all administrative organizations, a line of command developed within the National Intelligence Council—including a Chairman and Vice-Chairman, who had clear roles in organizing the work, and formalized procedures for coordinating within the Intelligence Community. The terms of reference for proposed NIEs are developed by this council, contributions to be used in preparing draft NIEs are submitted by members in the Community, and one person is designated to prepare a working draft for review at a coordination meeting of representatives from members of the National Foreign Intelligence Board. An agreed draft—when agreement exists—is prepared for submission to the NFIB. Where there is disagreement, the points of variance are set out clearly, thus highlighting the issues for policy levels.

But the overall objective remains unchanged, whatever the machinery. This objective is the production of a clear summary of the subject, consideration of its significance, and formulation of alternative future developments. Sometimes the summary can provide a reliable forecast;

even in times of uncertainty, it still can highlight the issues. In some cases it describes how foreign governments may react to various courses of action from which U.S. policymakers must choose. This latter function comes close to the making of policy, which must be handled carefully in order to preserve the objectivity of the analytical effort.

NOTES

1. *Change and Habit: The Challenge of Our Times*, by Arnold S. Toynbee, Oxford University Press, London and New York, 1966, pages 7–8.

2. *Church Committee Report*, Book I, page 267. It is believed by some that the USSR has a similar problem, whereby senior officials prefer to do much of their own analysis. Conventional wisdom in Western intelligence circles seems to hold that the USSR conducts limited analysis of intelligence, with the KGB and GRU concentrating on validation of the reliability of reporting instead of subjecting it to the critical analysis employed in the United States. A U.S. publication in 1963, based on an earlier NKVD textbook (the NKVD was a precursor of the KGB), ridiculed the American concept that "hypotheses of national importance" can be expected from those who submerge themselves in paper and books. That publication stated: "The political significance of the information is evaluated by the policymaking members of the government and the Party Presidium." See the related discussion in *Intelligence Requirements for the 1980's: Analysis and Estimates*, edited by Roy Godson, Consortium for the Study of Intelligence, Washington, D.C., 1980, pages 17–18. See also *KGB: The Secret Work of Soviet Agents* by John Barron, Reader's Digest Press, Pleasantville, N.Y., 1974, page 77.

To the extent that it is correct to state that the KGB and GRU did not in earlier times engage in analysis—in the production of "finished intelligence," as we think of it—we must take into consideration other developments. In 1967 efforts were made as a result of the Twenty-Third Congress of the Communist Party in the previous year to strengthen the study of the noncommunist world. Several special institutes were created within the Academy of Sciences, organized on a geographic basis. The greatest importance to us is the Institute on the USA and Canada. Others include the institutes on the Far East (IDV), Oriental Studies (IVAN), Africa (IA), Latin America (ILA), and World Economy and International Relations (IMEMO). Consciously patterned after Western "think tanks," they were declared—by the Twenty-Fifth Congress of the Communist Party in 1976—to have corrected the defects noted in 1966. See *The Armed Forces of the USSR*, by Harriet Fast Scott and William F. Scott, Westview Press, Boulder, Colo., 1979, pages 81–85. There can be no question that the results of the studies conducted by these institutes have their impact on the Soviet government's policymaking processes.

Even if the KGB and GRU did not perform analysis as we think of it prior to the mid-1960s, it is safe to say that some form of analysis was conducted in the Soviet government. There must have been some screening of the hundreds of thousands of raw reports received and some forwarding of selected reports to the higher echelons, much as is done in the United States government. Whatever the staff support of senior levels might be for processing that information, it is certain that the policymakers themselves did not screen all reports. Sufficient time would not have been available. In addition, there are "desk officers" in the Foreign Ministry who must be familiar with developments, and some form of analysis obviously exists there in support of foreign policy—and always has been.

3. One of the better pieces of exposition in the *Church Committee Report* (Book I, pages 268–269) states the problem of certainty as follows: "Clearly what is needed is a realistic understanding by both producers and consumers about the limits of intelligence: what it can and cannot do. As a former senior analyst explained to the Select Committee, what intelligence *can* do is to follow the behavior of foreign leaders and groups over a long period of time in order to get a sense of the parameters within which their policies move. American policymakers are not then likely to be greatly surprised by foreign behavior even though intelligence analysts might not be able to predict precise intentions at any given moment with respect to a given situation. Nor can analysts be expected to predict human events when often the actors themselves do not know in advance what they will do. As the Schlesinger Report said: 'In a world of perfect information, there would be no uncertainties about the present and future intentions, capabilities, and activities of foreign powers. Information, however, is bound to be imperfect for the most part. Consequently, the intelligence community can at best reduce the uncertainties and construct plausible hypotheses about these factors on the basis of what continues to be partial and often conflicting evidence.' To expect more may be to court disappointment. Despite this recognition on the part of many policymakers, if analysis is not correct, there is often the charge of an 'intelligence failure.' Good intelligence or accurate predictions cannot insure against bad policy, in any case. For example, as the current Deputy Director for Intelligence maintains, the pessimistic CIA estimates on Vietnam had little or no effect on U.S. policy decision there. Vietnam may have been a policy failure. It was not an intelligence failure. Similarly, the United States had intelligence on the possibility of a Turkish invasion of Cyprus in 1974. The problem of taking effective action to prevent such an invasion was a policy question and not an intelligence failure."

4. *Strategic Intelligence*, by Sherman Kent, Princeton University Press, Princeton, N.J., 1949.

5. Ibid., page 199.

6. Ibid., pages 64–65.

7. Ibid., page 74.

8. Ibid., pages 108–109.

9. See *Intelligence Requirements for the 1980's: Analysis and Estimates*, Ch. 2, "Comparative Historical Experience of Doctrine and Organization," by Angelo Cordevilla, page 30.

10. *Strategic Intelligence*, pages 200–201.

11. *Church Committee Report*, Book I, pages 271–272. Subsequently, as noted therein, the Reagan Executive Order 12333, section 1.5 (k), provides that the

DCI is responsible for "ensuring that appropriate mechanisms for competitive analysis are developed so that diverse points of view are considered fully and differences of judgment within the Intelligence Community are brought to the attention of national policymakers." During the Colby-Bush period, an experiment was run in which the work of the regular estimators, on a controversial topic, was compared with that of a panel of nongovernment experts. There were significant differences between the two groups; later events seemed to support the findings relating to outsiders (or the "B-Team," as it was known). Out of this followed rationales to the effect that the B-Team findings were not supported by the facts available, which were answered by the assertion that the A-Team employed faulty methodology in handling the facts. Assuming some basis for both views, the experiment provides an illustration of the uncertainties of some types of analysis; indeed, basic attitudes and instinct are not to be discounted entirely, just as available facts may not reveal the whole truth of a situation.

12. "Ethics and Intelligence," by E. Drexel Godfrey, *Foreign Affairs*, April 1978, page 633. See also a statement quoted in the *Church Committee Report*, Book I, pages 266–267, on the relationship between policy levels and intelligence: "If the policy-intelligence relationship is to work, there must be mutual respect, trust, civility, and also a certain distance. Intelligence people must provide honest and best judgments and avoid intrusion on decisionmaking or attempts to influence it. Policymakers must assume the integrity of the intelligence provided and avoid attempts to get materials suited to their tastes."

13. *Church Committee Report*, Book I, pages 99–100.

14. *Church Committee Report*, Book IV, page 56. See also Book I, pages 260–261.

15. *Church Committee Report*, Book IV, page 55.

16. See *Soviet Military Power*, Government Printing Office, Washington, D.C., 1984, edition, issued annually by the U.S. Department of Defense. See also *American and Soviet Military Trends*, by John M. Collins (a Congressional Research Office employee), Center for International Strategic Studies, Georgetown University, Washington, D.C., 1978, 1981; *The Military Balance 1984–1985*, International Institute for Strategic Studies, London, Autumn 1984; *Strategic Survey 1983–1984*, International Institute for Strategic Studies, London, 1984; and *The Armed Forces of the USSR*, which outlines the history of the Soviet armed forces and describes the development of current tactical and strategic doctrine.

17. *Soviet Military Power*, 1981 edition, pages 39–40.

18. *Church Committee Report*, Book IV, pages 56–57.

19. Ibid., pages 58–59.

20. *Intelligence Requirements for the 1980's: Elements of Intelligence*, edited by Roy Godson, Consortium for the Study of Intelligence, Washington, D.C., 1979, Ch. 3, "Analysis and Estimates," by Daniel O. Graham, page 23.

21. *Intelligence Requirements for the 1980's: Analysis and Estimates*, Ch. 3, "Evaluating Intelligence Estimates," by David S. Sullivan, page 56.

22. *Cold Dawn*, by John Newhouse, Holt, Rinehart & Winston, New York, 1973, page 101.

23. *Arms, Men and Military Budgets*, edited by Francis P. Hoeber and William Schneider, Jr., Crane, Russack & Co., New York, 1977, pages 288–295. See also

Estimated Soviet Defense Spending, National Foreign Assessment Center, Central Intelligence Agency, Washington, D.C., June 1978 (SR 78–10121).

24. *Church Committee Report*, Book I, page 267.

25. *Arms, Men and Military Budgets*, pages 47, 331.

26. See Note 16 in this chapter.

27. *U.S. Intelligence Agencies and Activities: The Performance of the Intelligence Community*, Hearings before the Select Committee on Intelligence, U.S. House of Representatives, Ninety-Fourth Congress, First Session, Part 2, Government Printing Office, Washington, D.C., 11 September–31 October 1975, pages 881–893.

28. Ibid., page 712.

29. Ibid., page 886.

30. Ibid., page 888.

31. *Church Committee Report*, Book I, pages 272–273. The committee was critical of current reporting, categorizing it as "incremental analysis." A more balanced presentation can be found in the *Washington Quarterly*, Summer 1980, in an article by Richard K. Betts, "Intelligence for Policymaking," page 119: "The kind of intelligence that is most frequently likely to be useful, therefore, lies in the middle range: analyses of specific problems that marshal recent information acquired through multiple channels, link it with relevant data from the past, outline the range of possible implications, and estimate probabilities without attempting to state definitive or sweeping conclusions." Betts was describing the level of analysis that exists between the daily reporting of interesting developments bearing on current policy and the more sweeping National Intelligence Estimates. Depending on circumstances, both the current reporters and the estimators have contributed to these intermediate forms of analysis. The Betts article is well worth reading in full.

32. *Church Committee Report*, Book I, page 321.

33. *Strategic Intelligence*, page 98.

34. *Church Committee Report*, Book I, pages 74–77. See also pages 270–271, where the point is made in a broader sense.

35. Ibid., page 75.

36. Letter from the CIA Public Affairs Officer, 6 January 1983.

13

COUNTERINTELLIGENCE

There is one evil I dread, and that is, their spies. I could wish, therefore, the most attentive watch be kept. . . . I wish a dozen or more of honest, sensible and diligent men, were employed . . . in order to question, cross-question, etc., all such persons as are unknown, and cannot give an account of themselves in a straight and satisfactory line. . . . I think it a matter of importance to prevent them from obtaining intelligence of our situation.
—General George Washington, 1776[1]

Counterintelligence—work directed at countering hostile intelligence operations—seems generally accepted as authorized by law. It has not been subjected to the same technical legal arguments experienced by other forms of intelligence activity. It has, however, been the subject of some concern with respect to its possible trespass on civil rights. When it appears that Americans may be involved in foreign intelligence operations against the United States, they become the subject of counterintelligence interest by the government's intelligence and security organizations. The thought of subjecting those people to secret surveillance is offensive to some—an attitude reinforced by government actions during the protest era of the 1960s and 1970s. The entire subject warrants careful review.

Just as there are people with grave reservations about counterintelligence and its impact on our open society, there are also those who feel that the activity should be strengthened to better deal with the external threat. Strongly argued and contradictory cases have resulted, complicating assessments of the issues by the uninitiated. Even in the intelligence agencies the work is not widely known, given that its great sensitivity has placed it behind such a curtain of mystery that definitions have not been clarified and rationales have been left obscure. To write about the subject, therefore, is to risk being challenged from all sides, particularly by those "inside" who sometimes view as an act of ignorant presumption any comment by those not directly involved.

It is useful to note the varied definitions and concepts that have found their way into print, if only to convey the sense of an absence of agreed principles. It might also be noted that the reorganization of CIA's counterintelligence activities in 1973 produced some new views and intense feelings that did not help clarify the issues.

The *Church Committee Report* offers as useful a general description of counterintelligence as has been provided. The introductory statement to its discussion of the subject put the matter as follows:

> Counterintelligence (CI) is a special form of intelligence activity, separate and distinct from other disciplines. Its purpose is to discover hostile foreign intelligence operations and destroy their effectiveness. This objective involves the protection of the United States Government against infiltration by foreign agents, as well as control and manipulation of adversary intelligence operations. An effort is made to both discern and deceive the plans and intentions of enemy intelligence services.[2]

As a footnote to the Church Committee's description, it should be kept in mind that "hostile foreign intelligence operations" are, at the point of their penetration of our government, conducted by U.S. citizens. In the British vernacular, such persons are called "moles," a term that has gained some currency in the United States as well. Foreign intelligence operatives cannot walk in and out of secure areas or have access to classified information stored there. Those secrets can be obtained only through a betrayal of trust by one of our own.

Soviet intelligence gives special attention to recruiting U.S. citizens.[3] In the United States, with its strongly developed attitude on the rights and privileges of citizens, this focus can pose special problems in counterintelligence work. Counterintelligence officers are not as free to pursue an enemy when he is one of our own as they would be if he were a foreigner operating abroad. This point will not be belabored here, but it is a material consideration within the work itself.

The Church Committee's generalized description allows for a variety of activities ranging from relatively passive defense to aggressive operations. It spares the reader the tangle of semantics that has developed over the terminology relating to the subject. The fact is that those who have specialized in counterintelligence, or discussion of it, have been unable in a number of cases to agree on the definitions of what is involved,[4] and sometimes over what it should be.

Some seem to support the narrowest defensive role for counterintelligence, limiting its function to barring foreign espionage against the United States.[5] Others extend the activity to both domestic traitors and to aggressive action against foreign intelligence organizations hostile to our nation. They also feel that U.S. counterintelligence should concern itself with foreign clandestine attempts to manipulate public developments in this country. Some would broaden the range of counterintelligence work to include not only analysis of our own security vulnerabilities and the threat of hostile intelligence services—traditional functions of security and counterintelligence work—but also analysis of security measures to determine "how best to test a new weapons system" and how to "conduct a field maneuver."[6] One writer, noting that one of "the most critical and difficult tasks facing the U.S. intelligence community is the detection of strategic or geopolitical deception," has discussed the sort of aptitudes needed by CI personnel for such work.[7]

The differing perceptions about the scope of counterintelligence become more confusing still when one considers the definitions offered by different writers on the subject. Former DCI Allen Dulles—obviously an authority—viewed the term *counterintelligence* as referring to the results or product of the activity, reserving the term *counterespionage* for the activity itself.[8] Others feel that counterintelligence and counterespionage are distinct activities, with counterintelligence concerned primarily with Americans who are betraying their trust and counterespionage concerned with foreign spies.[9] This last view has obvious flaws, insofar as the traitor and the foreign operative are an integral entity—opposite sides of the same coin. The Church Committee, after first giving the description quoted earlier in this chapter, ventured further, treating counterintelligence as the overall activity, with the subcategories of "security" and "counterespionage" constituting its two main fields.[10] That formulation is not universally accepted. Another writer divides counterintelligence into "passive counterintelligence" and "active counterintelligence,"[11] with the functions listed under the two categories matching those under the sub-categories of the Church description, although they bear different names.

Whatever the purists may say, there is some logic in considering security and counterintelligence together. Conceptually and in practice, there is a necessary working relationship between the administration of an organization's internal security program and the conduct of its counterintelligence operations. Some government agencies that have both functions tend to separate them organizationally while ensuring that they are coordinated; some merge them.

This author considers administrative security and counterintelligence operations to be separate, while accepting in practice some dual interests and sometimes considerable overlap between the two. Counterintelligence is viewed as an operational activity in the clandestine field, directed toward thwarting hostile intelligence operations and against the organizations themselves. Counterintelligence, as a general activity, also includes special staff work in support of these activities.

As terrorism became an important factor in everyday life, counter-terrorist responsibilities were assigned to the FBI and CIA in their respective jurisdictions. Terrorism can be treated as a special subcategory of counterintelligence, and here it is subsumed in the discussion of counterintelligence. Some forms of counterterrorist activity will also be considered in the context of paramilitary programs.

THE NATURE AND SIZE OF THE PROBLEM

One of the difficulties in counterintelligence work is identifying operational targets. Who is attempting to steal classified secrets? And where? It is not just a paranoid notion that "the other side" is engaged in intensive operations against us. It is so. Then what is the nature and size of the problem?

A former Soviet intelligence officer who had defected from the Chief Intelligence Directorate of the Soviet General Staff, the GRU, once stated: "The Soviet Union not only has the world's most powerful secret service. It has the world's *second* most powerful secret service too"[12] (emphasis in original). There is considerable public awareness in the West of the Soviet Union's primary intelligence organization, the KGB (*Komitet Gosudarstvennoy Bezopasnosti*). It may be news to some that the USSR has yet another intelligence service, the GRU (*Glavnoye Razvedyvatelnoye Upravleniye*), which is so formidable that its members claim superiority over all intelligence organizations in the world (with the exception of the KGB). That suggests something of the importance to the Soviets of their intelligence effort, and of the task of defending against it.

The United States is the primary target of Soviet intelligence operations.[13] Abroad these operations focus on the offices and residences of U.S. ambassadors, senior foreign service personnel, CIA officers, and defense attachés. "Great attention" is also given to U.S. personnel with access to encrypted or other secret correspondence, such as code clerks, secretaries, and typists.[14] Inside the United States, recruitment attempts are made against executive branch personnel as well as members of congressional staffs.[15] The mission of counterintelligence is to block those activities. Outside the United States the CIA has primary jurisdiction, with the military services concentrating on Soviet activities directed at their extensive personnel and facilities. Within the United States the FBI has jurisdiction, cooperating with the military services and, on occasion, with CIA—specifically when its foreign operations move here or if it has some special support to provide.

Given the emphasis of Soviet intelligence operations against U.S. citizens and facilities, how extensive is their organization? The KGB has both security responsibilities inside the USSR and foreign intelligence functions. Estimates of the KGB's total strength run from 410,000 members at the national level in the USSR[16] to some 490,000.[17] In addition, each Republic and Autonomous Region in the USSR has its own KGB structure. Some 175,000 to 300,000 KGB personnel are organized into a formal military force known as the Border Guards,[18] with another 65,000 in the elite Kremlin Guard.[19] That leaves some 125,000 to 280,000 at the national level to direct and manage internal security programs and engage in foreign intelligence.

The GRU is limited to intelligence duties. Unlike the KGB, it has no internal security responsibilities. Its headquarters staff is estimated to have some 2,000 officers,[20] not including field personnel. In addition to foreign intelligence, it assigns personnel to the various military commands for typical military staff intelligence duties.[21] The GRU is generally subordinate to the KGB in its foreign intelligence operations.[22]

Perhaps most significant to this discussion is the estimate that 10,000 KGB personnel are engaged in clandestine activity directed against foreign countries.[23] When this figure is matched with the estimate that about one-third of the 10,000 Soviets assigned to official installations abroad (excluding military and economic aid missions) are KGB and GRU officers,[24] it would appear that the proportion of clandestine to official positions is high.

In addition to Soviet intelligence activities, it is known that the East European satellite nations conduct clandestine operations against U.S. personnel and installations under Soviet direction. These nations, and Cuba, are effective extensions of Soviet capabilities. Although the separate East European services are not large by Soviet standards, the total number of intelligence personnel assigned abroad by these services approaches the number that the Soviets have similarly assigned.[25]

The FBI reported that, in 1979, of the 1,079 Soviet officials then on a regular tour of duty in the United States, 40 percent were positively identified as KGB or GRU intelligence personnel. Conservative estimates of the unidentified intelligence officers raised the total to more than 60 percent. Another report states that as of September 1978 there were 1,300 Soviet and 700 East European officials assigned to the United States in diplomatic, media, and trade work. Moreover, Soviet and East European personnel serving abroad in areas other than intelligence work carry out intelligence assignments for the KGB and GRU.[26]

In the fifteen-year period from 1960 to 1975, Soviet representation in the United States trebled. In 1974, for instance, some 4,000 Soviets entered the United States in various capacities; the number was less than 500 in 1972. In the year prior to September 1978 some 60,000 Soviet Bloc visitors came to the United States. Of these, 14,000 were described as commercial, scientific, or cultural people, with some 40,000 being merchant seamen free to enter the 40 ports that had been opened to them. It must be assumed that at least some of them had intelligence assignments. Of the 400 or so Soviet students attending school in the United States under an exchange program in the period 1962–1974, more than 100 were identified as Soviet intelligence agents.[27] Added to all of these is the unknown number of "illegals" who have established residence in this country. An illegal is an operative who gains admission under false credentials and establishes residence under some innocent cover to carry out clandestine work. Some illegals are detected from time to time, but the size of the program is not known. The detection of illegals "presents a most serious problem to the FBI. . . . [T]heir presence is obscured among the thousands of legitimate emigrés entering the United States annually."[28]

The key unknown is the number of Americans who have been recruited to serve the interests of the Soviet Union in clandestine operations against the United States. They are more difficult to identify than the Soviet intelligence officers, who at least are recognized as Soviet personnel to be watched. The starting point for discovering which Americans may be involved in serving Soviet interests is usually an uncertain one. If uncertainty plagues much of the work of intelligence in general, it is even greater in the specialized activity of counterintelligence. The problems involving both uncertainty and numbers are considerable. Counterintelligence approaches convey something of the difficulty encountered.

Although it differs in nature from counterintelligence, counterterrorist intelligence is addressed in this book in the context of counterintelligence because of some similarities. Terrorists constitute a less tangible target since they usually do not have the stable, identifiable base associated with intelligence operators. Some terrorist groups consist of a mere handful of individuals with no governmental sponsorship, who share a common attitude and are willing to commit violence in its name. There is little to guide intelligence officers to them. Even terrorists with government sponsorship do not need recurring official contacts, as the reporting requirement of espionage does not exist. Espionage operations, on the other hand, have a continuing operational focus, with recurring contacts, thus increasing the chance of detection. Terrorist activity can be likened to lightning, which seldom strikes twice in the same spot. It is clear that counterterrorist intelligence operations present special problems.

IDENTIFICATION OF HOSTILE INTELLIGENCE OPERATIONS

The necessary and unavoidable working assumption of counterintelligence is that there are far more hostile intelligence operations under way than have been detected. It is assumed that the Soviets have had more success in recruiting Americans than we know. The first task for counterintelligence personnel is to detect hostile activities, or at least to develop leads that may help make them known. This starts with the identification of those involved.

All intelligence is concerned with people and things, and counterintelligence, in particular, focuses on the individuals engaged in clandestine operations against us. In the beginning, key actors are not known and seldom can be identified by direct methods. This phase of counterintelligence has been likened to searching for a small needle in a large haystack, or groping for an unfamiliar object in a large, dark, and cluttered room. Where to start is a problem in itself.

Counterintelligence work has sometimes been regarded as similar to police work[29] because there are shared investigative techniques. However, counterintelligence officers seldom know with certainty that an offense has taken place. Even if it is assumed that espionage is happening, not known is where, much less by whom. Secrets are stolen by trusted citizens whose records are clear and for whom there is no real reason for distrust.

Hostile espionage does not advertise itself. There are no forced doors or windows, no battered bodies or missing possessions. A secret can be copied with a camera or pencil, or can be carried off in someone's head. Law enforcement officers at least know when someone has been burgled or murdered and can thus commence the investigative techniques familiar to readers of mystery novels. But counterintelligence officers seldom have this tangible beginning.

Not only do counterintelligence people usually have a different starting point for their work, their basic objective differs somewhat from that of law enforcement officers. The first purpose of counterintelligence is to block hostile penetrations of our government's secrets. Prosecutions may result, but frequently there is insufficient evidence for prosecution. The objective often is simply to bar further acts rather than to gather evidence for use in court. Again, the analogy between law enforcement and counterintelligence seems strained. Despite this bleak picture, there are ways of identifying persons involved in espionage against us.

An obvious focal point for identifying hostile espionage operatives is the Soviet intelligence officers. That there has been considerable success over the years in making these identifications is evident in the statistics cited earlier in this chapter. When Soviet, East European, and

Cuban intelligence operatives are identified, surveillance of them can lead to the identification of colleagues in their own bureaucracy, as well as to that of agents and collaborators.

The security and intelligence services of allied governments have the same interests in Soviet espionage that we have. There is considerable exchange of information on the subject, which adds to the basic operational data used in shaping our own counterintelligence activities. Sometimes allies are able to report on Americans in touch with known hostile intelligence organizations and terrorists. And, indeed, they do.

Soviet defectors have been helpful in pinpointing successful penetrations of the U.S. or allied governments. Even when such sources exist, they can name specific individuals only occasionally; for investigative purposes, however, they can describe places of penetration. With such leads, our own security and counterintelligence officers have been successful in discovering the individuals involved.[30]

In the absence of the kind of outside help just described, a starting point may be no more than identifying the location at which classified information has been compromised. This identification provides at least an initial point for internal inquiry, and may lead to the source of the compromise. However, even if the source is discovered, it is possible that no espionage has occurred. In our society, "leaks" of classified information may be purely personal acts, however much they may help the Soviets. Still, all such incidents must be investigated to determine whether the problem is a matter for administrative discipline or a foreign intelligence operation.

There are other ways in which penetration of the U.S. security system may be discovered. An individual may report suspected espionage. Such allegations cannot be ignored, but the counterintelligence officer must keep in mind the possibility that however well intended, the informant may not be well informed. And sometimes allegations may be made maliciously. Of course, the conduct of a person engaged in espionage may attract attention, this raising questions about what he or she is doing. Whatever the origin of suspicion, counterintelligence officers must decide how to handle the problem. There may be no tangible facts on which to proceed. The operational problem becomes that of finding a balance between what is necessary and what is appropriate, without trespassing on a person's privacy and legitimate rights. The Church Committee, commenting on that issue, summarized the remarks of a CIA officer as follows:

The task is difficult, technically, and raises sensitive legal and ethical questions. As the CIA Deputy Director for Operations testified, the "U.S. counterintelligence program to be both effective and in line with traditional

American freedoms must steer a middle course between blanket, illegal, frivolous and unsubstantiated inquiries into the private lives of U.S. citizens and excessive restrictions which will render the Government's counterintelligence arms impotent to protect the nation from foreign penetration and covert manipulation."[31]

Indeed, realistic standards must be established for what should be done to protect the basic rights of citizens and of noncitizens entitled to the same legal privileges. Concern for such procedures was heightened by the zealotry of certain intelligence organizations during the public disorders of the 1960s and early 1970s, when questions arose within the government as to whether there were ties between foreign sources and those engaged in the protests.

In counterterrorist work even special security precautions cannot provide a sure defense. Such precautions are relatively static, and they can be assessed by the terrorists for planning to circumvent them. As pointed out earlier, counterterrorist intelligence operations face more problems in identifying the terrorists for countering actions. Sometimes disaffected members of terrorist groups become sources of information on both individuals and planned operations. In addition, counterintelligence officers can identify persons with dubious attitudes and affiliations, and place them under surveillance. The eventual decimation of the European Baader-Meinhoff gang was the result of intensive work by European security and intelligence officers, who were assisted by increasing knowledge of the gang's movements and plans as its activities continued over a long period. There have been successes, and there will be failures, in working against such groups.[32]

SURVEILLANCE

Those seeking to regulate the conduct of counterintelligence operators have focused on the surveillance of Americans in its various forms. Both physical and electronic surveillance activities were involved. In 1978 the Congress enacted the Foreign Intelligence Surveillance Act,[33] after accepting the need for electronic surveillance in certain circumstances but establishing procedures and reviews for approving it. Similar legislation was not enacted for physical surveillance.

The 1978 Act provided that, with presidential authorization, the Attorney General may either petition the courts for electronic surveillance warrants or issue such approvals himself. Both actions would be reported to the Congress—the court-issued warrants on an annual basis and those issued by the Attorney General on essentially a concurrent basis.[34] The 1978 Act avoided trying to anticipate all the circumstances under which electronic surveillance should be authorized, apparently recognizing a place for human judgment in this complex area.

The Foreign Intelligence Surveillance Act did not specify which government agencies would conduct electronic surveillance operations. Practically speaking, its primary impact was on activities inside the United States. The FBI, the three military agencies, and NSA were the ones affected primarily. CIA, which had not conducted clandestine "audio operations," as they are known, in the United States since 1968, remained essentially unaffected by this aspect of the law. Both the Carter Executive Order of 1978 and the Reagan Executive Order of 1981 provided that CIA not engage in such operations inside the United States.[35] Of course, if the occasion should arise for CIA to seek counterintelligence surveillance of "United States persons" abroad, the procedures would apply.

The Carter Executive Order went further than the 1978 Foreign Intelligence Surveillance Act in applying additional requirements to the conduct of physical surveillance. This involves observing the activities of an individual by following and watching, much as in television cops-and-robbers shows. The Carter directive stated that the FBI could conduct physical surveillance of United States persons "only in the course of a lawful investigation." Other intelligence agencies were forbidden "any physical surveillance . . . against a United States person" except in specific circumstances. The exceptions made it clear that the purpose was to restrict physical surveillance, except in bona fide intelligence cases. The language in one of the exceptions presented a problem in semantics, providing that physical surveillance could be conducted "outside the United States and the person being surveilled [sic] *is reasonably believed* to be acting on behalf of a foreign power, engaging in international terrorist activities, or engaging in narcotics production or trafficking"[36] (emphasis added). The requirement of reasonable belief is somewhat vague and leaves room for subjective judgments. If read narrowly it could pose insuperable obstacles to most surveillance operations.

Investigation in counterintelligence cases is required partly to ascertain if a basis for further action exists at all. There may be only a question, perhaps raised to the level of tentative suspicion. The basis for real or reasonable belief must often await the results of an inquiry of some sort. Such an inquiry, in most cases, would involve some form of surveillance. In this way, a person's associations and activities are determined. It should be clear that the language of the Carter Executive Order presented practical problems.

The Reagan Executive Order replaced the Carter directive. It maintained the jurisdictional provisions of the latter—with the FBI inside the United States, CIA abroad, and the military services coordinating with one or the other of those two organizations when operating in their area of primary jurisdiction. The Reagan provision on physical surveillance of Americans abroad was stated as follows: "Physical surveillance of a United States person abroad to collect foreign intelligence [shall not be authorized] except to obtain significant information that cannot reasonably be acquired by other means."[37]

In essence, the Congress has set the procedures for electronic intelligence operations by requiring review—on the merits of each case— outside the Intelligence Community. The Executive branch has provided separately for physical surveillance in intelligence cases, seeking realistic standards without making such surveillance impossible. It can be assumed that further attempts will be made to find practical formulations that provide for balance between national need and individual rights. For the present, these provisions seem to afford a workable approach to the matter.

FILES AND COUNTERINTELLIGENCE

That the U.S. intelligence organizations have accumulated voluminous files on Soviet intelligence organizations and activities is to be expected. These files provide one means for developing leads to hostile intelligence activities. Another source of information are the files resulting from security investigations of applicants for government employment, or of those seeking employment with private firms that have classified government contracts. These investigations, in addition to periodic reinvestigations, produce extensive information on people—and some of this information has counterintelligence significance. The government's organization for such work is extensive.

The Department of Defense has a number of investigative agencies charged primarily with conducting security inquiries. The Defense Investigative Service (DIS) focuses almost exclusively on security investigations inside the United States for clearance of military and civilian personnel in the department, as well as employees of Defense contractors. DIS has a computerized index that records previous security clearances and references to all past investigations in the Department. It does not maintain all the files, but it does record which counterintelligence and investigative agency holds them. In 1975 this index had references to files on 15 million Americans. DIS relies on the military services for investigations outside the United States.[38]

The organization of the three military services for security and counterintelligence functions varies. For years the U.S. Army Intelligence Agency (USAINTA) handled security investigations and counterintelligence work for the Army in the United States. Overseas, where military units directly under the Assistant Chief of Staff for Intelligence (ACS/I) were stationed (e.g., Germany and Korea), those organizations carried out the investigative work. Where ACS/I units were not stationed, USAINTA handled the work. In 1977 USAINTA was merged with the Army Security Agency (and other organizations), forming the U.S. Army Intelligence and Security Command (INSCOM), which reports to ACS/I. In the Navy all domestic and foreign investigations and counterintelligence activities are carried out by the Naval Investigative Service (NIS), which reports to the Director of Naval Intelligence (DNI). All Air Force investigations are conducted by the Air Force Office of Special Investigations (AFOSI), which reports to the Inspector General.[39] Overseas, in the absence of the FBI, the military services have conducted investigations of those civilian groups composed primarily of Americans living abroad and considered "threats" to security.[40]

CIA's Office of Security conducts investigations similar to those done in the Department of Defense by checking the background of applicants for employment and those involved with private commercial firms engaged in classified work with the Agency. Some 900,000 files had resulted from this, as of the time of the intelligence investigations in the mid-1970s. Ninety percent of these investigations were made on American citizens. About one third of the files had been retired to inactive status in archives.[41] It was estimated that between 500 and 800 files were on "dissident organizations" and 12,000 to 16,000 names were indexed to those particular files.[42] "Indexing" of names means only that they are included in card files or computer indexes to show where the name is recorded should some future interest develop concerning the individual named. As will later be discussed, this reference capability is important to security and counterintelligence analysis.

CIA's Operations Directorate—the organization with primary counterintelligence responsibility in that agency—had some 750,000 files on individuals at the time of the Rockefeller report in 1975, some 57,000 of whom were American citizens (possibly another 15,000 were also Americans but were not identified as such). The practice, for reasons that will be noted later, was to index all names appearing in all reports from the field, resulting in some 7,500,000 entries. An estimated 115,000 of these were Americans.[43]

In 1967 CIA began a special foreign counterintelligence program known as Operation CHAOS, which continued until 1972. This operation started at the direction of the White House, which was struck by parallels between the positions of antiwar groups and the propaganda line of the Soviet Union. CIA's task was to identify overseas any foreign influence that may have existed. That mission was well within its counterintelligence charter.[44] In the five years over which the program ran, it failed to produce evidence of Soviet influence. Over that period CIA developed some 13,000 files, including 7,200 on Americans. The documents in those files contained the names of more than 300,000 persons and organizations, which were entered into a computerized index.[45] The files consisted primarily of materials provided by the FBI, which were used initially for possible reference but were added to as the program developed. The CHAOS file and records system existed in addition to the usual CIA filing systems mentioned earlier.

In 1972 CIA's Inspector General criticized CHAOS for its relatively indiscriminate standards.[46] That led to a review that reduced the files by about two-thirds. Those remaining were incorporated into the regular counterintelligence records system. CHAOS, as a separate program, was terminated.

The FBI, during the twenty-year period from 1955 to 1975, conducted 740,000 investigations of "subversive matters" and 190,000 investigations of "extremist matters" in the United States. These activities produced some 480,000 files on "subversion" investigations and over 33,000 on "extremism."[47] In 1975 the Bureau, serving as a "clearing house" on domestic intelligence, had about 6,500,000 files at headquarters and a general index consisting of more than 58,000,000 index cards.[48]

The Internal Revenue Service (IRS) conducted limited collection of material on certain categories of individuals, based on a list of 10,000 names derived from a Department of Justice index service.[49] The National Security Agency (NSA) also collected information on individuals requested by other agencies in the Intelligence Community, disseminating some 2,000 items of information between 1967 and 1973.[50] The function of these two agencies supported the counterintelligence activities of other organizations. The procedures under which this support was given have been tightened.

This summary provides a sense of the extent of the U.S. security effort, especially as reflected in the numbers of files that it produces on Americans. The fact that the government has files on Americans has troubled some observers, even though these files were developed primarily as the result of routine security checks. The reported numbers have reinforced the negative reservations of some. Yet the files serve a real purpose, both in verifying the reliability of persons involved in classified work and, occasionally, in helping identify hostile intelligence operations. The actual use of the files has not received the attention it warrants, and an understanding of the basic nature of this function is not widespread.

The vast majority of the security files simply contain normal data on normal people that validates their suitability for access to classified information. However, individuals with highly dubious interests and connections sometimes apply for classified work. Usually the security investigation discloses "derogatory information," and a clearance is not granted.

The extent of information gathered in a security investigation varies with the individual. As noted earlier, the procedure involved usually follows a normal pattern, but when questions arise about an individual they must be resolved by careful inquiry. Someone whose personal record is clear may have close associations with others who cannot be trusted with classified materials, or there may be foreign connections that raise questions. The range of possibilities is infinite. Often the questions are resolved and the individual is accepted. Of course, some may occasionally slip through the screening process, but even in such cases their basic files contain information that may later be of use.

Following completion of the investigation, security files are retained for extended periods of time. If the person under investigation is employed, the file becomes part of his or her normal record. If the applicant is not employed, investigation records are retained for possible future reference. The individual may reapply for employment or seek employment in some other work involving classified materials. It is regular procedure for government organizations, in processing applications for employment, to check with other government agencies for information in their files. This "national agency check" had its origins in executive orders issued by Presidents Truman and Eisenhower.[51] In instances of counterintelligence interest, the same cross-checking procedures can be followed.

Most agencies conduct periodic reinvestigations of employees who work with classified information to ensure that the original clearance remains valid. The applicants—and employees subject to reinvestigation—are required to fill out forms that provide a variety of personal biographical information, such as dates, places of residence over a period of years, education, organizational affiliations, character references, and the names of immediate family members. This information is not considered an invasion of privacy; the individuals agree to it as a condition of employment.

There are other ways of developing information on persons of counterintelligence interest that may lead to opening files on them. One of the more interesting of these is a regular procedure employed in clandestine intelligence operations. When an operations officer meets his or her agent, it is routine procedure to "debrief" the agent as a matter of both management procedure and operational security. Experience has shown that agents sometimes have operational opportunities, or access to desired information, that they don't recognize. They may also come into contact with individuals who are hostile to their mission.

Through the information that case officers obtain from agents, they can ensure the best possible use of the agent (i.e., no missed opportunities) and help him or her avoid identifiable risks. To do this the case officer writes both "contact reports" (operational intelligence) and informational reports. Contact reports record where the agent went, how he or she traveled, the names of persons encountered, and so on. They sometimes reveal significant details that neither the agent nor the case officer had recognized.

All names mentioned in the contact reports are excerpted for indexing. If, over a period of time, the agent—or other agents, for that matter— have a number of encounters with the same individual, that coincidence signals the need for closer review. Possibly the individual in question may be engaged in counterintelligence activity against our own clandestine operations. If so, precautions must be taken. First, all filed references to that person are assembled into a new file, which becomes the basis for counterintelligence analysis. However tenuous this approach may seem, the fact is that operations—and possibly lives—have been saved by it.

The process just described refers primarily to foreign operations. It also applies to American citizens who may attract attention in some way. In certain instances, the process has provided valid leads to the identification of individuals working for the Soviets.

The files may also contain a great deal of meaningless and irrelevant information that has come from security inquiries and other sources. For instance, much of the material gathered in the course of security investigations is flawed, sometimes untrue, and occasionally malicious. Yet, even the most prejudiced informant may provide some information that is valid and significant. All information is recorded and, to the extent possible, cross-checked. The uneven quality of the material explains why the FBI refers to it as "unevaluated information." This is not to say that it is useless. Some of the less impressive information may, perhaps to the surprise or relief of the file custodians, prove valuable.

It is easier to agree in principle that much of the miscellaneous data in the files ought to be eliminated than it is to pick and choose what is to go. There will always be an element of subjective judgment involved. Those responsible for carrying out the counterintelligence mission feel that less damage is done by retaining marginal material than by excluding it. For instance, it was easier for CIA's Inspector General to criticize the establishment of files on individuals in the CHAOS program, thus making formal CI cases on the basis of uncritical acceptance of requirements from another agency, than it would have been to select for discard the materials in those files that were retained when the operation ended. As most of the information came from the FBI—where copies remained—

large scale destruction of files was less difficult than it otherwise would have been.

As the Church Committee, commenting on the materials in the FBI's files, noted:

> The Committee has found that there are massive amounts of irrelevant and trivial information in those files. The FBI has kept such data in its filing system on the theory that they might be useful someday in the future to solve crimes, for employee background checks, to evaluate the reliability of the source, or to "answer questions or challenges" about the Bureau's conduct.[52]

The Rockefeller Commission reached similar conclusions about the CIA files:

> Although maintenance of most of the indices, files, and records of the Agency has been necessary and proper, the standards applied by the Agency at some points during its history have permitted the accumulation and the indexing of materials not needed for legitimate intelligence or security purposes.[53]

These criticisms are generally valid in principle. There is some feeling, however, that such unqualified statements reflected legal tests of what would be usefully admissible as evidence in a court of law. Investigators on the staffs of the Senate Committee and Presidential Commission, many of them attorneys, may have forgotten the myriad useful details they collected in developing a case for trial—details that helped their understanding of the case even though they were not admissible as evidence. In any event, counterintelligence and security do not have court proceedings as their first purpose. They look for indications of problems as a basis for further action that may be appropriate. They often get the first indication of a problem from odds and ends of information that became fully meaningful only after additional inquiry.

The Church Committee recognized in principle something of the problem, saying that "espionage investigations must be initiated on the basis of fragments of information, especially where there may be only an indication of a suspicious contact with a foreign agent and limited data as to the specific purposes of the contact."[54] The leads too often are slim, indeed, but seemingly meaningless fragments frequently fit other bits of information to provide the first indication of a problem. They often yield enough information to raise questions in the minds of persons tuned to the intricate characteristics of counterintelligence, questions that can be answered only by more thorough investigation.

The stakes are high. Hostile espionage is carefully obscured from us, and only intense vigilance, utilizing available and permissible means, will provide defenses against hostile clandestine operations. The files are a critical feature in this work.

SPECIAL COLLECTION PROGRAMS

Aside from the files, where else can counterintelligence officers turn for leads to possible hostile clandestine operations against the United States? Who is in touch with Soviet officials, and what does this information mean? Two means of communication, other than by personal contacts that can be observed by surveillance, are the mails and international telecommunications. In tapping those areas one must know what is permissible. What is acceptable during a war declared by Congress, for instance, is subject to certain limitations in other circumstances.

Shortly before World War II, FBI personnel were trained in opening the mail of Axis diplomatic installations in Washington, D.C.[55] This technique was suspended by U.S. intelligence agencies following the war, until mid-1952 during the Korean War. As stated in the Rockefeller Commission report: "At the height of the so-called cold war, the CIA initiated the first of a series of programs to examine the mails between the United States and Communist countries for purposes of gathering intelligence."[56] The main operation was conducted in New York until 1973. Sampling operations of two- or three-weeks duration were conducted in San Francisco during 1969, 1970 and 1971; in New Orleans in 1957; and for about a year in Hawaii during 1954–1955. All these operations were concerned with international mail between communist countries and the United States. The New York operation handled some 4,350,000 pieces of mail during its lifetime, examining the outside only of more than half the total, photographing the covers of approximately 33,000 items, and analyzing the contents of some 8,700 letters. The FBI found the project valuable for purposes of internal security. CIA acquired addresses for mailing programs into the Soviet Union and as a source for intelligence on Soviet censorship techniques, secret writing, and counterintelligence leads.[57]

The Rockefeller Commission concluded that the New York project was in violation of statutes, and that CIA support of the FBI's internal security function violated the National Security Act of 1947.[58] The Church Committee agreed.[59] The Department of Justice took the matter for investigation and possible prosecution. In January 1977 the same department released to the press a lengthy document that stated, in part:

> Although the Department is of the firm view that activities similar in scope and authorization to those conducted by the CIA between 1953 and 1973 would be unlawful if undertaken today, the Department has concluded that a prosecution of the potential defendants for these activities would be unlikely to succeed because of the unavailability of important evidence and *because of the state of the law that prevailed during the course of the mail openings program.* (Emphasis added.)[60]

The Justice Department's investigation produced evidence that a number of presidents, in addition to several postmasters general, had approved or were at least aware of the program, thus raising the question of adequate approval in this unique period.

Whatever the legality of the program when it was initiated by CIA, it seems agreed that such a broad program—however selective the targets—would be illegal today unless approved by the President in the event of armed conflict, under the War Powers Act. Single mail openings can be authorized by search warrant under a law passed in 1970, but a general counterintelligence program such as that conducted in New York for some twenty years would not be allowed under existing conditions.

Technical means for listening in on communications are discussed in the *Church Committee Report*,[61] although its examples primarily concerned single operations. The National Security Agency (NSA) began to intercept overseas communications of selected Americans in the early 1960s, at the request of Army intelligence.[62] A "watch list" of persons in whom the intelligence agencies were interested was compiled. Computers were programmed to select out communications involving those names.[63] Such blanket activity is now barred by the Foreign Intelligence Surveillance Act of 1978; each separate case requires issuance of a warrant.

DOMESTIC OPERATIONS

Some observers have been concerned that overzealous counterintelligence activities may have invaded the privacy and possibly the civil rights of individuals. Accordingly activities of the intelligence services during the period of protest over Vietnam in the 1960s and 1970s, when the issue assumed important dimensions, will be reviewed briefly here.

CIA's CHAOS program was a foreign intelligence operation requested by the President, but it has been criticized as intruding illegally in domestic operations. While it was concerned with foreign influences on internal political activities, its basic direction was overseas. American agents were used, but were instructed not to engage in domestic operations. One problem arose from steps taken to procure "credentials" for these agents when they traveled overseas. They joined activist and dissident groups as regular members so that when they went abroad they had a record of sympathetic and participating membership, making them acceptable there. The case officer for three of these agents, as a training exercise, had them draft reports as though they were on a live assignment. He liked the reports and put them into the normal reporting channel, contrary to instructions. A fourth agent was used almost exclusively in reporting on domestic organizations. These instances were contrary to CIA's charter under the 1947 Act.[64]

CIA's largest domestic activity in relation to protest activities occurred in 1967 and 1968 during the demonstrations in Washington, D.C. CIA's Office of Security employed about a dozen private citizens living in the area who joined some of the activist organizations to learn their plans for demonstrations, specifically against CIA facilities in the Washington area. One of the informants reported evidence of foreign funding for one of the groups, which was reported to the FBI; the agent was then transferred to the Bureau for handling.[65] Although the rationale for this activity was understandable, it was contrary to the limitations of the 1947 Act and was phased out as the Washington police developed a similar capability in 1968.

CIA's Office of Security had other operational tasks that should be noted here[66] to convey a sense of the activity normal to security operations, and how the capabilities for one type of work may be applied to other situations in unusual circumstances. In the twenty-eight-year period of CIA's existence prior to the Rockefeller Commission's inquiry, the CIA Office of Security had conducted some 163 surveillances of individuals inside the United States, other than routine investigations and reinvestigations of applicants and employees. Ninety of these arose from 76 investigations of employees and former employees, as a result of security questions raised about them. Eleven of those placed under surveillance in these investigations were not employees but contacts of those in question, and the surveillance was intended to identify them and determine their interests. Forty-nine foreign nationals were also watched by the Office of Security inside the United States during that period. Thirty-eight of these were CIA operatives, and eleven were defectors. It should be noted that CIA had been assigned responsibility for defectors by the National Security Council, as a service of common concern. Of the cases not arising from a direct CIA responsibility (as with the defectors) or from an employment relationship, seven were persons

reported to be plotting to kidnap the Vice-President and assassinate the
DCI, six were newsmen who were followed to try and identify the
sources of classified information reported in their columns and news
stories, and eleven were other foreign nationals who were placed under
surveillance to investigate questionable activities. The great majority of
these cases were well within CIA authority. A few were not, thus
violating the restrictions on internal security. Without reference to the
question of legality, these activities were carried out with the agreement
of the FBI.

During that time the Office of Security conducted thirty-two telephone
"wiretaps" in the United States, the last of which occurred in 1965 and
was approved, incidentally, by Attorney General Robert Kennedy. The
Office of Security also conducted thirty-two audio, or "bugging," operations in the United States, the last of which occurred in 1968 when
the rules were changed. CIA is now barred from electronic surveillance
in the United States. Executive Order 12333, Section 2.4 (c) (1), provides
that all agencies may conduct physical surveillance of present or former
employees.

Over the years, the FBI has agreed that CIA and other members of
the Intelligence Community would be responsible for the security of
their own employees. In fact, the National Security Council had assigned
primary responsibility to them for protecting intelligence sources and
methods within their respective organizations. The Bureau was reluctant
to conduct certain types of investigations, especially security leaks to
the media.[67] The DCI, with statutory responsibility for protecting intelligence sources and methods, but with limitations on internal security
functions, was presented with something of a dilemma by the Bureau's
policy. This situation led to the surveillance of the news reporters noted
earlier.

The FBI, during the period in which CIA conducted its overseas
CHAOS program, initiated a counterintelligence program within the
United States under the acronym of COINTELPRO. The Bureau levied
requirements on CIA concerning individuals traveling abroad; these
requirements constituted the basis for the CIA effort under CHAOS.
FBI targets were political action groups, especially radical dissident
organizations, in a search for evidence of possible foreign influence or
domestic communist involvement. Such a general program fell within
the FBI's mission. The Bureau, however, did not confine its program to
that objective, but also conducted itself as an *agent provocateur*, stimulating
controversy within some of the groups to discredit individual members
(some well known) and generally seeking to cause troubles within the
ranks of the organizations. Although a conservative defensive counterintelligence program was proper, application of such techniques to bona

fide American groups was inappropriate. The program was discussed in some detail in the *Church Committee Report*, including a variety of operational techniques.[68]

The U.S. military services also conduct counterintelligence programs within the United States. There is an obvious interest in hostile intelligence and sabotage operations against military installations and personnel, an interest that intensified as the perceived need for security precautions rose. This concern has existed from earliest times, as indicated in George Washington's statement at the head of this chapter and in the actions of the Continental Congress noted in Chapter 7.

During the 1960s, when organized protest and civil disturbances became a matter of concern to senior government officials, pressures were brought on the Army to increase its work against protest groups. Even Attorney General Ramsey Clark, whose liberal image is well established, stated that "every resource" should be used in the domestic intelligence effort. He criticized the Army for not being more selective in the reports it was sending to the Department of Justice.[69] The Army, subject to several such proddings, responded by increasing its attention to protest groups and their members and establishing files associated with that work. Although it did not go to the same lengths as those of the FBI's COINTELPRO, it did engage in harassment of some of the groups.[70] It also conducted surveillance programs, using both physical and technical methods. These activities did not occur without some reservations at senior army levels. When the activity was revealed in 1970, it was terminated.[71] The military services continue to have counterintelligence programs within the United States, but they are more focused on possible hostile operations against their installations and personnel, in coordination with the FBI.

RECRUITMENT OF THE OPPOSITION

Efforts are made to recruit agents for general intelligence purposes among the officials of Soviet Bloc countries, particularly KGB or GRU officers. This is one of the more difficult tasks faced by CIA. Ideally, such agents will stay "in place," as normal officials of the Soviet government, while remaining responsive to operational direction from a U.S. case officer. When Soviet officers are sufficiently dissatisfied with their lot in life to deal with U.S. intelligence personnel, they are more susceptible to defecting than to taking the risk of working "in place." Defectors are valuable to counterintelligence work by virtue of the details they can give on organization, personalities, and programs, but an agent in one of those organizations, working in place, is the acme of counterintelligence achievement. A mere description the concept is sufficient to raise the issue of the sensitivity of such operations.

Identifying a person recruited by a hostile intelligence service to work against us, and turning that agent to our purpose, is known as "doubling" an agent—hence the term *double agent*. Such agents continue to appear responsive to the directions of the hostile intelligence service while reporting to U.S. case officers and carrying out their instructions. The direction of penetrations and double agents is a difficult and uncertain task. For instance, a recruited Soviet official may return home and not be seen for months or years. Communications and contact can be uncertain, and we cannot be sure that the recruitment will "stick."

The penetration of a hostile service and the doubling of agents open a number of doors for operational options, in addition to acquiring information about the organization, its personalities, and its activities. These operations afford the opportunity of planting misleading information that will distort what the other side knows, or thinks it knows. Such deception is most sophisticated, requiring that an agent's credibility be maintained by giving him or her real intelligence, judged to not be harmful, in order that the deceptive reporting be considered reliable. The summary review of the Church Committee on this subject provides useful reading for those who want more detail.[72]

MANAGEMENT OF COUNTERINTELLIGENCE

A number of distinctive qualities are unique to counterintelligence, but two features stand out and require special attention when organizational arrangements are being made.

The feature most frequently recognized—one that gives counterintelligence a character of its own—is the requirement for security. In penetrations or double-agent operations, protecting the operation and those involved is critical. Adherence to the statutory obligation to "protect intelligence sources and methods" is as great here as in any other activity, and greater than in most. Counterintelligence operations are therefore given special security protection. Normally they are handled on a strict system of access compartmented from other activities, with special lists of individuals who have been cleared for the subject matter.

A less generally recognized feature of counterintelligence is the attitude and intellectual approach of CI operators. Some speak humorously of the tendency toward indirect approaches on the part of the counterintelligence officer, who is trained to deal with problems that really defy direct approaches. One former counterintelligence officer refers to "the tortuous logic of counterintelligence."[73] The fact is that counterintelligence concerns itself with the obscured or hidden target, where professionally sharpened instinct is sometimes essential. In seeking out an unknown adversary, counterintelligence delves into the subconscious of individuals to divine their motives and conduct. The role is often that of devil's advocate in questions involving people and in designing approaches to find the answers. Some characterize the challenging, questioning approach of counterintelligence personnel as paranoid. Nevertheless, the task requires approaches and attitudes, only cursorily described here, that are qualities to be developed and nurtured for the insights they produce to intricate problems.

Organizational arrangements must provide for these distinctive characteristics. Doing so sometimes creates conflicts with the requirements of other intelligence organizations. The elusive element of balance is the responsibility of management. That issue was highlighted in CIA by the reorganization of counterintelligence in 1974. CIA's Counterintelligence Staff (CI Staff) had long held both operational functions and the usual staff-like role of a support element. DCI Colby removed the operational functions from CI Staff, assigning personnel involved in those activities to the operational area divisions referred to in Chapter 3. CI Staff became a sort of specialized organization that staffs usually are considered to be.[74] There was considerable controversy over the degree to which the Staff should retain certain special operations, for which some felt it to be uniquely qualified.

Some believed that the Agency's CI Staff had complicated CIA operations in the field, bypassing the field stations and dealing directly with its own agents as well as with allied services, for which liaison relations were usually the responsibility of the local station. That tended to degrade the importance of the station in its relations with its liaison services, and threatened the station with the introduction of operations that might conflict with or disrupt other sensitive activities.[75]

In earlier times, CIA had tried to conduct two types of operations overseas separately. When the government originally became involved in Covert Action, CIA first was given a semi-independent Office of Policy Coordination (OPC). Started as a planning activity, this office soon ran its own overseas activities. There was competition for clandestine agents between OPC and CIA's Office of Special Operations (OSO).[76] DCI Bedell Smith brought the two together in a new directorate (known at the time as the Directorate of Plans, later titled the Directorate of Operations), which was actually the CIA's Clandestine Service. This action resulted in a single CIA authority in each country in which there was representation. OPC evolved into the Covert Action Staff (CA Staff) serving in the traditional staff role, but with some operations of its own. However, it was required to coordinate closely with the operating divisions of the Clandestine Service, and it functioned in the field under the authority of the chief of station.[77]

Elimination of recurring coordination difficulties was one of the reasons for reorganizing CI Staff. Colby, whose career had been with the Clandestine Service, apparently shared critical views concerning the impact on orderly management of CI Staff's relatively independent activity in the field. He seems to have held a fairly firm view about having clear lines of command authority. As DCI he took actions on at least three occasions that in retrospect seem to have had this view in common.[78]

The reduced CI Staff retained responsibility for maintaining files and for their analysis, as had initially been directed in NSCID No. 5.[79] However, there was concern among counterintelligence officers that transfer of its officers to the operating divisions had reduced the Staff's analytical capabilities, including as it did the special cadre of trained counterintelligence analysts. Further, some believed that this transfer would result in reducing the time those officers would have to devote to counterintelligence matters in favor of Foreign Intelligence (FI) matters—that is, espionage—which were more likely to be recognized and rewarded in that new environment.

Close on the heels of the changes in CI Staff, and perhaps as a result of them, came a general counter thesis contending that all counterintelligence should be centralized in one agency. That idea has attracted little, if any, support, with the possible exception of the Reagan transition team of 1981, which seemed to endorse the principle. However, according to one commentator:

An independent counterintelligence agency would soon become another monstrous expensive bureaucracy interfering, delaying, disrupting and attempting to usurp the essential functions of each agency. The supra-agency could not effectively and efficiently assume the functions and responsibilities vital to the internal requirements of the counterintelligence or intelligence services.[80]

Consolidation into one separate agency would also bring together into one place all of the most sensitive operational secrets, such that one hostile penetration would permit more extensive damage than would occur with the information dispersed among the operating agencies. Pressures in favor of community-sharing of access to the computer files would arise, thus raising the specter of the vulnerability of computers to manipulation. Such considerations would cause every intelligence organization to create some independent CI function of its own, to protect its operations. The pressures for such duplication would be intense.

The Church Committee recommended that oversight of counterintelligence be institutionalized within the Executive branch of government, in the NSC structure. The Carter administration's Executive Order 12036, Section 1-3, formed a Special Coordination Committee (SCC) with this purpose, among others, in mind. The Reagan administration's arrangement of the NSC has not been so specific, but the Senior Interagency Group (Intelligence) and with the subordinate Interagency Group on intelligence are the probable locations for such matters within the NSC structure.

Essentially, management of counterintelligence should be reserved for the separate agencies, subject to policy direction by the NSC. Primary jurisdiction within the United States should remain with the FBI, with CIA retaining jurisdiction abroad. Each agency is responsible for adequate staffing to conduct its special analytical and staff support functions, and to handle its operational tasks in the field. Counterintelligence is a function vital to national security, which in turn is vital to our society.

NOTES

1. *Intelligence in the War of Independence,* a Bicentennial Publication of the Central Intelligence Agency, Washington, D.C., 1976, page 21.

2. *Church Committee Report,* Book I, page 163. Another definition and description of what is involved, and had long been classified, is recorded in the *Church Committee Report,* Book III, pages 684–685. It is a portion of a directive of the National Security Council (NSCID No. 5), which read as follows: "Counterintelligence is defined as that intelligence activity, with its resultant product, devoted to destroying the effectiveness of inimical intelligence activities and undertaken to protect the security of the nation and its personnel, information and installations against espionage, sabotage and subversion. Counterintelligence includes the process of procuring, developing, recording, and disseminating information concerning hostile clandestine activity and of penetrating, manipulating or repressing individuals, groups or organizations conducting such activity." That directive, in addition to giving CIA primary responsibility for conduct of counterintelligence operations abroad, directed all agencies to provide CIA with counterintelligence information appropriate for a central file.

3. *KGB: The Secret Work of Soviet Agents,* by John Barron, Reader's Digest Press, Pleasantville, N.Y., 1974 (cited hereafter as *KGB*). See Appendix C, pages 346–378, entitled "The Practice of Recruiting Americans in the USA and Third Countries," based on a KGB textbook by that name. Barron is the lay authority on the KGB; the introduction to his book credits FBI, CIA, and DIA personnel with assisting in its preparation. See also *Intelligence Requirements for the 1980's: Counterintelligence,* edited by Roy Godson, Consortium for the Study of Intel-

ligence, Washington, D.C., 1980, Ch. 6, "Soviet Intelligence in the United States," pages 161–199, by Herbert Romerstein. Also useful is the chapter in *Facing Reality*, by Cord Meyer, Harper & Row, New York, 1980, pages 312–330, entitled "The Soviet Apparat: KGB."

4. *Intelligence Requirements for the 1980's: Counterintelligence*, page 1.

5. *The Intelligence Establishment*, by Harry Howe Ransom, Harvard University Press, Cambridge, Mass., 1970, page 14. See also "Ethics and Intelligence,' by E. Drexel Godfrey, *Foreign Affairs*, April 1978, page 639, in which the following statement appears: "If counterintelligence is to survive, it should be organized on a purely defensive basis as a protection against foreign penetration of the U.S. intelligence services and their technical capabilities." Mr. Godfrey seems to have omitted consideration of the mission to include protection of all national secrets, not just those of the intelligence agencies.

6. *Intelligence Requirements for the 1980's: Counterintelligence*, page 34.

7. Ibid, pages 76–77, 264–268. One line of reasoning suggests that because of training and experience, CI personnel are more likely to discern deception on the part of a foreign power. While it is certain that CI personnel can have penetrating insights that may prove correct, the usual analysts would maintain that they seek the same end, when the facts warrant it. Those familiar with a thesis once held in a group of counterintelligence personnel, to the effect that the Sino-Soviet split of the 1960s was a grand deception plot, may question the unqualified advantages of applying special CI analysis across the board.

8. Quoted in *Intelligence Requirements for the 1980's: Counterintelligence*, Ch. 2, "What is Counterintelligence?" by Arthur A. Zuehlke, page 15.

9. Sherman Kent, in *Strategic Intelligence*, gives little space to counterintelligence. At one point (page 3) he refers to counterintelligence and counterespionage, in succession, and then, in the same sequence, as dealing with traitors and foreign spies, respectively. Kent seems to have viewed CI as concerned with traitors, and CE as concerned with foreign spies. For another interpretation of Kent, see *Intelligence Requirements for the 1980's: Counterintelligence*, pages 13–15.

10. *Church Committee Report*, Book I, page 166.

11. *Intelligence Requirements for the 1980's: Counterintelligence*, pages 26–27.

12. "Inside the G.R.U.," by Robert Moss, *Parade*, 6 September 1981, page 6.

13. *Church Committee Report*, Book I, pages 559, 561. The First Chief Directorate of the KGB is responsible for foreign intelligence operations, the First Department of which is responsible for operations against the United States and Canada. The Church Committee stated the matter as follows: "Traditionally, the numerical designation 'First' has been assigned to the department that operates against the 'main enemy' of the U.S.S.R. The United States has been that enemy since World War II."

14. *Church Committee Report*, Book I, page 561.

15. Ibid., page 164.

16. Ibid., Book I, page 558.

17. *KGB*, page 71 (footnote).

18. *Church Committee Report*, Book I, page 558, states that there are over 175,000 Border Guards, whereas *KGB*, page 85, puts the total at some 300,000. The figure is given as between 200,000 and 300,000 in *Intelligence Requirements for the 1980's: Counterintelligence*, page 102.

19. Ibid., page 558.

20. Ibid., page 560. Figures were not given for clerical personnel.

21. "Inside the G.R.U.," op. cit., page 7.

22. Different·sources offer different views as to the relationship between the KGB and GRU. "Inside the G.R.U." suggests considerable independence on the part of the GRU in its operational activity abroad, and at page 7 states that it controls an elite corps of some 30,000 *Spetsnaz* (Special designation) troops, trained in terrorism and sabotage. Most authorities accept the fact that the KGB controls the *Spetsnaz* (see *Intelligence Requirements for the 1980's: Counterintelligence*, pages 87–100). One source credits both the KGB and GRU with conducting training in terrorism and sabotage in Czechslovakia—functions that are consistent with the *Spetsnaz*. See *The Terror Network*, by Claire Sterling, Holt, Rinehart & Winston, New York, 1981, page 221.

23. *Church Committee Report*, Book I, page 558.

24. Ibid., page 561. The Church Committee figure of 10,000 in 1975 must be viewed in the light of a later report of 12,000 Soviet intelligence officers assigned outside the USSR. See *Intelligence Requirements for the 1980's: Elements of Intelligence*, page 61.

25. *Church Committee Report*, Book I, pages 561–562.

26. Ibid., pages 163–164; *Intelligence Requirements for the 1980's: Elements of Intelligence*, page 51.

27. *Church Committee Report*, Book I, pages 163–164.

28. *Church Committee Report*, Book I, pages 164–165.

29. *The Intelligence Establishment*, page 14.

30. An example of how a security indiscretion can lead to a successful counterintelligence action is found in a sequence of media reports in the last half of 1984 and the first half of 1985. On 13 September 1984 the ABC "World News Tonight" claimed that U.S. government agencies had reported to the U.S. Senate Select Committee on Intelligence that there was a possibility the Indian government might order an attack on a Pakistani nuclear reactor. This was followed by news stories in the *Washington Post* and the *New York Times* on 15 September. The *Times* stated that the two senior members of the Senate Select Committee on Intelligence were concerned about such an attack. The *Post*, while reporting the story, quoted government officials as discounting it as "alarmist." *Time* magazine, on 4 February 1985, reported Indian government action to arrest officials charged with selling secrets to foreigners. The *Time* story stated: "The current investigation was apparently triggered last September, when reports [were published] in U.S. newspapers based on leaks from a CIA briefing to a congressional committee in Washington."

If the media was correct in its reports about the briefing of the Senate committee, and if *Time* is correct in attributing the Indian counterintelligence actions to those leaks, we have a classic example of how important intelligence sources can be lost. Still to appear in the press is one of those investigative reports revealing what actions, if any, were taken to ascertain the source of the leaks and the steps taken to discipline the guilty parties.

31. *Church Committee Report*, Book I, page 165.

32. An example of how meticulous police work and counterintelligence effort can eventually unravel not only the nature of terrorist organizations but even the relationships among some of them can be found in "Terror Network, U.S.A.," by Eugene H. Methvin, *Reader's Digest*, December 1984, pages 109–119.

33. *Title 50 U.S. Code*, Sections 1801–1811.

34. *Title 50, U.S. Code*, Sections 1802–1803. The special surveillance court, established by the 1978 Act, is reported to have issued 518 warrants for electronic surveillance during the first fifteen months of its existence (by the end of 1980). No applications for warrants were rejected. (See *The Puzzle Palace*, by James Bamford, Houghton Mifflin, Boston, 1982, pages 370–371.) This figure compares with a total of 773 telephone wiretaps and microphones installed by the FBI for the five-year period (1970–1974) preceding the congressional investigations that led to the 1978 Act—an average of 154 a year for that period (see *Church Committee Report*, Book III, page 301). That average is considerably lower than the level of activity observed since the 1978 Act. Even if allowance is made for special NSA operations and the occasional CIA counterintelligence activities directed against Americans abroad, the new procedures appear not to have reduced the level of such operations. Apparently reasons of operational necessity have prevailed.

One source has reported that the surveillance court issued 322 warrants in 1980, and that the number rose to 437 in 1982. The authors writing on the subject did not, of course, have access to the confidential records that would disclose the considerations presented to the court in making its decisions. Those records might have provided qualitative understanding for what is otherwise an unrefined statistic. The implication, in the treatment by the authors, was that the court, by never refusing an application, was in some way derelict. Given the "minimization" purpose of the Surveillance Act, it can be safely stated that an application would not be made without supportable grounds. Further, the authors seem to feel that electronic surveillance is limited to remote processes (telephone taps and communications intercept), whereas those familiar with the work are aware that more than occasionally it is necessary to gain access to private quarters to install electronic devices. Such questions are unlikely to inhibit academic deductions. See "Secrecy, Foreign Intelligence, and Civil Liberties: Has the Pendulum Swung Too Far?" by Duncan L. Clarke and Edward L. Neveleff, *Political Science Quarterly*, Vol. 99, No. 3, Fall 1984.

35. *Executive Order 12036*, Section 2-202 (January 1978); *Executive Order 12333*, Section 2.4 (a) (December 1981).

36. *Executive Order 12036*, Section 2-206. The provision for "reasonable belief" has its origins in existing standards of evidence in the practice of criminal law. Under current court procedure, if evidence offered in a criminal prosecution is judged to have been obtained by means that violate the constitutional injunction

against unreasonable search, it cannot be introduced into the proceedings. The principle seems unquestionable, but the formula for narrow application to intelligence activities has been criticized strongly and may yet become modified in some respect.

Some consider counterintelligence to be just another form of law enforcement (see Note 29 in this chapter), and it seemed natural to such thinking simply to extend the practices of criminal law to counterintelligence. But the purposes of counterintelligence and of law enforcement differ. Law enforcement seeks to prosecute the criminal, whereas counterintelligence seeks to stop espionage and thus may not progress to court proceedings. The stakes are also vastly different, in that espionage differs from common crimes against persons and property.

The *Church Committee Report*, Book I, pages 174–175, addressed the general question as follows: "The type of activity which is most easy to detect and which may indicate possible espionage does not always satisfy the normal standard of 'reasonable suspicion.' As a study prepared by the Fund for the Republic stated: 'The problems of crime detection in combatting espionage are not ordinary ones. Espionage is a crime which succeeds only by secrecy. Moreover, spies work not for themselves or privately organized crime "syndicates," but as agents of national states. Their activities are therefore likely to be carefully planned, highly organized, and carried on by techniques skillfully designed to prevent detection.' Consequently, espionage investigations must be initiated on the basis of fragments of information, especially where there may be only an indication of a suspicious contact with a foreign agent and limited data as to the specific purposes of the contact.

"In addition, prosecution is frequently not the objective of an espionage investigation. For one thing, the government may desire 'to avoid exposing its own counter-espionage practices and information.' In addition, the purpose of the investigation may be to find out what a known foreign agent is looking for, both as an indication of the espionage interest of the foreign country and as a means of insuring that the agent is not on the track of vital information. Since foreign agents are replaceable, it may be a better defense not to expel them from the country or otherwise halt their activities, but rather to maintain a constant watch on their operations. This also means investigating in a more limited fashion many of the Americans with whom the foreign agent associates, in order to determine what the agent may be interested in learning from them." Clearly, there is more than the usual law enforcement work in this activity, and standards of criminal law may not be naturally transferable in every respect.

37. *Executive Order 12333*, Section 2.4 (d).

38. *Church Committee Report*, Book I, page 358.

39. Ibid., page 358–359. The description of the functions of USAINTA, NIS, and AFOSI are from the *Church Committee Report*. The brief comment on the formation of INSCOM is from a letter of 27 January 1983 from the Director of Counterintelligence, Office of the U.S. Army Assistant Chief of Staff for Intelligence.

40. *Church Committee Report*, Book III, pages 818–822.

41. *Rockefeller Commission Report*, page 246.

42. Ibid., page 157.

43. Ibid., pages 242, 243.

44. *Facing Reality*, pages 212–213.

45. *Rockefeller Commission Report*, page 130.

46. *Church Committee Report*, Book II, page 102; Book III, pages 705–706.

47. *Chuch Committee Report*, Book II, page 167.

48. Ibid., page 262.

49. Ibid., page 95.

50. *Church Committee Report*, Book III, page 743.

51. *Executive Order 9835*, 12 Fed. Reg. 1935 (1947); *Executive Order 10450*, 18 Fed. Reg. 2489 (1953).

52. *Church Committee Report*, Book II, page 263.

53. *Rockefeller Commission Report*, page 250.

54. *Church Committee Report*, Book I, page 174.

55. *Church Committee Report*, Book III, page 561.

56. *Rockefeller Commission Report*, page 101.

57. Ibid., pages 105–115.

58. Ibid., page 115.

59. *Church Committee Report*, Book III, pages 561–636. The committee treated the subject in more detail than did the Rockefeller Commission, but the two were essentially in accord.

60. Department of Justice press release, 14 January 1977.

61. *Church Committee Report*, Book IV, pages 109–119.

62. *Church Committee Report*, Book II, page 108. Subsequently, other agencies requested similar coverage.

63. For a detailed review of NSA activities, see *Church Committee Report*, Book III, pages 735–783. See also *The Puzzle Palace*, which covers the techniques in considerable detail.

64. *Rockefeller Commission Report*, pages 137–142, 149. Although these four cases were in violation of instructions, and contrary to the limitations of the 1947 Act, they were clearly not "massive" programs much less an "ambitious domestic operation," as it was termed as late as 1984. See "Secrecy, Foreign Intelligence, and Civil Liberties: Has the Pendulum Swung Too Far?" page 494.

65. *Rockefeller Commission Report*, pages 152–155.

66. Ibid., pages 160–168. This is a full discussion of the subject.

67. Ibid., pages 163–164.

68. *Church Committee Report*, Book II, pages 10–18, 65–93; Book III, pages 1–185.

69. *Church Committee Report*, Book III, page 797.

70. Ibid., page 802.

71. Ibid., Book III, pages 804–806.

72. *Church Committee Report*, Book I, pages 166–169. See also *Intelligence Requirements for the 1980's: Counterintelligence*, pages 16–21.

73. *Intelligence Requirements for the 1980's: Counterintelligence*, page 40.

74. *Church Committee Report*, Book I, pages 171–172.

75. An interesting discussion of the problems presented by independent CI operations in the field can be found in the chapter by Eugene Franz Burgestaller, in *Intelligence Requirements for the 1980's: Counterintelligence*, pages 247–250.

76. *Church Committee Report*, Book I, page 145, footnote 11.

77. Ibid., pages 143–147. See also the comments by Burgestaller cited in Note 75.

78. Not only did Colby reduce CI Staff's independent operations, limiting its functions to those of basically staff support; he also tightened controls on CA Staff, eliminated a group known as the Central Cover Staff (which had labored with some progress toward developing a viable, but independent, system for centrally managed operational cover for clandestine operatives), and cut back the staff of the Inspector General (whose inquiries throughout the Agency were considered by some to be an invasion of the prerogatives of command). He later told a close acquaintance that the latter of these actions was a mistake, and the Inspector General's staff was increased to more than double its previous size. Colby had an energetic management bent, as will be remembered by those who worked at implementing the system known as Management by Objective, which proposed and validated programs for the Agency's budget. His innovation in the area of establishing collection requirements for the Intelligence Community and his replacement of the Office of National Estimates with the new system for National Intelligence Officers were further samples of this activist quality. Had he not been so pressed by the investigations of the 1970s which consumed so much of his time and attention, he might have produced more initiatives, making the Agency into a somewhat different organization than it had been.

79. See Note 2 in this chapter.

80. *Intelligence Requirements for the 1980's: Elements of Intelligence*, page 56.

14

COVERT ACTION/ SPECIAL ACTIVITIES

> *. . . to do nought is in itself almost an act.*
> —Dante Gabriel Rossetti

The early record of the National Security Council's decisions to launch a broad Covert Action program by the U.S. government, and the first organizational steps after it was assigned to CIA, has been covered briefly in Chapter 3. Following the first uncertain organizational arrangements, which were accompanied by rapid growth, Covert Action came to have an established place among the instruments of U.S. foreign policy. Its purpose is to influence international developments, and the theater of action is most often in some foreign country. Soviet expansionist policy, in selecting the areas for extension of its influence and power, often determines the major U.S. undertakings in this type of activity. In such instances, the United States is faced with the decision of whether or not to play a more positive role in the affected area.

American courses of action may range from anticipatory programs to stunt the growth of communist organization in its early stages, to meeting it head on in its later, well-established, phases. A U.S. covert program may involve no more than attempts to influence political opinion through propaganda campaigns as reinforcement for overt support. It may include support for moderate political groups against radical Marxist movements. Occasionally special activities have involved force, in supporting a foreign government's opposition to communist subversion, terrorism, and insurgency. The situations are always fluid, and the details often uncertain and surely not arranged to our choosing. When the United States decides on a Covert Action program, it does so as part of a broader government policy.

Henry Kissinger, writing in a reflective mood after his service with the Nixon and Ford administrations, made this observation on Covert Action:

> Whether and to what extent the United States should seek to affect domestic developments in other countries is a complicated question, the answer to which depends on a variety of elements, including one's conception of the national interest. Presidents of both parties have felt the need for covert operations in the gray area between formal diplomacy and military intervention throughout the postwar period.[1]

Kissinger further commented on the undiscriminating criticisms of those who opposed some forms of counterintervention in other nations, observing that the same critics have supported the principle of intervention in other instances in which it fit their political preferences. The issue is neither easy to resolve nor always clear after a decision has been taken.

The record does indicate that national leadership has been unwilling to accept the role of bystander to developments that are judged important to the national interest. If resulting policy has not met with uniform success—which reinforces public criticisms of it—the outcry would also be great if the United States stood on the sidelines, wringing its hands and issuing pious statements of principle. For example, the Truman administration's policy of containing Soviet expansionism—which appears fairly positive in retrospect—became an issue at the time for not being forceful enough.[2] The fact is that problems of foreign policy relating to Soviet initiatives more often present dilemmas than opportunities for the sort of programs that most Americans would prefer to pursue.

DIRECTION AND CONTROL

Although CIA did not have exclusive jurisdiction over Covert Action within the U.S. government, for some three decades it has had the primary role and has been involved in the major programs. Accordingly, this discussion will focus on CIA and its activities.

Some elements of the media have portrayed CIA as an independent, freewheeling organization, striking out for itself in all manner of Covert Action programs. Senator Church was persuaded, in the initial phases of the Senate investigating committee's work, to believe that CIA could safely be accused of being a "rogue elephant" out of control. As noted earlier, that characterization had to be withdrawn.

From the early days of the post–World War II era, when CIA was put into the business of Covert Action, the requirement for coordination and clearance in the government was firm. The Office of Policy Coordination was the first effective instrument of the government's post-war Covert Action program, with policy guidance coming from the Departments of State and Defense. Its function was envisioned as planning and handling coordination of CA programs. In June 1948, NSC directive 10/2 replaced the original NSC directive, and a "10/2 Panel" was established to review Covert Action proposals. That arrangement continued through 1952. From 1953 to 1955 the DCI coordinated proposals with NSC committees, first with the Psychological Strategy Board, and then with the Operations Coordination Board when that board took over the function. Provision was made for presidential review on a selective basis. In 1955, as a result of the *Hoover Commission Report*,[3] two new NSC directives were issued. They remained in effect until 1970,[4] providing basic policy guidelines for the critical period of CIA's major Covert Action operations during the ensuing fifteen years.

With the 1955 directive a new review group was established within the NSC structure, known as the Special Group. It consisted of representatives of the Secretaries of State and Defense and, for the first time, a representative of the President. The Special Group was to meet regularly to review and approve Covert Action programs proposed by CIA or others. In fact the meetings of the Special Group were irregular, due—as the Church Committee recognized—to the fact that there was a special relationship between the Secretary of State (John Foster Dulles) and the DCI (Allen Dulles), who were brothers, and President Eisenhower. They transacted considerable business on a personal basis.[5] Secretary Dulles fell ill, resigning in April 1959; weekly meetings of the Special Group began early that year. When the Kennedy administration took office in 1960, the weekly meetings were moved to the White House, where they were chaired by the President's representative. In 1964 the Special Group was renamed the 303 Committee because its former name and function had been exposed.

In 1970, NSDM 40 rescinded previous NSC directives on covert action, and the successor to the 303 Committee was named the 40 Committee. Under the new procedures the DCI was to obtain policy approval from the 40 Committee for all major and/or politically sensitive covert action programs. Added to the procedures of the committee was a formal annual review.[6] This arrangement was in effect when the congressional investigations commenced in the mid-1970s. Following the investigations, arrangements for review and approval were changed again by President Ford's Executive Order.

The Carter Executive Order in 1978 (EO 12036, Section 1-3) created a Special Coordination Committee (SCC) under the National Security Council. Among the committee's duties were the review of all Special

Activities and submission of recommendations for action to the President. This provision reflects the statutory requirement for the President to report to the Congress on Covert Action/Special Activities under the Hughes-Ryan Amendment to the Foreign Assistance Act of 1974, then in effect. While expanding the review and approval process, EO 12036 also continued the basic concept of coordination and review within the government, which had existed in one form or another from the earliest days following passage of the National Security Act of 1947.

The Reagan Executive Order (EO 12333, section 1.2) did not specify the form in which reporting to the President would be handled, stating only that there would be "such committees as may be necessary." By the time of the Reagan directive, the Hughes-Ryan Amendment had been replaced by the Intelligence Oversight Act of 1980, which also required reporting by the President to the Congress. Although the specific arrangements for handling this particular subject by the Reagan NSC have not been publicized, it is clear that the basic function is similar to that under the Carter administration.

This quick trip through the various arrangements for coordinating covert action programs within the Executive branch, and their review and approval at the NSC level, highlights the provisions for direction and control. Whatever the controversies that whirl around the different programs—and even the basic concept of covert action—it should be clear that Covert Action programs are formal products of the government's foreign policy machinery. Discovery of this fact caused Senator Church to retreat from his "rogue elephant" statement.

CIA's covert action programs were officially sanctioned, but CIA was not alone in the activity. Other members of the Intelligence Community also conducted covert action programs of various types; for example, toward Cuba during the Eisenhower and Kennedy administrations, and under the Johnson and Nixon administrations during the war in Southeast Asia. It is not at all clear that the non-CIA covert action programs were given the same review accorded those of CIA. The investigative committees seem not to have recognized this aspect of the government's activities, so their findings are silent on the point.

Under the Reagan Executive Orders, CIA has been designated the sole executive agent for the government in Covert Action/Special Activities, except in the event of declared war or specific presidential action to the contrary.[7] Two general categories of activity will be discussed below: political action and propaganda. Others will be covered later.

POLITICAL ACTION

Cold war developments increased the importance of political stability and orientation of the so-called developing nations in the minds of U.S.

policymakers. Those nations lacked important attributes of viable societies. National identity was uncertain, and institutionalized arrangements and attitudes necessary for managing national affairs, which are
taken for granted in Western societies, were either minimal or nonexistent. What those nations needed most was to be left alone to sort
out their own problems and establish their own patterns, with some
economic and technical assistance from the more fortunate nations. They
were vulnerable to revolutionary opposition; the opposition, whatever
its form, was highly vulnerable to communist infiltration and exploitation.

The older but also less-developed nations did have established social
and governmental systems with hierarchies accustomed to managing
public affairs. Whatever their adequacy for pre–World War II days, they
would prove somewhat antiquated for the demands of a changed and
changing world. Those older nations suffered many of the problems of
economic and social backwardness experienced by the new nations. But
new or old, these nations suffered the basic problems that could cause
political restiveness on the part of their people. The ability to meet
expectations and demands of the new age was limited by the quality
of organization, by the level of development of existing national resources,
and by custom and attitude.

Barring the intrusion of other forces, U.S. tradition and capabilities
had prepared the United States for contributing to the resources needed
by those nations. In essence, that assistance was envisioned as reinforcing
the economies of the less-developed nations, encouraging social and
political progress as they began to solve their problems. The tendency
was to work through existing governments and social structures, which
provided the mechanisms for management and social order. It proved
difficult, however, to extend economic and technical assistance without
becoming involved in arrangements for their use. As our familiarity
with the established norms of those societies developed, so did judgments
about the entitlement of the governments, as distinguished from the
needs of their people. Political reform tended to become a condition
for aid, rather than a result of it. Hence the creation and implementation
of policies became even more difficult to achieve.

In the early post–World War II period, it was less difficult to see
to the heart of a problem and produce relatively clear-cut policies that
attracted support. This can be explained in part by the striking novelty
and challenges of early post–World War II Soviet policy. With the passage
of time, and given the continuing nature of the problem, something of
a sophisticated *ennui* seems to have set in as the recurring crises lost
their novelty.

In the 1940s the Soviets created clear issues on which people could
take positions. Soviet pressure on Greece and Turkey gave rise to the
Truman Doctrine. The overthrow of the governments in Eastern Europe

and the subjugation of those nations, given the perceived threat to Western Europe, produced NATO. The Soviet sponsored invasion of South Korea evoked the UN and U.S. effort to block it. These crises demanded considerable effort, wearying those who preferred to do other things, but they did lead to policies that seemed to be containing Soviet expansionism on its periphery. Then Soviet interests broadened beyond the neighboring territories of the USSR, taking on a global nature that was new in many ways.[8] The Third World became a prime target for projection of Soviet influence and power, especially as decolonization occurred.

The extension of Soviet policy beyond its periphery impacted on the problems facing U.S. policy. There were legitimate grounds for political opposition to the governments in many of those lands. Communist tactics, of course, were to align with or infiltrate opposition groups. The communists usually were well prepared for this sort of activity, and their influence often became significant. Opposition to a government often took the form of violence, deliberate terrorist acts, and armed rebellion. Many Third World governments, not inclined to look benignly on opposition in any event, reacted strongly and often in ways that were oppressive. Political views in those countries often became polarized, and for distant democracies, the issues were blurred by alternatives.

U.S. policymakers would prefer to deal with stable and open societies. A degree of order is necessary for economic progress, and the objective of U.S. aid was to help lay the economic base for social evolution. It is disturbing to witness oppression by an incumbent, with whom the United States must deal if its larger purpose is to be achieved. Whatever the reservations about incumbent governments, the strong sense of opposition to communist-dominated revolutionary movements has often caused U.S. policymakers to settle for preserving governments on which they must base their hopes for progress. Those governments frequently have been driven into a siege state of mind that tends to limit their ability to produce and carry out progressive programs. Such a development is, obviously, one of the Soviet objectives.

Given the broader purposes of the policies just summarized, U.S. policymakers often face a dilemma when a government with more warts than soul is threatened with a communist takeover. Our preference is a better government, so change is not entirely undesirable. But a communist state is the antithesis of our hopes for those peoples. The question is what to do. On occasion, the United States has supported noncommunist forces in opposition to the government, as in Iran and Guatemala in the 1950s. But such actions have the character of a desperate last resort to salvage a failing policy. Too often, when some covert action operation is undertaken and succeeds, later results have not proven to provide better conditions. The successor government often is not susceptible to American influence and may start a new cycle of unprogressive policy and practice. Despite these reservations, there have been instances that have contributed to a better course of events.

Two such cases of major U.S. political action programs in support of moderate forces were the elections in West Europe in the 1940s and those in Chile in the 1960s. The first case has been largely ignored, despite its success, and the second has been lost in the dramatic misrepresentations of the U.S. role in Chile in 1973. The objective of U.S. policy in both instances was to assist moderate political forces to stave off the real threat of communist political ascendancy in those countries. These programs are major undertakings, with all the techniques and trappings of modern national political campaigns: opinion polls, selection of issues for the campaign, identification of key political figures, development of their organizations, and planning and conduct of media campaigns—all with adequate financing to carry the plan through to fruition. However, major campaigns of this kind are not the rule. They are costly and difficult to control. Identification and support of a few individual candidates, when that seems suited to the problem, is the more normal course. Such activity can have long-range benefits.

Relationships that develop in the course of shared political experiences have lasting qualities. Governments elected with U.S. assistance are more likely to be receptive to embassy initiatives, although, as noted earlier, this is not always the way things turn out. Individual politicians who hold office with the help of foreign supporters are also likely to be favorably disposed. Whatever the degree of the individual public officials' friendliness, at least radical destabilizing elements have been excluded from the government. Experience shows that regardless of a government's—or an individual's—predisposition to be responsive to those who have helped that government or individual, personal or perceived national interest often has proven the stronger bond when U.S. views conflict with the views of those in power. The United States has been unable or unwilling to have puppets. If Americans want unqualified responsiveness from foreign public officials, they had best recruit functionaries from within the country's bureaucracy.

It has been common practice throughout history for governments to attempt to develop "agents of influence" who are prominent enough, or have sufficient special access, to be able to influence policymakers. Where these individuals are sympathetic to U.S. policies and willing to help, they can be very useful. However, there is usually an element of independence associated with these persons. In any event, the number is limited—certainly there are fewer now than during the early post-

World War II days when there was less national stability around the world than there seems to be at present.

One aspect of the support given governments as part of aid programs is sometimes characterized by political action. A government subject to extensive subversion needs a strong police force and internal security service. Accordingly, among the programs provided by the United States is police training, administered by the U.S. Agency for International Development (AID). CIA, too, has provided help in developing counterintelligence organizations and techniques targeted on local Soviet representatives and indigenous communist parties that may be working with the Soviets. CIA is in a position to conduct mutually useful exchanges with the local government's security services. Depending on the state of matters, CIA representatives can collaborate in harassment programs to discredit the Soviets in their subversive activities. That sort of action is a mixture of counterintelligence and covert action.

There are many different situations in which political action may be appropriate. Each case must be designed to fit the local situation and issues. That political action programs can work has been demonstrated, and that they can fail should be warning of the pitfalls such activities hold.

PROPAGANDA

One special area of activity is propaganda, which is related to political action although properly considered a distinct specialization. The word *propaganda* has been given a negative connotation by some, as though everything produced by it is untrue. But one dictionary defines propaganda as "the systematic propagation of a given doctrine or allegations reflecting its views and interests. Material disseminated by the proselytizers of a doctrine."[9] By definition, then, it is no more than a matter of advancing one's view. Assuming that one's creed or position is based on informed and honest conviction, that definitions allows for—and even argues in favor of—using the truth to support and advance the position at issue. This concept has had particular relevance since World War II.

The Cold War created a need to persuade others of the significance of Soviet global policy and of the relative positions of the opposing sides. As one writer put it: "Dwight D. Eisenhower and Harry S. Truman agreed on at least one thing. They said it in substantially the same words in 1952, 'We cannot hope to win the cold war unless we win the minds of men.'"[10] The same author, emphasizing the belief that "we can progressively win men's minds" emphasized that "in the contest . . . truth can be peculiarly the American weapon." By and large, U.S.

propaganda since World War II has operated within the positive principles implicit in the forthright presentation of issues as we view them, with limited departures from those principles that will be mentioned below.

United States propaganda is conducted in a number of ways, both overt and covert. Presidential press conferences and addresses are given wide coverage. Department of State press releases and statements, the work of the U.S. Information Agency, the Voice of America programs, and the broadcasts and publications of Radio Free Europe (RFE) and Radio Liberty (RL) all contribute to conveying the American view of the world to others.

RFE and RL have been targeted toward the East European nations and the USSR, respectively, to broaden the understanding of listeners. For many years RFE and RL were supported covertly by CIA. Their programs were subject to general government policy directives and operated openly as privately supported organizations. As a result of congressional debates in 1971, the two "Radios" (as they were known) were given independent status in 1973 under a congressionally chartered Board for International Broadcasting, funded openly by the U.S. government.[11] All these instruments of information and propaganda have been purveyors of reliable fact, thus reflecting the basic belief that in the long run candor is important to success in bringing others to our views. If our information and propaganda programs are to be viable, much depends on their credibility.[12]

In addition to the various means of information/propaganda activity that can be pursued by the U.S. government, CIA was given the task of conveying the United States' message to the peoples of other lands by other means. In addition to the Radios, this involved

> the placement of news stories in the foreign press, criticized *inter alia* in 1976 by the U.S. Senate's Church Committee Report. (We should point out that, while such stories *could* be notional, the CS [Clandestine Service] has always understood, as most advertisers do, that the truth is often the most powerful argument) (emphasis in original).[13]

Such activity requires establishing operational contacts with foreign media, whose people are also potential sources of intelligence. The ability of these individuals to place news stories in local papers and radio and television stations is something of a dividend to operations managers and case officers, who may even be able to use them occasionally as agents of influence.

Policy guidance for programs on the Radios and for press placement was coordinated in Washington before being sent to the field.[14] Press placement is fairly direct. Stories from other areas are provided operational contacts to be reprinted in local newspapers. Their previous publication elsewhere gives them additional credibility for both publishers and readers. Editorials favorable to the U.S. position may also be provided. The volume of press placement has been impressive. It must have contributed to at least a subconscious appreciation for the U.S. position. Although there is no reliable method for measuring total impact, there have been recurring indications of its usefulness.

The exception to this basic approach is known as "black propaganda"—the placing of an apparently authentic story that is either artfully distorted or completely fabricated. During the intense days of the Cold War, it was used in various areas to create local problems for the USSR. The Soviet Union still uses this device—sometimes artfully but often crudely.

Whatever ability we had to influence public opinion in West Europe after World War II has been largely lost. The European press became so diverse and sophisticated that, with existing resources, media propaganda campaigns can expect marginal results, if any. On the other hand, the Soviet Union, through its international organizations, is able to carry out intensive propaganda campaigns that get considerable coverage for the organizations and their demonstrations. Communist international fronts have been most effective in the so-called peace movement in Europe during the early 1980s.[15] A U.S. program to off-set that situation would require reactivating the organizational structure used so extensively in the earlier Cold War days. That structure was severely cut back following a press campaign in what came to be known as the "Ramparts Flap" of 1967, discussed in Chapter 19. The revelations at that time, followed by aggressive media coverage, resulted in basic changes in operating capabilities.

Some use can still be made of European newspapers. A news story placed in one of them can be cited elsewhere as having an apparently authentic source. This activity generated some concern in the Church Committee, as will be noted later.

In addition to press placement activities, CIA also supported a number of general publishing programs. Scholarly works were commissioned on subjects believed to be useful if distributed to Third World audiences. Usually the authors were not aware of CIA sponsorship, although CIA representatives sometimes monitored the preparation of a book to ensure that certain subject matter was included. There appears to have been no significant criticism of the content of these works. The publishing program also included translation of literary classics and minor works of humorous propaganda nature, distributed to foreign lands through the mails. Some of the printing was done in the United

States.[16] The program was terminated in 1967 following the report of the Katzenbach Committee after the Ramparts Flap.

The Church Committee was uneasy about both the overseas press placement program and CIA publishing activities. This uneasiness was based on the perception that overseas press placements might find their way back into the United States and contaminate the U.S. press,[17] and that the books might be accepted without knowing that CIA was behind them. The Church Committee did no substantive evaluation either of the basic press placement program or of the quality of the books. The working assumption seems to have been that they were suspect because of their origin.

As noted earlier, the great majority of press placements were news stories already printed elsewhere. The Church Committee did acknowledge that CIA had briefed senior officials in the U.S. government when "black" or other deceptive propaganda might be reprinted from the foreign press, to prevent our policymakers from being misled.[18] The committee also acknowledged that pains had been taken to brief senior executives in the U.S. media to ensure that care be exercised in handling news items reported on CIA-controlled wire services.[19] In effect, where the Church Committee believed there was danger of domestic contamination by our own propaganda—either in the government or in the media—steps had been taken to eliminate the risk. In any event, the danger that pro-American propaganda might be considered newsworthy enough by the wire services to report back to the United States is not a likely one.

As a practical matter, the CIA covert press program is not a threat to the integrity of the U.S. press. The author of the section of the *Church Committee Report* who dealt with the program did not get very far into its subject but, rather, simply raised a dubious issue without developing it factually.

NOTES

1. *The White House Years*, by Henry Kissinger, Little, Brown, Boston, 1979, pages 658–659.

2. It was the Truman administration, as noted in Chapter 3, that gave CIA its Cold War activist mission. At the very first meeting of the National Security Council—in December 1947, after passage of the National Security Act of 1947—CIA was assigned the function that came to be known as Covert Action and then, later, as Special Activities.

Some sixteen years later, more than ten years after he left office, Truman was reported to have second thoughts about CIA's covert action role. A syndicated article under his name appeared in a number of newspapers (e.g., in the

Washington Post on 22 December 1963, under the caption "Harry Truman Writes: United States Should Hold CIA to Intelligence Role") that were critical of CIA's Cold War activist role.

The Truman NSC not only assigned a Covert Action role to CIA, but it broadened the mandate in just a few months. This was reported to the Congress in early 1948, as part of the legislative process to complete CIA's charter in the Central Intelligence Agency Act of 1949. And the Congress made appropriations for this purpose over the ensuing years. The patterns of activity that followed were formed during the Truman administration, whatever reservations Truman may have developed at a later date.

There is some question as to just how much Truman actually shared the reservations set forth in the 1963 newspaper article. Former DCI Allen Dulles showed him the article and reported that the former president "seemed quite astonished at it. In fact, he said it was all wrong." A former DDCI (in the company of an individual who later became DDCI) discussed the article with an assistant of the former president, who stated that it was he who had written it. It was the conclusion of one writer, in *Studies in Intelligence*, a CIA publication (Vol. 17, No. 3, Fall 1973), that not only did Truman not write the article, but that he did not see it before it was published.

Cited in *Donovan and the CIA*, by Thomas Troy, at page 528, is a handwritten note by Truman to Sidney Souers, seeming to comment favorably on the article. Souers, in addition to drafting the intelligence section of the Eberstadt Report, became the first DCI under the NIA arrangement. He left that post in 1946, after getting the CIG launched, and was replaced by Lt. Gen. Hoyt Vandenberg. Souers returned to Washington upon passage of the 1947 Act and served as Executive Secretary of the NSC through 1950. He was very much a part—with Truman—of the process that set the pattern for CIA's role in the Cold War. Whatever reservations Truman may have developed later, his role and that of Souers, in setting that pattern when it was their responsibility to do so, is very clear.

3. A portion of the Hoover Report is quoted in Chapter 17 of this book.

4. The *Church Committee Report*, Book I, page 51, provides the following key provisions of the directive: (1) Create and exploit problems for International Communism. Discredit International Communism, and reduce the strength of its parties and organization. (2) Reduce International Communist control over any areas of the world. (3) Strengthen the orientation toward the United States of the nations of the free world, accentuate, wherever possible, the identity of interest between such nations and the United States as well as favoring, where appropriate, those groups genuinely advocating or believing in the advancement of such mutual interests, and increase the capacity and will of such peoples and nations to resist International Communism. (4) In accordance with established policies, and to the extent practicable in areas dominated or threatened by International Communism, develop underground resistance and facilitate covert and guerrilla operations.

As indicated in the *Church Committee Report*, the directive dealt with means as well as objectives, stating: "Specifically, such [covert action] operations shall include any covert activities related to: propaganda, political action, economic warfare, preventive direct action, including sabotage, anti-sabotage, demolition, escape and evasion and evacuation measures; subversion against hostile states or groups including assistance to underground resistance movements, guerillas and refugee liberation groups; support of indigenous and anticommunist elements in threatened countries of the free world; deception plans and operations and all compatible activities necessary to accomplish the foregoing."

5. Ibid., page 52.

6. For a review of the evolution of NSC involvement and direction of Covert Action, see *Church Committee Report*, Book I, pages 45–61, 141–149.

7. *Executive Order 12333*, Section 1.8 (e), provides that CIA shall "conduct special activities approved by the President. No agency except the CIA (or the Armed Forces of the United States in time of war declared by Congress or during any period covered by a report from the President to the Congress under the War Powers Resolution [87 Stat. 855]) may conduct any special activity unless the President determines that another agency is more likely to achieve a particular objective."

8. *Church Committee Report*, Book I, pages 146–147.

9. *The American Heritage Dictionary of the American Language*, Houghton Mifflin, Boston, 1969.

10. *Truth Is Our Weapon*, by Edward W. Barrett, Funk & Wagnalls, New York, 1953, page ix. See also *Soviet Propaganda*, by Baruch A. Hazan, Keter Publishing House, Jerusalem, 1976, Ch. 1, "The Definition," pages 9–15. The American Declaration of Independence in 1776 was, among other things, a propaganda statement of the revolutionary cause, the Continental Congress already having created the Committee of Secret Correspondence "for the sole purpose of corresponding with our friends in Great Britain, Ireland and other parts of the world."

11. *Facing Reality*, by Cord Meyer, Harper & Row, New York, pages 134–135.

12. Ibid., page 112.

13. *The Clandestine Service of the Central Intelligence Agency*, by Hans Moses, Association of Former Intelligence Officers, McClean, Va., 1983, page 12. See also *The Man Who Kept the Secrets*, by Thomas Powers, Alfred A. Knopf, New York, 1979, page 80. The basic techniques are known to and practiced by the Soviets as well. See *Intelligence Requirements of the 1980's: Covert Action*, Ch. 5, "Trends in Soviet Covert Action," by Donald Jameson.

14. *Facing Reality*, page 117.

15. "The KGB's Magical War for 'Peace,'" by John Barron, *Reader's Digest* (Book Section), November 1982, pages 225, 231–236.

16. *Church Committee Report*, Book I, pages 193–195.

17. Ibid., pages 197–201.

18. Ibid., pages 200–201.

19. Ibid., page 199.

15

COVERT ACTION OPERATIONS

Be not too tame neither . . . : suit the action to the word, the word to the action; with this special observance, that you o'erstep not the modesty of nature.
—William Shakespeare, *Hamlet*, III, ii, 1

When the term *covert action* was applied for reasons of administrative convenience to a somewhat disparate collection of activities, it included an array of unevenly matched disciplines. Although such terms as *psychological warfare* and *paramilitary activity* did not disappear, the more inclusive phrase tended to blur the distinctions between them. Yet, different qualifications were called for in those assigned to the different types of work. The intellectuals who studied problems around the world, conceived political campaigns, and designed propaganda embodied a set of aptitudes different from those who engaged in aggressive and daring action. It is the latter activities that have attracted the greater controversy, not only because of their nature but also because of the policies they are designed to advance.

Presidents seem not always to have distinguished between the two (and occasionally these activities do overlap), sometimes directing courses of action that seem chancy at best. Even the Church Committee spoke favorably of CIA's influence on the elections in West Europe during the period after World War II; they had succeeded, without later negative repercussions. It is the programs of aggressive action, involving the risk or use of violence, that have attracted the main criticisms. Several programs in particular have been controversial. The Church Committee studied a number of them in considerable depth.

The Church Committee's approach to the general subject of covert action reflected awareness of the notoriety it had received,[1] reinforced by at least a visceral reservation on the part of some of the committee members about clandestine activities.[2] The committee nevertheless concluded that the function should be retained among the instruments of

226

U.S. foreign policy implementation. Given its reservations about the activity, the discussion leading up to Committee acceptance of this function is interesting. Although starting on a negative note, the *Church Committee Report* provides insights into the problems facing policymakers when confronted with challenges they judge cannot be handled in normal channels.

In attempting to establish a frame of reference for its review, the *Church Committee Report* made the following comment:

> The record of covert action review by the Congress suggests that net judgments as to "success" or "failure" are difficult to draw. The Committee has found that when covert operations have been consistent with, and in tactical support of, policies which have emerged from a national debate and the established processes of government, these operations have tended to be a success. Covert support to beleaguered democrats in Western Europe in the late 1940s was in support of an established policy based on strong national consensus. On the other hand, the public has neither understood nor accepted the covert harassment of the democratically elected Allende government. Recent covert intervention in Angola preceded, and indeed preempted public and congressional debate on America's foreign policy interest in the future of Angola. The intervention in Angola was conducted in the absence of efforts on the part of the executive branch to develop a national consensus on America's interests in Southern Africa.[3]

The two examples cited by the Church Committee—Chile and Angola—demonstrate both the misleading nature of popular perception and the difficulty of making sweeping judgments on such issues.

CHILE

In the introduction to its discussion of Chile, the Church Committee's final report contains this categorical statement: "In Chile, the United States attempted to overthrow a democratically elected government."[4] The statement was not elaborated on. To some it would convey more than it actually says; at best it is imprecise, and it does warrant a review of what actually happened in Chile.

First, among published versions of the Chile affair, the impression has been created by some that CIA either was responsibile for causing the 1973 coup that overthrew the government of Salvador Allende Gossens or was at least involved in some way. The Church Committee's staff examining this point in a lengthy study printed for committee use, but not issued as a committee report, gave the following question and answer: "Was the United States *directly* involved, covertly, in the 1973 coup in Chile? The Committee found no evidence that it was"[5] (original emphasis). The study did describe CIA's program to keep the democratic organizations in Chile viable in the face of Allende's assault on them but tried to raise an inference that there may have been some undiscovered ties between what the Chilean Army did and CIA's relationships with various organizations. Despite the study's editorializing,[6] it does present an interesting compilation of the types of covert action in existence over a ten-year period.

Why did Chile prompt such a variety of U.S. activity, over such a long period of time? Chilean stability had been judged important to the United States. It had been "chosen to become the showcase for the new Alliance for Progress" of the Kennedy Administration. Between 1962 and 1969 Chile received more economic aid per capita than any other country in the hemisphere, as well as liberal credit through private channels.[7]

The Chilean political scene was not entirely free of destabilizing forces of its own; given the long-standing radical-leftist political activity involving communist and radical socialist cooperation. Salvador Allende, a perennial presidential candidate, had run strongly in 1958, with the more conservative candidates and parties experiencing difficulties. His known radical Marxist orientation was a source of concern to U.S. policymakers, and CIA was assigned a number of covert action programs aimed at organizing opposition to established communist groupings.[8] Finally, a major program was launched in 1964 to support moderate forces in the election of that year, not unlike the programs in Western Europe in the late 1940s. They were successful at the time.

Somewhat late in the 1970 election race, CIA was instructed to develop a major effort. Its work was limited to what was called "spoiling actions," which were intended to cause problems for Allende as distinguished from the positive programs in support of his opponents.[9] In a three-way race Allende gained a plurality of slightly more than 36 percent of the vote. His two opponents had a total of almost 63 percent, the runner-up having slightly over 35%.

In the absence of a majority, the election would be settled by the Chilean congress. Unless Allende's two opponents could combine their 60 percent popular vote, it seemed likely that the congress would declare Allende president. President Nixon directed that the possibility of encouraging such a combination be explored. He also instructed CIA to find out if there were elements of the armed forces—known to have grave reservations about Allende—that might move to prevent his accession to power. This could have included a coup. After a futile survey of the scene, CIA reported that it was unable to develop the necessary support for such a move, and Allende was elected president.

What was the full nature of the concern with Allende? Socialists and leftist democrats were not a new phenomenon in the world. The United States had experienced no difficulty in finding accommodation with most of them. Allende was different. His close associations with Cuba and Soviet-controlled organizations were well known. U.S. Ambassador to Chile Edward Korry stated that in the 1970 elections there was certain knowledge "that the Soviet Union and other Communist governments and organizations provided substantial sums for covert political action to the Communist Party, to the Socialist Party, and to Allende himself."[10]

Allende's Socialist Party was in a coalition with the more conservative Communist Party. Allende, himself, was quite candid during the course of the election as to what victory would mean: "Cuba in the Caribbean and a Socialist Chile in the Southern Cone will make the revolution in Latin America." Soon after the election, Allende met secretly with Latin American revolutionaries. He pledged them covert support. As Ambassador Korry wrote:

> In 1970, as in 1963, we know beyond a shadow of a reasonable doubt that an Allende government intended to use the process and laws of what it called formal democracy to eliminate and replace it with what is called popular democracy. (From 1961 to 1970, the Embassy, like the majority of Congress, agreed that such a development would do serious harm to U.S. interests and influence-for-good in the world.)[11]

The danger that the man represented as a dedicated Soviet-oriented Marxist was clear to those who were informed.[12] Whatever the emphasis of the Church Committee on the electoral processes by which Allende had come to power, when Nixon's effort to prevent his coming to power failed, it was not difficult to predict the problems that lay ahead for Chile. As former Secretary of State Henry Kissinger later wrote: "It was the first, and so far the only, time in modern history that a democratic process has come so close to producing a Communist takeover."[13]

The Nixon appraisal proved correct. Allende set out to take Chile's society apart. The private sector was attacked aggressively. The government undertook to destroy the middle class. Social disintegration was deliberately advanced. Acts ruled unconstitutional by the courts were continued. Armed insurrectionists were equipped and trained for some form of civil war. The economy rapidly disintegrated, with inflation rising to an annual level of 300 percent in 1973.[14]

Despite its constitutional tradition—or because of it—the Chilean military rose against Allende before he could complete his task and ousted his government. Leftists and other political elements have alleged

CIA sponsorship, or at least hinted at some role in the coup. That allegation provided the primary basis for attacks on the United States because of its "intervention" in Chile. Despite authoritative documentation that CIA was not involved, this propaganda has continued—with some echoes in the U.S. press as well.

After 1970, the task assigned to CIA was that of trying to maintain the independent and democratic organizations and elements of Chilean society until the elections scheduled for 1976. As a result, private groups, including some elements of the free press, received funding to help them survive. In its information-gathering role, CIA attempted to keep informed on the course of events. But in the end it was the Chilean military—on its own initiative—that moved to save what had not already been destroyed.

Emotions ran high, and dramatic charges were leveled in all directions. Liberal groups in the United States joined the attack on U.S. policy and pressed for sanctions against the military regime that replaced Allende. Henry Kissinger addressed one aspect of the matter as follows:

> It is ironical that some of those who were so vociferous in condemning what they called "intervention" in Chile have been most insistent on governmental pressure against Allende's successors. The restrictions on American aid to Chile have been far more severe against the post-Allende government than during Allende's term of office.[15]

What does all this reveal about the Chile affair, other than that it has been full of controversy?

First, there had been a consensus over the years about Chile's importance to the United States in the Western Hemisphere. The facts recorded in the Church Committee's staff study speak convincingly on this subject, as did Ambassador Korry. But that consensus was not relevant to the events in 1970, when the effort to block Allende's accession to power failed. If the consensus that had existed was lost in subsequent events, and with the propaganda that followed Allende's fall, that was after the fact.

Beyond that, the story of Chile helps demonstrate the pitfalls of popular news reporting. Allende was not an American-type liberal who merely wanted to reform a backward country. His conduct in office seemed to bear out the evaluation that led President Nixon to try and prevent his accession to power. Nor was the United States involved in the coup against Allende. Out of the chaos he created, the military rose up in a home-grown move to oust him. Certainly the issue was not as simple as the rhetoric of the Church Committee presented it (i.e., as an American ouster of a democratically elected government).

What was the responsibility of a U.S. president who had every reason to know the dangers that Allende represented? Was he to sit by and watch the subversion of a country judged important to U.S. interests in the Western Hemisphere? If not, what steps were appropriate, if any were feasible at all? President Nixon first tried to block Allende's accession to power. Failing that, he then sought to preserve the democratic forces in Chile so they could remain viable for future elections. The dilemmas were significant. Whatever the different views, the President believed his policies, which he judged appropriate for the situation, to be in the national interest.[16]

However one may reach independent conclusions on the topic, the Chile affair was not exactly an apt case to cite in support of the Church Committee's views.

ANGOLA

The introductory comments of the Church Committee, quoted above, also referred to a program of aid to anticommunist elements in Angola. President Ford, in his memoirs, described the situation as follows:

Using $100 million worth of Soviet-supplied weapons and assisted by some five thousand Cuban combat troops, the pro-Communist Popular Movement for the Liberation of Angola (MPLA) was winning control of the country. For the past several months, we had been providing limited amounts of military assistance to forces sympathetic to the West. So had the French. But by the middle of December, it had become clear that our aid was insufficient. We would have to supply more. We had no intention of sending U.S. military personnel to Angola, but about $25 million worth of arms might give the pro-West forces there a chance. The French agreed to work in conjunction with us.[17]

By a vote of 54 to 22, the Senate, in December 1975, blocked any further aid to the noncommunist forces in Angola. Reflecting on the situation, President Ford wrote:

How can the United States, the greatest power in the world, take the position that the Soviet Union can operate with impunity many thousands of miles away with Cuban troops and massive amounts of military equipment, while we refuse any assistance to the majority of the local people who ask only for military equipment to defend themselves? This abdication of responsibility by a majority of the Senate will have the gravest consequences for the long-term position of the United States and international order in general.[18]

The Soviet-supported forces won control of the Angolan government. President Ford felt that instead of criticizing the Senate, people tended to blame him for what he viewed as a failure. History, in its tendency to work in cycles, has led some to believe that congressional attitudes toward U.S. policy on Angola in 1975 seem ready to force a repetition in Central America in the 1980s.

Pursuing the "consensus" thesis, the Church Committee contended that it was the failure of the Executive to develop a consensus that caused the program to fail.[19] Whether it would have failed if the Senate had not withdrawn support for the anticommunists must remain speculative. That there was not a supporting consensus in the Senate is clear, but there were other factors involved. At that time, the Executive branch also was the subject of congressional efforts to establish a new balance in the conduct of foreign affairs, following Vietnam and Watergate. That process undoubtedly affected the way in which this issue was handled by the Congress. The Ford administration, considered something of an interregnum, had a most limited national constituency, which reduced its influence with the Congress. If the Executive branch cannot avoid responsibility for failure to defend its program successfully, neither can the Congress avoid ultimate responsibility for its actions on matters of national interest. To hear it contended that there must be a consensus for an issue to be treated on its merits is at best an interesting, if aberrant, theme.

Citing Angola in support of its thesis, the Church Committee seems, again, to have chosen a case less than fully appropriate for the point it wanted to make.

More recently the Angolan government reportedly has become less than enthusiastic over its ties with the USSR and Cuba. It has not provided the bases the Soviets have sought, and the numerous Cuban military forces there have not made themselves popular. On the other hand, the Angolans have been quite positive in response to commercial overtures from major western corporations, seeing in them an opportunity for economic development that the Soviets do not provide. If the government is not overthrown by some Cuban-Soviet action, there may be a chance to reverse the apparent losses of 1975.

Whatever one's view of the Angola and Chile cases, they do provide a point of departure for considering other controversial instances in which United States policy supported forces that sought to affect the composition of other governments.

COUPS D'ETAT

In six cases, presidents of the United States, in what they deemed grave situations, supported a change in the leadership of foreign nations:

Jacobo Arbenz Guzman of Guatemala in 1953; Muhammed Mossadeq of Iran in 1954; Fidel Castro of Cuba in the 1960–1962 period; Rafael Trujillo of the Dominican Republic in 1961; Ngo Dinh Diem of South Vietnam in 1963; and Salvador Allende Gossens of Chile in 1970. Of these six, four were overthrown with U.S. encouragement or support. (There are a few other instances of similar American involvement, which will not be treated here.) Emphasis is in on the separate programs, with brief detail on each case to help understand the circumstances. Those interested in additional detail are referred to four of the cases detailed in a special report of the Church Committee.[20]

The two cases not covered in depth by the Church Committee were the Guatemalan and Iranian incidents of the early 1950s. In each instance CIA was designated the action agency, its approach being to encourage and support indigenous elements opposed to the governments in question.

1. *Iran.* President Eisenhower became concerned with the deteriorating stability of Iran, accompanied by the strong organizational activity of the Soviet-controlled communist Tudeh Party that was working to exploit the opportunity for revolution. Iran's location, between the USSR to the north, and at the head of the Persian Gulf to the south, increased the sense of the strategic significance of the country, and its oil. Shortly after the fall of the Shah, Iranian military forces, with popular demonstrations in the streets of Teheran, overthrew Mossadeq's government. The Shah was returned to power.

2. *Guatemala.* President Eisenhower's concern in this case also was based on a combination of domestic deterioration and strategic concerns. The perceived far-left orientation of the Arbenz government—with considerable communist infiltration into policy positions—was made more ominous by rapid changes instituted in political and economic arrangements within the country. The conviction grew that Arbenz was pointing towards a Marxist resolution. Guatemala is strategically located in Central America, some 800 miles from the Panama Canal. It could serve as a base for further spread of communist ideology and influence to adjoining areas. These strategic considerations raised the general concern to a high level. However, a small insurgent force, bolstered by considerable propaganda, convinced Arbenz that he could not prevail, and he fled.

In these two instances the Eisenhower Administration acted in response to apparent threats to the stability of areas felt to have strategic significance for the United States. It moved to forestall developments that would be most difficult to reverse were they left to continue in the direction they appeared to be moving.

Eisenhower's understanding of the dangers in those two nations has been challenged since that time on interpretations of fact that differ from his. The apparently hostile forces then in existence were virtually eliminated, so threats to U.S. interests cannot be measured with certainty today and probably will remain the subject of disagreement. That organized communism did not become a serious threat for some three decades afterward speaks to one aspect of the matter, although the ensuing history of those nations has not been a progressive one. It doubtless is such post-coup experience that reinforces the reservations of those opposed to engaging in any such activities at all.

Part of the problem in cases such as these, in which retarded social and economic development dictates reform, is that the nations in question are the ones most likely to be vulnerable to communist subversion. U.S. policymakers have often concluded that the threat of communist revolution is a more compelling consideration than the alternative of inaction. Those who believe that action must be taken because inaction ensures a worsening of the situation point to Nicaragua, where a despotic government was opposed by a mix of reformers, businessmen, and communists. The United States stood aside, making it clear that it did not favor the incumbent government, which was overthrown. Then the independent noncommunists were eliminated from the new government, and Nicaragua began to export leftist revolution and violence to adjoining countries. Ultimately, Nicaragua became a destabilizing force in the area.

The other four cases are documented in detail in the Church Committee's study entitled *Alleged Assassination Plots*. They are summarized below.

1. *Chile*. President Nixon's concern over the significance of Allende's Marxist orientation and revolutionary intent was covered earlier in commenting on the Church Committee's introductory remarks about Covert Action. When CIA found itself unable to prevent Allende's election to the presidency in 1970, which might have involved a coup, that course of action was dropped. Nixon's 1970 appraisal of Allende seemed borne out by Allende's attack on his nation's social and economic structure in apparent preparation for a Marxist revolution.

Allende's death at the time of the 1973 coup by the Chilean military, followed by allegations of CIA involvement, brought the affair to the attention of the Church Committee in the context of its study of assassination plotting. As noted earlier, CIA was not involved in the 1973 coup, its 1970 exploration of some course of action that could have involved the Chilean military having aborted. One interesting historical footnote emphasizing blurred popular perceptions, was the statement attributed to Señora Allende when she left Chile following the 1973 coup, that her husband had died by his own hand.

2. *The Dominican Republic*. President Eisenhower believed the Trujillo regime to be a weak link in opposing the spread of communism in the Caribbean. As summarized by the Church Committee:

Trujillo's rule, always harsh and dictatorial, became more arbitrary during
the 1950s. As a result, the United States' image was increasingly tarnished
in the eyes of many Latin Americans.

Increasing American awareness of Trujillo's brutality and fear that it
would lead to a Castro type revolution caused United States' officials to
consider various plans to hasten his abdication or downfall.[21]

State Department and CIA officials dealt with Dominican opponents
of Trujillo, encouraging them to oust him. State Department records
make it clear that Department officials believed the only way the objective
could be realized was with Trujillo's death.[22] It also became apparent
that the Dominicans planning the coup felt the same way and planned
to kill him. This was known in the White House,[23] where the Kennedy
Administration had taken over the operation from the Eisenhower
Administration. No positive action was taken to modify the plans of
the coup group. Trujillo was killed in an ambush.

3. *South Vietnam.* Ngo Dinh Diem was installed as president of
South Vietnam following the Geneva Accords in 1954. This was done
with American support, for he was a nationalist figure untained by past
ties with the former colonial power, France. President Diem's early
achievements in drawing together the new nation and inaugurating social
reforms were impressive and encouraging. Then his early reforms lost
their impetus, and he became increasingly withdrawn and unresponsive
to American initiatives.

As the communists renewed their program of terror and war, and
as Diem's regime employed repressive measures against domestic dis-
sidents, many American officials came to believe that he did not have
the qualities needed so desperately for the demands that lay ahead.
President Kennedy, Ambassador Henry Cabot Lodge, and the Department
of State concluded that Diem should be replaced. Word was passed to
the South Vietnamese military, which had become opposed to Diem,
that if they moved against him the successor government would be
recognized by the United States.[24]

The CIA chief of station, who had proved less than enthusiastic
over the decision, was transferred on grounds of his association with
Diem's brother.[25] A military officer assigned to CIA was designated as
the go-between with the military.[26] The South Vietnamese army moved
against Diem in the presidential palace. He escaped with his brother
to a church, where they were captured. Both were killed.

4. *Cuba.* The Eisenhower and Kennedy programs to bring down
Fidel Castro and his government are considered in the next chapter, in
the context of paramilitary operations. In conjunction with the Bay of
Pigs, CIA sought the assassination of Castro. Because the criminal

syndicate—the Mafia—had access to Cuba at the time and was believed to have contact with persons close to Castro, their help was enlisted.[27] The plan to be conducted in conjunction with the Bay of Pigs operation of 1961, was called off when the invasion failed.[28]

The Kennedy Administration developed an intensive covert action program against Cuba to supplement its diplomatic efforts.[29] In the latter part of 1962, the earlier relationship with members of the Mafia was renewed and the plot to assassinate Castro reactivated.[30] It, too, made little progress, but was still being planned at the time of the Cuban missile crisis in October 1962. It was terminated in early 1963.[31]

While the record is clear that general programs against Castro's government were the result of presidential decision, it is not so clear about presidential awareness of the first plot to assassinate Castro. There is, however, considerable circumstantial evidence that the White House did know about the reactivated program of 1962.[32] In this respect, the Castro plot differs from the clear involvement of American presidents in the other operations summarized above. This point was the subject of considerable speculation during the various investigations, when an attempt was made to ascertain the extent and level of approval for these activities. This final question must remain unresolved, whatever the facts suggesting an answer.

In each of the above instances there was a presidential sense of grave national interest. The resulting decisions to change a foreign government were made at the highest level of the U.S. government. The role given to government agencies—usually with CIA as the primary instrument of action—was similarly the result of presidential decision. Rationales employed by the presidents are apparent, although the facts on which they based their decisions have been contested in some cases. Some critics would oppose such actions regardless of the facts.

As the legal considerations of intervention and counterintervention will be discussed in Chapter 18, they will not be dealt with in detail here. However, it would seem that policymakers who face decisions in these areas must be as certain as possible that perceived dangers are real, given that there always are unknowns, and that national interest is measurably important. Such a general statement of principle is probably too broad to satisfy some, for the circumstances surrounding a particular case cannot be spelled out in advance with much confidence. The best guarantee that decisions will be as wise as possible seems to rest in the procedures of the government.

The machinery in the National Security Council, where the President's advisers in the government are brought together to give their best advice, reinforces the likelihood of a valid and balanced judgment. One would hope that the procedures for reporting to the Congress reinforce the sobriety of such judgments, although they may introduce an additional element of uncertainty into the equation. But in all such cases, the judgment is not that of the intelligence agencies, which provide the best information they have on the situation in question and sometimes will be given a role in carrying out a decision.

ASSASSINATION

Coups d'états involve the likelihood of some level of violence, since incumbents are unlikely to leave office without some resistance. Even if not so planned, the key figures may lose their lives. When they do, whether planned or not, the issue of assassination comes up.

The Church Committee considered its review of this subject "an unpleasant duty,"[33] thus undoubtedly reflecting a general instinctive reaction of the American public to reject assassination as "a tool of foreign policy."[34] The committee, however, was aware that the issue could be complicated under certain circumstances. Aside from the extensive detail that it gathered on assassination planning and possibly related activities, it left aspects of the subject basically untouched.

Despite the Church Committee's categorical rejection of assassination as a tool of foreign policy, its final proposal took the form of a statute to ban assassination—except in time of war.[35] The rationale for the exception was not recorded, but it highlights the dilemmas facing those who apply general principles to international affairs. Without defining what constitutes peace, the committee's conclusion makes apparent, at least in this one area, that what is improper in time of peace can become acceptable in time of war. This sort of open-ended ambivalence seems to affect many when considering covert action, even in its less unattractive forms.

The Church Committee undertook to distinguish between intervention in its various forms, which includes coups that may result in the unplanned deaths of political leaders, and deliberate plans to assassinate someone. Its formulation of the issue was stated as follows: "Once methods of coercion and violence are chosen, the probability of loss of life is always present. There is, however, a significant difference between a coldblooded, targeted, intentional killing of an individual foreign leader and other forms of intervening in the affairs of foreign nations."[36] This presentation downgrades the cause-and-effect relationship of a general movement to overthrow a government and the casualties that may stem from it. Different persons may react to this conceptualization differently, but the committee's handling of it leaves the question somewhat unsettled. Not only was the subject an unpleasant one for the committee, but it seems to have proved more difficult than its general summary would suggest,

If we view the question somewhat more directly than the Church Committee felt able to do, it seems inevitable that an effort to overturn a hostile foreign government must rely on indigenous forces, which cannot be controlled with any degree of confidence.[37] The most conscientiously planned operation, intending to avoid the deaths of those to be removed, carries with it the clear risk that deaths will occur anyway. One must believe that most mature officials would recognize this. Broad policy decisions, however, tend to leave details for others to work out and may leave some basic policy implications untouched.

There is one additional aspect of the question that should be considered. That is the question of tyrannicide, and of the effect it may have on the thinking of policymakers. Those who accept literally the biblical injunction against killing will turn away from violence in any form that may produce deaths. Our domestic law is not so unequivocal in that it establishes different levels of culpability in taking the lives of others, including the acceptance of it in the event of self defense. Whatever the proper interpretation of the scripture, a theological concept has developed over the centuries, in which some Christian sects hold that "tyrannicide is defensible and right in circumstances where, if the oppressor were an alien, war would be justified, and provided that the grievance is considerable, that the circumstances offer no milder means of redress, and that the killing is not simply an act of revenge."[38] That summary is addressed to situations in which individuals may be justified in rising against a ruler exercising oppressive rule of their own country. The general principle is applicable in shaping national policy toward other governments, and it will be one factor in considerations over whether a foreign tyrant will be ousted. It is not irrelevant to observe that following World War II, the victors formed courts of law to try and punish senior leaders on the losing side, passing death sentences on some. The war was over, but some of the motivations remained.

During the Church Committee investigation, the question of assassination was debated among members of the committee's staff. Apparently it also was brought to the attention of committee members. One aspect of the issue, as discussed among the investigators, was whether any of them would have condoned assassinating Adolf Hitler. The question was that of balancing one man's life against the estimated 40 million who died under Germany's oppression of its own and conquered peoples, and in the war Hitler unloosed on the world. The Church Committee was unable to handle this difficult question in the context of its general attitude on the subject, and did not touch on it in its report. However, Senator Barry Goldwater raised the question rhetorically, without answering it, because he felt that it should have been faced:

> The Select Committee may be faced with a dilemma that cannot be resolved: tyrannicide. The appalling atrocities committed by Hitler and Stalin raise a question which may be unanswerable but which needs to be carefully examined because the human carnage they created cries out for it. Stated another way, should a President of the United States have the right to aid the destruction of either a Josef Stalin or Adolf Hitler in peacetime? Assassination during wartime does not seem to be at issue. Here we have a fundamental question which may have confronted Presidents in the past, and which could confront a future President.[39]

The Committee, as a whole, failed to treat this question, although it was recognized by members of its staff and by committee members. Awkward considerations arose that complicated treating the issue.

Respected past presidents of both political parties had sought the ouster of foreign governments. Those programs always carried the possibility of casualties, and in some instances there was positive knowledge of planned violence. In a few cases assassination was planned, with apparent knowledge at least among close advisers of those who were president at the time. Caution was a factor in the Church Committee members' handling of the issue.

In its final report, the Church Committee was to accept in principle the role of covert action in foreign policy. This involved the problem of inability to anticipate future events and the actions that then might seem necessary. But that sort of problem did not lend itself to the crisp, unequivocal conclusions that best serve the presentation of investigative reports by the Congress.

Even if one were to accept the principle of tyrannicide in the abstract, the difficult question would remain as to who would weigh the degree of wickedness of a specific tyrant, and at the same time evaluate the threat to national interest that may convince some future president to seek that tyrant's ouster. But this problem, too, is not amenable to legislative solution, beyond the existing provisions for the Executive-Legislative consultation and reporting already established.

The issue is not clearly resolved. As Senator Goldwater stated, it may not even be answerable. Such uncertainties affect the way in which a problem might be faced. The legislation recommended by the Church Committee on this point has not been enacted into law. Past directives forbid assassination, as does the Reagan Executive Order.[40] The present book such as can only emphasize the complexity of an issue such as this, without attempting to resolve it.

NOTES

1. The *Church Committee Report*, Book I, page 141, recorded uncritically a statement by former Secretary of Defense Clark Clifford: "The knowledge regarding such operations has become so widespread that our country has been accused of being responsible for practically every internal difficulty that has occurred in every country of the world." Numerous charges have been made of the U.S. responsibility for a wide variety of events with which the United States had no connection. Implicit in the Clifford comment is the thought that much of what is laid at the door of the United States was without basis in fact. Most of the charges appeared first in the foreign media, sometimes moving into the U.S. press when found newsworthy. No notice seems to have been given the role of Soviet propaganda in this phenomenon, either by Mr. Clifford or by the Church Committee.

2. See the related discussion in Chapter 19 of this book.

3. *Church Committee Report*, Book I, page 154.

4. Ibid., page 142.

5. *Covert Action in Chile 1963–1973*, Staff Report of the Select Committee to Study Governmental Operations with Respect to Intelligence Activities, United States Senate, 94th Congress, 1st Session, 1975, printed for use by the Select Committee, page 2.

6. Henry Kissinger, in *White House Years*, Little, Brown, Boston, 1979, page 658, characterized the study as "tendentious," opining that "there is no evidence that the authors of the report tried to weigh the concerns about an Allende victory that we felt so acutely at the time." Senator Goldwater was also very critical of the staff's approach. See *Church Committee Report*, Book I, page 578 ff.

Following the election, and Allende's taking office, CIA's Operational Directive (OD) for its Chile station, in addition to calling for support of democratic elements, provided that contacts be developed among Chilean military circles for possible future action. CIA had been prepared neither for the task given it in the 1970 election nor for the action ordered afterwards by the President. Now it was to develop a contingency capability if called on again. The Church Committee's inquiry found no progress on this task. See *Church Committee Report*, Book I, page 158. Had CIA been called on to carry out some major action, its resources for complying would have been limited with respect to ties with the military.

7. *Covert Action in Chile 1963–1973*, page 4.

8. Ibid., page 9.

9. Ibid., pages 9, 12.

10. *Church Committee Report*, Book I, page 579.

11. Ibid., page 580.

12. *Church Committee Report*, Book I, pages 578–585. See also *White House Years*, pages 654–657; and *Years of Upheaval*, by Henry Kissinger, Little, Brown, Boston, 1982, pages 374–377.

13. *Years of Upheaval*, page 375.

14. *Church Committee Report*, Book I, pages 580–583; *Years of Upheaval*, op. cit., pages 378–385, 391–394, 396–400.

15. *White House Years*, page 658. Kissinger gives what is probably the most detailed review by an "insider" on how developments in Allende's Chile moved toward a Communist dictatorship. Those wishing to review the subject in more detail will find the chapters in his two books fascinating reading. After reviewing the economic concessions made to Chile during the Allende regime, and Allende's attack on Chilean society, Kissinger observes: "Chilean democracy was 'destabilized' not by our actions but by Chile's constitutional President." See *Years of Upheaval*, pages 378–383.

16. Kissinger describes the decision to support the democratic parties and groups as follows: "The ominous developments in Chile in the first year of Allende's term . . . led us to reexamine our covert action program. No effort to promote a coup was considered. What we sought was to help the democratic parties and groups to resist Allende's systematic efforts to suppress them. Our aim was to keep the opposition groups alive so that they might compete in the various elections provided by the Chilean Constitution and ultimately in the next Presidential election in 1976" (*Years of Upheaval*, page 382). Kissinger's critics may question his statements as deceptive and self-serving, but his presentation of the events is impressive and convincing. Richard Nixon does not devote much space to the question, but he does mention briefly the moral considerations involved in helping those in the position of suffering Allende's program. See *The Memoirs of Richard Nixon*, Grosset & Dunlap, New York, 1978, pages 489–490. Although Nixon's statements may be criticized as self-serving, it is safe to say that his account is an accurate reflection of his best judgment at the time.

17. *A Time to Heal*, by Gerald R. Ford, Harper & Row/Reader's Digest Association, Inc., New York, 1979, page 345.

18. Ibid., Pages 345–346.

19. *Church Committee Report*, Book I, page 154.

20. *Alleged Assassination Plots Involving Foreign Leaders: An Interim Report of the Select Committee to Study Governmental Operations with Respect to Intelligence Activities*, U.S. Senate, 94th Congress, 1st Session, Report No. 94–465, November 20, 1975 (cited hereafter as *Alleged Assassination Plots*).

21. *Alleged Assassination Plots*, page 191.

22. Ibid., page 195.

23. Ibid., pages 191, 262.

24. Ibid., pages 218–219.

25. *The Pentagon Papers*, Bantam Books, 1971, page 173; *The Lost Crusade*, by Chester L. Cooper, Dodd, Meade, New York, 1970, page 218.

26. *Alleged Assassination Plots*, pages 221–222.

27. Ibid., page 74.

28. Ibid., page 82.

29. Ibid., pages 139–147.

30. Ibid., page 83.

31. Ibid., page 84.

32. Ibid., pages 83, 123, 138, 141, 161. See also the comments made by Senators Baker and Goldwater, on pages 307–326, 342. Of course, Attorney General Robert Kennedy was deeply involved in the Cuban program (see page 140).

33. Ibid., page 2.

34. Ibid., pages 1, 257.

35. Ibid., pages 1, 283–284, 289–290.

36. Ibid., page 6.

37. Ibid., pages 256–257.

38. *The Oxford Dictionary of the Christian Church*, edited by F. L. Cross, Oxford University Press, London, New York, Toronto, 1958, page 383.

39. *Alleged Assassination Plots*, page 343.

40. *Executive Order 12333*, Section 2.11.

16

PARAMILITARY OPERATIONS

The tension between liberal values and the apparent needs of power in dealing with the enemies of those values is . . . expressed in a hundred ways. . . . Nowhere . . . was that tension more evident than in the area christened, in the early 1960s, "counterinsurgency."

—William Bundy[1]

The disparate character of the activities that were drawn together under the rubric of "covert action" was pointed out earlier. Perhaps the greatest disparity lies in the qualities required to develop and implement a sophisticated propaganda campaign on a complex political problem, in contrast to the talents and skills needed to conduct guerilla warfare or paramilitary operations. The latter activities have attracted the most public notice, especially since the Congress has taken to publicizing past paramilitary operations and exposing current ones.

Paramilitary activity may involve no more than supplying limited quantities of arms to groups working against antidemocratic elements. It may provide contingency plans for so-called stay-behind programs, which train and equip indigenous forces in areas that may be overrun, enabling them to conduct irregular warfare behind the lines of a future invader.[2] Or paramilitary activity may expand to support major military campaigns. This chapter deals with the larger operations.

The Church Committee felt that paramilitary activities "are an anomaly, if not an aberration, of covert action." It saw the activity as costly, controversial, and "difficult, if not impossible, to conceal."[3] Presumably the committee would not have opposed such activity on the grounds of cost and controversy alone. Its indictment on concealment seems to be based on a semantic misunderstanding of the word *covert*. The intended results of paramilitary operations are, in fact, overt, whether attributable or not.

It was noted earlier that the term *covert action* was the product of administrative convenience, without unique substantive significance. In any event, although most covert action will have an overt result, the secrecy that it hopes to achieve has to do with the absence of acknowledged sponsorship. The Boston Tea Party in 1774 was an overt act, but the identities of those involved remained for historians to reconstruct from imperfect sources. In modern international affairs this protection of sponsorship has been given the name "plausible denial." When denial of sponsorship serves policy purposes, the disclaimer makes it possible to keep open channels for formal diplomatic exchanges, a field in which artificial appearances often prevail. Official acknowledgment of an event may compromise diplomatic relations, but so long as a covert act is not publicized—so goes the concept—it is plausibly deniable.

The Church Committee also expressed the belief that paramilitary activity carries with it the possibility of escalating into major military commitments.[4] While theoretically correct, the same can be said of overt programs conducted by the U.S. Army's Special Forces, or even of normal diplomatic activity. In fact, more wars have come from failed diplomacy than from U.S. paramilitary activities. The underlying problem with this whole line of thought, however, is that U.S. involvement in paramilitary activity invariably comes in response to situations arising from the actions of others that raise an issue of U.S. national interest.

As the larger paramilitary programs have been most publicized, they are the ones that cause the most concern. Assuming that consensus can be reached that the United States has an interest in preventing a foreign attempt to destroy a friendly government, the question becomes one of whether the Congress can bring itself to act on that point and, if so, whether CIA alone can handle truly large operations. CIA's capabilities are limited by the lack of large logistical organizations and staffs, which are normal to the military services.

CIA's two best-known large paramilitary involvements are the Bay of Pigs invasion, and the Agency's operations in the Laotian theater of the Indo-China War. A brief review of each should help develop some sense of what is involved.

BAY OF PIGS

The Eisenhower and Kennedy administrations mounted major programs to weaken and overturn Fidel Castro's government. These programs involved major diplomatic initiatives, propaganda, economic measures, and clandestine programs. At some point in the process, President Eisenhower concluded that there was enough opposition to Castro among the Cuban people that an invasion by exiled Cubans could lead to a popular uprising that would sweep Castro from power, not unlike the disintegration that preceded Batista's fall.

Direction of the invasion was assigned to CIA, with military and other government staff personnel detailed for planning and support. Recognizing the chance of failure, the planners initially picked a site from which the invaders could withdraw if necessary into nearby mountainous terrain and continue to operate as externally supported insurgents.

When President Kennedy took office, he wanted to lower the "noise level" of the operation, and directed that its location be changed. The Department of State felt it important that, unlike the original site, the new one have an existing air strip. The new site became famous for the Bay of Pigs landing.[5]

There were many deficiencies in planning and support, tragically revealed in the defeat of the Cuban brigade. In retrospect, had basic evaluations been more realistic, the support might have been more nearly commensurate with the requirements, or the operation might have been cancelled. Some say there were too many voices in the plan, and others feel there were not enough, but no one contended that it failed for lack of a consensus—a cause of failure offered by the Church Committee for those Covert Action programs that did not succeed. Public opinion strongly supported the government's Cuban policy, and continued to do so as the Kennedy administration pressed ahead energetically with an anti-Castro program after the Bay of Pigs failure.

There have been a number of authoritative accounts of the Bay of Pigs, and the details will not be recounted here. But what would have been its significance had it succeeded? In other words, why, in the first place?

Had the Bay of Pigs operation overthrown Castro's government, a Soviet base less than 100 miles off the United States coast would have been eliminated. The significance of that fact became startlingly clear during the Cuban missile crisis in October 1962. Cuba now serves as a base for Soviet submarines and patrol aircraft and, reportedly, for a combat-ready Soviet brigade as well. Soviet aircraft, with a capability for delivering nuclear weapons, have been introduced into the Cuban air force, and Cuba serves as a strategic base for clandestine operations into Central and South America.

As President Kennedy summed up the Bay of Pigs, "victory has a hundred fathers, defeat is an orphan." If the reasons for undertaking the project were clear, its rationale became blurred by the mistakes and ultimate failure. The lasting lesson—if there is one—is that a major paramilitary program should not be undertaken, whether by the regular military establishment or by CIA, without adequate support. This lesson, in turn must be based on a realistic appraisal of the problem. One might apply the same reasoning to the abortive prisoner-rescue mission in Iran in 1981.

Many felt the Bay of Pigs dictated that CIA never be given a major military operation again. This one had proved beyond its capacities to manage successfully.

LIBYAN AIR RAID
U.S. AIR FORCE
USED

THE WAR IN SOUTHEAST ASIA—LAOS

Following the Geneva Accords in 1954, which settled for the time being the war in Indochina, there was a period when Laos was officially neutral. The communists and other elements shared in the government. By 1960 the communists had withdrawn and had taken on an independent role based in the two northeastern provinces. With North Vietnamese support, the Laotian communists began to expand their interests. The Kennedy administration was faced with a complex array of problems in helping the country maintain its stability and independence.[6] In 1961, the administration decided to give CIA "the management of a large military operation" there, in support of the noncommunist elements. At least one commentator believed the decision was taken

> because of the desire of the U.S. to minimize any violations of the Geneva Accords and later because of the State Department's conviction that U.S. military management of the resistance support effort would bring increasing difficulties of political control and very possibly would inevitably lead to pressure to commit American combat forces.[7]

CIA's primary role was that of in-country logistical support of the Laotian military forces, which spread its people from northwest Laos to the lower panhandle in the south. The problems proved to be more than just military logistics. When the Meos were forced to evacuate the Plaine Des Jarres, support for all of their people became part of the task. U.S. governmental participation was extensive. The Agency for International Development (AID) provided all manner of community support to the Laotians. The Department of Defense participated in the logistical task outside Laos. U.S. military aircraft flew missions in the northern area, including airlifting some Laotians on military operations. Commercial air lines under contract to AID and CIA carried out endless supply missions throughout the country. The ambassador in Vientiane was actively engaged in detailed direction of the operation. As was not the case in the Bay of Pigs operation, U.S. governmental resources and support were adequate and it was possible to develop the organization to handle it.

Laotian forces supported by the U.S. government achieved their main mission of holding the Laotian communists, supported by North Vietnam, away from the main population centers of the country. It was not believed feasible, however, to prevent the North Vietnamese from using eastern Laos as a transit route to, and a base area for, military operations against South Vietnam and into Cambodia. There were only limited forays by Laotian troops to interdict the so-called Ho Chi Minh Trail.

Because of political considerations, CIA was assigned the task of supporting a large military operation—a war. For other reasons, it might have been preferable for the U.S. military to be given the task, but CIA was able to handle it effectively with strong governmental support. If large military operations preferably should be assigned to the military, the occasion may recur when policymakers again will settle on a paramilitary approach. In that case, adequate resources and support are the essential ingredients for success once the decision is taken.

In fact, CIA did not have enough people available for the Laos program. It was necessary then, as has been the case from time to time since then, to employ additional personnel on relatively short-term contracts. Retired senior noncommissioned officers and former junior commissioned officers were hired for the Laos operation. In any event, when the U.S. withdrawal occurred in 1973, the Laotians were left to their own devices. South Vietnam collapsed in 1975, and Laos went with it.

In the early 1970s, the present author visited a small CIA post "up country" in Laos, where a number of young staff officers were assigned, amidst the relatively primitive living conditions of the local villagers. As often happens in times of war, periods of considerable activity alternated with those of relative inactivity. During periods of low activity, the young CIA officers launched their own private Peace Corps effort. They obtained literature on the subject and helped the villagers dig deep wells, construct sanitary drainage, and build fish ponds. To their embarrassment, the CIA men found themselves being approached for the kind of advice traditionally provided by the village elders. In deference to the established social structure, those seeking advice were directed as gently as possible to their elders. This heart-warming incident merely emphasizes the basic qualities of the average American who finds himself or herself in a foreign environment in which there is a constructive role to play—an interesting projection of the American sense of global service to a local opportunity for improving the lot of those who, in this case, were being defended against a foreign tyranny.

EL SALVADOR AND NICARAGUA

As this is being written, the media are filled with the political controversy over the Reagan administration's policy toward Central America and the Caribbean. Although the larger issue is regional in nature, the current focus has been on Nicaragua and El Salvador, whereby the former has been supporting an armed insurgency against the latter. The situation is worth examining, as it illustrates the pitfalls awaiting the conduct of policy in the unconventional situations that often lead to covert action programs.

U.S. policy was supportive of the anti-Somoza forces in the revolutionary period, when they were representative of a broad cross-section of the Nicaraguan populace. When Somoza fell, the United States gave interim economic aid and followed with support for significant international credit.[8] As the new government took power it excluded the noncommunists from the ruling body, and familiar forms of communist authoritarian control were instituted. An early turn toward Cuban and Soviet alignment was followed by a major military buildup, with equipment and guidance from those sources as well as growing support for armed insurgency in the area. El Salvador, progressing in the democratization of its government and society since 1979, became the main target of the Nicaraguan-supported insurgency.[9] The Carter administration began to reduce its support, and the successor Reagan administration found itself facing what it judged to be a move to extend Soviet influence and policy into the area. The intelligence showing strong Soviet and Cuban support was extensive.

The proximity of Guatemala to the Panama Canal had been a factor in President Eisenhower's decision in 1954 to oppose the Arbenz regime. It was viewed then as posing the imminent establishment of a communist base in the region, and as providing a point from which military strikes against the Panama Canal could be launched. Nicaragua, several hundred miles closer to the canal, and evidencing considerable hostility toward the United States—with Soviet and Cuban alignment—presented the same issue, in more modern terms. As one observer noted: "More than half of all U.S. seaborne trade passes through the Caribbean Basin, including half of the U.S. crude oil imports. In a European crisis, supplies for U.S. allies would also pass through the region."[10] This point was emphasized by the Cuban/Soviet-supported coup that took over little Grenada, followed by steps to make it into an important military bastion that would extend communist military capabilities in the area. The dramatic military operation in 1983 to save Grenada was but a part of the broader policy the Reagan administration had been developing.

The so-called Caribbean Initiative of Reagan envisioned a major economic aid program in the area, directed at the endemic backwardness that plagues the societies there. Military support for Honduras, deemed a future target of Nicaragua, developed rapidly. El Salvador received special attention in both economic and military aid, as its reformist government worked at breaking the cycle of corruption and repression of the former rightist regime.[11] Napoleon Duarte has now won two important elections in this program, but his government remains under attack by the revolutionaries. As his retrained military has increased its effectiveness, and as Nicaraguan aid seems reduced for the time being in the face of the rising threat of U.S. involvement, cautious optimism is appropriate. But the basic issue remains alive.

The Reagan Administration, viewing Nicaraguan support for the terrorist insurgency in El Salvador, decided to add to its program support for the various exile groups known as the "Contras," organized to oppose the Nicaraguan regime. As with the anti-Somoza movement earlier, these groups consist of a broad cross-section of the Nicaraguan people, including former anti-Somoza leaders who feel that the revolution was "stolen" by the communists.

CIA was assigned to provide support for the Contras, by covert means. The initial objective was to interdict the movement of arms from Nicaragua, across Honduras, to the insurgents in El Salvador. As must be recognized in such cases, the Contras have their own agenda and control will be a continuing problem. The Church Committee made this point in its earlier studies.[12] The Contras aim at ousting the communists, and President Reagan in one of his rhetorical moments seemed to support that objective.

Two incidents drew dramatic attention to the covert program. First, ports in Nicaragua from which arms were being shipped along the coast to the insurgents in El Salvador were mined. The Congress (the House of Representatives in early 1984 and the Senate, after a series of postponements, in March) was informed of this development. When the mining became public, members of the intelligence oversight committees, challenged in terms of violation of international law, disclaimed any knowledge of it. When it was made clear that the Congress had been informed, there were complaints that the information had not been sufficiently emphasized and that it was badly timed. An administration spokesman commented on the broader issue as follows: "Under international law, we have the right to help them [the Salvadorans] undertake offensive action in pursuit of a defensive policy."[13] The administration decided not to contest the issue in the International Court on the stated grounds, among others, that to prove its case would compromise intelligence sources and methods. There was a general negative public reaction to that decision.

At some point the CIA concluded that the Contras were using excessive force in their forays into Nicaragua. Seeking guidelines to control this activity, a U.S. Army Special Forces manual for guerilla warfare, prepared during the Kennedy administration, was sent to the field, where it was translated under the supervision of a CIA contract employee. Apparently it was not reviewed in Washington. One section of the pamphlet, on psychological warfare, outlined a procedure for removing local officials in public ceremonies. In the process of translation, the term *neutralize* was used in such a way that it could have been interpreted as meaning that assassination was appropriate. That brief section in the ninety-page pamphlet gained considerable publicity, and the U.S. Senate Select Committee on Intelligence issued a strong criticism of CIA's management and control of the program.[14]

The publicity of the mining of the four harbors and the incident involving the manual, combined with the remarks by President Reagan about making the Nicaraguan government say "uncle," crystallized into criticism of a covert program to overthrow a government. Lost along the way was the original reason for the program. The shift in public and congressional opinion is an interesting phenomenon that future policymakers, and those who implement policy, should bear in mind.

It seems clear that there were flaws in CIA's management and control of the program, whatever the general purposes of the activity. And the President's somewhat cavalier remarks did nothing to retrieve public support for the program. Although the Congress has neither repudiated the President's broader Caribbean Initiative nor barred economic and military aid to El Salvador and Honduras, it is not inconceivable that political perceptions could move away from such a program if the President is unable to restructure his approach and public presentation. For the moment it appears that the Congress is not prepared to support a covert program against Nicaragua, even though that country is viewed as an aggressor by the President. In fact, the Congress seems to support legislation that extends to Nicaragua, as a matter of U.S. law, a right against retaliation that does not exist under international law for aggressor nations.

With the apparent failure of the Reagan administration to retain congressional support for the exile forces, the major covert action feature of the program seems over for the time being. Following a new mission to Moscow by the Nicaraguan leader in April 1985, Reagan declared economic sanctions against the country. The general situation can only be observed at the present writing, before events have reached their culmination and history has made its eventual judgments. In this connection, intelligence involvement seems to be limited for the present to the role of intelligence collection.

COUNTERINSURGENCY AND COUNTERTERRORISM

Programs to counter armed, communist-dominated insurrections came to be known during the Kennedy administration as counterinsurgency. Usually such insurgencies had passed through a period of political organization, accompanied by the ugly and disruptive terrorism directed at society in general that has become so familiar. As pointed out in the chapter on counterintelligence, in settled societies terrorist acts are handled by security forces (the FBI in the United States) and the police. Should the revolutionary program evolve into organized military operations, it becomes a form of armed insurgency that the incumbent government must meet with some countering action, if it is to preserve itself.

Organized terrorism is an established part of armed insurrection, which is generally directed against formal institutions of the society under attack, in contrast to the more random incidents characterizing pre-insurgency terrorism. Dealing with terrorism that is part of an armed insurgency involves many of the techniques of counterintelligence. However, the environment is different, and the techniques must be adapted to the situation. An excellent description of counterintelligence operations in a paramilitary situation can be found in William Colby's book, *Honorable Men*.[15] A brief summary of this activity is useful.

In nonmilitary situations, the first step in counterintelligence work is identification of the opposition. As information is gathered it is analyzed as a basis for planning operations. In a counterinsurgency situation, in which the enemy usually employs some form of clandestine organization, counterintelligence has the same basic problem, but different techniques are employed. It is necessary to capture the enemy to gather knowledge about the organization. Working through indigenous elements—as is usual in counterinsurgency programs—teams of specially trained personnel undertake missions for the express purpose of taking captives. By interrogating prisoners, these teams are able to identify those on the other side, their organization, and their locations. This information then becomes the basis for operations against them.

There is sometimes room for disagreement between the intelligence people and the military. The first group may wish to delay action until the enemy network is thoroughly known; to attack often results in a reorganization of the net, and work on analysis must then start anew. By contrast, the military is often impatient to strike.

Whatever the general problem, the United States will continue to be confronted with insurgencies around the world. Each, by itself, may not seem a matter of major significance. But on a cumulative basis over time, such insurgencies become a serious phenomenon that must be faced. If such insurgencies are to be dealt with when U.S. action seems appropriate, they must be recognized and acted on before the situation is beyond retrieval. As one authority described the long-term situation:

> Despite heavy camouflage, Soviet-sponsored "wars of national liberation" have been exposed in such diverse locations as Chad, Lebanon, Namibia, Oman, South Africa, Sudan, Thailand, and Zimbabwe. The dangerous magnitude of involvement with insurgencies must be understood by Americans who shape or influence our policy.[16]

That authority went on to quote the new Soviet constitution, which states: "The Soviet Union is committed to strengthening the position of world socialism, of supporting the struggles of peoples for national liberation and social progress."

Former DCI Colby, speaking before the Church Committee, observed that in some crises the United States has been faced with two alternatives short of nuclear war: sending in the Marines or doing nothing. He clearly felt that supporting counterinsurgency programs can sometimes provide an alternative.

Where possible future counterinsurgency operations are concerned, both political and operational factors need to be taken into account. The Congress is not an institution in the usual sense, with dependable continuity and straight-line thinking. Political appearances often become as important as the substance of the issues at hand, and ambivalence may be their product. Partisanship sometimes influences policy and is often blind to national interest.

Given that the success of CIA's programs depends in great part on secrecy, the Agency suffers the burden of being assigned covert action programs that, more than ever, are likely to be the subject of negative publicity emanating from no less a source than the Congress. There long have been many in CIA who would prefer paramilitary operations to be assigned elsewhere, especially if they are large operations. But an unbroken succession of national administrations from Truman through Reagan has turned to CIA to carry out such programs in the sort of difficult situations that our time in history produces.

The Department of Defense's Rapid Deployment Force (RDF) is the formal organization of the military services intended to handle brush fires, and it clearly is limited to that sort of situation. The Army's Special Forces are being restored to the position they had during the

Kennedy administration, and there is no reason that their training could not include some of the relationships that CIA has had in the past with foreign forces engaged in counterintelligence activities. Nevertheless, situations will continue to occur in which CIA's clandestine experience makes it an optimum instrument of national policy. Of course, cooperation in the field between the Special Forces and CIA has worked in the past—especially in Vietnam[17]—and could provide a partial solution in future situations. Joint planning is a real possibility, and, reportedly, steps are being taken in the Department of Defense to coordinate the special elements of the various military services. But whatever the future decisions and arrangements may be, paramilitary operations should not be undertaken unless they are adequately supported and unencumbered by inflexible legislative restrictions. Broad strategy had best be worked out between the Legislative and Executive branches, with publicity limited to an irreducible minimum.

NOTES

1. *The Counterinsurgency Era*, by Douglas S. Blaufarb, Free Press, New York, 1977, page x.
2. *Honorable Men: My Life in the CIA*, by William E. Colby, Simon & Schuster, New York, 1978, pages 82–85.
3. *Church Committee Report*, Book I, page 154.
4. Ibid.
5. *Bay of Pigs*, by Peter Wyden, Simon & Schuster, New York, 1979, pages 90, 100–101.
6. *Kennedy*, by Theodore Sorensen, Simon & Schuster, New York, 1979, pages 639–648.
7. *The Counterinsurgency Era*, page 147. The entire chapter on the Laotian problem (pages 128–168) provides a succinct summary of a large story. Former DCI Colby's view of the Laotian operation, and the problem it posed by virtue of being conducted by an organization that operates in "secret," can be found in *Honorable Men*, pages 191–202. Colby felt that: "a large scale paramilitary operation does not fit the secret budget and policy procedures of CIA."
8. *Strategic Survey 1979*, The International Institute for Strategic Studies (Chronologies), London, 1980, page 137.
9. "Central America," by Clete Di Giovanni, Jr., and Alexander Kruger, *Washington Quarterly*, Summer 1980, pages 176–178.
10. *Guatemala: A Complex Scenario*, by Louis S. Segesvary, CSIS Significant Issues Series, Vol. 6, No. 3, Center for Strategic International Studies, Georgetown University, Washington, D.C., 1984, page 2.
11. A summary of the progress of the Duarte regime after 1979 is given by former Ambassador Robert White in an article in the *Center Magazine*, Center for the Study of Democratic Institutions, November/December 1981, pages 7–8.

12. *Alleged Assassination Plots*, pages 256–257.

13. *Time*, 10 December 1984, page 43.

14. See *Washington Post*, 31 October 1984; and *Wall Street Journal*, 2 November 1984. See also "CIA Manual Traced to Vietnam Era," by Philip Taubman, New York Times News Service, printed in *Courier-Journal*, Louisville (Ky.), 29 October 1984. See also "CIA Will Discipline 'Low-Level' Workers Involved in Manual," by David Hoffman, *Washington Post*, 11 November 1984.

15. *Honorable Men*, pages 266–271. The chapter in which the counterintelligence work is described also treats the wider responsibilities of the much-maligned Phoenix program. Colby stated during the war that the program silenced some 60,000 authentic communist operatives—a claim received by the media with some skepticism. Afterward, Colby's statements were confirmed by top communists in Vietnam. See *Vietnam*, by Stanley Karnow, Viking Press, New York, 1983, page 602.

16. *The Third Option*, by Theodore Shackley, McGraw-Hill/Reader's Digest Press, New York, 1981, page 23.

17. *Honorable Men*, pages 166, 169, 173, 219.

Part Three

CONSIDERATIONS AFFECTING INTELLIGENCE

17

INTELLIGENCE UNDER AMERICAN LAW

A government of laws. . . .

The legality of U.S. government intelligence activities was commented on extensively in the 1970s, by both the media and the various investigative bodies that conducted inquiries into the general subject. The Executive branch of the government had long accepted the basic legality of the activities in question, as had congresses of the past, but a new generation on the Hill challenged this view. An imaginative range of assertions was advanced during that period concerning the basic legal authority for many intelligence activities. Most of the questions were handled, in one way or another, in reports of the investigative bodies, with subsequent congressional action seeming to have disposed of the remainder.

Some of the answers to questions raised during the investigations would seem, today, to be so apparent that further discussion should be unnecessary. However, the issues were raised in such dramatic form, both in the media and other literature, that one using reference material from the 1970s might conclude that the whole subject remains open. Therefore, the issue of legality will be addressed in some detail. One still finds recurring press commentary that apparently is based on inaccurate presentations made more than a decade ago. It is almost impossible to treat the subject without reference to the issues emphasized in the 1970s. Perhaps a point and counterpoint approach for considering this matter will serve to highlight the issues involved and help clarify the way in which they were resolved and how they stand.

Technical legal arguments advanced against the underlying authority for some intelligence activities often were mixed with basic opposition to the activities themselves in any form, legal or not. Advocacy sometimes seemed to infect the purportedly objective legal views devised to argue the issue. Some of the dramatic publicity of the times reflected this view, thus also affecting the tone of public commentary. One example—not precisely a legal point—is the recurring appearance in the media of a statement by Senator Frank Church made in 1975, early in the investigation by the Senate committee that he chaired, in which he characterized CIA as a "rogue elephant." The senator contended that the Agency operated out of control of the government, raising the inference that, in some way, its activities were illegal. The fact that the final report of his committee found the charge to be untrue, which he confirmed when confronted by the press, seems not to have found as prominent a place in the media as did the initial statements.[1] In addition, one still sees the editorial language that first appeared in news stories published by the *New York Times* in late December 1974, alleging "massive" surveillance of U.S. citizens by CIA, inside the United States, allegedly in violation of its legislative charter. Those two stories, more than anything else, started the move toward the investigations that began in 1975. Yet the first of these stories has been discredited for its gross distortions and imbalance,[2] whereas the second was completely untrue.[3]

One point should be noted at the outset. The United States Congress has left the basic statutory framework for the U.S. intelligence organizations essentially as it had stood for many years. The same basic missions assigned these organizations over the years by an unbroken succession of national administrations remain intact. Previous congresses, which knew in general, if not in detail, what was involved in the intelligence operations, seem to have had their actions ratified by a more recent congress, which, in 1980, declined to enact a variety of restrictive and detailed legislation that had been prepared by the critics of intelligence.

Always subject to some evolution given changing times and requirements, as well as the perceptions of national leadership, the basic framework and nature of U.S. Intelligence Community organizations and programs has been remarkably constant over the years. The reason for this is that they serve the needs of our time. Whatever the future adjustments, and whatever reorganizations and realignments there may be, the basic missions and functions will continue essentially as they have been, until there is a change in the nature of the world in which we live.

Chapter 3 reviewed the process by which the CIA legislative charter took shape, with respect to both the limitations on security activities within the United States and the intelligence collection activities that were understood thoroughly by the Congress to be part of the organization's mission. The early addition by the National Security Council of covert action to the new Agency's tasks was described. Each of these three areas of activity became the subject of challenges to CIA's authority. They will be discussed in the following sections.

CIA'S DOMESTIC ROLE

The provision limiting CIA's role in internal security matters became the basis for charges that CIA was denied *any* functions in the United States. At least some of those advancing this view seem not to have been familiar with the actual language of the statute, much less with its background. Although this view recurs from time to time, it has no serious support any longer; nevertheless, its repetition contributes to an uneasy reservation about the activities CIA is authorized to engage in.

In Chapter 3 it was noted that the language pertinent to CIA's domestic role arose from questions of bureaucratic jurisdiction, at least at first. Nevertheless, allocation of responsibilities, especially between the CIA and the FBI, required further arrangement when overlaps of interest and authority occurred. Legislative attempts to fix everything by means of intricate language often fall to earth. Just as the distinction between Departmental Intelligence and National Intelligence proved less than perfect, so did the limitations of jurisdiction in this instance. The FBI and CIA did work out jurisdictional arrangements, informally at first, with a more formal agreement in 1966.[4] The FBI retained primary jurisdiction over domestic counterintelligence, the field of activity in question. The CIA was required to coordinate with the Bureau when some special situation inside the United States presented the question of how it should be handled. The military services, while not subjected to the statutory limitations of CIA in this respect, also had to coordinate with the Bureau.

Without reference to the original reason for the 1947 limitation, critics of CIA sought to interpret the language so as to bar CIA from all activities inside the United States, and not just those listed in the 1947 Act. This view received so much circulation in the media that the Rockefeller Commission felt it necessary to comment on the subject rather specifically. One can infer from the treatment in the Rockefeller report the nature of some of the assertions that had been made on this point:

> Although Congress contemplated that the focus of the CIA would be on foreign intelligence, it understood that some of its activities would be conducted within the United States. The CIA necessarily maintains its headquarters here, procures logistical support, recruits and trains employees,

tests equipment, and conducts other domestic activities in support of its foreign intelligence mission. It makes necessary investigations in the United States to maintain the security of its facilities and personnel. Additionally, it has been understood from the beginning that the CIA is permitted to collect foreign intelligence—that is, information concerning foreign capabilities, intentions, and activities from American citizens within this country by overt means.[5]

The Rockefeller Commission's report also addressed the question of CIA's operational activity with reference to foreign nationals "temporarily within the United States." Such activities are in coordination with the FBI. The Rockefeller Commission stated it thus:[6] "These activities appear to be directed entirely to the production of foreign intelligence and to be within the authority of the CIA." The Senate's Church Committee discussed these clandestine domestic activities without taking issue with their basic nature.[7]

It is clear that CIA engages in proper foreign intelligence activities inside the United States. Congress knew this when it passed the 1947 Act. There are limitations in the 1947 Act, however, and these must be observed; but they are not to be interpreted narrowly or applied unreasonably.

CIA'S INTELLIGENCE COLLECTION

The 1947 Act makes no specific reference to collection of intelligence by CIA. The reason for that, as recorded in the *Church Committee Report*, was based in part on the Executive branch's reluctance to make collection a matter of official public record, which inclusion in legislation would have accomplished.[8] Critics of CIA clandestine collection activities used the resulting absence of an express provision as a basis for challenging any collection activities by the CIA. The Rockefeller Commission spoke on the issue as follows:

Some witnesses during the Congressional hearings [on the 1947 Act] opposed giving CIA any responsibility for collection of intelligence and urged that the authority of the National Security Council to assign additional functions to the CIA be deleted so that the CIA could not collect intelligence. *The Congress did not agree.* Although two congressmen expressed disapproval of any CIA collection, the general provisions were not challenged during the floor debates. They remain in the statute as authority for the CIA to collect intelligence at the direction of the National Security Council. (Emphasis added.)[9]

The Church Committee, facing the same set of arguments, made the following statement on the subject:

> The language of the National Security Act, its legislative history, and the post-enactment interpretation by the Congress itself indicates that the Act can legitimately be construed as authorizing clandestine collection by the CIA. The Select Committee's record shows that the legislating committees of the House and Senate intended for the Act to authorize the Agency to engage in espionage.[10]

Both investigating groups felt that clarity would be served if the 1947 Act were amended specifically to authorize the CIA to collect intelligence, regardless of how clear that provision already was by normal standards. The generic word *collect* seems to be broad enough to serve the purpose, without opening the U.S. Government to propaganda attacks for acknowledging that it engages in espionage. Such legislation has not been enacted, having been lost along with unacceptable proposals rejected by the Congress in 1980. Whatever the benefits of clarification, it is certain that the Congress intended for CIA to engage in intelligence collection, and it does so under the authority of the 1947 Act and by direction of the NSC.

CIA AND COVERT ACTION

Covert action is one area that led to a challenge of CIA's legal right to engage in any action programs. The term is essentially one of convenience that emerged in the 1960s as a means of gathering a variety of disparate activities under one administrative umbrella for the purpose of financial management. It has been defined variously, but the definitions always leave something to be desired because of the different activities carried on under the name. One definition attributed to CIA by the *Church Committee Report* is as useful as most: "clandestine activity designed to influence foreign governments, events, organizations, or persons in support of the United States foreign policy conducted in such a manner that the involvement of the U.S. government is not apparent."[11]

More recently, the term *special activities* has been used—in the Intelligence Oversight Act of 1980, and in EO 12333—in lieu of *covert action*, partly to provide a euphemism for an activity that had acquired some notoriety because of controversies over some covert programs. It is a bland term that connotes the separation of some activities from the usual realm of intelligence work. This discussion will emphasize the legal issues inasmuch as covert action was discussed in depth in earlier chapters. Some general background is useful, however.

During World War II, the Office of Strategic Services (OSS) conducted special operations referred to as unconventional warfare, generally falling into two subject areas: Political and Psychological Warfare (PP) and Paramilitary Warfare (PM). These operations had other names, as well, but the two just mentioned have survived. PP encompassed such activities as radio broadcasts, propaganda leaflets, and programs intended to demoralize the enemy by political activities, whereas PM involved sabotage, guerilla operations, and other means of violence. Those elements of the OSS that engaged in this latter activity were transferred to the U.S. Army in late 1945.[12]

Various wartime studies of a new intelligence structure, particularly those by Ferdinand Eberstadt and Robert Lovett, made no mention of these special activities. The transfer to the Army of those elements of OSS engaged in paramilitary activities indicates that they were not contemplated as part of a postwar organization, nor is there any indication that they were considered in the process of enacting the National Security Act of 1947. That is not to say that special intelligence operations were not being considered elsewhere in the government. The wartime Coordinating Committee of the Departments of State, War and Navy (SWNCC) had begun to address the question of Soviet aggression in Europe and the Middle East, and had already made proposals for covert programs to counter them.[13]

One might note the phenomenon of independent momentum in separate courses of bureaucratic action, each pursuing its own purpose. Initial planning for the 1947 national security legislation had preceded both development and recognition of Soviet postwar expansionist policy. The process of devising lasting national security machinery for peacetime had foreseen neither the Cold War that was to come nor the requirements it would place on U.S. policy, much less what the instruments of that policy would be. The need to counter Soviet expansion was recognized elsewhere in the government but was not included in the processing of the 1947 Act. Yet, at the first meeting of the new National Security Council in December 1947, a directive was issued to develop a program of clandestine activity to meet Soviet expansionism. CIA was singled out as the "logical agency to conduct such operations."[14] The following June, as awareness of the situation developed, the NSC broadened CIA's mission in the field, apparently assuming that the function was being assigned under NSC authority in the 1947 Act to give CIA "other functions and duties."[15]

The CIG General Counsel—when the matter was under study—recorded reservations about relying on that section of the 1947 Act used by the NSC as authority for assigning these covert missions to CIA. His opinion at the time was this: "It is our conclusion, therefore, that neither M.O. [morale operations] nor S.O. [special operations] should be undertaken by CIA without previously informing Congress and obtaining its approval of the functions and the expenditure of funds for those purposes."[16]

Whatever the sequence of cause and effect, in early April 1948 the DCI testified before CIA's oversight committee, reporting that CIA already had been involved in supporting moderate political forces against communist elements in a West European election, and that it was encountering security problems in acquiring certain materials such as weapons silencers and explosives (for use in unspecified circumstances).[17] There can be no question that the activities involved Political and Psychological operations (PP) and Paramilitary operations (PM). There could have been no misunderstanding because of the description that was given, unconcealed by bureaucratic jargon. No reference was made to something that later came to be known as *covert action*, as that phrase had not yet emerged.

The occasion for this candid testimony was the request by CIA for additional legislation granting it authority to protect the security of its clandestine activities, which might have been revealed by exposure to normal government accounting and reporting procedures. In a very real sense, this was the enabling legislation that had been mentioned during the process of enactment of the 1947 Act, with special features because of the nature of the work. The Congress, knowing what it was that had to be protected—a part of which later came to be known as covert action—passed the Central Intelligence Agency Act of 1949, to give CIA the protection and authority it needed for those activities.[18]

The fact of knowing approval is quite clear. The literal-minded may contend that legislative approval for protection of known categories of activity does not, of itself, constitute explicit or specific approval of those activities, and that it therefore has not been authorized. Yet, over the years CIA returned many times to its oversight committees in the Congress, requesting financial support for its various clandestine activities, both espionage and covert action. The Congress responded with the sort of support that is most meaningful in government—appropriations—fully aware of the activities for which the money would be spent.

In 1962, the CIA General Counsel—the same man who had stated his reservations in 1947 about engaging in covert activities without congressional approval—wrote:

Congress has continued over the years since 1947 to appropriate funds for the conduct of such covert activities. We understand that the existence of such covert activities has been reported on a number of occasions to the leadership of both houses, and to members of the subcommittees of the Armed Services and Appropriations Committees of both houses. It can be said that the Congress as a whole knows that money is appropriated to CIA and knows generally that a portion of it goes for clandestine activities, although knowledge of specific activities is restricted to the group specified above and occasional other members of Congress briefed for specific purposes. In effect, therefore, CIA has for many years had general fund approval from the Congress to carry on covert cold-war activities, which the Executive Branch has the authority and responsibility to direct.

It is well-established that appropriations for administrative action of which Congress has been informed amount to ratification of or acquiescence in such action. (A number of U.S. Supreme Court cases are cited). Since the circumstances effectively prevent the Congress from making an express and detailed appropriation for the activities of the CIA, the general knowledge of the Congress, and specific knowledge of responsible committee members . . . are sufficient to render this principle applicable [with further legal citations].[19]

The authors of the *Church Committee Report* took issue with this, arguing that "the whole Congress" did not, in fact, know.[20] It must be kept in mind that, during the period in question, the Congress had elected to organize itself under the leadership of a handful of powerful political figures who personally handled many decisions under the authority delegated to them. Whether that fact constituted a dubious delegation of responsibility by the members can be argued, but the fact that they did so is undeniable. That is the way Congress organized itself.[21] A later congress might change the law and practice for the future, but it cannot rewrite the record or deny the acts of those earlier congresses. Imagine the chaos if all the legislation shepherded through by those powerful committee chairmen was declared not to be the law.

In principle, "the whole Congress" was on notice through its chosen leaders and representatives, and legally can be considered as knowing. Beyond that, it was generally known that CIA had been given primary responsibility for contesting Soviet subversive activities around the world. The press during that period quoted members of the Congress to that effect from time to time. It is interesting to note that in the time since the Congress has reorganized its oversight of intelligence activities, it has institutionalized the secrecy that previously was practiced by individual leaders. The contention regarding widespread knowledge has subsided.

Relevant to this discussion is a set of actions taken in the Congress that revealing something of the congressional perceptions in effect prior to the investigations of 1975–1976. In 1974 Representative Michael

Harrington's version of secret testimony to the Congress by DCI Colby on CIA's role in Chile found its way into the press. Misrepresenting Colby's testimony, Harrington gave new currency to the word *destabilize*, alleging that to be Colby's characterization of CIA's function in Chile.[22] The House Committee confronted Harrington, extracting a reluctant admission that the charges were incorrect. However, the charges did lead to moves in both houses of the Congress.

Following Harrington's "revelation," Representative Elizabeth Holtzman proposed the following legislation in September 1974: "After September 30, 1974, none of the funds appropriated under this joint resolution may be expended by the Central Intelligence Agency for the purpose of undermining or destabilizing the government of any foreign country."[23]

That proposal was defeated. It was followed by this proposal made by Senator James Abourezk:

Illegal activities in foreign countries—(a) no funds made available under this or any other law may be used by any agency of the United States Government to carry out any activity within any foreign country which violates or is intended to encourage violation of, the laws of the United States or of such countries.

(b) The provisions of this section should not be construed to prohibit the use of such funds to carry out any activity necessary to the security of the United States which is intended solely to gather intelligence information.[24]

That, too, failed. New legislation was proposed in December 1974 by Senator Harold Hughes and Representative Leo Ryan as an amendment to the Foreign Assistance Act, as follows:

Limitations on intelligence activities—(a) no funds appropriated under the authority of this or any other Act may be expended by or in behalf of the Central Intelligence Agency for operations in foreign countries, other than activities intended solely for obtaining necessary intelligence, unless and until the President finds that each such operation is important to the national security of the United States and reports, in a timely fashion, a description and scope of such operation to the appropriate committees of the Congress, including the Committee on Foreign Relations of the United States Senate and the Committee on Foreign Affairs of the United States House of Representatives. (b) The provisions of subsection (a) of this section shall not apply during military operations initiated by the United States under a declaration of war approved by the Congress or an exercise of powers by the President under the War Powers Resolution.[25]

This proposal, which came to be known as the Hughes-Ryan Amendment, became law.

In these three developments certain facts stand out. First, the Congress declined to accept the Holtzman and Abourezk proposals, which would have brought an end to at least some of CIA's covert action programs abroad (Holtzman) or to all government-sponsored covert action programs (Abourezk). Second, the Congress did approve a new and formal structuring for the reporting of covert action programs to the Congress in place of the less institutionalized practice of the past.

The Church Committee is literally correct in stating that the Hughes-Ryan Amendment "does not on its face provide any new authority for the President or the CIA."[26] This amendment did, however, recognize what already was known to be going on, under the long-standing approvals of past Congresses; it also specified the manner in which the activities were to be reported to the Congress in the future.

The Hughes-Ryan Amendment did present problems in practice. The Executive branch felt that the prescribed reporting procedure involved too much exposure of sensitive operations to too many individuals. CIA already reported to its then-established oversight committees, the Armed Services Committees of the two houses, as well as the Appropriations Committees of both houses. As a result of Hughes-Ryan, two more committees were added to these four—the Foreign Affairs and Foreign Relations committees. Following the investigations, when each house established a special committee for oversight of intelligence, the total was raised to eight committees, including their members and staffs.

In 1980, when the supporters of extensive new legislation failed to attract enough support for their proposal to pass, the Congress did agree to enact the Intelligence Oversight Act of 1980, which replaced the Hughes-Ryan Amendment, as well as providing that the oversight committees be kept "fully and currently informed of all intelligence activities." This, of course, would include covert action programs. The new Act reduced the onerous reporting load from eight to two committees, extended the reporting obligation to all government programs as well as to those of CIA, and tightened the reporting requirements from a "timely fashion" to advance notice, with special provisions for handling especially sensitive activities.

Hughes-Ryan preceded the investigations, while the 1980 Act followed them by several years. The two acts have at least two things in common. They both recognize the existence of the covert action (special activities) programs of the United States government, and they both formalize or institutionalize the procedures for reporting them to the Congress.

Related not to the legal status of covert action, but to its more general place in the government's policy resources, the final judgment of the Church Committee was significant. The committee was uncomfortable with many aspects of covert action, and worried over what to do about it. Its conclusion was phrased as follows:

> Given the open and democratic assumptions on which our government is based, the Committee gave serious consideration to proposing a total ban on *all* forms of covert action. The Committee has concluded, however, that the United States should maintain the option of reacting in the future to a grave, unforeseen threat to United States national security through covert means.[27] (Original emphasis.)

The legal status of covert action among the instruments of national action no longer can be questioned seriously, and the practical requirement for it seems well established. The issue seems to have been resolved by the Congress, in its actions over the years. It has endorsed retention of the capability for covert action in the name of national security and provided procedures for reporting such action to the Congress. If it becomes the general view that more specific authority is required beyond that of the 1980 Act, the time may come when legislation for that purpose will be enacted. Until that time, it is clear that the general legal status of covert action/special activities is well established.

Although covert action is legal under U.S. law, individual programs of the Executive branch are subject to congressional review. Just as the Congress saw fit to terminate support for the anticommunist forces fighting Soviet and Cuban-supported Marxist forces for control of Angola, it has the power to prohibit programs in Central America directed against the spread of communism there. Whatever the rationale for such action, that is the way the governmental system is arranged.

COUNTERINTELLIGENCE

Counterintelligence activities have produced a number of controversial incidents. Some clearly involved violation of the law. Others, though legal, became the subject of debate because they involved U.S. citizens as objects of government surveillance.

Some of the problems of counterintelligence have arisen because, by definition, it is concerned with foreign intelligence operatives engaged in clandestine operations against the United States. Those foreign agents rely on U.S. citizens who have been entrusted with national secrets. Counterintelligence agents must try to identify involved Americans, thus leading to what the media sometimes has referred to as "spying on

Americans" (see Chapter 13). Assuming that overly aggressive conduct can be kept in hand, the issue considered here is that of basic legality.

There has been very little specific legislation on counterintelligence as such. There are legislation and court decisions that buttress the role of the FBI in domestic intelligence. The Internal Security Act of 1950— passed over President Truman's veto—reinforces the FBI's special role in this respect. Further, the Communist Control Act of 1954 specified that the Communist party was "not entitled to any of the rights, privileges, and immunities attendant upon legal bodies created under the jurisdiction of the laws of the United States." This Act opened the Communist party to surveillance by the FBI. In 1956 the Supreme Court recognized the role of the FBI intelligence activities aimed at "Communist seditious activities," although the Court seems to have narrowed the application of the Act in overturning conviction of second-level communist leaders.[28]

The Church Committee did not develop the same extended legal arguments on counterintelligence that it advanced on the subject of CIA's espionage and covert action. It did touch on the question briefly as follows:

> The legislative history of the 1947 Act and the 1949 Central Intelligence Act recognizes that the CIA would perform training and other functions in the United States in support of its overseas intelligence efforts.
>
> Like foreign intelligence, the term "counterintelligence" is not dealt with explicitly in the 1947 Act. In the broad sense, however, counterintelligence may be viewed as one facet of "foreign intelligence activities."
>
> . . . Although it was not expressly addressed by the Congress during the passage of the 1947 Act, it is hard to imagine, for example, that foreign intelligence collection was implicitly authorized [as the Committee report acknowledged elsewhere to be the case], but that the Congress precluded CIA efforts *abroad* to ascertain hostile threats to the security of its own operations or to learn about enemy espionage (original emphasis).[29]

Similarly, the Church Committee did not contest general counterintelligence activities by the military services, although it expressed the opinion that they lacked specific legislative authority. In stating this view, the committee failed to consider the provisions of the National Security Act of 1947 that extended broad if unspecified authority to the military services for intelligence activity, as noted earlier. Instead, the Committee concentrated on specific instances in which the manner of conducting various operations was questioned, as distinguished from the question of whether counterintelligence itself is a proper function.[30]

Concerned with methods, the Congress did, in 1978, enact the Foreign Intelligence Surveillance Act, which established procedures for issuing warrants for electronic surveillance and activities associated with that work.[31] But the counterintelligence mission itself has not been challenged and remains essentially intact. It is an accepted part of the business of intelligence organizations, with the FBI, the three military services, and CIA sharing the mission in various ways.

NOTES

1. *Church Committee Report*, Book I, pages 427, 587. A recent example of the perpetuation of this notion can be found in a book review in the *Political Science Quarterly*, Vol. 97, No. 4, Winter 1982-1983, page 706.

2. *Honorable Men: My Life in the CIA*, by William Colby, Simon & Schuster, New York, 1978, pages 391–392, 425. See also *Rockefeller Commission Report*, pages 9–10.

3. *Rockefeller Commission Report*, page 221.

4. *Church Committee Report*, Book II, page 97.

5. *Rockefeller Commission Report*, page 11.

6. Ibid., page 221.

7. *Church Committee Report*, Book I, page 438; Book VI, page 261.

8. Ibid., pages 129 and 485 and footnote 47 on page 486. In addition, there was some concern expressed about stirring up additional controversy over the main issue of the 1947 Act—that of unification of the armed services. The *Church Committee Report*, Book IV, page 15, states this aspect of the question as follows: "Under the Act, CIA's mission was only loosely defined, since the efforts to thrash out the CIA's duties in specific terms would have contributed to the tension surrounding the unification of the services. . . . The Act did not alter the functions of the CIG. Clandestine collection, overt collection, production of national current intelligence, and inter-agency coordination for national estimates continued, and the personnel and internal structure remained the same."

Whatever the questions raised by those challenging the various authorities of CIA, the Congress knew of the activities already under way, and that they would be continued. These activities included both overt and clandestine collection of intelligence. The *Rockefeller Commission Report*, at page 11, summarized emergence of the later issue as follows: "[The] apparent statutory ambiguity, although not posing problems in practice, has troubled members of the public who read the statute without having the benefit of the legislative history and the instructions to the CIA from the National Security Council."

9. *Rockefeller Commission Report*, page 51.

10. *Church Committee Report*, Book I, page 127. See also pages 128–131.

11. Ibid., page 475.

12. Ibid., page 483.

13. Ibid., page 490; Book IV, Pages 26–27.

14. Ibid., page 490.

15. Ibid., pages 490–491.

16. Ibid., page 489.

17. Ibid., page 494.

18. Ibid., page 133.

19. Ibid., page 497.

20. Ibid., pages 498–499.

21. Ibid., page 150; Book IV, pages 39–40, 51–55. See also *Honorable Men*, pages 182–183. Former DCI Colby was heard on numerous occasions to say that CIA always had done business with the Congress the way the Congress organized itself to do business, and always stood ready to do so.

22. *Inquiry into Matters Regarding Classified Testimony Taken on April 22, 1974, Concerning the CIA and Chile,* Hearing before the Special Subcommittee on Intelligence of the Committee on Armed Services, 93rd Congress, Second Session, September 25, 1974, Government Printing Office, Washington, D.C., 1975. Representative Harrington had been given access to secret testimony by DCI Colby, subject to the committee rules requiring that there be no release of information from that testimony except on committee decision. Mr. Harrington had written a letter that found its way into the press, in which he (Harrington) stated that CIA had the mission to "in Mr. Colby's words 'destabilize' the Allende government." Representative Harrington was called before the committee to testify under oath on his possible violation of rules. See pages 23–24, where the following exchange is recorded:

> *Mr. Bob Wilson.* I want to commend you for bringing a new word into our vocabulary—destabilize. I have read the total testimony and never once was that word used. You invented it and it is beautiful.
>
> *Mr. Harrington.* That is to the real credit of Bill Colby.
>
> *Mr. Slatinshek.* If I may interrupt at this point, Mr. Colby did not use the word "destabilize" in his testimony.
>
> *Mr. Bob Wilson.* That is what I said.
>
> *Mr. Slatinshek.* In fact, he wrote a letter to the *New York Times* to this effect.
>
> *Mr. Harrington.* That is what I said.
>
> *Mr. Slatinshek.* I am sorry I missed that.

The word was too catchy to not be attractive to the media, which has used it ever since. And Soviet propaganda uses it regularly in its activities as well.

23. *Church Committee Report*, Book I, pages 502–503.

24. Ibid., page 504.

25. Ibid., page 506.

26. Ibid.

27. Ibid., page 159.

28. *Church Committee Report*, Book II, page 41.

29. *Church Committee Report*, Book III, page 684.

30. Ibid., pages 793 ff.

31. *Title 50, U.S. Code*, Sections 1801–1811.

18

INTELLIGENCE UNDER INTERNATIONAL LAW

. . . and the law of nations.

International law on the relations between nations usually involves two general types of principles. One reflects the preferences for how nations should deal with one another and is usually found in declarations of principles by international bodies such as the United Nations. The other comes into play when one nation operates outside the general principles, violating the integrity and society of another—openly, or clandestinely through surrogates. In the latter case the question becomes that of what the nation under attack or its allies are entitled to do in response. The application of these principles must relate to the facts.

The intelligence activities of nations are a part of the foreign policy practice of the major nations of the world. It is clear from the investigations of the Presidential Commission and the U.S. Senate that U.S. intelligence activities are firmly based in U.S. policy and law. The reports of the investigative bodies did not provide the same extensive discussions on questions of international law. The Rockefeller Commission was concerned primarily with CIA activities inside the United States, whereas the Church Committee barely touched on issues of international law. It commented only generally on espionage under international law as follows: "It is generally illegal in the countries against which it is aimed, but its widespread practice by nation states makes the status of espionage under international law ambiguous."[1] This is the lone comment on the point in the Church Committee's report. It is noted that the laws of a nation that make espionage conducted against it illegal, within that country, are not international law. They are matters of domestic law, although some contend that they should have the same status as international law. Beyond that the *Church Committee Report* seems to

271

suggest that, in the real world, international practice accepts espionage. Although that seems to be the case, there are contrary views.

One view is that essentially all clandestine intelligence activities are illegal under international law. This position appears to be based on international documents produced during the post–World War II period. The opposing view, of course, is that clandestine activities are legal in the broad sense, having long been accepted in practice. As a practical matter, the first of these views has given way before the second in the face of the international situation.

Following World War II, with the objective of completing the structure of peace and order that the United Nations was to provide, attempts were made to codify a coherent body of legal principle. Those principles have the ring of progress when they are accepted, but when they are out of step with the challenges of the times, or when they conflict with the interests of sovereign states, they tend to be inadequate for the task. In the postwar era, Soviet expansionist policy destroyed what chance there may have been for establishing a real foundation for an effective system of international law and order.

It is not necessary to emphasize in any detail that international law is a subject of uncertain standards. It is not really analagous to the domestic law of nations, which is enforced by police authorities and courts. In some areas of international commercial affairs there is a form of law, but in major political matters the exercise of national sovereignty presents more demanding imperatives. Scholars may postulate theories and argue for ideals, but events and national interests dictate how nations will conduct themselves. To recognize this is not cynicism but acknowledgment of a fact of life.

This chapter will first summarize the basis for the view that secret intelligence operations have doubtful status at international law.

INSTITUTIONALIZED PRINCIPLES FOR THE CONDUCT OF NATIONS

Earlier objections to clandestine activities on the part of United States government agencies have been mentioned. Those reservations reflect basic beliefs about how nations should conduct themselves. A well-known scholar in the field, Quincy Wright, maintained in 1961 that various clandestine activities were in violation of international law. His key conclusion was that "in time of peace . . . espionage, and in fact, any penetration of the territory of a state by agents of another state in violation of local law, is also a violation of international law imposing a duty upon states to respect the territorial integrity and political independence of other states."[2] Although this excerpt addresses the specific question of espionage only, the principle would extend to include covert action as well. In any case, it serves to present the issue quite directly.

The Church Committee's brief comment on espionage under international law has been noted. On the subject of covert action, the committee seemed initially to lean toward Professor Wright's view, in observing that "many covert operations appear to violate our international treaty obligations and commitments."[3] However, the committee progressed to the conclusion (noted in Chapter 17) that covert action should be retained as an instrument of national security policy. Despite the committee's conclusion, the basis for the general reservations about both espionage and covert action was Article 2 of the United Nations Charter, which states:

> All members shall refrain in their international relations from the threat or use of force against the territorial integrity or political independence of any State, or in any other manner inconsistent with the purposes of the United Nations.

In 1965, consistent with Professor Wright's 1961 statement, the U.N. General Assembly elaborated the concept in a resolution:

> No State has the right to intervene, directly or indirectly, for any reason whatever, in the internal or external affairs of any other State. Consequently, armed intervention and all other forms of interference or attempted threats against the personality of the State or against its political, economic and cultural elements are condemned.

Similar language appears in Articles 18 and 19 of the Charter of the Organization of American States (OAS).

Again, in 1970, the General Assembly approved a Declaration of Principles of International Law, reiterating the proscription against threats and use of force, as set out in Article 2 and in the 1965 Resolution, stating that any such threats or use of force "are in violation of international law."

The foregoing principles are subject to the interpretation that they bar any involvement by one nation in the affairs of another, regardless of the circumstances. There are obvious exceptions to such an unqualified view. The most literal interpretation will not be read as barring the giving of requested assistance in the event of natural calamities, or economic aid, or even military support against an invasion. Though phrased so as to apply primarily to overt acts, the statement can be interpreted as pertinent to clandestine acts as well, given its reference to intervention "directly or indirectly." But no distinction is made between overt and covert forms of action, as a result of which the two would seem to have equal status. One is no better or worse than the other.

In addition to these declarations by the United Nations, in 1961 an international convention was completed in Vienna concerning diplomatic relations between nations. Certain protection was assured by host governments to the official installations of foreign nations, along with certain privileges for the diplomatic and consular personnel assigned to them. Article 41 of the agreement provides the following:

> 1. Without prejudice to their privileges and immunities [i.e., official representatives assigned to a foreign land], it is the duty of all persons enjoying such privileges and immunities to respect the laws and regulations of the receiving State. They also have the duty not to interfere in the internal affairs of that State.

> 2. All official business with the receiving State entrusted to the mission by the sending State shall be conducted with or through the Ministry of Foreign Affairs of the receiving State or such other ministry as may be agreed.

> 3. The premises of the mission must not be used in any manner incompatible with the functions of the mission as laid down by the present Convention or by other rules of general international law or by any special agreements in force between the sending and the receiving States.

The provisions of the Vienna Convention would appear, on their face, to preclude officially accredited representatives from one country to another from engaging in espionage or covert action. However, instead of promulgating new principles of international law, the Convention was largely a codification of existing practice, which was subject to the vagaries of the international climate. Further, whatever the force of law of the principles summarized earlier, the Vienna Convention was handled in such a way as to raise questions about its status as international law.[4]

In a larger sense, the effectiveness of all these principles depends very much on the environment in which they are to apply. The unique situation that developed following World War II, continuing to the present, became the major influence on the manner in which international affairs were to be conducted.

THE INTERNATIONAL ENVIRONMENT

The objective of world peace based on an application of codified rules of international conduct has considerable appeal. It is particularly attractive to Americans, imbued as they are with the principle of the rule of law. Unfortunately, the conditions necessary if such a system is to flourish have been denied by events. The record of the developments creating this situation is clear, as are the results at international law, in which the rules of society must relate to the state of society.

At the close of World War II, U.S. policymakers did not envision clearly the events that would follow. They could foresee a period of military occupation of the defeated nations. The performance of this responsibility occasioned a striking demonstration of uncommon generosity and enlightenment. The defeated lands were patched together and set on a new road. U.S. leaders envisioned an even larger task, that of international reconstruction, with the United States playing a leading role in restoring the vitality of other disrupted national systems, thereby helping to build the stability of a world at peace.

The rapid demobilization of the U.S. armed forces emphasized the peaceful purposes of the United States. In the four months following the end of the war in September 1945, nearly 6,000,000 uniformed men and women returned to civilian life.[5] The rate of demobilization continued apace. Interim programs for relief of the war-torn lands commenced while longer range plans were under development. The programs for reconstruction were for both friend and foe. U.S. initiatives were largely responsible for final agreement on establishing the United Nations, in the face of last minute Soviet reservations. Americans hoped that the U.N. would become the instrument of world order and stability. It was a period of high ideals and optimism.

The USSR, in contrast to the U.S., saw the postwar dislocations as an opportunity for vigorous exploitation to advance its national ambitions. It maintained its massive forces essentially intact, particularly in East Europe and in the Soviet zones of occupation in Germany and Austria. The presence of the Soviet Army was used to advance the USSR's long-range ambitions.

The expansionist nature of Soviet policy soon became evident. The USSR sought to annex the Iranian province of Azerbaijan, which had been occupied by Soviet forces during the war. Turkey was pressured for concessions along its border with the Soviet Union, and for special privileges in use of the Bosporus and Dardanelles waterway between the Mediterranean and the Black Seas. The new government of Greece came under attack by an externally supported communist armed insurrection. These latter two events led to extension of U.S. support to Greece and Turkey. That program, which focused on the eastern Mediterranean, became known as the Truman Doctrine and established a precedent for later response to Soviet expansionism. Soviet-supported factions in the East European nations maneuvered for control of the

governments there, with the large Soviet military force looming men-
acingly over it all. The important role of the Soviet Army in the
communization of Eastern Europe has been recorded in Soviet writings.[6]

By the end of 1948, the USSR had eliminated the last vestige of
noncommunist influence in the governments of Eastern Europe. Poland,
Czechoslovakia, Hungary, Romania, and Bulgaria shared the earlier fate
of Latvia, Esthonia, and Lithuania, which had been absorbed in 1939
following the cynical agreement between Nazi Germany and the USSR.
The Soviet occupation zone of Germany was cordoned off from the rest
of the German people and made into a separate country joined to the
Soviet Bloc. Although Albania and Yugoslavia succeeded in pursuing
their own form of communism, any facade of independence in the other
East European lands was destroyed by the ruthless suppression of
Hungary in 1956 and Czechoslovakia in 1968. The latter event produced
a formal ideological rationale in support of the action as being in defense
of "socialist systems." This came to be known in the West as the
Brezhnev Doctrine.

Early in this period, nations of Western Europe were subjected to
intensive, highly organized, and heavily financed campaigns of communist
subversion and disruption. Soviet-controlled international organizations
with national affiliates campaigned to install communist power in the
area.[7] Soviet leadership later acknowledged—somewhat ruefully, perhaps—that the failure to communize France and Italy at the time was
due to the absence of the Soviet Army from those areas.[8]

The Soviet-sponsored attack on South Korea in 1950 should have
banished any doubts on the part of those inclined to dismiss a calculated
Soviet policy of expansionism. The Cold War had become established
fact.

Revisionist historians have tried to assign to U.S. and other Western
powers much of the blame for failure of the peace, and fail it did.
Western leaders must acknowledge their mistakes; yet they were not
mistakes of original initiative but of response to aggressive Soviet policies.
Western policy was essentially reactive, with a considerable defensive
quality.

The West sought accommodation by negotiation and pursued political
avenues for implementing wartime agreements that called for restoration
of independence to the lands overrun by German troops. Without detailing
events, suffice it to say that the putative instrument of international
law—the United Nations—proved largely ineffectual. The UN functioned
in the early days of the Korean War primarily because the Soviet Union
and its satellite nations boycotted it and were not present to block the
action to unite against North Korean aggression.[9]

WESTERN RESPONSE TO SOVIET POLICY

Even before the Korean War the United Nations had proved unable to cope with the tensions resulting from Soviet policy. It was unable to establish an international peacekeeping force; it had no way of enforcing its general declarations of law and principle; and nations were obliged to rely on their own resources. What came to be known as the "West," in this so-called East-West confrontation, had been put on the defensive and it responded by resorting to old fashioned alliances.

The North Atlantic Treaty Organization (NATO) was formed in 1949 under Article 51 of the UN Charter, to organize against the Soviet threat. Article 51 authorized collective action by members. At one point the legality of NATO under Article 51 was questioned from the left and by some legal scholars on the grounds that collective action should be limited to response to actual attack, and then only after UN consideration and decision. Acceptance of that view would have barred advance planning among allies, even in the face of clear danger. This was not the last time that legalistic arguments were to be advanced against actions taken by Western nations in response to Soviet policy. Without yielding to such rationales, the Western nations resorted to traditional practice under long-standing international law—also justifiable under Article 51—and organized for their defense. Any support that had been attracted to the narrower interpretation of Article 51 seems to have subsided when the USSR and its East European allies formed the Warsaw Treaty Organization in 1955. Other regional defense alliances were formed, but they lacked the stability and staying power of NATO.

The underlying rationale for international defense arrangements is well established in international law. The right to self defense lies in the very nature of statehood. The following statement, consistent with numerous similar summations, puts it thus:

> The primary right of a state is clearly the integrity of its personality as a state, since the existence of the state is the necessary condition of any other rights that it may claim. At times [this right] is described as "national security," or as "the right of self-preservation," or the "right of self-defense," the "fundamental law," "the first law of nature," to which all other laws are subordinate.[10]

U.S. law supports this broad principle. The United States Supreme Court endorsed the general concept prior to the beginning of this century: "To preserve its independence, and give security against foreign aggression, and encroachment, is the highest duty of every nation, and to attain these ends nearly all other considerations are to be subordinate."[11]

It is central to the principle of self-defense that when a nation perceives danger it can take action under the concept of anticipatory defense.[12] Alliances and arming for defense are a natural part of such action.

Because international law accepts the perceptions of national leader as the basis for the courses of action they choose, it is useful to restate the way in which the Western leaders saw Soviet policy. First, they had a basic philosophical objection to the brutal system itself and to its extension to other nations. Further, the unremitting pressures of Soviet policy, in seeking to extend its influence and control to other lands, gave its policy a threatening quality. Concern was expressed over the long-range cumulative effect that extension of Soviet influence and control around the world would have on the vital interests of the noncommunist West.

Geopolitical considerations acquired new dimensions in the thinking of Western policymakers. A continuing accumulation by the USSR of satellite nations and client states around the world could give the Soviet Union the capability of launching major programs against the West. Such a threat gave numerous distant areas a new level of importance to the United States and its allies. Consider, for example, the problems likely to arise if all the oil-producing nations in the Middle East were to fall under Soviet domination. But even before these general concerns developed, massive Soviet ground forces poised in Eastern Europe were seen as a threat to Western Europe. Western responses were stimulated by that threat.

However one might describe modern international affairs, the word *peace* is hardly appropriate. This is recognized in general acceptance of the term *Cold War*. As Patrick Henry put it so pointedly many years ago, when debating British colonial policy prior to the outbreak of the Revolutionary War: "Gentlemen may cry peace, peace—but there is no peace!"[13] It was in response to a similarly uncertain situation that U.S. and other Western leaders developed policies for self defense. Not only did they rearm and form alliances in key areas, but they also devised an array of programs with which to meet far-flung Soviet initiatives. Among the instruments of Western security were clandestine intelligence operations. These included espionage to gain information on Soviet activities and on relevant world situations, and covert action programs to help resist Soviet subversion of the weaker and more vulnerable nations.

INTERVENTION AND COUNTERINTERVENTION

If the United States is to play an active role in international affairs, it will be confronted with situations it would prefer to avoid. Each situation will bring with it difficult decisions regarding whether or not to take action, and if so, what course seems most appropriate under the circumstances. Some action usually is unavoidable; depending on how one chooses to describe whatever is done, it is in some way an intervention in the situation at hand.

Unilateral intervention by a great power in the internal affairs of other nations is objectionable to most Americans. But not all intervention falls into that category. Nevertheless, when the word *intervention* is used to describe U.S. involvement, an indiscriminate, negative reflex often follows, regardless of the facts. Those who are critical of positive U.S. involvement tend to intensify their criticism when a policy includes some covert features. Some examples of the many forms of intervention will help establish a frame of reference for this discussion. U.S. assistance to help counter Soviet pressures on Iran, Turkey, and Greece was touched on earlier, as was U.S. assistance in rebuilding the economies and political stability of Western Europe, and U.S. leadership in the UN defense of South Korea. These larger programs often included covert features designed to deal with certain aspects of Soviet aggression.

Considered in Chapters 15 and 16 were a number of cases in which presidents decided to intervene, for reasons of national interest, in various situations around the world. In some instances the intervention was intended to defeat communist threats to the survival of weak governments. However controversial the separate instances, they represent in each case the best decision available at the time, in the light of contemporary perceptions and information then at hand.

Those who hoped that the Cold War of the 1940s to the 1960s had ended during détente must recognize that the Soviet Union supported the North Vietnamese during that time in their campaign to conquer not only South Vietnam but also Laos and Cambodia, all of which fell in 1975. Some believe that the second Cold War started in 1975, when the USSR extended its influence and power to Africa in Angola, Mozambique, and Ethiopia.[14] The United States did try to intervene in the Angolan affair, which the Congress stopped. The USSR's blatantly open aggression against Afghanistan differed only in the tactics used. In that latter case, even had the Carter administration been inclined to intervene openly, geography would have prevented it. As with the subjugation of Eastern Europe, the United States could only protest.

The communist success in capturing the Nicaraguan revolution and, then, in seeking to extend itself into El Salvador coincided with the attempt to make little Grenada into a strategic bastion in the Caribbean, as part of an obvious move to improve the foothold in the area that Cuba already provided. The United States did intervene decisively in Grenada, and it has been attempting to support the Salvadoran government against the externally supported insurrection there—not without some congressional opposition. However one views these various developments, it surely appears that the problem of Soviet expansionism remains; moreover, the question of what to do about it has become an important issue in the U.S. political system.

There are instances in which national consensus has supported some form of intervention even when national security is not immediately at stake. Whenever the United States tries to persuade other nations to observe more humane practices toward their citizens—surely a laudable goal—it interferes in their internal affairs. Friendly nations (e.g., Iran and Nicaragua, before their revolutions) felt the displeasure of basic U.S. liberalism. The USSR, not exactly an ally, has experienced U.S. pressure to liberalize its emigration policies, especially with respect to its Jewish citizens. Although the motivation behind these policies is understandable, they nevertheless raise the question of meddling in the affairs of others.

Even the laudable economic aid programs of the United States involve it directly in the internal affairs of other nations. U.S. policymakers have been reluctant to extend material support to economic development programs of other nations if that support does not promise some measurable contribution to their economic well-being. A condition of aid, therefore, often involves U.S. overview and approval of planning, followed by inspection of the actual use of aid. Critics of this approach describe it as having "strings attached," an attitude reinforced when concessions in foreign policy are added to the package. However reasonable this attitude may appear to Americans, it has rankled the sensitivities of some recipients who feel that it is only an excuse for a U.S. intrusion into their affairs.

The range of possible U.S. action is broad. It can involve simply a refusal to extend economic aid or to engage in special trade arrangements. Economic sanctions of a broader nature, for instance, are a form of interference with the policies and practices of other nations, especially when designed to achieve objectives bearing on internal conduct. The question arose most recently when the Reagan administration attempted to pressure the Soviet Union to ameliorate conditions imposed on the Polish people.

There is an ambivalence—even an inconsistency—on the part of some critics of U.S. foreign policy concerning this question. As mentioned earlier, former Secretary of State Henry Kissinger observed that those who criticized U.S. political and economic policies toward Chile in the 1970–1973 period advocated even stricter sanctions against Allende's successors.[15] Similarly, those who organized to criticize the human rights issue in Nicaragua prior to the fall of Somoza have been singularly silent—or defensive—concerning that country since then, despite grim reports of ensuing repression.

Whatever the forms of intrusion into the affairs of a nation, by overt courses of action, such intrusion seems an established feature of international practice. It is in the context of the so-called East-West contest that the question of clandestine activities arises.

Most of the nations included in the U.S. aid program have basic economic problems and retarded social systems that are vulnerable to communist exploitation. It is U.S. policy to improve economic conditions, encourage social progress, and contribute to internal stability. To reinforce stability during what must be a difficult evolutionary period, economic aid often includes some program of assistance to internal security forces, as noted earlier.

The hoped-for period of transition in these nations must be recognized as uneven and certainly less rapid than most Americans would want. The development of U.S.-style political practice is limited by many factors, not the least of which is the cultural tradition of the indigenous people. Economic development, and U.S. pressures, produce a number of new forces. Opposition elements emerge, and if the system does not find a place for them—or even if it does—they are subject to infiltration by leftist revolutionaries who will maneuver for control of the movements and who prefer violence for solving internal problems; orderly change does not serve their purpose. Depending on developments, U.S. policy-makers may find themselves faced with the problem of a country important enough to merit help in its development but moving instead toward the ragged edge of successful communist subversion and disintegration.

Soviet intervention exists in many forms, and its programs of subversion are widespread. The press has reported official estimates that the Soviet Union spends the equivalent of $200 million annually in support of "national liberation" movements,[16] in addition to the internal financial arrangements of the indigenous communist parties. The rate of Soviet investment scheduled for a given country can be increased dramatically if developments make it seem propitious to do so. This was the case in Angola, as noted earlier. When President Ford sought to increase aid to the noncommunist forces in Angola, the Congress barred that action on the grounds that it constituted intervention in the affairs of another country.[17] The basic nature of the issue was lost in controversies over details of how U.S. aid was to be given, and how CIA—the action agency in that case—was to disengage following the congressional action.

The difficulty of offsetting or countering an established revolutionary program is considerable. Such a policy is faced with the problem of establishing itself in an environment in which indigenous revolutionary forces are already present. In anticipation of such difficulties, the equipping and training of the security forces of a U.S. client is often part of an aid package. When the incumbent government has difficulty in holding its own, the issue of further involvement arises.

It is the USSR that picks the locales for expansion of its influence and power, making the weaker nations of the world the arena for such confrontations as may occur with the United States if the United States decides to intervene. If the United States decides to respond, the question is whether it will be overt, clandestine, or a mix of both. Typically it is both, with the balance between the two varying with the assessment of the problem. Although it is customary in the United States for some to view the question as though only their country engages in such action, in fact others have been similarly involved; both Western European nations and Third World nations have, indeed, acted to help defend the governments of smaller powers from subversion.[18] Such actions are not in violation of international law.

International law and practice, as a corollary to the right of self-defense, recognizes the general principle of acting to prevent unlawful intervention by one state in another state.[19] This principle provides the legal basis for action in countering the intervention of others—overt or covert—if legal reasons are required in this unhappy world. It is proper to think of this activity as counterintervention, akin to the countering character of counterintelligence and counterinsurgency.

The existence of a legal rationale for counterintervention will not reduce the objections of those who challenge such action in general, nor will it eliminate criticisms of past instances. Some early cases of clandestine U.S. activities in unstable nations with strong overtones of communist involvement have been criticized when communist influence failed to materialize afterward. In other instances, it did materialize when the countering action failed.

It is Soviet practice to disguise or conceal its hand, thus blurring the fact of its involvement in the first place. When the United States and other Western nations decide to engage in counterintervention, critics may seek to give that intervention a sinister character. Foreign policy is always open to some disagreement, but when a policy is misrepresented as involving unwarranted or illegal intervention in the affairs of another nation—regardless of the facts—the debate in a country such as the United States can become intense.

Whatever the wisdom of a chosen course of counterintervention, it has a place in international law and practice. Perhaps this country is tending toward abandonment of the option for clandestine counterintervention by reducing its capabilities to do so and by challenging the secrecy with which such activities must be conducted. But the need to counter the subversion of nations important to United States interests will recur. Although overt means of action are available—economic aid, military equipment and training of indigenous forces, and political initiatives in the United Nations—they often are limited in their effectiveness. Nevertheless, it is safe to say that in some future crisis, serious consideration will be given to the possibility of at least some clandestine operations in whatever course of action is selected.

NOTES

1. *Church Committee Report*, Book I, page 437.

2. Professor Wright's statement was introduced into the *Congressional Record* on 2 October 1974 by Senator Mark Hatfield.

3. *Church Committee Report*, Book I, page 142.

4. *The Codification of Public International Law*, by R. O. Dhokalia, Manchester University Press, England, 1970, page 314. That authority stated, in part: "It is unfortunate that the Convention has based the law of diplomatic immunity on the concept of reciprocity, which . . . in essence amounts to a denial of the existence of a rule of law and of legal duty. The insertion in the Convention itself of a unilateral right to vary its application . . . may encourage a tendency to generalize and perpetuate encroachment upon diplomatic immunity." Although the emphasis in that discussion is on diplomatic immunity under the Vienna Convention of 1961, the same line of reasoning applies to diplomatic responsibilities, in the context of the discussion in this book.

5. *Year of Decision*, by Harry S. Truman, Doubleday, New York, 1955, page 510.

6. Letter from the Central Committee of the Communist party of the Soviet Union to the Communist party of Yugoslavia, 4 May 1948. This letter cited the role of the Soviet Army in the communist success in Yugoslavia, observing that the absence of the army in France and Italy had contributed to the failure in those countries. See also "Liberation of Poland by Soviet Troops in 1944-45," by A. D. Bagreev, in the Soviet journal *Questions in History*, 28 June 1955. This concept of the role of the Soviet armed forces has continued into more current thinking. See *The Armed Forces of the USSR*, by Harriet Fast Scott and William F. Scott, Westview Press, Boulder, Colo., 1979, pages 56–59. Those who look to the past for possible courses of future action may find some illumination in the 1939 draft of the protocol between Nazi Germany and the USSR. Although the protocol was not formalized because of events, it did provide that "the area South of Batum and Baku in the general direction of the Persian Gulf is recognized as the focal point of the aspirations of the Soviet Union" (*Soviet Documents on Foreign Policy*, Vol. 3, page 478). Some might suggest that the Soviet Union's adventure in Afghanistan forty years later indicates the durability of its long-range strategic objectives.

7. Some of the story of this period, and the role given to CIA, is told in *Facing Reality*, by Cord Meyer, Harper & Row, New York, 1980, pages 94–138. See also *Church Committee Report*, Book I, pages 144–145, 179.

8. See Note 6, supra.

9. *The March of Democracy: The History of the United States*, Vol. 7, Record of 1949–1958. Charles Scribner's Sons, New York, pages 37–38.

10. *International Law*, 4th ed., by Charles G. Fenwick, Appleton-Century-Crofts, East Norwalk, Conn., 1965, page 271. See also *Elements of International Law*, 8th ed., by Henry Wheaton, Little, Brown, Boston, 1866, Part 2, Chapter 1, Section 61, for a general consideration of related issues.

11. *Chinese Exclusion Case*, 130 U.S. 581, 9 S. Ct. 623, 630, 1899.

12. *International Law*, page 274; Oppenheim's *International Law*, 7th ed., edited by H. Lauterpacht, Longman, New York, 1948, pages 265 ff.; *International Law*, by Charles C. Hyde, 2d ed., Little, Brown, Boston, 1945, page 247.

13. *Great Americans Speak*, edited by Frederick C. Packard, Jr., Charles Scribner's Sons, New York, 1948, page 4. Patrick Henry may have received some inspiration for his phrasing from the King James Bible, Jeremiah 6:14.

14. "Soviet War Has Little to Show for Cold War that Began in 1975," by Joseph C. Harsch, *Christian Science Monitor*, reprinted in the *Lexington Herald-Leader* (Kentucky), 2 December 1984.

15. See the discussion of Chile in Chapter 15.

16. "Terror: A Soviet Export," by Robert Moss, *New York Times*, 2 November 1980.

17. *Honorable Men*, pages 421–423; *Facing Reality*, pages 243–270; *The Third Option*, by Theodore Shackley, McGraw-Hill/Reader's Digest Press, New York, 1981, pages 125–140.

18. See "Coup and Counter-Coup," by Steven R. David, *Washington Quarterly*, Autumn 1982, pages 189–201.

19. See *International Law*, by Charles C. Hyde, pages 248–249. See also *International Law* by Charles G. Fenwick, pages 275 ff., for a general discussion of the question of one nation intervening in another when conditions appear to threaten the intervenor. Of special interest is *Intervention and Regional Security*, by Neil Macfarlane, International Institute for Strategic Studies, London, Spring 1985. At page 23 the following summary appears: "The UN General Assembly has on a number of occasions endorsed a prohibition of 'armed intervention' in internal conflicts. But General Assembly resolutions on the subject do not explicitly prohibit assistance to established governments. In this sense, they uphold what remains the predominant principle of international law; that the 'incumbent government is entitled to assistance from other states while rebels are not—at least until they have been accorded the status of belligerents.' Mainstream legal thinking on intervention is, therefore, selective in inhibiting interventionist behaviour; to the extent that states take it seriously, it constrains intervention against established regimes while permitting it in their support."

For a thorough discussion of what post–World War II legal principles were intended to achieve in the area of intervention and counterintervention, the problems encountered in trying to fit general principles to the actual situations, and how this matter should be viewed, see "The Right to Intervene," by Lloyd Cutler, in *Foreign Affairs*, Fall 1985, pages 96–112. For a discussion of considerations leading to counterinsurgency policies, see also *Special Operations in US Strategy*, edited by Frank R. Barnett, Hugh B. Tovar, and Richard H. Shultz, National Defense University Press/National Strategy Information Center, Washington, D.C., 1984, pages 64–65.

19

PRINCIPLES AND
STANDARDS OF CONDUCT

Gentlemen do not read each other's mail.
                    —Henry L. Stimson, 1929

The principles that guide a free society are reflected in its laws; in international affairs they color the nation's foreign policy. It is clear that the conduct of secret and clandestine intelligence operations is fixed in U.S. law, and it is established policy that these activities are an integral part of the management of national security and the conduct of foreign policy.

The standards and principles of conduct that do or should guide intelligence work have attracted varied comment over the years. Extremes range from those who oppose virtually all intelligence activity on the part of the U.S. government to those who feel that anything serving the purpose should be permitted. Prevailing standards and practice are well between the extremes, often varying with the importance and requirements of a given situation.

Basic issues of principle and standards seem generally settled for the present, but they are certain to be raised again in some form. The question of ethics in intelligence rests first on the broader subject of foreign affairs and national security, since the sole duty of intelligence is to support those important elements of national policy in our disordered world.

AN OVERVIEW OF THE SUBJECT

The remark at the head of this chapter attributed to Secretary of State Stimson highlights a visceral reservation held by some regarding intelligence activities in general and how they would prefer to conduct foreign policy. When Stimson became Secretary of State under President

Hoover, he learned of an activity supported by the Department of State known as "the Black Chamber." That activity involved the decoding and reading of the secret communications of other nations. Stimson ordered the support terminated, later giving as the basis for his action the judgment that "gentlemen do not read each other's mail." The person reporting the incident summarized Mr. Stimson's attitude as follows: "He regarded it as a low, snooping activity, a sneaking, spying, key-hole peering kind of dirty business, a violation of the principles of mutual trust upon which he conducted both his personal affairs and his foreign policy."[1]

The two military services and the Coast Guard obviously did not share the Secretary's view, as they continued the similar activities they were then conducting.[2] That action by the services ensured, when World War II came twelve years later, that the technical expertise for this specialized work existed. It was the successful deciphering of Japanese codes that enabled U.S. naval commanders to deploy forces for the Battle of Midway, credited with being the turning point of the war in the Pacific. Secretary Stimson, who returned to public service during the war as Secretary of War, is reputed to have become an avid consumer of this kind of intelligence. Mr. Stimson's personal and high-minded standards of the 1920s simply proved inapplicable to the situations confronting the United States from the 1940s on. The incident displayed with unusual clarity a basic aspect of the role of personal attitudes in the conduct of foreign affairs.

There is an important place in U.S. foreign policy for the application of ethical standards. Those who make U.S. foreign policy consider themselves guided by broad moral principle, as well as by valid national interest. As pointed out in Chapter 18, the first duty of a government is to protect the national interest, a responsibility not to be compromised by conflicting abstractions. Policymakers try to balance broad principle and necessary actions in each situation that must be addressed. It is not an easy task.

Discovering the best balance is important. When differences arise from an inability to agree on the balance between principle and practice, the divergence can become so marked as to obscure better courses of action that may lie between the extremes. Polarization of views tends to complicate rational solutions. In the heat of controversy, the contesting sides often tend to criticize not only one another's judgments but their moral principles as well. One example is the debate over the war in Southeast Asia. U.S. officials who decided on involvement in a war, to defend the noncommunist people of the area from imposition of a brutal dictatorship, subsequently were charged with waging a war of aggression, an immoral war. Those who opposed the war on what they judged to be moral grounds succeeded in bringing an end to U.S. involvement. They now are charged with blind support for aggression by the North Vietnamese, against not only the South Vietnamese but the Cambodians and Laotians as well. There is an irony in the tragic results, with both sides in the American debate accused of dubious guiding principles. Neither is likely to accept full blame for its contribution to the debacle. The situation does illustrate the difficulty of bringing to bear on complex international issues what otherwise might seem appropriate moral judgments. Worth considering briefly is the way in which different approaches can emerge from a society such as that of the United States, where a general consensus on conduct exists.

Various factors in the United States produce different approaches to major issues. Perhaps this is to be expected in a large and diverse land such as ours, whatever the general consensus. Different environments present different problems to the inhabitants, which in turn produce differing appreciations for how to meet challenging situations. There also is a social tradition that emphasizes attention to high principle. But this tradition is somewhat offset by an innate practical quality that values reality over ephemeral notions.

Abstract principle is generally subject to modifications in accommodating the requirements of daily life. There seems to be something of an unconscious acceptance of such accommodations, usually within generally sensed if undefined limits. Sometimes referred to as "situational ethics," the practice is based on the recognition, conscious or not, that what is wrong in one set of circumstances may be quite acceptable in another.

Beyond the geographical and sociological influences on differing attitudes toward conduct, there are some basic philosophical considerations that have their roots in our national history. The historian Page Smith, in the third volume of his history of the United States, *The Shaping of the Young Republic*, commented on the early development of a fundamental dichotomy that he saw in public philosophy—one that has expressed itself in American attitudes over the years. He observed that most of the founding fathers were adherents of the Christian faith. The prevailing concept at the time accepted the flawed nature of humankind, arising from the doctrine of original sin, and the purposes of life in this world in preparation for the next. In the minds of the founding fathers, one problem in writing the Constitution was that of providing for the liberties of the citizens and, at the same time, protecting them from their human shortcomings. They sought guidance in the experience of ancient Greece and republican Rome, finally designing our republican system with its distinctive checks and balances. Contrary to these considerations, in Page Smith's understanding of it, was the

European Enlightenment's optimistic and philosophical faith in mankind. This view was distinguished by an unqualified idealism involving democratic concepts, so appealing to most of us. Dr. Smith saw this idealism as having become the predominant force in American attitudes on public issues.

In considering the impact of the democratic approach on foreign affairs, Smith quotes Felix Gilbert, who observed that the American ethos tries to ensure that

> [there] should be no difference between the "moral principles" which rule the relations among the individuals and the "moral principles" which rule the relations among states. . . . Diplomacy should be "frank and open." Formal treaties would [then] be unnecessary. . . . Foreign policy and diplomacy . . . owed their importance to the fact that rulers followed false ideals and egoistic passions instead of reason. The logical consequence was that in a reformed world, based on reason, foreign policy and diplomacy would become unnecessary. . . . [T]he new world would be a world without diplomats.[3]

Dr. Smith does not argue it, but his presentation raises the dilemma that faces those whose general principles and absolute ideals must find a place in the real world. Such individuals invariably will collide with practical people who may be impatient with what strikes them as irrelevant application of abstract notions.

Page Smith's selection of Felix Gilbert's observation does serve to highlight the gap between abstract principle and reality. This gap can pose special problems, especially in the world of international affairs, if the standards and traditions of social conduct inside the United States are applied rigidly to the situations encountered among and within nations. George F. Kennan, considered a liberal intellectual, grappled with the issue in considering both morals and law. Speaking of U.S. policy in the context of that question, he said: "I see the most serious fault of our past policy formulation to lie in something that I might call the legalistic-moralistic approach to international problems."[4]

He attributes the compulsion to devise international agreements and institutions that would achieve a structure for international law and order—and reason, too, for that matter—to the belief that Anglo-Saxon concepts of law really can be made to work in some international system. In his view, some believed our constitutional system, contrived for the thirteen American colonies, to be adaptable to the needs and nature of other nations. He observes, more pointedly, that

> the American concept of world law ignores those means of international offense—those means of the projections of power and coercion over other

peoples—which by-pass institutional forms entirely or even exploit them against themselves: such things as ideological attack, intimidation, penetration, and disguised seizure of the institutional paraphernalia of national sovereignty. It ignores, in other words, the device of the puppet state and the set of techniques by which states can be converted into puppets with no formal violation of, or challenge to, the outward attributes of their sovereignty and their independence.[5]

Mr. Kennan seems to be saying that the usual American approach to law does not recognize, or provide for recognizing, attacks on sovereignty through other than overt aggression. It is fair to observe that this phenomenon is one of the reasons for a lack of clarity on the part of those who find it difficult to view subversion of a country as a basis for countering action.

At a later time, writing about how to apply one's personal standards to the relatively amoral international scene, Mr. Kennan had this to say:

We Americans have evolved certain concepts of a moral and ethical nature which we like to consider as being characteristic of the spirit of our civilization. I have never considered or meant to suggest that we should not be concerned for the observation of these concepts in the methods we select for the promulgation of our foreign policy. Let us, by all means, conduct ourselves at all times in such a way as to satisfy our own ideas of morality. But let us do this as a matter of obligation to ourselves, and not as a matter of obligation to others. Let us do it in order that we may be able to live easily with ourselves. But let us not assume that our moral values, based as they are on the specifics of our national tradition and the various religious outlooks represented in our country, necessarily have validity for people everywhere. In particular, let us not assume that the *purposes* of states, as distinct from the methods, are fit subjects for measurement in moral terms.[6] (Emphasis in original.)

In looking at an external milieu, different from the one in which we live, he observed the following:

Morality as a general criterion for the determination of the behavior of states and above all as a criterion for measuring and comparing the behavior of different states—no. Here other criteria, sadder, more limited, more practical, must be allowed to prevail.[7]

The problem becomes one of how to proceed, once the understanding is reached that our familiar standards at home frequently do not adapt to the standards of international life. The policies that our nation shapes and seeks to implement are to be judged as much by what needs to be done as by how it is to be done. Broad principles need not be betrayed in defending the nation's interest and advancing its cause. The fact remains that, in shaping a consensus in this country, general perceptions of right and wrong may collide head-on with the pragmatic approach of those concerned with solving knotty problems. Often, neither side will prevail absolutely.

Perhaps those who advance simple, if abstract, principles must find satisfaction in the tempering influence they have on those responsible for acting. And those who believe that direct action is required may find satisfaction in the fact that something is being done instead of marking time while philosophical concepts consume the time and energy of the body politic. Only occasionally does one extreme or the other fit the requirements of critical events. It is a happy occasion when both fit the case.

The genius of our political system has been its usual ability to find a balance in contested public issues. In periods of crisis, the need to find the mean quickly leaves less time for developing a consensus, when differences have arisen over how to proceed. Given the American penchant for solving problems and putting them behind us, it should not be surprising that the unending nature of the post–World War II crises, with their intractable character, have burdened the partnership between the Executive and Legislative branches of our government. Certainly the open-ended quality of this situation frustrates those who know that domestic problems are intensified as a result of the priorities of foreign affairs.

The virulent force produced by the mixing of traditional Russian expansionism with the revolutionary drive of so-called Marxist ideology has produced the Cold War, which cannot be blinked away. In responding to the Cold War, the United States and Western leaders have had to face the world as it is and not as we would like it to be. The resulting wide range of policies and programs to protect the environment in which Western society and values can endure includes secret intelligence activities. These activities will continue for the foreseeable future.

As pointed out earlier, the principle right and duty of a nation is to defend its interests. This has led U.S. policy to include a significant feature of what the French so gracefully term *real politique*, in which problems are dealt with as they are and not as one might prefer them to be. This is not a cynical approach to the responsibilities of foreign policy, but a pragmatic attempt to cope with the actual problems that beset the world in which it is our lot to be a leader of the West. It does not mean that action can follow any direction at will, disregarding all moral considerations. It merely recognizes the complexity of functioning in the sort of world that faces us.

The purpose of this brief philosophical detour is to examine the environment for which policy must be made, and to raise the question how policy decisions must be shaped to fit the conditions in which it is to be implemented. All this should be done with due attention to both the basic standards of our society and the practical requirements of policy. Just as quick judgments leading to dubious policies must be kept in mind, so must quick judgments of the standards to fit a given situation be weighed carefully to ensure that they are relevant to the facts. As with foreign policy, so will it be with that subordinate function of it—intelligence. The sole purpose of foreign intelligence lies in the domain of foreign affairs, and it must be judged in that context.

WHAT STANDARDS WERE EXPECTED
FOR INTELLIGENCE?

There apparently were no detailed considerations of standards of conduct when the National Security Act of 1947 became law. However, the general activities anticipated under that act, and the reservations that some held about them, were considered. Those opposing creation of the Central Intelligence Agency, including the authority given it, made it a matter of record.

Espionage relies on subverting the loyalties of some citizens of other nations. It was known that CIA's predecessor organization, the Central Intelligence Group, engaged in espionage and that the practice would continue. Counterintelligence, although barely touched on in the hearings, had received considerable publicity as the result of FBI activities during World War II. They involved acts to identify and block, or neutralize, hostile espionage against this country, including surveillance of those who supported the fascist principles of Germany and Italy. What became known as covert action—now known euphemistically as special activities—although not considered when the 1947 Act was passed, was outlined candidly to the Congress in 1948 when special security authority was sought in the Central Intelligence Agency Act of 1949. Covert operations were supported over the years and institutionalized by the Hughes-Ryan Amendment in 1974 and by the Intelligence Oversight Act of 1980. There was no misunderstanding as to what was involved, and the Congress accepted this fact in principle, in the face of vocal opposition from those who opposed such activities.

There were many unknowns in the 1940s. Had the Congress addressed the more detailed questions of conduct, it would have been hard-pressed to produce any reliable or relevant set of standards. Clark Clifford, an adviser to presidents over several administrations and Secretary of Defense under President Johnson, had been involved in drafting the 1947 Act. He described the uncertainties at the time as follows: "The law that was drawn in 1947 was of a general nature and properly so, because it was the first law of its kind. We were blazing a new trail."[8]

Speaking about that portion of the 1947 Act that stated CIA would do such other things as the NSC directed, in addition to those specified in the Act, Clifford further noted: "Because those of us who were assigned to this task and had the drafting responsibility were dealing with a new subject with practically no precedents, it was decided that the Act creating the Central Intelligence Agency should contain a 'catch-all' clause to provide for unforeseen contingencies."[9] Experience since then has only emphasized the unpredictability of events and the requirements they produce. The Congress, anticipating the unexpected, provided the authority to ensure that the government could act as needed in the world that was developing after World War II.

Congress did not involve itself in detailed questions of conduct, other than to approve the kinds of activities that had been opposed by some as a matter of principle. It appears to have avoided seizing the nettle in those early days. One member of Congress, Senator Leverett Saltonstall, with refreshing candor, revealed the early congressional attitude in speaking in 1956 on the relations between Congress and the CIA:

> It is not a question of reluctance on the part of CIA officials to speak to us. Instead, it is a question of our reluctance, if you will, to seek information and knowledge on subjects which I personally, as a member of Congress and as a citizen, would rather not have, unless I believed it to be my responsibility to have it because it might involve the lives of American citizens.[10]

Senator Saltonstall was a member of the Senate's oversight committee at the time. His statement indicates that what he knew in general led him to avoid wanting to know more. It reflected both his sense of the need for security and the simple fact that there *may* be more than he would care to know, whether that feeling was correct or not. It was not uncommon in CIA to hear officers comment on their offering to brief members of Congress about programs that later developed controversial aspects. Such offers often were declined, although strongly encouraging comments based on a general understanding of what was involved were often included.

Whatever the posture of the Congress, statements of members, appearing in the press from time to time, made clear the understanding that intelligence organizations had a special assignment to enter the fray with the Soviets. As the Church Committee described it, intelligence had a unique role to play in "the gray, shadowy world between war and peace."[11] As former Secretary of State Dean Rusk put it, the intelligence mission was to contest with the Soviets in "the back alleys of the world."[12]

There were few formal standards of conduct in the early days. The lessons of experience were to become a major force in shaping the direction those events were to take. New tasks were assigned before the groups that were to handle them had even been established. Performance, innovation, and flexibility were the challenges of the times. Inexperienced people, in unprecedented circumstances, obviously would err.

Errors did occur, particularly in the earlier years, but the salient fact is the relatively small number of them. It is significant that they were identified and corrected by the intelligence people; any careful reading of the *Church Committee Report* reveals that the recitation of these problems had a strongly historical quality. The intelligence organizations had demonstrated a marked capability for learning and self-correction, a trait seldom attributed to those inhabiting large organizations.

In the absence of early congressional guidance beyond the clear expectation that secret activities would be involved, what general terms of reference were there for setting standards of conduct? The people involved were products of American society, which obviously had an effect on their approaches. But what more could they draw on? The range of views runs from the uneasy reservations of Secretary Stimson's 1929 attitude to the sentiment expressed in a Top Secret report produced by the second Hoover Commission.

Former President Hoover had first headed a special commission to study organization of the Executive branch of government following World War II. He next headed a similar commission following the Korean War. The report of the second commission contained the following statement:

> As long as it remains national policy, another important requirement is an aggressive covert psychological, political, and paramilitary organization more effective, more unique, and if necessary, more ruthless than that employed by the enemy. No one should be permitted to stand in the way of prompt, efficient, and secure accomplishment of this mission.
>
> It is now clear that we are facing an implacable enemy whose avowed objective is world domination by whatever means and at whatever cost. There are no rules in such a game. Hitherto acceptable norms of human conduct do not apply. If the U.S. is to survive, long-standing American

concepts of "fair play" must be reconsidered. We must develop effective espionage and counterespionage services and must learn to subvert, sabotage, and destroy our enemies by more clever, more sophisticated, and more effective methods than those used against us. It may be necessary that the American people be made acquainted with, understand and support this fundamentally repugnant philosophy.[13]

That statement—however stark and unqualified—suggests that there is room only for ruthless derring-do and a regular application of negative standards of conduct to intelligence operations. In fact, it is somewhat naive in its dramatic rhetoric. Clandestine activities do not require the sort of mind-set envisioned in the Hoover report. There are many reasons for a contrary approach. The dramatic attitude proposed by the language of the report inevitably would produce numerous actions that would be counterproductive in work that must avoid undue publicity.

There is an undeniable element of risk in clandestine operations, but that risk can be reduced by the cautious adherence to operational security practices. The risk is accepted. On occasion, hard decisions on courses of action will have to be made and resolved in terms of the requirements and circumstances. The questions must be asked: "How necessary is it? How great are the risks?" But in intelligence, as distinguished from the waging of war, situations requiring decisions that involve the use of force are subject to high-level review. In real practice a balance is struck, as it obviously must be, between the Stimson and Hoover views, with occasional diversion toward one side or the other depending on the situation of the moment and the perceptions of the time.

Secretary Stimson's criticism of Communications Intelligence has died away. It is no longer a challenged activity, although some of the means by which it was collected have attracted critical comment. The same cannot be said about clandestine programs, despite the clear policy decision that this country will engage in them. This affirmation of earlier decisions, following full congressional review and action, has not removed the nagging concerns of some. The rest of this chapter will consider the main issues of principle and practice that have been raised in this connection.

AGENT RELATIONS

Central to all clandestine activity is the foreign agent, without whom secret operations abroad could not be conducted successfully. This *sine qua non* has been questioned by some observers who feel that foreigners who work for another country against their own have compromised their integrity and reliability and are subjected to various abuses as part of the agent relationship. To the contrary, it should be apparent that the successful agent should be treated according to his or her worth. The relationship between the agent and the U.S. case officer is critical to the success of their undertaking. Yet this relationship has been described in negative terms that would lead one to believe that this is not so.

One of the most caustic descriptions of the relationship between case officer and agent was by a respected former CIA officer, E. Drexel Godfrey, who served as a senior officer in CIA's analytical organization. While his contact with clandestine activities was limited, he developed strong feelings about the nature of his work, expressed in an article published in the *Foreign Affairs* magazine. His comments follow:

> The highest art in [clandestine] tradecraft is to develop a source that you own "lock, stock and barrel." According to the clandestine ethos, a "controlled" source provides the most reliable intelligence. "Controlled" means, of course, bought or otherwise obligated. Traditionally it has been the aim of the professional in the clandestine service to weave a psychological web around any potentially fruitful contact and tighten that web whenever possible. Opportunities are limited, but for those in the clandestine service who successfully develop controlled sources, rewards in status and peer respect are high. The modus operandi required, however, is the very antithesis of ethical interpersonal relationships.[14]

First, before considering the standards observed in clandestine operations, we should note that the Clandestine Service (of CIA) does not automatically consider a "controlled source" to be the most reliable source of intelligence. Many factors are involved in determining the reliability of clandestine intelligence reporting, whether from a controlled source or from some other source. The one constant is uncertainty, which operations managers try to bring within acceptable limits (as discussed in Chapter 9 in the context of clandestine collection). Each source is subject to cross-checking with other current reporting, and a retrospective record is maintained to determine reliability over a period of time. But a controlled source may be a mediocre reporter, while a volunteer collaborator may prove unusually valuable. Beyond this point, Mr. Godfrey's other comments provide a basis for discussion of the general question of relationships with agents. It is helpful to go back in time a bit.

In the early post–World War II days, when U.S. clandestine operations had to establish themselves almost simultaneously with creation of the mission, many factors played on the work. Few of those assigned to operational tasks had experience in peacetime clandestine operations. Some had wartime exposure to the work, but despite certain similarities the requirements differed in important respects.

The early postwar environment did help solve some of the immediate problems. In Western Europe, for example, many people were ready to help out of gratitude to the Americans for what they had done and what they were doing. Refugees from Eastern Europe were eager to free their homelands and then to oppose further Soviet expansion. The relations established in those days provided a valued clandestine resource that lasted for many years. These relations did not consist of cynically recruited individuals, nor were they handled with intricate psychological techniques; on the contrary, they began were formed on the basis of comrades in arms. This fact strongly influenced operational style and the practices that were to follow. Had there been an operating doctrine for psychological manipulation, which there was not, there would have been few trained to follow it. It wasn't needed in any event.

Over the years many volunteers have emerged—so many, in fact, that a term developed to describe them—"walk-ins." Many sought out U.S. representatives to offer help. The most valuable single espionage agent since World War II, Soviet Colonel Penkovskiy, contacted Western intelligence operatives on his own initiative and worked for them until he was apprehended by Soviet authorities.

Not all agents are engaged in working against their own lands. It is not at all uncommon for a citizen of a "third country" (i.e., other than the United States or the USSR) to agree to assist in some mission against the Soviets. Such relationships are commonplace enough that it is customary to clear the arrangement with the authorities of the prospective agent's government, if an ally.

Not all agents are volunteers in the sense described earlier. They have to be sought after on a highly selective basis. Stated in its simplest terms, the task is to identify persons who have access to desired information and prescribed personal qualities and who appear susceptible to a clandestine relationship. Individuals have different motivations that may lead them to accept such a relationship. Their reason may involve perceived sharing of ideological principles, resentment of their own government's conduct, personal bitterness with career progress, mistreatment of members of their family, simple financial need, or the mere challenge of adventure. There is obviously some "psychology" involved in the evaluation of the prospective agents and in dealing with them. Specialists at headquarters can help toward these ends by contributing assessments of the stability and quality requisite to clandestine relationships. If a prospect lacks the necessary qualities, he or she may become a source from whom information is elicited, although never considered for clandestine assignment. The U.S. operative must be sensitive to the interests and reactions of the prospect and responsive to preferences in order to maximize the common ground with those individuals. But it is easier to talk about psychological webs than to weave them.

Many factors enter into the management of an agent relationship. A stronger factor than psychological manipulation is personal rapport— genuine personal relations. This is the true strength of the American case officer. Plain old-fashioned salesmanship should not be overlooked during the recruitment phase. Experience has shown that it is sometimes useful to bring in another case officer to be introduced for the recruitment only, usually a person with talents of personal magnetism and instinct unique to that individual. But the final "pitch," as the proposal is known, is seldom made on a serious prospect until the individual has been fully evaluated and developed and the time has been judged propitious.

Once the relationship with an agent has been established, it must mature. The case officer must take pains to ensure that the agent knows what is involved, how to do it, and how to be secure in his or her movements. An objective of the relationship is to develop the agent's responsiveness to direction. This is achieved through a mix of training, adjustment of the agent to the requirements of the work, personal motivation, and financial rewards. Many of the familiar techniques of personnel management are involved, as a balancing consideration to the sinister-sounding notions of psychological web-weaving.

The intent is for an agent to develop a degree of responsiveness that equates with "control," but the basic element of uncertainty is always present and must be kept in mind. Agents who come to be considered as "controlled" have, on occasion, elected to end the relationship when it no longer serves their purpose, and some have demonstrated rather independent qualities. There are too many variables characterizing both sides of the relationship for it to be viewed in cut and dried terms. Much depends on the personal quality and talent of the case officer, and on the willingness of the agent.

The effective case officer must develop a viable personal relationship with his or her agent. The trust and respect between them, which proceed from their personal ties, are important to the mutual undertaking. Were the relationship based solely on the cynical manipulation depicted by Godfrey, this trait would reveal itself in many subtle ways to the agent. The result could well be resentment, which in turn might well be expressed in the sly revenge of deliberately misleading reporting.

"Case officering" involves many responsibilities if relations between agent and case officer are to be balanced. As in other fields of endeavor, the contented agent is the better performer. So the "care and feeding of agents," as some refer to it, is an important part of this balancing act. Beyond this, however, there is a deep sense of responsibility for the agent, omitted from Mr. Godfrey's summary.

One of the provisions of the National Security Act of 1947 is relevant to this responsibility. A provision usually considered in relation to other issues, it provides the basis for an article of faith in agent handling. The provision states: "The Director of Central Intelligence shall be responsible for protecting intelligence sources and methods from unauthorized disclosure." That broad statement, seemingly limited to security considerations, has extended to the personal responsibility of the case officer for the agent. It is more than the impersonal protection of intelligence sources for the mere purpose of avoiding the loss of information. It involves both personal and institutional responsibility for the safety and welfare of the agent.

If one questions—as some do—CIA's high sensitivity about revealing the details of its operations, it is because of the risk of life that is involved. In sum, the case officer is trained in profound responsibility for the agent. That ethic is central to effective clandestine operations. It is seldom matched, and never surpassed, in any other line of endeavor.

Operations managers are conscious of a by-product of the case officer's special responsibility for the agent. It sometimes leads the case officer to be overly solicitous for the welfare of the agent, seeking additional rewards for performance. Or a case officer may take extra precautions in the conduct of operations, thus unnecessarily retarding progress. Further, in sharing in the success of their work with the agents, many case officers come to identify strongly with them. This is such a well-known tendency that, in the way of bureaucratic humor for recurring situations, it has come to be known as "falling in love with your agent." Managers stay on the alert for signs of undue favoritism toward an agent on the part of the case officer. This tendency may occasionally present a management problem, but it is also an easily recognizable reflection of a basic American ethic in the relationship of people—one applied to a line of work that is not familiar to most. Overall, there is considerably more to the relationship between agent and case officer than described in the narrow, negative presentation by Mr. Godfrey.

PRIVATE AMERICANS AND CLANDESTINE ACTIVITIES

It was clear from the beginning that U.S. citizens were to be involved in clandestine activities, at least as employees of the government's intelligence organizations. One must assume that the Congress did not intend for public servants assigned to the work to be set apart in some way from the main stream of American thought and conduct, however unique their assignments. After all, they were carrying out public policy. It was implicit that the general propriety of it was accepted by the Congress, first in 1947, then over the ensuing years, and ultimately in the actions taken in the latter half of the 1970s.

Ratification of intelligence activities as public policy did not deter those generally opposed to the work. In a sense it only changed their general approach to the tactical one of attacking in detail. Without surrendering their general opposition to clandestine activities, the critics shifted to specific issues, some of which were considered in earlier chapters. One issue was the involvement of private citizens in their government's secret programs. Objections were brought to the attention of the Church Committee's staff during the inquiries, in the process of which ambivalent thinking gained them some sympathetic attention focused especially on those private citizens with ties to selected categories of institutions. The Church Committee authors set the stage for consideration of this aspect of the inquiries as follows:

> Clandestine activities that touch American institutions and individuals have taken many forms and are affected through a wide variety of means: university officials and professors provide leads and make introductions for intelligence purposes; scholars and journalists collect intelligence; journalists devise and place propaganda; United States publications provide cover for CIA agents overseas.
>
> These forms of clandestine cooperation had their origins in the early Cold War period when most Americans perceived a real threat of a communist imperium and were prepared to assist their government to counter that threat. As the communists pressed to influence and control international organizations and movements, mass communications, and cultural institutions, the United States responded by involving American private institutions and individuals in the secret struggle over minds, institutions and ideas. Over time national perceptions would change as to the nature and seriousness of the communist ideological and institutional threat. Time and experience would also give increasing currency to doubts as to whether it made sense for a democracy to resort to practices such as the clandestine use of free American institutions and individuals—practices that tended to blur the very difference between "our" system and "theirs" that these covert programs were designed to preserve.[15]

This formulation of the state of affairs at that time warrants some examination. First, it recognized an undeniable consensus in the country for policies opposing Soviet expansionism. It then declared that consensus had eroded. To the extent that such an erosion actually occurred, it would necessarily have happened in the period immediately following the Vietnam-Watergate controversies, coinciding with the inquiries of the Church Committee. Without developing factual support for that perception of change, the report then used it to question the propriety of private citizens' participation in the nation's secret programs against the Soviet Union, and through them the institutions with which they were associated. The Church Committee, claiming a growing concern on the part of the public with this question, then described the method by which it undertook to address the issue:

> In approaching the subject the Committee has inquired: Are the independence and integrity of American institutions in any way endangered by clandestine relationships with the Central Intelligence Agency? Should clandestine use of institutions or individuals within those institutions be permitted? If not, should there be explicit guidelines laid down to regulate Governmental clandestine support or operational use of such institutions or individuals? Should such guidelines be in the form of executive directives or by statute?[16]

Proceeding further with the belief that public concern over this point was increasing, the Committee's report added that it also: "looked not only at the impact of foreign clandestine operations on American institutions but has focused particular attention on covert use of individuals."[17]

The *Church Committee Report* was correct in stating that during the early days of the Cold War, when Soviet policy included extensive use of communist-controlled international organizations, the United States took countering action by giving secret support to U.S. organizations actively opposed to Soviet communism, as well as to foreign organizations.[18]

The United States, as an open society, is not the ideal place from which to mount secret operations abroad. Yet, in one way or another, every secret U.S. operation conducted abroad originates in the United States. Special procedures have had to be devised to meet the challenges of communist front organizations engaged in advancing Soviet interests.

The techniques for supporting the international activities of private organizations were complex. First, confidential contacts had to be established to ascertain if there was a basis for cooperation. Some organizations have accepted funds that expand what they were doing already. Some have welcomed guidance as well. Various arrangements are possible, depending on the individuals and circumstances. Where cooperation is agreed upon, arrangements had to be made for channeling funds so they would not be attributed to official U.S. sources.

Some corporate entities were established solely to receive funds from the government; they would then pass these funds to established foundations, which, in turn, would pass them on to an action organization. This intricate arrangement provided protection from tracing the source of funds, although, as is the case with many large operations, it involved the risk that security would gradually erode over the years.

The best-known case involving the support of a private organization concerned the National Student Association. A detailed review of that case history will illustrate some of the approaches to such an operation and some of the difficulties that can arise.

NATIONAL STUDENT ASSOCIATION

The National Student Association had experienced some frustrations in participating in Soviet-sponsored conferences and youth festivals. To strengthen its role in such activities, the Association sought financial support. It was turned down by both the Congress and the Department of State, perhaps because it was considered to be too far to the left. At some point the State Department pointed it toward CIA, which agreed to provide funding for the organization's international activities. Funds were to be used primarily for U.S. students to attend international forums in which they could express their views in their own way.[19]

Some of the practical considerations this presented to a government agency are quickly apparent. The National Student Association had declared positions at variance with official U.S. government policy. Recognizing this fact, but also concerned with the unhindered Soviet organizational and propaganda activity advancing that country's policies, CIA officials saw the importance of having another voice on the scene. The resulting concept was strikingly sophisticated and, at the same time, a statement of faith.

The contrast at international gatherings between the rigid party-line posture of the communists and the patent individualism and enthusiasm of American youth would be dramatic to those free to make such comparisons. In fact, the impact on the uncommitted and Third World individuals attending those gatherings was dramatic. There is a chemistry in young people not to be denied. Further, confronted with the challenge of communist organization for manipulating meetings, the Americans developed their own expertise for performing in that environment. It is clear that the costly international youth festivals and congresses became an unprofitable investment for the Soviet Union, which had provided the main financing for the gatherings. Whatever the initial reservations about CIA's decision, the program became a resounding success. The Church Committee reported that a few of the hundreds of young people who took part in this program accepted intelligence tasks, such as observing—to the extent they were able—indications of

Soviet counterintelligence activities and reporting what they saw. One student was asked to purchase a piece of Soviet-made equipment.

In maintaining the secure basis of the relationship, CIA had an interest in the type of individuals who led the National Student Association. Leadership changed annually, and continuation of the relationship required that the persons elected to office be discreet and trustworthy, whatever their general political views. To this end, CIA helped screen prospective new leaders for these qualities, without otherwise being involved in their selection. The Church Committee felt that these developments "underline the basic problem of an action-oriented clandestine organization entering into a covert funding relationship with private organizations."[20] But there was no evidence of any meddling with the policies of the organization, nor any corruption of its integrity. The Committee's objection was to the clandestine nature of the relationship, in the absence of any consideration of the fact that overt funding from the government would have required the approval of policies and activities, sometimes interfering in them.

In 1967, after the relationship between the National Student Association and CIA had existed for some fifteen years, a former member of the organization told what he knew about the relationship. His statement was printed in *Ramparts*, a left-wing publication on the west coast. When this version was matched with the disclosures made by a congressional committee in 1964, numerous similar relationships between CIA and other private organizations were revealed. The ensuing excited handling of the story by the media was told in *Facing Reality* by the person responsible in CIA for the overall program at the time.[21]

THE RAMPARTS FLAP

Publication of the *Ramparts* story was followed by other publicity in the more prominent media, and the affair came to be known in intelligence circles as the Ramparts Flap. Media coverage was extensive and liberal criticism strong.

The view of liberal critics was typified by the Americans for Democratic Action (ADA), which charged that CIA funding of voluntary organizations "indicated a serious perversion of the democratic process." ADA's rhetoric seemed unconcerned that the program was a product of the political system. The Congress—the elected law-making body—had been kept informed and encouraged the programs. The activities had been approved by senior officials in a succession of elected national administrations. The relationships had been entered into voluntarily by the members of the student organization concerned, originally at their own initiative. ADA had to admit that what resulted was not out of line with U.S. policy, and that in fact it had achieved "in many cases positive advances" of that policy.[22]

In the face of intense media publicity, President Johnson: "moved quickly to contain the damage. To head off a wide-ranging congressional investigation of all clandestine financing by CIA . . . the President appointed a special three-man committee."[23] The President's committee— the so-called Katzenbach Committee—met in 1967 in an emotion-charged atmosphere created by media handling of the issue. It focused on a number of simple, practical considerations. There were additional operational activities that had not been exposed by the media campaign, some of which were expected to continue. They had to be protected. At the same time, a number of activities that had been exposed could not be continued, as their usefulness had been compromised by the exposure. There was both a need to protect what had not been compromised and to close out what no longer was useful. As stated in *Facing Reality:*

> Once the curtain of secrecy had been torn and many of the funding channels exposed, there was no way through which [CIA] could reconstruct a secure method of providing discreet assistance to the overseas activity of the organizations we had previously assisted. If these groups were to receive governmental assistance in the future, it would have to be supplied through open government grants and be subject to annual public review and authorization by the Congress.
>
> Most of the elected leaders of the voluntary organizations with whom we had cooperated were reluctant to accept this conclusion. . . . Some organizations took the position that they would prefer to do without any government funds if grants would have to be made a matter of public record.
>
> The political sensitivity of their relations with foreign groups was such that they would be severely damaged by a public admission of dependence on U.S. government funding.[24]

There was also the traditional question of using public funds to support privately operated activities, even though these funds were intended to advance difficult foreign policy objectives. The report of the three-man committee concluded that

> it should be the policy of the United States Government that no federal agency shall provide any covert financial assistance or support, direct or indirect, to any of the nation's educational or private voluntary organizations.[25]

Soviet propaganda had joined the U.S. media in playing the story broadly. The President's committee stated that the proposed policy would "make it plain in all foreign countries that the activities of private American groups abroad are, in fact, private." President Johnson approved the recommendations. However, he appeared not to have considered it a major issue as he did not refer to it in his memoirs.

POST-RAMPARTS DEVELOPMENTS

In accordance with the Katzenbach recommendations, CIA ended its financial support to a large number of domestically based organizations; it also terminated the relationships that had been exposed but it continued to fund a number of foreign-based organizations and private commercial concerns, neither of which had been barred by the new policy.

When the Church Committee took up the problem eight years later, it did so with the belief that the Katzenbach restrictions were too narrowly focused. It criticized the Katzenbach approach as having concerned itself primarily with security matters—despite the broader statements of that group's conclusions—saying there had been no "significant rethinking of where the boundaries ought to be drawn in a free society."[26]

The Church Committee focused on three categories of institutions in American society—educational institutions, religious organizations, and the media. Its approach differed from that of the Katzenbach Committee by emphasizing the role of individuals employed by those organizations, or associated with them in other ways, even though the organizations were not involved.

The Church Committee first addressed the "academic community," which it felt should be defined in broader terms than the formal organizations themselves, to include "the full range of individual scholars and school administrators, ranging from department heads to career counselors and to Ph.D. candidates engaged in teaching."[27] The committee felt that those individuals should, in some way, be restricted in their independent, extracurricular activities, at least so far as their associations with clandestine activity were concerned. The underlying attitude for this position was that there may be some corrupting influence on academic integrity stemming from the clandestinity of the activity.

The Church Committee felt that it could not criticize open professional contacts between academia and the government's intelligence agencies (although that inevitably would entail some confidential considerations), but its reservations about relationships with covert activities were clear. The activities cited with disfavor are of doubtful relevance. Making introductions of foreigners to intelligence officers was bothersome to the Church Committee authors. Yet, if such an introduction progressed to a clandestine relationship, the scholar making the introduction was most unlikely to know of it. In addition, some scholars wrote material for propaganda purposes, which would have a doubtful element of harm. Some agreed to collect intelligence abroad, usually in circles where scholars move. But there was no showing that any of these activities had in any way compromised the integrity of the academicians or the quality of their regular work.

The Church Committee, concerned with protecting the reputations of religious institutions,[28] undertook to substitute its judgment for that of the church people who had accepted cooperation with CIA in circumstances they had felt compatible with their mission. Although the number of cases was acknowledged to be "small,"[29] the restrictions proposed were to have blanket application.

The Committee also expressed its concern that U.S. journalists passed valuable information to U.S. intelligence officers, fearing that in some way it would endanger the reporting they would file with their employers.[30] It also spoke of journalists helping prepare propaganda—an infrequent event—as further risking their objectivity. This description was accompanied by a sort of essay on propaganda, not really relevant to the issue of the role of individual citizens in covert activities.

The conclusion of the Church Committee's review of this subject cannot be credited with consistency. Because of constitutional considerations, it did not propose legislation restricting the relationships of academicians with intelligence agencies. Instead, it proposed that academia impose upon itself restrictions that, as law, in the Committee's words, would have been: ". . . unenforceable and in itself an intrusion on the privacy and integrity of the American academic community."[31] It did feel free to propose legislation that would bar any covert paid or contractual relationship with the clergy.[32] Perhaps there was some feeling that this proposal would be safely within traditional concepts of separation of church and state. It failed to devise a similar recommendation concerning journalists, although its reservations were clear.

There is an interesting aspect to this portion of the *Church Committee Report*, differing from the treatment given most of the subjects that it addressed. Usually there was sufficient factual material in the discussion for the careful and knowledgeable reader to identify alternative positions, if the report's conclusions were unconvincing. In this discussion, however, the Church Committee treatment is distinguished by its adherence to hypothesis, and the absence of significant factual support for its conclusions. Had there been supporting data there would have been no security reasons for not describing it in the report. The treatment leads to some further consideration, as to why it differs from so much of the remainder of the report.

One congressional source suggests that the Church Committee's attitude was stimulated by the views of a privately funded group that had advanced strikingly similar positions.[33] It had waged a campaign against intelligence, with the leading personality in the organization favoring reduction of "the collection of raw data by technical and clandestine means,"[34] a position hardly designed to strengthen the intelligence effort. The group in question "share[d] office space on Capitol Hill under the aegis of the Fund for Peace, a group associated with the Soviet-controlled World Peace Council (WPC)."[35] However intriguing these comments, they really do not add to the Church Committee's presentation; rather, they only emphasize the different quality of this section of the report from most of the rest of it.

The Church Committee proposals were not enacted into legislation, although they reportedly are still among those favored by some of the staff of the Senate Select Committee on Intelligence. Such actions as there were on these matters were, instead, taken at the initiative of the Executive branch.

EXECUTIVE REGULATION

The Central Intelligence Agency, in response to the Katzenbach Committee's proposals, adopted new rules for covert relations with individuals in voluntary organizations. This action coincided with a general reduction in the number of its covert action programs occurring at the time. However, later presidential Executive Orders essentially superseded those administrative regulations. President Ford issued regulations on the subject, but these were short lived, inasmuch as the period during which he held office after issuance was limited.

The Carter administration, in its Executive Order of January 1978, addressed the problem of persons associated with private organizations engaging in clandestine activities with U.S. government intelligence agencies. It provided the following:

No agency within the Intelligence Community shall enter into a contract or arrangement for the provision of good(s) or services with private companies or institutions in the United States unless the agency sponsorship is known to the appropriate officials of the company or institution. In the case of any company or institution other than an academic institution, intelligence agency sponsorship may be concealed where it is determined pursuant to procedures approved by the Attorney General, that such concealment is necessary to maintain essential cover or proprietary arrangements for authorized intelligence purposes.[36]

Although this Executive Order applies to organizations, it clearly includes the role of individuals, inasmuch as intelligence operations deal with individuals as distinguished from institutions. With the exception of the relatively unqualified limitation on academic institutions, the order permits activities to continue essentially as the intelligence organizations had functioned previously. Security considerations have always been a central factor in determining how an operational relationship is to be established. It is usually preferable for senior management in a private organization to be aware of a special relationship with an employee, if security considerations do not rule that out.

The Reagan administration, in December 1981, issued a new Executive Order replacing that of the Carter administration. On this point the new order provided:

> Agencies within the Intelligence Community are authorized to enter into contracts or arrangements for the provision of goods or services with private companies or institutions in the United States and need not reveal the sponsorship of such contracts or arrangements for authorized intelligence purposes. Contracts or arrangements with academic institutions may be undertaken only with the consent of appropriate officials of the institution.[37]

This provision modified the stated preference for working with senior officials, although those relationships doubtless will continue for practical reasons. It also continued the special exclusion of persons in academic employment from dealing with their government's intelligence operatives on clandestine matters, although it is permissible if approved by officials of the institution.

NOTES

1. *Church Committee Report*, Book I, page 323; Book VI, page 118.

2. *Church Committee Report*, Book I, page 355; Book VI, pages 123–131. An extended description of Secretary Stimson's 1929 action, the ensuing steps by the services, and Stimson's later attitude when war came is given in *The Puzzle Palace*, by James Bamford, Houghton Mifflin, Boston, 1982, pages 16–41.

3. *The Shaping of the Young Republic*, by Page Smith, McGraw-Hill, New York, 1980, page 225. See also this fine article with a different emphasis: "America Ideals Versus American Institutions," by Samuel P. Huntington, *Political Science Quarterly*, Vol. 97, No. 1, Spring 1982, pages 1–37.

4. *American Diplomacy, 1900–1950*, by George F. Kennan, University of Chicago Press, Chicago, 1951, page 95. Some thirty-five years after publishing

American Diplomacy, Kennan seems to have been questioned by "the younger generation" about his earlier views. In an article in *Foreign Affairs* (Winter 1985/86, Vol. 64, no. 2, pp. 205–218) titled "Morality in Foreign Affairs" he elaborates on his earlier writing. Distinguishing between personal standards and the responsibilities of government in its "obligation . . . to the *interests* of the national society" he reviewed the problems of making foreign policy. Although he regretted some of the by-products of this approach, he held rather faithfully to his earlier conclusions.

5. Ibid., p. 98
6. *Realities of American Foreign Policy,* by George F. Kennan, Princeton University Press, Princeton, N.J., 1954, pages 47–49.
7. Ibid.
8. *Church Committee Report,* Book I, page 16.
9. Ibid., page 144.
10. Ibid., page 149.
11. Ibid., page 9.
12. Ibid.
13. *Church Committee Report,* Book I, pages 9, 50.
14. "Ethics and Intelligence," by E. Drexel Godfrey, *Foreign Affairs,* April 1978, page 630.
15. *Church Committee Report,* Book I, page 179.
16. Ibid, page 180.
17. Ibid.
18. The main international communist front organizations have been listed in numerous places. The following list contains the main groups: the World Peace Council (WPC), with the International Institute for Peace (IIP); the World Federation of Trade Unions (WFTU); the World Federation of Democratic Youth (WFDY); the International Union of Students (IUS); the Women's International Democratic Federation (WIDF); the International Association of Democratic Lawyers (IADL); the World Federation of Scientific Workers (WFSW); the International Organization of Journalists (IOJ), with the International Committee for Co-operation of Journalists (ICCJ); the International Federation of Resistance Fighters (FIR); and the International Radio and Television Organization (OIRT). See *Facing Reality,* by Cord Meyer, Harper & Row, New York, 1980, pages 106–107. The international fronts have literally hundreds of affiliate organizations around the world. For instance, the National Lawyers Guild in the United States is reported as being affiliated with the IADL. See *Broken Seals,* Western Goals Foundation, Alexandria, Va., 1980, page 81.
19. *Church Committee Report,* Book I, pages 184–185.
20. Ibid., page 185.
21. *Facing Reality,* pages 86–94.
22. Ibid., page 90.
23. Ibid., pages 91–92.
24. Ibid., page 92.
25. *Church Committee Report,* Book I, page 187.
26. Ibid., page 188. For the entire discussion of the issue, see pages 179–203.

27. Ibid.

28. *Church Committee Report*, Book I, page 201.

29. Ibid., page 202.

30. Ibid., page 192.

31. Ibid., page 191. The report also proposed that CIA give notice to senior authorities in educational institutions when employees of those organizations are to be involved in clandestine activities.

32. Ibid., page 203.

33. *Broken Seals*, page 97.

34. Ibid., page 22.

35. Ibid., page 23. See also Note 16, supra.

36. *Executive Order 12036*, 43 Federal Register 18, page 3675, January 1978, Section 2-303.

37. *Executive Order 12333*, 46 Federal Register 235, page 59941, December 8, 1981, Section 2.7.

20

THE FUTURE

If it ain't broke, don't fix it.

There is no question that the United States government will, for the indefinite future, continue to need a complex and comprehensive intelligence system as a critical part of its national security apparatus. As long as the world continues in its present restless state, there will be a basic requirement for good factual knowledge and objective reporting on the questions that confront policymakers and planners.

Difficult policy decisions inevitably reflect political, economic, and military judgments—and occasionally subjective bias. The more difficult the decisions, the more likely they are to be controversial. It follows that information assembled by the nation's intelligence system—often the basis for policy judgments—may also be controversial, in its substance as well as with respect to the organization that produced it. The intelligence system will be the forum for many such controversies, and itself will sometimes be the target of those who seek to influence the source for the views they espouse.

Most observers would agree that if a national intelligence system did not exist, one would have to be created. Were a new system to be designed starting from scratch, managerial arrangements and bureaucratic controls would probably differ materially from those now in effect. Whatever the new administrative alignments, the basic missions and programs now in existence would have to be provided for. Those programs would carry with them certain imperatives for coordination and control that would compel procedures closely parallel to those now in use. Although all this would produce differences, many similarities would also be present, for the substance of the intelligence business would be essentially the same, whatever the organizational arrangements.

The sprawling nature of the existing system is tempting to those who feel certain that there could be better arrangements and procedures for directing and controlling things. There are so many people working at so many different problems, sometimes at odds in purpose and viewpoint, that in the abstract it seems there is considerable room for improvement. As a result, it is not at all unusual to hear, within the Intelligence Community, general discussion of how better to order the workings of the entire system. It was interesting, in this respect, to observe that DCI Casey put into effect a reorganization of CIA's Intelligence Directorate on a geographic basis, in place of the long-standing organization based along substantive and functional lines.

This chapter will examine a few of the ideas for change that have been advanced at one time or another. First, however, it is useful to review the major virtues of the present system so as to achieve some perspective on the proposals for change. Some of the most important positive features stem directly from the National Security Act of 1947, while others reflect maturing refinements over nearly forty years of evolution since then.

THE PRESENT SYSTEM

First, the fears of those who foresaw a militarist incubus in our government—one that would make political judgments subject to military reporting—should be allayed. Firm provision has been made for civilian control: The President and his senior cabinet officers in the National Security Council preside over the general national security program, of which intelligence is an important part; civilians can be designated as Director of Central Intelligence; and when a military officer holds the post, he or she is barred from certain types of ties with the military. "National intelligence" cannot be dominated by military "departmental" interests.

Beyond the narrower issue of military control over national intelligence, a major strength of the present system is the centering influence of the DCI. The absence of pre–World War II arrangements for sharing intelligence and coordinating its analysis was highlighted in the inquiries into the Pearl Harbor debacle. That was one of the basic reasons for establishing a central intelligence service. The 1947 Act requires the sharing of intelligence between the services—something once resisted by the military—and authorized the DCI to ensure that this provision is observed.

Although the military services initially held back from the development of a process for producing government-wide intelligence estimates, General Walter Smith, DCI in the early 1950s, instituted a system for producing what became the National Intelligence Estimate. That process, which has continued in one form or another, constitutes the governmental appraisal of important situations around the world. Although the National Intelligence Estimate is produced under the aegis of the DCI and is treated by some as a CIA estimate, it is the coordinated product of all those agencies involved in the work. Some agencies may wish to dissociate themselves from the final product, but if they are not in agreement with the majority there is provision for their dissent to show clearly, which highlights the issue for further consideration at policy levels.

The military services retain their analytical organizations, which concentrate on the special problems that confront them. They must study military forces around the world in order to be able to plan for war. And if war were to come, they must be in a position to follow and react to its progress, in support of their forces in the field. This control of their own analytical resources is critical to national security in war and peace.

The Secretary of Defense has the Defense Intelligence Agency (DIA) to manage the department's overall intelligence needs relative to the global considerations that confront policymakers in our government. Whatever the strengths of the separate military intelligence agencies, their focus and orientation are directed toward their special areas of responsibility—no matter how global some involvements might be— and a broader perspective is needed by the Secretary of Defense. The DIA provides just that.

The Department of State has Foreign Service Officers stationed around the world, supported by the Bureau of Intelligence and Research (INR) and the regional bureaus in Washington. State is the major collector of political intelligence. Its global orientation, in addition to its concern with both national and regional issues, ensures an important focus in its contributions to the work of the Intelligence Community.

It was not until 1976 that the DCI was given authority over the national intelligence budget by President Ford. That authority, which carried with it direct influence over the government's formulation of its intelligence program, has been continued by succeeding administrations. It involves measuring achievements, determining needs, setting priorities, and coordinating the allocation of tasks, thus providing a means for ensuring not only that unnecessary duplication among the numerous organizations is avoided but also that the overall program is reasonably comprehensive and coherent. Although the national intelligence budget is but a small part of the national security budget, and even a smaller fraction of the total federal budget, it *is* costly. Still this central review and control is an important aspect of the government's management of its affairs.

Of course, CIA has intelligence activities beyond those of the independent departments' special interests that it is able to pursue without the distractions of advancing policy and departmental interests.

There are other organizational features of the present national intelligence system to which some observers attach greater importance than those just noted. Among them are the manifold informal channels of cooperation that have grown up within the separate agencies and departments as well as between them. These channels do not show on organization charts or in formal administrative orders and descriptions, but they contribute as much to the working of the system as do all the formal procedures that attract the attention of outside observers. There was a long period in which this kind of coordination was not the case, but over the years practical need triumphed over parochial interests. The functioning of these personal and informal avenues of cooperation is a critical part of the system's operation today.

The Intelligence Community is not arranged as a command organization, with neat lines of subordination and command being provided for every unit. When important issues surface that do not lend themselves to easy resolution, the apparent sense of disorder becomes disturbing to many outsiders, who would change existing arrangements so that the system would function with less difficulty.

Some believe—as does this author—that the vital missions assigned to the departments and agencies that house the intelligence organizations produce attitudes and purposes that must not be stifled in a rigid chain of command. Disagreement is healthy if handled professionally by individuals who know why they are taking particular positions. It simply is not always easy to mesh specialized departmental views with broader national views. Yet if a truly balanced and comprehensive national posture is to be achieved, it must be the product of responsible, considered judgments and not the arbitrary decisions that sometimes are the product of organizational unity. A monolithic system carries with it many weaknesses as well.

Perhaps the most important attribute of the present system is that it works. Given the different interests and missions within the system, it is fair to say that it works very well.

POSSIBLE CHANGES

Ideas abound on how to arrange things better, usually stimulated by a current difficulty or contest among the agencies involved. This book has reviewed the changes that have been made over the years, some of which have resulted from new perceptions of need and some intended to meet the personal preferences of individuals who happen to be in a position of power at a given moment. It was no surprise that during the investigations of the mid-1970s, various proposals for reorganization were considered—more of them by the Church Committee than by other investigative bodies.

The Church Committee spent about a year and a half in its inquiry into the entire intelligence system. Members of its staff tested every function and wondered how things might be improved. At the end, the committee produced few organizational proposals, concentrating instead on procedures and restrictions. It did recommend legislative charters for the main intelligence organizations, but they were formalistic in some respects, adding little of a substantive nature to what already existed. If all of those proposals had been enacted, they would have limited the Executive branch in future organizational changes, serving to lock in place arrangements that might be outgrown.

One idea toyed with by Church Committee staff employees had to do with the status of the Director of Central Intelligence. The concept of a centering force in the Intelligence Community seemed to have appealed to them. But there was an uneasy sense of conflicting responsibilities between the DCI in his community role and his more specific responsibility for heading an operating agency. One notion was that the DCI's Community role would be enhanced by separation from the Agency, with the DCI being moved to the White House staff area. The practical problem with any such change was that it would deprive the DCI of independent intelligence support, and would end up making him something of an assistant to the Assistant to the President for National Security Affairs. In the long run, it would remove the DCI from the active role he has come to have. In becoming something of a disembodied head, he would lose much of the bureaucratic clout so important in Washington's hierarchies. The idea was dropped, interesting as it was.

Another idea given a test flight during the Church Committee inquiry was that of abolishing the Defense Intelligence Agency (DIA). Some suspected that this idea had originated in one or more of the military services' intelligence agencies. At any rate, DIA's performance was questioned.[1] Some CIA personnel argued that DIA provided the Secretary of Defense an essential handle on the overall Defense intelligence program, which otherwise would be fragmented among the separate departmental organizations. The Church Committee concluded that DIA had an important role and that action should be taken to strengthen it rather than diminish it in any way.[2]

The Church Committee had come to the inquiry with sweeping reservations about covert action programs. That attitude was based on the belief, which had found some currency in the media, that the various programs were independent adventures, mainly those of CIA. This had led to Senator Church's early "rogue elephant" charge. Opposition to all such activities was argued before the Church Committee, one view being that all covert action should be barred by statute. The credibility of that position was impaired by the assertion of the main proponent that there should be no career intelligence officers engaged in "covert collection of intelligence by human means."[3] Presumably amateurs should make such collections openly. The same witness is quoted elsewhere as favoring a reduction of the "collection of raw data by technical and clandestine means."[4] Yet it is technical collection that has supported arms control agreements. The Church Committee concluded its inquiry on this range of issues by leaving clandestine collection programs intact, specifically stating that covert action should be retained for use when needed.[5] In essence, the Church Committee favored retention of controversial programs that, if discarded, would have had a significant effect on the organizations that had been assigned responsibility for such activities. It is important to keep in mind that the intelligence agencies were left with their basic missions unchanged; indeed, the Church Committee proposed that they be continued, if at the same time circumscribed by a number of restrictions.

Perhaps the most serious approach by a knowledgeable and responsible individual is to be found in Ray S. Cline's book *Secrets, Spies and Scholars*. The author was a former Deputy Director of CIA, with senior service abroad. He later served as Director of the Department of State's Bureau of Intelligence and Research.

Cline's approach covers the gamut, from how the NSC should conduct its affairs to a reorganization of the structure of at least some of the Intelligence Community. He would start by raising the DCI to cabinet stature, "equal in rank with the Secretaries of State and Defense and entitled to report directly to the President on policies and broad programs of the whole intelligence community, the budget for which he should prepare and defend before the Congress."[6] One might question that cabinet rank makes one equal to the Secretaries of State and Defense, but DCI Casey was given that rank by President Reagan (a move on which this author has reservations) and does, in fact, report to the President as well as participate in NSC meetings.

Cline would extend to the DCI "broad supervisory control over all intelligence agencies, including an independent, new, purely analytical and estimative agency to be established by Congressional legislation."[7] That would amount to more than the coordinator's role given the DCI by the 1947 Act. Cline would name the new organization the Central Institute of Foreign Affairs Research (CIFAR), and it would "consolidate the work of the main analytical staffs now in CIA, State, and Defense.

It should also work out, on an interagency basis, directives for overt, technical, and clandestine intelligence collection agencies to be attached to Defense, State, other Cabinet departments, or to the National Security Council itself."[8] The proposal is stated in very general terms, leaving considerable latitude for how the administrative pieces could be arranged. The DCI would chair the NSC's Committee on Foreign Intelligence, which can be equated with the Reagan Administration's Senior Interagency Group (Intelligence), which is now chaired by the DCI.

Under the Cline rearrangement, CIFAR would replace CIA at the headquarters at Langley, Virginia, and the present CIA clandestine service would be scattered among various departments and agencies—for purposes of security and anonymity—subject to direction by the DCI and the Foreign Intelligence Committee and with collection requirements specified by CIFAR. A Clandestine Service Staff would be attached to the DCI in his new location at the White House offices to support him in this function.

There is enough generalization in the Cline proposal to leave room for adjustment when the imperatives of departmental organization would require retention of functions instead of transferring them to CIFAR. As noted earlier, the separate military services need special departmental analytical capabilities, both for planning in time of peace and in the event of war.[9] The services would have to retain those activities; moreover, experience with the creation of DIA shows that they would probably maintain both their size and their functions in any case, even if some of their functions were taken over formally by a new organization.[10] The Secretaries of State and Defense will continue to require independent analytical resources, which simply cannot be replaced by the interests of some organization located elsewhere. On reflection it should become apparent that basic, practical considerations would result in so many important compromises to the concept of government-wide consolidation of analytical resources that many similarities to the present system would be the result. The change might prove to be one mainly in name rather than in fact.

The scattering of clandestine activities around the government, while probably welcome to the military, which would receive many of them, would be unacceptable to the Department of State, so far as its own organization is concerned. If such a dispersion was carried out, a basic management problem would be maintenance of the standards unique to clandestine work—the critical elements of professionalism, discipline, and operational control. Those qualities are difficult to realize in an organization with less than effective line command.

One stated reason behind this proposal was to help conceal the clandestine organization from a prying press. It should be emphasized that it is not the clandestine organization, per se, that attracts attention, but the more dramatic covert action programs. Clandestine collection programs have not received publicity. And among the covert action programs, low-key propaganda activities, and even occasional use of agents of influence have not attracted the media attention given to paramilitary activities. In fact, much covert activity does not require the sort of extra protection that the Cline proposal is designed to provide.

Cline took a different tack regarding organizational handling of covert action. His proposal was to dispense with a permanent organization for conducting covert action, and to assign it to one of the existing organizations when the decision is made to engage in such activity. It does not seem practical to have "specially trained personnel"[11] waiting in the wings, with no organizational home, to exercise the controls and disciplines so important for the more usual clandestine activities. Perhaps the only organization with a standby capability for covert action—and one of the more dramatic paramilitary kind, at that—would be the Army's Special Forces.

A more recent proposal is contained in a short article in *Foreign Policy*, by Allan E. Goodman.[12] Dr. Goodman is a talented, responsible observer who spent considerable time at a senior level in the analytical work of CIA during the 1970s, and now serves as Associate Dean of the Georgetown University School of Foreign Service in Washington. Dr. Goodman has cited a number of situations in which intelligence failures have been charged. A number of these incidents have occurred as he states them; some are arguable. He has also noted charges of a tendency on the part of DCI Casey to have objective analysis revised to meet policy positions that Casey supports within the administration. Goodman points to a bill sponsored jointly by conservative Senator Barry Goldwater (Chairman of the Senate Select Committee on Intelligence) and liberal Senator Patrick Moynihan (senior Democratic member of the committee) that would have provided that the DCI should be a career civilian or military intelligence officer.[13] If this bill had passed Casey would have had to return to private life, as he was not a career intelligence officer.

The Goodman proposal follows the Cline proposal, insofar as it would consolidate the government's intelligence analysis with all its collateral functions in a single agency devoted to analysis alone. But Goodman goes further than Cline. He would bring together, in another agency, all the collectors to "establish a central collection agency, able to command and mix human and technical collectors to use each effectively."

The problem with the Goodman approach is that it would mix apples with oranges, from the point of view of management. The separate departments, as the proposal reads, would be deprived of their essential, specialized types of analysis. And mixing within one entity the clandestine collection of CIA and the military services with the highly complex systems of the large cryptologic agencies and the overhead reconnaissance programs would create a monster organization, combining so many disparate problems that focus and effective control would be a greater obstacle to efficiency than the arrangements now in existence.

If Goodman is correct in implying that intelligence is not shared, then the DCI is derelict in monitoring compliance with the requirement for sharing. But that should be the cause for corrective administrative action and not the basis for rearranging all the pieces now in place.

Although there might be some advantage or convenience, at the national level, in having all analysis take place under one roof, there are numerous operating disadvantages as well. It has been demonstrated that inherent in large organizations are problems that defy reasonable management. The bureaucratizing of procedure—necessary to maintain some semblance of control—would stifle initiative and suppress dissenting ideas and insights. Private enterprise has found the value of some decentralization for purposes of management control, and to centralize everything into one large organization would create a wide range of new and frustrating problems.

Not to be overlooked in both the Cline and Goodman proposals is the question of how a single analytical organization could produce a true "national estimate." A one-dimensional quality would inevitably emerge, with the single analytical organization developing its own special cant and view, free from the sort of challenges that are a valuable feature of the present system.

IS MAJOR REORGANIZATION DESIRABLE?

No one can challenge Allan Goodman's complaint that there are gaps in the performance of the present intelligence system. But the system provides for closing such gaps. Perhaps no system can control all events completely. Certainly the system Goodman proposes would create as many problems as it is intended to resolve.

Both those who have worked in the analytical environment and those who have worked with the analysts can testify to the delicate requirements for managerial balance in the work. Sherman Kent spoke eloquently of this matter in his book, *Strategic Intelligence*, parts of which have been cited earlier.

Despite its problems, the present system contains the necessary structure and procedures for continuous improvement. The technical specialists work on their problems, reduce data to sensible intelligence, and pass it on to those who need it. In comparing views with one another, the area specialists develop something of an informal consensus before an issue ever moves up the chain of command. Where problems cannot be agreed upon, usually among agencies, provisions for dissent are entirely adequate. Where there is substantive dissent, that should be enough of a signal for those at policy levels to call for a thorough review of the issue at stake. Nothing is suppressed, and views tend to find expression within the system.

Key to the functioning of the current system, which works remarkably well despite the opposing biases that exist in a large government, is the unrecorded myriad of informal channels of communication that have developed over the years. Formal procedure does not take over from reason, and form is easily modified for special situations. Were some major attempt at reorganization to occur, with significant changes in command and control within the system, all the strongly functioning informal channels would be done long-lasting harm. They might never be reestablished. Crowding large analytical organizations into one place would create more havoc than enlightenment.

The present author feels that any major reorganization along the Cline and Goodman lines would be seriously disruptive. Over a prolonged period clarity and coherence would be lacking. And during the time in which the system was in the hands of innovators, the nation's policy-makers would be relatively blind to critical developments that might occur while the administration was being rearranged. Effective management of those aspects that are not felt to work as well as desired should be the subject of continued determined attention, but improvement through major rearrangement would both prove illusory and ultimately endanger the working system for unproven, theoretical change.

The requirements for intelligence coverage continue. A major part of that coverage is timely—"real time" in the intelligence world—reporting on critical situations around the world. The nation cannot afford to let down its guard while it gets a new blueprint for handling the difficult problems that currently exist would remain for any successor organization that might be created. The present system soundly meets the requirements of running the intelligence business. It should not be changed recklessly, just because it suffers the malady common to all administrative systems—imperfection. In short, evolutionary change has met past needs, and should be allowed to continue as new requirements and conditions demand.

WHAT DIRECTION TO TAKE?

Instead of major organizational change in the Intelligence Community, what is needed is continued close attention to the substantive content of the various programs conducted by its members. The numerous intelligence organizations are the first line of managerial responsibility, and they will be held accountable in their departments, as well as within the Intelligence Community, for their performance. The DCI—with his Intelligence Community Staff—has the organization and procedures for providing a coherent overview of activities. The Congress, in its legislative oversight capacity, should focus on this aspect of the work.

The two costly and important collection programs—Signals Intelligence and Overhead Reconnaissance—should be kept under continuing review to ensure that they are complying with Community guidance and that they have the capabilities needed to provide the intelligence required by national policymakers and planners. The present system provides for this assurance. The Congress's interest should address the question of capabilities, executive direction, and results. Judgments about the systems must take into consideration not only the needs for peacetime but also the capabilities that would be essential in times of war. In this latter respect, operational resources for wartime are analagous to the general military readiness of our national defense. They must exceed purely peacetime needs in order to accommodate wartime expansion. The determination that no *unnecessary* redundancy exists is an appropriate area for congressional study.

Clandestine collection has always been the subject of changing perceptions. After CIA developed its resources and skills, its activities were shifted about the world as policymakers judged changing needs. Witness the emergence of Third World decolonization after World War II and the growing Soviet interests there. While CIA once began to focus its clandestine efforts against the so-called classical target of the Soviet Bloc, it soon became clear that policy levels wanted reporting of events in other parts of the world as well. For example, collection and reporting were insufficient for adequately judging the deterioration of the Iranian government prior to the fall of the Shah. The extent of reporting interests must be determined clearly and set for the long term; clandestine resources cannot be made to appear at the wave of a magician's wand. A long-range view with adequate programming is needed.

Analysis must continue to be organized on a comprehensive basis, not unlike its current arrangement, with attention given to the personnel and equipment resources needed to cope with a wide range of subject matter. This is important for State, Defense, and the military services, as well as for CIA.

There seems to be a growing requirement for both the traditional counterintelligence work directed against hostile espionage and the related activity of identifying and blocking terrorists. In the past few years, a growing number of official Soviet representatives have been expelled from various countries in which they were posted. Their expulsion could be a reflection of increased aggressiveness by the KGB and GRU during the time that Yuri Andropov—former head of the KGB—was at the helm in the USSR. In our own country FBI Director William Webster has stated that the United States currently has "more people charged with espionage . . . than at any time in our history." This phenomenon is attributed by Webster to a combination of increased Soviet technological espionage and the emergence of an attitude among many individuals, devoid of loyalty to the United States.[14]

Indications of mounting terrorist activity have also been observed throughout the world. Terrorism ranges from localized individuals and splinter groups disaffected with society and strike out in an almost random way at those around them, through elements of larger groups acting independently, to centrally trained and directed activities. The limited or informal organization of radical splinter groups makes such terrorists a difficult and less recognizable intelligence target than the international terrorist groups.

Both the KGB and GRU have training facilities in Czechoslovakia for terrorist activities. Third World students attending the Patrice Lumumba University in Moscow return to their homes trained in political activities and organization and prepared to work with activist organizations to subvert their own governments. These people can be identified for attention by the security forces of their homelands, which are often in cooperation with U.S. intelligence organizations. There is a continuing trail of Soviet connections with such individuals. Arms of Soviet Bloc manufacture are usually used in terrorist acts. Some arms shipments have been intercepted. Financial support is not always mysterious; banks may be robbed, but Soviet support is clear.[15] The fact that the political ideology of the international terrorist is often characterized by some form of Marxist thought constitutes more than symbolic coincidence. The track record of Marxist infiltration of groups organizing to oust an incumbent regime is quite clear. If ties to the Soviet Union are not always clearly demonstrable under rules of evidence in an Anglo-Saxon court, they are obvious to those who must work with the problem.

A number of actions can be taken to carry out counterintelligence and counterterrorist programs. The number of intelligence people assigned to this complex task can be increased. It was noted earlier that there have been reports of reinforced personnel strengths in CIA under the Reagan administration. Recently congressional sources have provided more specific information on the subject,[16] thus apparently reflecting a congressional readiness to provide the wherewithal for reinforcing such activities.

There are tangible physical-security precautions that can be taken against terrorists. Air travelers are familiar with the security screening process for passengers to reduce the threat of skyjackers, some of whom represent organized terrorist movements and some of whom are individuals with personal problems. Precautions have been taken in Washington to seal off the Congress, the White House, and other government offices from possible terrorist attacks, to counter a perceived threat that most would not question.[17] Such measures have caused concern for the effect they will have on our open society, but the Secret Service nevertheless has raised the question of more extensive precautions. It is clear, however, that there are limits to the effectiveness of physical barriers. The readiness of a suicidal terrorist to drive through the barriers into the Marine barracks in Lebanon provided a lesson that will last a long time. The Congress reacted by passing a bill, signed into law by President Reagan on 19 October 1984, that authorizes some $350 million for strengthening the security of official U.S. installations around the world. That bill also offers financial rewards for information on terrorist groups and plans, thus adding to the possible resources of those involved in counterintelligence and counterterrorist work. It also indicates the readiness of the Congress to support programs for dealing with the problem. The Congress must continue to be approached for such support as circumstances demand.

The type of terrorist activity that is part of an armed insurgency against an incumbent government, such as in Central America today, sometimes presents special problems. The Congress must come to grips with the problem, unencumbered by ideological confusion and artificial legalistic concepts that relate only peripherally to the facts. If the Congress is unable to clear its mind on this point, serious repercussions for our long-range national interests could occur.

When the substantive content of the U.S. intelligence program is understood in terms of the world we live in, a clearer attitude on its work and needs will be necessary, in place of the confused ambivalence that often is apparent in congressional debate.

Finally, to repeat George Washington's statement quoted at the head of Chapter 7:

The necessity of procuring good Intelligence is apparent & need not be further urged—All that Remains for me to add is, that you keep the whole matter as secret as possible. For upon Secrecy, Success depends in Most Enterprizes of the kind, and for want of it, they are generally defeated, however well planned & promising a favourable issue.

The members of the Executive branch who know the classified facts on a controversial subject must restrain themselves from leaking information that supports their view. Perhaps some measure must be taken to ensure that they observe this requirement. Members of the Congress too often seem not to understand the underlying requirement for security, taking public stands that compromise basic programs and the national interest. They must consider carefully what is involved and how to handle issues *within the structure of the Congress.* And the Congress, as an institution, must determine the extent to which it will exercise restraint on its own members, by depriving them of positions with access to sensitive information when they prove unable to respect it. Congressional staff employees can be dismissed out of hand, and should be, but members are another problem. A few of them seem to feel that their membership in the select club they inhabit at the will of their constituents carries with it a right to violate security, regardless of the larger national interest.

If this country is to have an intelligence system, there are certain conditions that must be accepted A few elected officials should not feel free to attack the system publicly on peripheral issues when the Congress, in the larger sense, has approved the system. Our elected representatives are authorized to act for all of us and are accountable to their constituents. But not all the actions they take are, or always should be, in public.

Some secrecy is essential in the conduct of international diplomacy and in national defense programs. Similarly, the secrecy characteristic of the intelligence activities that support U.S. foreign policy and national defense are necessary to their success. The tendency of some Americans to expose in detail the secret activities of their government is a source of concern to our allies, who share secrets with us. We have not found the balance between necessary public disclosure and unnecessary revelations, even though our political system ensures fully adequate accountability for both elected and appointed officials. And within our Executive branch there is an array of procedures and mechanisms for ensuring that programs are constructed and handled with reasonable responsibility.

As one takes a long look at the development of our national intelligence system, the broad judgment must be that it has been put together remarkably well and functions with great effectiveness. Indeed, it warrants a degree of support that it has not always received.

NOTES

1. *Church Committee Report*, Book I, pages 349–353.
2. Ibid., pages 463–464.

3. Ibid., pages 520–523.

4. Quoted in *Broken Seals*, Western Goals Foundation, Alexandria, Va., 1980, page 22.

5. *Church Committee Report*, Book I, pages 159ff.

6. *Secrets, Spies and Scholars*, by Ray S. Cline, Acropolis Books, Washington, D.C., 1976, page 265.

7. Ibid.

8. Ibid., pages 265–266.

9. *Church Committee Report*, Book I, page 325.

10. Ibid., page 349.

11. *Secrets, Spies and Scholars*, pages 267–268.

12. See "Dateline Langley: Fixing the Intelligence Mess," by Allan E. Goodman, *Foreign Policy*, Winter 1984-1985, No. 57, pages 160–179.

13. This bill, no. S-3019, lapsed with the end of the 98th Congress at the end of the first Reagan term. Such a bill may not be reintroduced, as it reportedly was intended to catch the attention of DCI Casey, whose alleged swashbuckling style upset the committee members.

14. "Investigators Are Dealing with a New Breed of Spy," *New York Times News Service*, reprinted in the *Lexington Herald-Leader*, (Kentucky), 21 December 1984, page A-13.

15. See *The Soviet Bloc and World Terrorism*, Paper No. 26, by Shlomi Elad and Ariel Merari, Tel Aviv University, Jaffee Center for Strategic Studies, Tel Aviv, August 1984. See also *The Terror Network*, by Claire Sterling, Holt, Rinehart & Winston, New York, 1981, which was cited Chapter 13 in the context of counterintelligence.

16. Representative Norman Mineta, of the House Permanent Select Committee on Intelligence (HPSCI), was quoted as saying that CIA has some 18,000 employees. If that figure is correct, the increase under the Reagan administration has been substantial. See "The CIA and Its Not-So-Secret War," by Christopher Dickey and Edward Cody, in the *Washington Post National Weekly Edition*, 31 December 1984, page 10.

17. "Washington's Security Blanket," by Saundra Saperstein, *Washington Post National Weekly Edition*, 8 January 1985, page 8.

THE NATIONAL SECURITY ACT OF 1947, PUBLIC LAW 253, JULY 26, 1947.

[The following is an excerpt.]

CENTRAL INTELLIGENCE AGENCY

SEC. 102. (a) There is hereby established under the National Security Council a Central Intelligence Agency with a Director of Central Intelligence, who shall be the head thereof. The Director shall be appointed by the President, by and with the advice and consent of the Senate, from among the commissioned officers of the armed services or from among individuals in civilian life. The Director shall receive compensation at the rate of $14,000 a year.

(b) (1) If a commissioned officer of the armed services is appointed as Director then—

(A) in the performance of his duties as Director, he shall be subject to no supervision, control, restriction, or prohibition (military or otherwise) other than would be operative with respect to him if he were a civilian in no way connected with the Department of the Army, the Department of the Navy, the Department of the Air Force, or the armed services or any component thereof; and

(B) he shall not possess or exercise any supervision, control, powers, or functions (other than such as he possesses, or is authorized or directed to exercise, as Director) with respect to the armed services or any component thereof, the Department of the Army, the Department of the Navy, or the Department of the Air Force, or any branch, bureau, unit or division thereof, or with respect to any of the personnel (military or civilian) of any of the foregoing.

(2) Except as provided in paragraph (1), the appointment to the office of Director of a commissioned officer of the armed services, and his acceptance of and service in such office, shall in no way affect any status, office, rank, or grade he may occupy or hold in the armed services, or any emolument, perquisite, right, privilege, or benefit incident to or arising out of any such status, office,

rank, or grade. Any such commissioned officer shall, while serving in the office of Director, receive the military pay and allowances (active or retired, as the case may be) payable to a commissioned officer of his grade and length of service and shall be paid, from any funds available to defray the expenses of the Agency, annual compensation at a rate equal to the amount by which $14,000 exceeds the amount of his annual military pay and allowances.

(c) Notwithstanding the provisions of section 6 of the Act of August 24, 1912 (37 Stat. 555), or the provisions of any other law, the Director of Central Intelligence may, in his discretion, terminate the employment of any officer or employee of the Agency whenever he shall deem such termination necessary or advisable in the interests of the United States, but such termination shall not affect the right of such officer or employee to seek or accept employment in any other department or agency of the Government if declared eligible for such employment by the United States Civil Service Commission.

(d) For the purpose of coordinating the intelligence activities of the several Government departments and agencies in the interest of national security, it shall be the duty of the Agency, under the direction of the National Security Council—

(1) to advise the National Security Council in matters concerning such intelligence activities of the Government departments and agencies as relate to national security;

(2) to make recommendations to the President through the National Security Council for the coordination of such intelligence activities of the departments and agencies of the Government as relate to the national security;

(3) to correlate and evaluate intelligence relating to the national security, and provide for the dissemination of such intelligence within the Government using where appropriate existing agencies and facilities: *Provided,* That the Agency shall have no police, subpena, law-enforcement powers, or internal-security functions: *Provided further,* That the departments and other agencies of the Government shall continue to collect, evaluate, correlate, and disseminate departmental intelligence: *And provided further,* That the Director of Central Intelligence shall be responsible for protecting intelligence sources and methods from unauthorized disclosure;

(4) to perform, for the benefit of the existing intelligence agencies, such additional services of common concern as the National Security Council determines can be more efficiently accomplished centrally;

(5) to perform such other functions and duties related to intelligence affecting the national security as the National Security Council may from time to time direct.

(e) To the extent recommended by the National Security Council and approved by the President, such intelligence of the departments and agencies of the Government, except as hereinafter provided, relating to the national security shall be open to the inspection of the Director of Central Intelligence, and such intelligence as relates to the national security and is possessed by such departments and other agencies of the Government, except as hereinafter provided, shall be made available to the Director of Central Intelligence for correlation, evaluation, and dissemination: *Provided however,* That upon the written request of the Director of Central Intelligence, the Director of the Federal Bureau of Investigation shall make available to the Director of Central Intelligence such information for correlation, evaluation, and dissemination as may be essential to the national security.

(f) Effective when the Director first appointed under subsection (a) has taken office—

(1) the National Intelligence Authority (11 Fed. Reg. 1337, 1339, February 5, 1946) shall cease to exist; and

(2) the personnel, property, and records of the Central Intelligence Group are transferred to the Central Intelligence Agency, and such Group shall cease to exist. Any unexpended balances of appropriations, allocations, or other funds available or authorized to be made available for such Group shall be available and shall be authorized to be made available in like manner for expenditure by the Agency.

EFFECTIVE DATE

SEC. 310. (a) The first sentence of section 202 (a) and sections 1, 2, 307, 308, 309, and 310 shall take effect immediately upon enactment of this Act.

(b) Except as provided in subsection (a), the provisions of this Act shall take effect on whichever of the following days is the earlier: The day after the day upon which the Secretary of Defense first appointed takes office, or the sixtieth day after the date of the enactment of this Act.

EXECUTIVE ORDER 12333
DECEMBER 4, 1981

Part 1

Goals, Direction, Duties and Responsibilities With Respect to the National Intelligence Effort

1.1 *Goals.* The United States intelligence effort shall provide the President and the National Security Council with the necessary information on which to base decisions concerning the conduct and development of foreign, defense and economic policy, and the protection of United States national interests from foreign security threats. All departments and agencies shall cooperate fully to fulfill this goal.

(a) Maximum emphasis should be given to fostering analytical competition among appropriate elements of the Intelligence Community.

(b) All means, consistent with applicable United States law and this Order, and with full consideration of the rights of United States persons, shall be used to develop intelligence information for the President and the National Security Council. A balanced approach between technical collection efforts and other means should be maintained and encouraged.

(c) Special emphasis should be given to detecting and countering espionage and other threats and activities directed by foreign intelligence services against the United States Government, or United States corporations, establishments, or persons.

(d) To the greatest extent possible consistent with applicable United States law and this Order, and with full consideration of the rights of United States persons, all agencies and departments should seek to ensure full and free exchange of information in order to derive maximum benefit from the United States intelligence effort.

1.2 *The National Security Council.*

(a) *Purpose.* The National Security Council (NSC) was established by the National Security Act of 1947 to advise the President with respect to the integration of domestic, foreign and military policies relating to the national security. The NSC shall act as the highest Executive Branch entity that provides review of, guidance for and direction to the conduct of all national foreign intelligence, counter-intelligence, and special activities, and attendant policies and programs.

(b) *Committees.* The NSC shall establish such committees as may be necessary to carry out its functions and responsibilities under this Order. The NSC, or a committee established by it, shall consider and submit to the President a policy recommendation, including all dissents, on each special activity and shall review proposals for other sensitive intelligence operations.

1.3 *National Foreign Intelligence Advisory Groups.*

(a) *Establishment and Duties.* The Director of Central Intelligence shall establish such boards, councils, or groups as required for the purpose of obtaining advice from within the Intelligence Community concerning:

(1) Production, review and coordination of national foreign intelligence;

(2) Priorities for the National Foreign Intelligence Program budget;

(3) Interagency exchanges of foreign intelligence information;

(4) Arrangements with foreign governments on intelligence matters;

(5) Protection of intelligence sources and methods;

(6) Activities of common concern; and

(7) Such other matters as may be referred by the Director of Central Intelligence.

(b) *Membership.* Advisory groups established pursuant to this section shall be chaired by the Director of Central Intelligence or his designated representative and shall consist of senior representatives from organizations within the Intelligence Community and from departments or agencies containing such organizations, as designated by the Director of Central Intelligence. Groups for consideration of substantive intelligence matters will include representatives of organizations involved in the collection, processing and analysis of intelligence. A senior representative of the Secretary of Commerce, the Attorney General, the Assistant to the President for National Security Affairs, and the Office of the Secretary of Defense shall be invited to participate in any group which deals with other than substantive intelligence matters.

1.4 *The Intelligence Community.* The agencies within the Intelligence Community shall, in accordance with applicable United States law and with the other provisions of this Order, conduct intelligence activities necessary for the conduct of foreign relations and the protection of the national security of the United States, including:

(a) Collection of information needed by the President, the National Security Council, the Secretaries of State and Defense, and other Executive Branch officials for the performance of their duties and responsibilities;

(b) Production and dissemination of intelligence;

(c) Collection of information concerning, and the conduct of activities to protect against, intelligence activities directed against the United States, international terrorist and international narcotics activities, and other hostile activities directed against the United States by foreign powers, organizations, persons, and their agents;

(d) Special activities;

(e) Administrative and support activities within the United States and abroad necessary for the performance of authorized activities; and

(f) Such other intelligence activities as the President may direct from time to time.

1.5 *Director of Central Intelligence.* In order to discharge the duties and responsibilities prescribed by law, the Director of Central Intelligence shall be responsible directly to the President and the NSC and shall:

(a) Act as the primary adviser to the President and the NSC on national foreign intelligence and provide the President and other officials in the Executive Branch with national foreign intelligence;

(b) Develop such objectives and guidance for the Intelligence Community as will enhance capabilities for responding to expected future needs for national foreign intelligence;

(c) Promote the development and maintenance of services of common concern by designated intelligence organizations on behalf of the Intelligence Community;

(d) Ensure implementation of special activities;

(e) Formulate policies concerning foreign intelligence and counterintelligence arrangements with foreign governments, coordinate foreign intelligence and counterintelligence relationships between agencies of the Intelligence Community and the intelligence or internal security services of foreign governments, and establish procedures governing the conduct of liaison by any department or agency with such services on narcotics activities;

(f) Participate in the development of procedures approved by the Attorney General governing criminal narcotics intelligence activities abroad to ensure that these activities are consistent with foreign intelligence programs;

(g) Ensure the establishment by the Intelligence Community of common security and access standards for managing and handling foreign intelligence systems, information, and products;

(h) Ensure that programs are developed which protect intelligence sources, methods, and analytical procedures;

(i) Establish uniform criteria for the determination of relative priorities for the transmission of critical national foreign intelligence, and advise the Secretary of Defense concerning the communications requirements of the Intelligence Community for the transmission of such intelligence;

(j) Establish appropriate staffs, committees, or other advisory groups to assist in the execution of the Director's responsibilities;

(k) Have full responsibility for production and dissemination of national foreign intelligence, and authority to levy analytic tasks on departmental intelligence production organizations, in consultation with those organizations, ensuring that appropriate mechanisms for competitive analysis are developed so that diverse points of view are considered fully and differences of judgment within the Intelligence Community are brought to the attention of national policymakers;

(l) Ensure the timely exploitation and dissemination of data gathered by national foreign intelligence collection means, and ensure that the resulting intelligence is disseminated immediately to appropriate government entities and military commands;

(m) Establish mechanisms which translate national foreign intelligence objectives and priorities approved by the NSC into specific guidance for the Intelligence Community, resolve conflicts in tasking priority, provide to departments and agencies having information collection capabilities that are not part of the National Foreign Intelligence Program advisory tasking concerning collection of national foreign intelligence, and provide for the development of plans and arrangements for transfer of required collection tasking authority to the Secretary of Defense when directed by the President;

(n) Develop, with the advice of the program managers and departments and agencies concerned, the consolidated National Foreign Intelligence Program budget, and present it to the President and the Congress;

(o) Review and approve all requests for reprogramming National Foreign Intelligence Program funds, in accordance with guidelines established by the Office of Management and Budget;

(p) Monitor National Foreign Intelligence Program implementation, and, as necessary, conduct program and performance audits and evaluations;

(q) Together with the Secretary of Defense, ensure that there is no unnecessary overlap between national foreign intelligence programs and Department of Defense intelligence programs consistent with the requirement to develop competitive analysis, and provide to and obtain from the Secretary of Defense all information necessary for this purpose;

(r) In accordance with law and relevant procedures approved by the Attorney General under this Order, give the heads of the departments and agencies access to all intelligence, developed by the CIA or the staff elements of the Director of Central Intelligence, relevant to the national intelligence needs of the departments and agencies; and

(s) Facilitate the use of national foreign intelligence products by Congress in a secure manner.

1.6 *Duties and Responsibilities of the Heads of Executive Branch Departments and Agencies.*

(a) The heads of all Executive Branch departments and agencies shall, in accordance with law and relevant procedures approved by the Attorney General under this Order, give the Director of Central Intelligence access to all information relevant to the national intelligence needs of the United States, and shall give due consideration to the requests from the Director of Central Intelligence for appropriate support for Intelligence Community activities.

(b) The heads of departments and agencies involved in the National Foreign Intelligence Program shall ensure timely development and submission to the Director of Central Intelligence by the program managers and heads of component activities of proposed national programs and budgets in the format designated by the Director of Central Intelligence, and shall also ensure that the Director of Central Intelligence is provided, in a timely and responsive manner, all information necessary to perform the Director's program and budget responsibilities.

(c) The heads of departments and agencies involved in the National Foreign Intelligence Program may appeal to the President decisions by the Director of Central Intelligence on budget or reprogramming matters of the National Foreign Intelligence Program.

1.7 *Senior Officials of the Intelligence Community.* The heads of departments and agencies with organizations in the Intelligence Community or the heads of such organizations, as appropriate, shall:

(a) Report to the Attorney General possible violations of federal criminal laws by employees and of specified federal criminal laws by any other person as provided in procedures agreed upon by the Attorney General and the head of the department or agency concerned, in a manner consistent with the protection of intelligence sources and methods, as specified in those procedures;

(b) In any case involving serious or continuing breaches of security, recommend to the Attorney General that the case be referred to the FBI for further investigation;

(c) Furnish the Director of Central Intelligence and the NSC, in accordance with applicable law and procedures approved by the Attorney General under this Order, the information required for the performance of their respective duties;

(d) Report to the Intelligence Oversight Board, and keep the Director of Central Intelligence appropriately informed, concerning any intelligence activities of their organizations that they have reason to believe may be unlawful or contrary to Executive order or Presidential directive;

(e) Protect intelligence and intelligence sources and methods from unauthorized disclosure consistent with guidance from the Director of Central Intelligence;

(f) Disseminate intelligence to cooperating foreign governments under arrangements established or agreed to by the Director of Central Intelligence;

(g) Participate in the development of procedures approved by the Attorney General governing production and dissemination of intelligence resulting from criminal narcotics intelligence activities abroad if their departments, agencies, or organizations have intelligence responsibilities for foreign or domestic narcotics production and trafficking;

(h) Instruct their employees to cooperate fully with the Intelligence Oversight Board; and

(i) Ensure that the Inspectors General and General Counsels for their organizations have access to any information necessary to perform their duties assigned by this Order.

1.8 *The Central Intelligence Agency.* All duties and responsibilities of the CIA shall be related to the intelligence functions set out below. As authorized by this Order; the National Security Act of 1947, as amended; the CIA Act of 1949, as amended; appropriate directives or other applicable law, the CIA shall:

(a) Collect, produce and disseminate foreign intelligence and counterintelligence, including information not otherwise obtainable. The collection of foreign intelligence or counterintelligence within the United States shall be coordinated with the FBI as required by procedures agreed upon by the Director of Central Intelligence and the Attorney General;

(b) Collect, produce and disseminate intelligence on foreign aspects of narcotics production and trafficking;

(c) Conduct counterintelligence activities outside the United States and, without assuming or performing any internal security functions, conduct counterintelligence activities within the United Stataes in coordination with the FBI as required by procedures agreed upon the Director of Central Intelligence and the Attorney General;

(d) Coordinate counterintelligence activities and the collection of information not otherwise obtainable when conducted outside the United States by other departments and agencies;

(e) Conduct special activities approved by the President. No agency except the CIA (or the Armed Forces of the United States in time of war declared by Congress or during any period covered by a report from the President to the Congress under the War Powers Resolution (87 Stat. 855)) may conduct any special activity unless the President determines that another agency is more likely to achieve a particular objective;

(f) Conduct services of common concern for the Intelligence Community as directed by the NSC;

(g) Carry out or contract for research, development and procurement of technical systems and devices relating to authorized functions;

(h) Protect the security of its installations, activities, information, property, and employees by appropriate means, including such investigations of applicants, employees, contractors, and other persons with similar associations with the CIA as are necessary; and

(i) Conduct such administrative and technical support activities within and outside the United States as are necessary to perform the functions described in sections (a) and through (h) above, including procurement and essential cover and proprietary arrangements.

1.9 *The Department of State.* The Secretary of State shall:

(a) Overtly collect information relevant to United States foreign policy concerns;

(b) Produce and disseminate foreign intelligence relating to United States foreign policy as required for the execution of the Secretary's responsibilities;

(c) Disseminate, as appropriate, reports received from United States diplomatic and consular posts;

(d) Transmit reporting requirements of the Intelligence Community to the Chiefs of United States Missions abroad; and

(e) Support Chiefs of Missions in discharging their statutory responsibilities for direction and coordination of mission activities.

1.10 *The Department of the Treasury.* The Secretary of the Treasury shall:

(a) Overtly collect foreign financial and monetary information;

(b) Participate with the Department of State in the overt collection of general foreign economic information;

(c) Produce and disseminate foreign intelligence relating to United States economic policy as required for the execution of the Secretary's resonsibilities; and

(d) Conduct, through the United States Secret Service, activities to determine the existence and capability of surveillance equipment being used against the President of the United States, the Executive Office of the President, and, as authorized by the Secretary of the Treasury or the President, other Secret Service protectees and United States officials. No information shall be acquired intentionally through such activities except to protect against such surveillance, and those activities shall be conducted pursuant to procedures agreed upon by the Secretary of the Treasury and the Attorney General.

1.11 *The Department of Defense.* The Secretary of Defense shall:

(a) Collect national foreign intelligence and be responsive to collection tasking by the Director of Central Intelligence;

(b) Collect, produce and disseminate military and military-related foreign intelligence and counterintelligence as required for execution of the Secretary's responsibilities;

(c) Conduct programs and missions necessary to fulfill national, departmental and tactical foreign intelligence requirements;

(d) Conduct counterintelligence activities in support of Department of Defense components outside the United States in coordination with the CIA, and within the United States in coordination with the FBI pursuant to procedures agreed upon by the Secretary of Defense and the Attorney General;

(e) Conduct, as the executive agent of the United States Government, signals intelligence and communications security activities, except as otherwise directed by the NSC;

(f) Provide for the timely transmission of critical intelligence, as defined by the Director of Central Intelligence, within the United States Government;

(g) Carry out or contract for research, development and procurement of technical systems and devices relating to authorized intelligence functions;

(h) Protect the security of Department of Defense installations, activities, property, information, and employees by appropriate means, including such investigations of applicants, employees, contractors, and other persons with similar associations with the Department of Defense as are necessary;

(i) Establish and maintain military intelligence relationships and military intelligence exchange programs with selected cooperative foreign defense establishments and international organizations, and ensure that such relationships and programs are in accordance with policies formulated by the Director of Central Intelligence;

(j) Direct, operate, control and provide fiscal management for the National Security Agency and for defense and military intelligence and national reconnaissance entities; and

(k) Conduct such administrative and technical support activities within and outside the United States as are necessary to perform the functions described in sections (a) through (j) above.

1.12 *Intelligence Components Utilized by the Secretary of Defense.* In carrying out the responsibilities assigned in section 1.11, the Secretary of Defense is authorized to utilize the following:

(a) *Defense Intelligence Agency,* whose responsibilities shall include;

(1) Collection, production, or, through tasking and coordination, provision of military and military-related intelligence for the Secretary of Defense, the Joint Chiefs of Staff, other Defense components, and, as appropriate, non-Defense agencies;

(2) Collection and provision of military intelligence for national foreign intelligence and counterintelligence products;

(3) Coordination of all Department of Defense intelligence collection requirements;

(4) Management of the Defense Attache system; and

(5) Provision of foreign intelligence and counterintelligence staff support as directed by the Joint Chiefs of Staff.

(b) *National Security Agency,* whose responsibilities shall include:

(1) Establishment and operation of an effective unified organization for signals intelligence activities, except for the delegation of operational control over certain operations that are conducted through other elements of the Intelligence Community. No other department or agency may engage in signals intelligence activities except pursuant to a delegation by the Secretary of Defense;

(2) Control of signals intelligence collection and processing activities, including assignment of resources to an appropriate agent for such periods and tasks as required for the direct support of military commanders;

(3) Collection of signals intelligence information for national foreign intelligence purposes in accordance with guidance from the Director of Central Intelligence;

(4) Processing of signals intelligence data for national foreign intelligence purposes in accordance with guidance from the Director of Central Intelligence;

(5) Dissemination of signals intelligence information for national foreign intelligence purposes to authorized elements of the Government, including the military services, in accordance with guidance from the Director of Central Intelligence;

(6) Collection, processing and dissemination of signals intelligence information for counterintelligence purposes;

(7) Provision of signals intelligence support for the conduct of military operations in accordance with tasking, priorities, and standards of timeliness assigned by the Secretary of Defense. If provision of such support requires use of national

collection systems, these systems will be tasked within existing guidance from the Director of Central Intelligence;

(8) Executing the responsibilities of the Secretary of Defense as executive agent for the communications security of the United States Government;

(9) Conduct of research and development to meet the needs of the United States for signals intelligence and communications security;

(10) Protection of the security of its installations, activities, property, information, and employees by appropriate means, including such investigations of applicants, employees, contractors, and other persons with similar associations with the NSA as are necessary;

(11) Prescribing, within its field of authorized operations, security regulations covering operating practices, including the transmission, handling and distribution of signals intelligence and communications security material within and among the elements under control of the Director of the NSA, and exercising the necessary supervisory control to ensure compliance with the regulations;

(12) Conduct of foreign cryptologic liaison relationships, with liaison for intelligence purposes conducted in accordance with policies formulated by the Director of Cenetral Intelligence; and

(13) Conduct of such administrative and technical support activities within and outside the United States as are necessary to perform the functions described in sections (1) through (12) above, including procurement.

(c) *Offices for the collection of specialized intelligence through reconnaissance programs*, whose responsibilities shall include:

(1) Carrying out consolidated reconnaissance programs for specialized intelligence;

(2) Responding to tasking in accordance with procedures established by the Director of Central Intelligence; and

(3) Delegating authority to the various departments and agencies for research, development, procurement, and operation of designated means of collection.

(d) *The foreign intelligence and counterintelligence elements of the Army, Navy, Air Force, and Marine Corps*, whose reponsibilities shall include:

(1) Collection, production and dissemination of military and military-related foreign intelligence and counterintelligence, and information on the foreign aspects of narcotics production and trafficking. When collection is conducted in response to national foreign intelligence requirements, it will be conducted in accordance with guidance from the Director of Central Intelligence. Collection of national foreign intelligence, not otherwise obtainable, outside the United States shall be coordinated with the CIA, and such collection within the United States shall be coordinated with the FBI;

(2) Conduct of counterintelligence activities outside the United States in coordination with the CIA, and within the United States in coordination with the FBI; and

(3) Monitoring of the development, procurement and management of tactical intelligence systems and equipment and conducting related research, development, and test and evaluation activities.

(e) *Other offices within the Department of Defense appropriate for conduct of the intelligence missions and responsibilities assigned to the Secretary of Defense.* If such other offices are used for intelligence purposes, the provisions of Part 2 of this Order shall apply to those offices when used for those purposes.

1.13 *The Department of Energy.* The Secretary of Energy shall:

(a) Participate with the Department of State in overtly collecting information with respect to foreign energy matters;

(b) Produce and disseminate foreign intelligence necessary for the Secretary's responsibilities;

(c) Participate in formulating intelligence collection and analysis requirements where the special expert capability of the Department can contribute; and

(d) Provide expert technical, analytical and research capability to other agencies within the Intelligence Community.

1.14 *The Federal Bureau of Investigation.* Under the supervision of the Attorney General and pursuant to such regulations as the Attorney General may establish, the Director of the FBI shall:

(a) Within the United States conduct counterintelligence and coordinate counterintelligence activities of other agencies within the Intelligence Community. When a counterintelligence activity of the FBI involves military or civilian personnel of the Department of Defense, the FBI shall coordinate with the Department of Defense;

(b) Conduct counterintelligence activities outside the United States in coordination with the CIA as required by procedures agreed upon by the Director of Central Intelligence and the Attorney General;

(c) Conduct within the United States, when requested by officials of the Intelligence Community designated by the President, activities undertaken to collect foreign intelligence or support foreign intelligence collection requirements of other agencies within the Intelligence Community, or, when requested by the Director of the National Security Agency, to support the communications security activities of the United States Government;

(d) Produce and disseminate foreign intelligence and counterintelligence; and

(e) Carry out or contract for research, development and procurement of technical systems and devices relating to the functions authorized above.

Part 2

Conduct of Intelligence Activities

2.1 *Need.* Accurate and timely information about the capabilities, intentions and activities of foreign powers, organizations, or persons and their agents is essential to informed decisionmaking in the areas of national defense and foreign relations. Collection of such information is a priority objective and will be pursued in a vigorous, innovative and responsible manner that is consistent with the Constitution and applicable law and respectful of the principles upon which the United States was founded.

2.2 *Purpose.* This Order is intended to enhance human and technical collection techniques, especially those undertaken abroad, and the acquisition of significant foreign intelligence, as well as the detection and countering of international terrorist activities and espionage conducted by foreign powers. Set forth below are certain general principles that, in addition to and consistent with applicable laws, are intended to achieve the proper balance between the acquisition of essential information and protection of individual interests. Nothing in this Order shall be construed to apply to or interfere with any authorized civil or criminal law enforcement responsibility of any department or agency.

2.3 *Collection of Information.* Agencies within the Intelligence Community are authorized to collect, retain or disseminate information concerning United States persons only in accordance with procedures established by the head of the agency concerned and approved by the Attorney General, consistent with the authorities provided by Part 1 of this Order. Those procedures shall permit collection, retention and dissemination of the following types of information:

(a) Information that is publicly available or collected with the consent of the person concerned;

(b) Information constituting foreign intelligence or counterintelligence, including such information concerning corporations or other commercial organizations. Collection within the United States of foreign intelligence not otherwise obtainable shall be undertaken by the FBI or, when significant foreign intelligence is sought, by other authorized agencies of the Intelligence Community, provided that no foreign intelligence collection by such agencies may be undertaken for the purpose of acquiring information concerning the domestic activities of United States persons;

(c) Information obtained in the course of a lawful foreign intelligence, counterintelligence, international narcotics or international terrorism investigation;

(d) Information needed to protect the safety of any persons or organizations, including those who are targets, victims or hostages of international terrorist organizations;

(e) Information needed to protect foreign intelligence or counterintelligence sources or methods from unauthorized disclosure. Collection within the United States shall be undertaken by the FBI except that other agencies of the Intelligence Community may also collect such information concerning present or former employees, present or former intelligence agency contractors or their present or former employees, or applicants for any such employment or contracting;

(f) Information concerning persons who are reasonably believed to be potential sources or contacts for the purpose of determining their suitability or credibility;

(g) Information arising out of a lawful personnel, physical or communications security investigation;

(h) Information acquired by overhead reconnaissance not directed at specific United States persons;

(i) Incidentally obtained information that may indicate involvement in activities that may violate federal, state, local or foreign laws; and

(j) Information necessary for administrative purposes.

In addition, agencies within the Intelligence Community may disseminate information, other than information derived from signals intelligence, to each appropriate agency within the Intelligence Community for purposes of allowing the recipient agency to determine whether the information is relevant to its responsibilities and can be retained by it.

2.4 *Collection Techniques.* Agencies within the Intelligence Community shall use the least intrusive collection techniques feasible within the United States or directed against United States persons abroad. Agencies are not authorized to use such techniques as electronic surveillance, unconsented physical search, mail surveillance, physical search, mail surveillance, physical surveillance, or monitoring devices unless they are in accordance with procedures established by the head of the agency concerned and approved by the Attorney General. Such procedures shall protect constitutional and other legal rights and limit use of such information to lawful governmental purposes. These procedures shall not authorize:

(a) The CIA to engage in electronic surveillance within the United States except for the purpose of training, testing, or conducting countermeasures to hostile electronic surveillance;

(b) Unconsented physical searches in the United States by agencies other than the FBI, except for:

(1) Searches by counterintelligence elements of the military services directed against military personnel within the United States or abroad for intelligence

purposes, when authorized by a military commander empowered to approve physical searches for law enforcement purposes, based upon a finding of probable cause to believe that such persons are acting as agents of foreign powers; and

(2) Searches by CIA of personal property of non-United States persons lawfully in its possession.

(c) Physical surveillance of a United States person in the United States by agencies other than the FBI, except for:

(1) Physical surveillance of present or former employees, present or former intelligence agency contractors or their present of former employees, or applicants for any such employment or contracting; and

(2) Physical surveillance of a military person employed by a nonintelligence element of a military service.

(d) Physical surveillance of a United States person abroad to collect foreign intelligence, except to obtain significant information that cannot reasonably be acquired by other means.

2.5 *Attorney General Approval.* The Attorney General hereby is delegated the power to approve the use for intelligence purposes, within the United States or against a United States person abroad, of any technique for which a warrant would be required if undertaken for law enforcement purposes, provided that such techniques shall not be undertaken unless the Attorney General has determined in each case that there is probable cause to believe that the technique is directed against a foreign power or an agent of a foreign power. Electronic surveillance, as defined in the Foreign Intelligence Surveillance Act of 1978, shall be conducted in accordance with that Act, as well as this Order.

2.6 *Assistance to Law Enforcement Authorities.* Agencies within the Intelligence Community are authorized to:

(a) Cooperate with appropriate law enforcement agencies for the purpose of protecting the employees, information, property and facilities of any agency within the Intelligence Community;

(b) Unless otherwise precluded by law or this Order, participate in law enforcement activities to investigate or prevent clandestine intelligence activities by foreign powers, or international terrorist or narcotics activities;

(c) Provide specialized equipment, technical knowledge, or assistance of expert personnel for use by any department or agency, or, when lives are endangered, to support local law enforcement agencies. Provision of assistance by expert personnel shall be approved in each case by the General Counsel of the providing agency; and

(d) Render any other assistance and cooperation to law enforcement authorities not precluded by applicable law.

2.7 *Contracting.* Agencies within the Intelligence Community are authorized to enter into contracts or arrangements for the provision of goods or services with private companies or institutions in the United States and need not reveal the sponsorship of such contracts or arrangements for authorized intelligence purposes. Contracts or arrangements with academic institutions may be undertaken only with the consent of appropriate officials of the institution.

2.8 *Consistency With Other Laws.* Nothing in this Order shall be construed to authorize any activity in violation of the Constitution or statutes of the United States.

2.9 *Undisclosed Participation in Organizations Within the United States.* No one acting on behalf of agencies within the Intelligence Community may join or otherwise participate in any organization in the United States on behalf of any agency within the Intelligence Community without disclosing his intelligence affiliation to appropriate officials of the organization, except in accordance with procedures established by the head of the agency concerned and approved by the Attorney General. Such participation shall be authorized only if it is essential to achieving lawful purposes as determined by the agency head or designee. No such participation may be undertaken for the purpose of influencing the activity of the organization or its members except in cases where:

(a) The participation is undertaken on behalf of the FBI in the course of a lawful investigation; or

(b) The organization concerned is composed primarily of individuals who are not United States persons and is reasonably believed to be acting on behalf of a foreign power.

2.10 *Human Experimentation.* No agency within the Intelligence Community shall sponsor, contract for or conduct research on human subjects except in accordance with guidelines issued by the Department of Health and Human Services. The subject's informed consent shall be documented as required by those guidelines.

2.11 *Prohibition on Assassination.* No person employed by or acting on behalf of the United States Government shall engage in, or conspire to engage in, assassination.

2.12 *Indirect Participation.* No agency of the Intelligence Community shall participate in or request any person to undertake activities forbidden by this Order.

Part 3

General Provisions

3.1 *Congressional Oversight.* The duties and responsibilities of the Director of Central Intelligence and the heads of other departments, agencies, and entities engaged in intelligence activities to cooperate with the Congress in the conduct of its responsibilities for oversight of intelligence activities shall be as provided in title 50, United States Code, section 413. The requirements of section 662 of the Foreign Assistance Act of 1961, as amended (22 U.S.C. 2422), and section 501 of the National Security Act of 1947, as amended (50 U.S.C. 413), shall apply to all special activities as defined in this Order.

3.2 *Implementation.* The NSC, the Secretary of Defense, the Attorney General, and the Director of Central Intelligence shall issue such appropriate directives and procedures as are necessary to implement this Order. Heads of agencies within the Intelligence Community shall issue appropriate supplementary directives and procedures consistent with this Order. The Attorney General shall provide a statement of reasons for not approving any procedures established by the head of an agency in the Intelligence Community other than the FBI. The National Security Council may establish procedures in instances where the agency head and the Attorney General are unable to reach agreement on other than constitutional or other legal grounds.

3.3 *Procedures.* Until the procedures required by this Order have been established, the activities herein authorized which require procedures shall be conducted in accordance with existing procedures or requirements established under Executive Order No. 12036. Procedures required by this Order shall be established as expeditiously as possible. All procedures promulgated pursuant to this Order shall be made available to the congressional intelligence committees.

3.4 *Definitions.* For the purposes of this Order, the following terms shall have these meanings:

(a) *Counterintelligence* means information gathered and activities conducted to protect against espionage, other intelligence activities, sabotage, or assassinations conducted for or on behalf of foreign powers, organizations or persons, or international terrorist activities, but not including personnel, physical, document or communications security programs.

(b) *Electronic surveillance* means acquisition of a nonpublic communication by electronic means without the consent of a person who is a party to an electronic communication or, in the case of a nonelectronic communication, without the consent of a person who is visably present at the place of communication, but not including the use of radio direction-finding equipment solely to determine the location of a transmitter.

(c) *Employee* means a person employed by, assigned to or acting for an agency within the Intelligence Community.

(d) *Foreign intelligence* means information relating to the capabilities, intentions and activities of foreign powers, organizations or persons, but not including counterintelligence except for information on international terrorist activities.

(e) *Intelligence activities* means all activities that agencies within the Intelligence Community are authorized to conduct pursuant to this Order.

(f) *Intelligence Community* and *agencies within the Intelligence Community* refer to the following agencies or organizations:

(1) The Central Intelligence Agency (CIA);

(2) The National Security Agency (NSA);

(3) The Defense Intelligence Agency (DIA);

(4) The offices within the Department of Defense for the collection of specialized national foreign intelligence through reconnaissance programs;

(5) The Bureau of Intelligence and Research of the Department of State;

(6) The intelligence elements of the Army, Navy, Air Force, and Marine Corps, the Federal Bureau of Investigation (FBI), the Department of the Treasury, and the Department of Energy; and

(7) The staff elements of the Director of Central Intelligence.

(g) *The National Foreign Intelligence Program* includes the programs listed below, but its composition shall be subject to review by the National Security Council and modification by the President:

(1) The programs of the CIA;

(2) The Consolidated Cryptologic Program, the General Defense Intelligence Program, and the programs of the offices within the Deaprtment of Defense for the collection of specialized national foreign intelligence through reconnaissance, except such elements as the Director of Central Intelligence and the Secretary of Defense agree should be excluded;

(3) Other programs of agencies within the Intelligence Community designated jointly by the Director of Central Intelligence and the head of the department or by the President as national foreign intelligence or counterintelligence activities;

(4) Activities of the staff elements of the Director of Central Intelligence;

(5) Activities to acquire the intelligence required for the planning and conduct of tactical operations by the United States military forces are not included in the National Foreign Intelligence Program.

(h) *Special activities* means activities conducted in support of national foreign policy objectives abroad which are planned and executed so that the role of the United States Government is not apparent or acknowledged publicly, and functions in support of such activities, but which are not intended to influence United States political processes, public opinion, policies, or media and do not include diplomatic activities or the collection and production of intelligence or related support functions.

(i) *United States person* means a United States citizen, an alien known by the intelligence agency concerned to be a permanent resident alien, an unincorporated association substantially composed of United States citizens or permanent resident aliens, or a corporation incorporated in the United States, except for a corporation directed and controlled by a foreign government or governments.

3.5 *Purpose and Effect.* This Order is intended to control and provide direction and guidance to the Intelligence Community. Nothing contained herein or in any procedures promulgated hereunder is intended to confer any substantive or procedural right or privilege on any person or organization.

3.6 *Revocation.* Executive Order No. 12036 of January 24, 1978, as amended, entitled "United States Intelligence Activities," is revoked.

THE WHITE HOUSE,
December 4, 1981.

BIBLIOGRAPHY

There is a growing body of literature on the U.S. government's intelligence system, much of which is cited in the notes throughout this book. Those wishing an even wider range of general sources can turn to the following three fine bibliographies:

Intelligence and Espionage: An Analytical Bibliography, by George C. Constantinides, Westview Press, Boulder, Colo., 1983.

Bibliography of Intelligence Literature, 8th ed., by Walter Pforzheimer, Defense Intelligence College, Washington, D.C., 1985.

Scholar's Guide to Intelligence Literature: Bibliography of the Russell J. Bowen Collection, edited by Marjorie W. Cline, Carla E. Christensen, and Judith M. Fontaine, published for the National Intelligence Study Center by University Publications of America, Frederick, Md., 1983.

The following are specific sources and books recommended for useful and generally reliable treatment of the subject:

Report to the President by the Commission on CIA Activities Within the United States, June 1975, GPO Stock No. 041-115-0074-8.

Final Report of the Select Committee to Study Governmental Operations with Respect to Intelligence Activities, U.S. Senate, 94th Congress, 2nd Session, Report No. 94–755, 26 April 1976 (six volumes).

Donovan and the CIA, by Thomas F. Troy, Center for the Study of Intelligence. Central Intelligence Agency, 1981.

Strategic Intelligence, by Sherman Kent, Princeton University Press, Princeton, N.J., 1949.

The U.S. Intelligence Community, by Lyman B. Kirkpatrick, Hill & Wang, New York, 1975.

Secrets, Spies and Scholars, by Ray S. Cline, Acropolis Books, Washington, D.C., 1976.

The CIA Under Reagan, Bush and Casey, by Ray S. Cline, Acropolis Books, Washington, D.C., 1981.

The Puzzle Palace, by James Bamford, Houghton Mifflin, Boston, 1982.

Honorable Men: My Life in the CIA, by William Colby, Simon & Schuster, New York, 1978.

Facing Reality, by Cord Meyer, Harper & Row, New York, 1980.

Intelligence Requirements for the 1980's. Five separate volumes under this general title, edited by Roy Godson and issued by the Consortium for the Study of Intelligence, Washington, D.C. The five volumes, with their titles and dates of issuance, are (1) *Elements of Intelligence,* 1979; (2) *Counterintelligence,* 1980; (3) *Analysis and Estimates,* 1980; (4) *Covert Action,* 1981; (5) *Clandestine Collection,* 1982.

Intelligence: Policy and Process, edited by Alfred C. Maurer, Marion D. Tunstall, and James M. Keagle, Westview Press, Boulder, Colo., 1985.

The Clandestine Service and the Central Intelligence Agency, by Hans Moses, Association of Former Intelligence Officers, McLean, Va., 1983.

National Security and the First Amendment, by John S. Warner, Association of Former Intelligence Officers, McLean, Va., 1984.

The Federal Loyalty-Security Program, by Guenter Lewy, American Enterprise Institute Studies in Political and Social Processes, Washington, D.C., and London, 1983.

Secrecy and Foreign Policy, edited by Thomas M. Franck and Edward Weisband, Oxford University Press, New York, London, and Toronto, 1974.

Foreign Policy and Congress, edited by Thomas M. Franck and Edward Weisband, Oxford University Press, New York and Oxford, 1979.

The Terror Network, by Claire Sterling, Holt, Rinehart & Winston, New York, 1981.

The Soviet Bloc and World Terrorism, Paper No. 26, by Shlomi Elad and Ariel Merari, Tel Aviv University, Jaffee Center for Strategic Studies, Tel Aviv, August 1984.

The Counterinsurgency Era, by Douglas Blaufarb, Free Press, New York, 1977.

KGB: The Secret Work of Soviet Agents, by John Barron, Reader's Digest Press, Pleasantville, N.Y., 1974.

Central Intelligence and National Security, by Harry Howe Ransom, Harvard University Press, Cambridge, Mass., 1958.

The Intelligence Establishment, by Harry Howe Ransom, Harvard University Press, Cambridge, Mass., 1970.

Soviet Propaganda, by Baruch A. Hazan, Keterpress Enterprises, Jerusalem, 1976.

U.S. Intelligence: Evolution and Anatomy, by Mark Lowenthal, Center for Strategic and International Studies, Washington, D.C., 1984.

ACRONYMS

The U.S. intelligence system has evolved in organizational arrangements, and has grown in size, since its creation in 1947 as a part of the government's national security structure. The actual facts relating to the system have been neglected, and even lost, in the dramatic controversies surrounding some of the activities. The result has been considerable misunderstanding over what the system actually is and what it has been. The decision was made by the present author, therefore in writing this book, that a description of some of the highlights of the history of the Intelligence Community would contribute to an understanding of it. This objective necessitated the naming of numerous organizations that came into existence along the way, some of which changed their names and some of which simply disappeared from the scene when their functions were assigned to other units. Thus provided was a plethora of bureaucratic data that must be confusing to some readers. Accordingly, a list of the more important acronyms is included here for those who may wish help in following events. Of course, the index will also be of help to those who wish further reference.

ACSI	Assistant Chief of Staff, Intelligence (Army and Air Force)
AFESC	Air Force Electronic and Security Command (formerly AFSS)
AFOSI	Air Force Office of Special Investigations
AIS	Army Investigative Services (merged into INSCOM)
ASA	Army Security Agency (merged into INSCOM)
CA	Covert Action
CPPG	Crisis Pre-Planning Group (in NSC structure)
CE	Counterespionage
CI	Counterintelligence
CIA	Central Intelligence Agency

CIG	Central Intelligence Group (preceded CIA)
COMINT	Communications Intelligence
COMIREX	Committee on Imagery Requirements and Exploitation
COMSEC	Communications Security
DAS	Defense Attaché System
DCI	Director of Central Intelligence
DIA	Defense Intelligence Agency
DIS	Defense Investigative Service
DNI	Director of Naval Intelligence
ELINT	Electronic Intelligence
EXCOM	Executive Committee (three man group directing overhead reconnaissance)
FBI	Federal Bureau of Investigation
FBIS	Foreign Broadcast Information Service
GRU	Glavnoye Razvedyvatelnoye Upravleniye (Soviet military intelligence organization)
HPSCI	House Permanent Select Committee on Intelligence
HUMINT	Human Intelligence
ICBM	Intercontinental Ballistic Missile
IG	Interagency Group (NSC structure)
INR	Bureau of Intelligence and Research (State Department)
INSCOM	U.S. Army Intelligence and Security Command
IOB	Intelligence Oversight Board (Presidential advisory group)
KGB	Komitet Gosudarstvennoy Bezopasnosti (Main Soviet intelligence and security organization)
KIQ	Key Intelligence Question
NFIB	National Foreign Intelligence Board
NFIC	National Foreign Intelligence Council
NIA	National Intelligence Authority (early administrative form)
NIC	National Intelligence Council
NIE	National Intelligence Estimate
NIO	National Intelligence Officer
NIS	Naval Investigative Service
NIT	National Intelligence Topics
NPIC	National Photographic Interpretation Center
NSA	National Security Agency
NSC	National Security Council
NSCID	National Security Council Intelligence Directive
NSDD	National Security Decision Directive
NSG	Naval Security Group

NSSD	National Security Study Directive
OMB	Office of Management and Budget (presidential budget office)
OSS	Office of Strategic Services (World War II predecessor of CIA)
PFIAB	President's Foreign Intelligence Advisory Board
PNIO	Priority National Intelligence Objectives
RADINT	Radar Intelligence
SIG	Senior Interagency Group (NSC structure)
SIG-I	Senior Interagency Group, Intelligence
SIGINT	Signals Intelligence
SSCI	Senate Select Committee for Intelligence
SSG	Special Situation Group (NSC structure)
SLBM	Submarine Launched Ballistic Missile
TELINT	Telemetry Intelligence
USIB	United States Intelligence Board (predecessor of NFIB)

INDEX

Abourezk, James, 265, 266
Academic community, 305–306, 307–308, 310(n31)
Academy of Sciences, 178(n2)
ACS/I. *See* Assistant Chiefs of Staff for Intelligence
ADA. *See* Americans for Democratic Action
Adams, Samuel, 170–172
Afghanistan, 279, 283(n6)
AFOSI. *See* Air Force, Office of Special Investigations
AFTIC. Air Force, Technical Intelligence Center
Agency for International Development (AID), 220, 246
Agents, 118–124
  debriefing, 195–196
  doubling, 203
  relations with, 295–299
  "third country," 297
Agents of influence, 124, 219–220
AID. *See* Agency for International Development
Air Force, 7, 41, 42, 45, 49, 61, 109–110, 160
  analysis function, 165–169
  Assistant Chiefs of Staff for Intelligence (ACS/I), 111, 163, 166
  Director of Central Intelligence and, 59
  Electronic Security Command, 130, 142(n5), 150
  Foreign Technology Division, 49
  Office of Special Investigations (AFOSI), 111, 193
  reconnaissance activities, 133, 136
  Technical Intelligence Center (AFTIC), 151
Air Force Security Service. *See* Air Force, Electronic Security Command
Albania, 276
Alleged Assassination Plots, 234
Allen, Richard, 17
Allende Gossens, Salvador, 227–231, 233, 234, 240(n6), 241(nn15,16), 270(n22), 280
Alliance for Progress, 228
Alliances, 277–278. *See also* North Atlantic Treaty Organization
"All-source" intelligence, 30, 97

Americans for Democratic Action (ADA), 303
Analysis. *See* Intelligence, analysis
Andropov, Yuri, 322
Angola, 227, 231–232, 267, 279, 281
Anticipatory defense, 278
Antiwar movement, 193–194, 199–200, 201–202
Appreciations. *See* Estimates
Arbenz Guzman, Jacobo, 70, 233
Argentina, 6
Armed Forces Security Agency, 130
Arms control, 127–129, 135, 140–141
Arms race. *See* Arms control; Military services; Soviet Union, monitoring; Strategic Arms Limitation Talks
Army, 36, 38(n14), 41, 42, 49, 61, 109–110, 116
  analysis function, 166, 169–172
  Assistant Chief of Staff for Intelligence (ACS/I), 163, 193
  counterintelligence operations, 192–193
  domestic intelligence, 202
  Intelligence Agency (USAINTA), 142(n5), 192–193
  Intelligence and Security Command (INSCOM), 111, 130, 142(n5), 150, 193
  Military Advisory Command, Vietnam (MACV), 170–172
  Secretary, 23
  Security Agency (ASA), 130, 142(n5), 193
  signals intelligence activities, 129
  Special Forces, 244, 252–253, 318
Articles of Confederation, 90
Articles of War, 89
ASA. *See* Army, Security Agency
Assassinations, 237–239, 250
Assessment, 118–119. *See also* Intelligence, analysis; National Intelligence Estimates
Assignments, 118
Assistant Chiefs of Staff for Intelligence (ACS/I) 111, 163, 166, 193
Assistant to the President for National Security Affairs. *See* National Security Adviser
Atomic Energy Commission, 41, 46, 69
Attorney General, 8, 46, 73, 190

353